SUCCESSFUL SG GARDENING

THE PRACTICAL GARDENER

Staff for Successful Gardening (U.S.A.)
Senior Associate Editor: Fiona Gilsenan
Art Editor: Evelyn Bauer
Art Associate: Martha Grossman

Contributors
Editor: Thomas Christopher
Editorial Assistant: Tracy O'Shea
Consulting Editor: Lizzie Boyd (U.K.)
Consultants: Tim Barr, Dora Galitzki, Mark D. Shulman, Ph.D., Dr. S. H. Smith
Copy Editor: Marsha Lutch Lloyd
Indexer: Sydney Wolfe Cohen

READER'S DIGEST GENERAL BOOKS
Editor in Chief: John A. Pope, Jr.
Managing Editor: Jane Polley
Executive Editor: Susan J. Wernert
Art Director: David Trooper
Group Editors: Will Bradbury, Sally French, Norman B. Mack, Kaari Ward
Group Art Editors: Evelyn Bauer, Robert M. Grant, Joel Musler
Chief of Research: Laurel A. Gilbride
Copy Chief: Edward W. Atkinson
Picture Editor: Richard Pasqual
Rights and Permissions: Pat Colomban
Head Librarian: Jo Manning

The credits and acknowledgments that appear on page 176 are hereby made a part of this copyright page.

Originally published in partwork form.

Library of Congress Cataloging in Publication Data

The Practical gardener.
p. cm. — (Successful gardening)
Includes index.
ISBN 0-89577-539-5–ISBN 0-89577-869-6(pbk.)
1. Gardening. 2. Landscape gardening. I. Reader's Digest Association. II. Series.
SB453.P675 1993
635.9—dc20 93-19529

Printed in the United States of America

Opposite: A narrow path snakes its way between beds resplendent with rhododendrons and azaleas, suggesting that the soil in this garden is acid. Glowing tulips and lemon-colored primroses complete the picture of a healthy garden.

Overleaf: Healthy plants, abundant flowers, and a well-tended lawn are a reflection of the gardener's practical experience and know-how.

THE READER'S DIGEST ASSOCIATION, INC.
Pleasantville, New York / Montreal

SUCCESSFUL SG GARDENING

The Practical Gardener

CONTENTS

Understanding your garden

Soil — a complex mixture of disintegrated rock, organic material, air, and microorganisms — is literally the foundation on which any successful garden is built. Whether you grow flowers, grass, shrubs, and ornamental trees, or vegetable and fruit crops, healthy plants need good soil to thrive and perform well. Fertile, moisture-retentive but well-drained loam soil is considered the ideal. However, most soil requires some kind of basic improvement.

Understanding your soil type is the key to improving it and will enable you to choose plants best suited for it. Simple soil-testing kits can assess acidity and alkalinity; other, equally simple tests can determine soil texture and water content. Once this information is obtained, you can correct nutrient imbalances and enhance structure and drainage, if necessary.

All soils profit from regular enrichment to maintain their fertility and moisture content. Bulky organic matter contributes texture to soil and provides food for plants. Its use is environmentally preferable to chemical fertilizers, which add nothing to soil structure and can build up to harmful levels in the soil if not used judiciously. Slower-acting organic fertilizers should be considered as an alternative. Compost — whether homemade or commercially produced — supplies plant nutrients while also boosting your soil's humus content.

Organic matter or specially designed materials applied as a surface cover, or mulch, provide extra benefits: mulched soil requires less weeding and less watering in dry areas. Mulch is also a natural insulator, keeping roots cool in summer and warm in winter.

Gardens around the country have different watering requirements. Careful planning, and techniques for coping with too little or too much water, can help you make the most of your garden environment.

Lime-haters Rhododendrons – and azaleas – will flourish only on moist, acid soils.

RECOGNIZING YOUR SOIL

Once you know your soil type, you can do a lot to improve and maintain it in good health, giving plants optimum growing conditions.

Healthy, well-balanced soil makes it easier to grow a variety of beautiful and productive plants. Not all plants will grow well in your garden's soil — soil types vary widely and it is impractical to try and transform one type into another. However, once you know what kind of soil you have in your garden, there are many ways you can improve it.

Knowing your soil

To improve a soil, first identify whether it is basically clay, silt, sand, or a mixture of these, which is known as loam. You can find out about the soil in your area by talking to neighbors and by working with the soil. Among the most dependable sources of information about soil types is the local Cooperative Extension or Agricultural Service. It usually has an in-depth regional soil survey available, as well as information on appropriate plants for your area.

Consider testing your soil for nutrient content and acidity/alkalinity. You can buy kits that are simple to use and give reasonably accurate readings. In addition, many Cooperative Extension or Agricultural Services will analyze a sample of your soil for you.

Your soil will fall roughly into one of four categories:

Clay soil is made up of minute mineral particles that tend to clump together. It is heavy and sticky to dig, as clay soil is generally poorly drained and aerated. When clay dries, it becomes rock-hard and cracks. To make the most of its natural fertility, you need to improve drainage and aeration by working in organic material, or a sharp sand, so that the texture becomes less compacted.

Silt soil is less finely textured than clay but still commonly suffers from poor drainage and inadequate aeration. Because this type of soil absorbs and drains water slowly, it erodes badly in heavy rains. However, it holds moisture very well in dry spells. Like clay soil, silt benefits from liberal doses of organic materials such as leaf mold.

Sandy soil is light and easy to work. Although it warms up quickly in spring, giving plants a good start, sandy soil drains so quickly that nutrients can be washed out. As a result, it needs plenty of organic matter and the careful addition of fertilizer.

Loam contains a good balance of

Loam

Clay

Sand

Silt

Developing a "feel" for soil is an important skill. Dig down 3–6 in (7.5–15 cm), to where plant roots grow. Scoop out a cupful of slightly moist soil, place it in a glass jar, and shake it thoroughly. Take some soil from the jar and rub it between your thumb and forefinger. Does it feel gritty? If so, that's a sign your soil is largely sand. Soil that feels smooth, like flour, is primarily silt; one that feels sticky and greasy is clay. Another way to identify texture is to take a spoonful of soil out of the jar and squeeze it in your palm. If the ball you've made falls apart almost as soon as you open your hand, the soil is sandy. If it crumbles when poked with your finger, then it is loam. If it keeps its shape after it is poked, it is either silt or clay.

clay, silt, and sand particles. It also has good texture and plenty of organic matter. You are lucky if you have loam soil, as it is the most easily cultivated of all soil types and holds water and nutrients well.

Acid and alkaline soils

Acidity or alkalinity is measured on a pH scale that ranges from 1.0 to 14.0. Something neutral, such as pure water, measures 7.0. Anything above that level is alkaline; below is acid. A pH reading that is between 6.5 and 7.0 suits the widest range of plants. Moderately acid soils have a pH of about 6.0, moderately alkaline soils have a pH of about 7.5. The ideal soil, a fertile, moisture-retentive loam, is slightly acid.

Sour (extremely acid) soils are often found in urban gardens, and can be corrected with powdered lime. Pulverized lime, available from garden centers, is the easiest to apply. Hydrated lime is quicker acting, but may be caustic to plants if you do not apply it carefully. Use 1/2 lb per sq yd (200 g per sq m), depending on the seriousness of the problem. Several months after adding the amendment to your soil, do another soil test to verify that you have added the correct amount of material.

Slight acidity is much easier to modify than excessive alkalinity. Plants in alkaline soil often show poor growth because they are unable to absorb trace elements such as iron and manganese. A bucketful of peat per sq yd (sq m) will increase the acidity of alkaline soils, but to apply this remedy to an entire garden could be both laborious and expensive. If your soil repeatedly tests alkaline, you may wish to landscape with plants adapted to that condition. If you still want to grow acid-loving plants, such as azaleas and rhododendrons, you can either create raised beds of acid soil (p.16) or grow these plants in containers filled with an appropriate soil mixture.

Humus for good soil

Good soil is composed of organic material and microorganisms that feed on it. Based on an accumulation of disintegrated rock, soil also contains a combination of chemical nutrients and humus. The latter ingredient is decayed organic matter, such as dead leaves that have been broken down by bacteria. Humus holds vital nutrients in a form that plants can absorb.

Two conditions are essential for humus to form: an adequate supply of air and a balanced provision

▲ **Earthworm activity** Worms are essential for a healthy garden. Their tunnels aerate heavy soils, and their feeding habits pull leaf litter underground, where it forms humus.

SOIL IMPROVER: WHAT TO DO WHEN

	SPRING	SUMMER	FALL
Dig/fork/hoe	Fork ground to loosen and aerate soil.	Hoe beds to keep down weeds and to aerate soil.	Dig beds before ground becomes too wet.
Manure	Mulch existing beds not dug and manured in fall. If planning to use stable manure in fall, begin composting it now.	None needed.	Incorporate manure at the bottom of trenches when digging new beds or beds for ornamentals and for vegetables (once every two years). If planning to use manure in spring, begin composting it now.
Fertilize	Sprinkle granular complete slow-release fertilizers onto soil and fork in lightly. Apply quick-acting fertilizers to specific plants to encourage their leaf growth and bud formation.	Apply quick-acting fertilizers, watering in or spraying as foliar feed, particularly to roses and tomatoes, and on "hungry" sandy soils.	Apply slow-release organic fertilizers when planting shrubs and trees.
Condition	Incorporate organic material, such as compost, leaf mold, or composted bark, to improve soil's texture and/or spread on a layer of mulch to conserve moisture, particularly on sandy soils.	None needed.	If soil is too dense or too free draining, incorporate bulky organic material when digging to improve texture. Every second year, add lime to soils that are too acid to increase their alkalinity; add gypsum to clay soils to break up their texture.
Water	In dry areas in late spring, water thoroughly, particularly sandy or clay soils.	Water ground thoroughly in dry weather, in morning or in evening.	Continue watering into midfall in dry spells.
Drain	Incorporate sharp sand and bulky organic material in poorly drained clay soils.	None needed.	In poorly drained soils, particularly clay, add sharp sand and bulky organic material, or build raised beds.

DOUBLE-DIGGING A BED

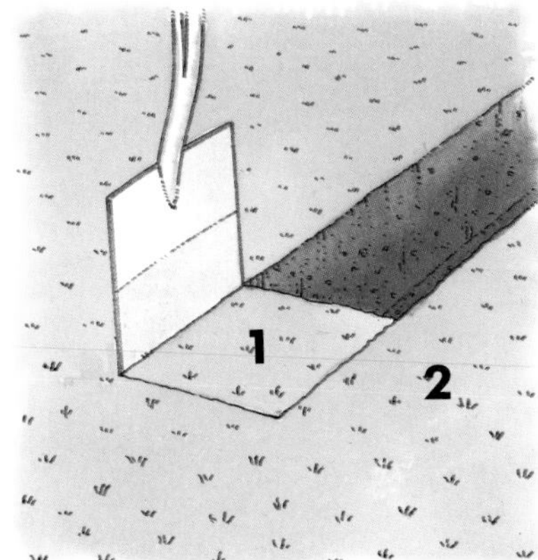

1 To dig a trench (**1**) 1 ft (30 cm) wide and one spade's depth deep: drive in the spade upright on all four sides of a square of earth. Then load the spade by sliding your hand down the shaft and bending your knees. Straighten your legs to take the strain off your back and lift the soil. Move the dug soil from the first trench to the far end of the plot.

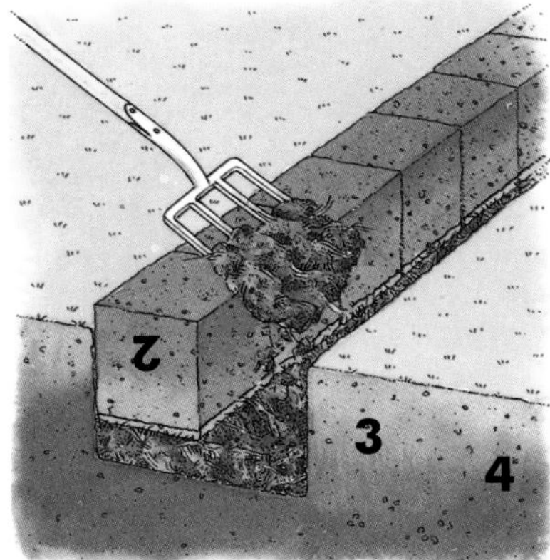

2 Remove any perennial weeds, such as dandelions and quack grass, from the soil. With a fork, evenly spread a layer of organic material in the trench. Dig the next strip (**2**) and turn it upside down into the first trench.

3 Continue in this way, trench by trench (**3, 4,** etc.), to the end of the plot, filling the final trench with the soil from the first one. Dig methodically, but don't overdo it — digging is tiring.

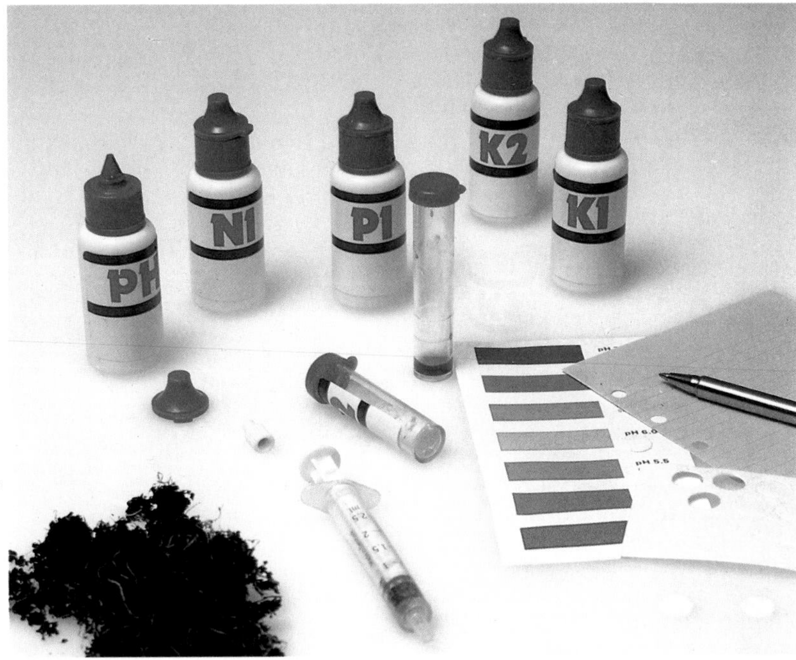

Soil-testing kits Adding drops of the chemicals in the kit to a sample of soil produces a liquid that, when it is matched against the color chart provided, indicates the acidity or alkalinity (pH) of the soil, as well as the presence of such nutrients as nitrogen (N), phosphorus (P), and potassium (K).

of water. Waterlogged soils, or those with very close textures, prevent the air from circulating freely, and so stop the beneficial process of decay.

Water is needed both for the action of soil bacteria and for the dissolving of nutrients. Fast-draining soil, which holds little or no moisture, parches easily and suffers from leaching — plant nutrients and minerals are washed out of the topsoil.

In addition to containing humus, a good soil must have a balanced nutrient composition, including not only the main nutrients required by plants — nitrogen, phosphorus, and potassium — but traces of other essential elements, such as copper and zinc.

Aerating the soil

Working the ground with a spade or fork is the most effective way of aerating waterlogged or dense, compacted soils. It's best to dig after annual flowers and vegetables have been cleared and before the ground becomes too wet. Soggy soils are heavy to work and there is a danger of compacting the ground, particularly on clay, while walking over it.

The action of frost in winter helps to break down soil that was turned over in fall. Raking in spring produces the fine, crumbly surface layer known as tilth — perfect for sowing seed or for planting seedlings.

In an established bed, such as a shrubbery or border, aerate the soil in spring — before growth starts — by turning it over with a fork. Throughout the summer, use a hoe to break up the soil around the base of plants, letting air into the soil and keeping the ground weed-free.

Adjusting the water balance

If an area of the garden is seriously waterlogged, water will lie in puddles after rain. It eventually evaporates rather than drains away. The simplest solution to improve drainage is to dig in plenty of organic material. If the entire garden tends to get waterlogged, you may find it more practical to dig drainage holes or build well-drained raised beds for your plantings (pp.13-14).

Conditioning soil texture

Bulky organic material, such as compost, helps to open up air spaces in the soil. It also gives substance to soil that is too free draining, thus increasing the soil's capacity to retain water.

If you have a clay soil, add sharp builder's sand, available at a local sand pit or a masonry supplier. It's composed of coarse, angular particles that break up the soil, which then becomes less dense, and thus easier to work, and more free-draining. You must dig in substantial quantities — at least a wheelbarrow load per sq yd (sq m). Powdered gypsum, added to the soil at a rate of ½ lb per sq yd (227 g per sq m) will "lighten" a clay soil by gradually binding its particles together. Both these treatments should be combined with additions of organic matter.

Mulching — covering the soil with an organic material, such as compost, leaf mold, or composted bark — conserves moisture and discourages weeds (pp.25–28). The mulch will also work its way gradually into the soil, improving its texture. Apply in spring or early summer when the sun has taken the chill off the ground and while the earth is still moist.

Enriching the soil

Organic material from animals (such as manure) and from composted plants aerates the soil and improves its texture and ability to retain moisture. But even more important, this active decaying matter produces humus.

Peat products — made from vegetable matter that was prevented from complete decomposition by lack of oxygen — come from bogs that take thousands of years to form. Peat has little nutrient value and should be used judiciously, since its sources are limited. There are many alternative products, such as composted bark, that can also be used as soil conditioners (pp.23-24).

Feeding plants

Applying chemical fertilizers — the inorganic alternative to compost — is the easiest way to boost the soil's nutrient content. But don't rely solely on these fertilizers — they don't produce humus and they can eventually reduce the soil quality. Use them as supplements to organic amendments.

Fertilizers come in various forms and perform different functions (pp.17–20). Add slow-release general fertilizers to the soil in early spring. Throughout the summer, apply quicker-acting liquid fertilizers. There are also special formulas for various plants, such as tomatoes and roses.

▲ **Alkaline-soil hydrangeas** The flowers of *Hydrangea macrophylla* are affected by soil pH. On alkaline or neutral soil they are pink or red.

◀ **Acid-soil hydrangeas** The same species on acid soil will have blue flowers. Bluing compounds containing aluminum sulfate can be added to neutral soils for a blue tint.

▼ **Lime haters** Acid-loving plants, such as heathers and conifers, can create a magnificent and colorful display on a very acid soil.

DRAINAGE

Waterlogged gardens are awful — if you don't know how to handle them. Here are techniques for improving poor drainage, and for learning how to live with it.

Every garden needs moisture to enable plants to flourish, and in most gardens the balance is about right; rain falls, seeps into the soil, and drains away naturally. But if something disturbs this natural process, the result can be a garden that is a soggy swamp.

Few plants can thrive with waterlogged roots, and wet soil is hard to work when digging and planting. Worst of all is a lawn that is always soft and wet underfoot; every step leaves a mark, and mud is carried throughout the house from the garden.

Waterlogging occurs for a variety of reasons. One of the most common problems — and the easiest to correct — is soil that has become compacted because it has not been recently worked. Heavy clay soils are particularly susceptible to this condition.

Water stands on the surface of compacted soil, never reaching plant roots. The result is undesirably shallow root growth. The solution is a vigorous program of double-digging, incorporating plenty of organic matter to help break up the soil and improve its water-holding capacity (p.11). For clay soils, adding a substantial dose of sharp builder's sand or lime will further improve their texture and drainage.

Sometimes a naturally occurring layer of compacted soil lies a foot or two below the surface. Known as "hardpan," it prevents water from draining, keeping the soil around the plant's roots perpetually wet, even when the soil at the surface has dried. The best way to resolve this situation is to pierce the hardpan with a pattern of drainage holes, similar to the ones you would find in the bottom of a flowerpot.

A comparable problem frequently occurs in the gardens of newly built houses. When clearing a site, builders often remove the topsoil and spread excavated material over the garden area. Then they inadvertently compact it with the movement of heavy machinery, and later cover everything up with a thin layer of topsoil or poor-quality subsoil. The end result is the same as that of a hardpan. But since the compacted layer lies closer to the surface, right in the root zone of garden plants, you will have to break up all the compacted soil. Again, the solution is to double-dig and to incorporate organic matter.

Before carrying out any of these measures, you should determine just how well your soil drains.

Gauging soil porosity

First, dig a hole about 2 ft (60 cm) square and 2 ft (60 cm) deep. Wait 24 hours (on a rainless day) to see if any water collects in the hole. If it does, the garden is suffering from waterlogging and you will need to correct the cause.

If the hole remains dry, fill it with water and see how quickly it drains away. If it empties in about 12 hours, drainage is too rapid — probably because the soil is very sandy. Drainage can be slowed down by enriching the soil with lots of organic matter. If the hole takes 24 hours to empty, drainage is adequate; if the water is still standing in the hole after 48 hours, the soil is probably too dense and needs breaking up thoroughly by double-digging.

If you moved into your house in the summer, you may not discover that you have a drainage problem until winter. The best way to spot a potential drainage problem is to look at how the garden grows; stunted, sickly looking shrubs, coarse turf, and bare patches of lawn are all telltale signs of drainage trouble.

Serious drainage problems

Some causes of poor drainage are not easily corrected. A layer of nonpermeable rock may run close to the surface, or a part of the garden may lie in an area where the water table — the natural level of groundwater — is particularly high. In the latter case, prolonged rainfall causes the water table to rise until it reaches the surface, resulting in standing water. The

To relieve waterlogging caused by hardpan, use a post-hole digger to punch drainage holes through the layer of impermeable soil. Space holes 2 ft (60 cm) apart.

Fill the holes with gravel to a level even with the top of the hardpan; the gravel will ensure that the drain stays open. Finish by replacing the topsoil.

only way to correct either of these problems is to install a network of subsurface drainage tiles to funnel water away from your garden — a project far too laborious and expensive for the average homeowner. It makes more sense in this situation to work with the natural condition of your garden rather than to try and change it.

One solution is to capitalize on the wet spots on your property by enhancing them with wetland plants, such as cardinal flower, royal fern, marsh marigold, sweet flag, or pickerel rush — in effect, creating a bog garden. In addition, you can take soil from the lowest areas and pile it up, creating dry, well-drained paths or even seating or play areas.

Raised beds

Another solution, one that allows the cultivation of more conventional garden plants, is to install raised beds for plantings.

A raised bed can be just an area of soil piled several inches deep, but the effect is more attractive and permanent if you frame the bed with stone, brick, or wood. By elevating the surface of the bed above the surrounding soil — and on a poorly drained site, you should make the bed a foot or even a foot and a half (30-45 cm) high — you will ensure that the bed will drain well.

Raised beds offer several other advantages. Because they are more exposed to the sun and air than the surrounding earth, they warm up faster in the spring than level beds. As a result, in cold-climate regions, raised beds can have the effect of lengthening the growing season by a few weeks. Also, as you fill a raised bed's frame with soil, you can make sure that the contents are free of rocks and are especially rich in organic matter. The finished bed will be far more productive than the surrounding soil. Raised beds also have a neat appearance that many gardeners like. And gardeners with back problems will find raised beds less taxing to work because, after the initial construction, there is less need to stoop when weeding or planting.

Success with raised beds depends on care in the planning and construction. Select a location that receives sun at least 6 hours a day. Before building, lay out the beds with stakes and string. Make sure that you will be able to reach the center of the beds while standing on the side. Usually, it's best to build them no more than four feet across. Also, choose rot- or rust-resistant materials: if using timbers, they should be a naturally rot-resistant wood such as cedar, or one that has been pressure-treated with a nontoxic wood preservative (ask for it at a lumberyard). Finally, you should use only galvanized fasteners.

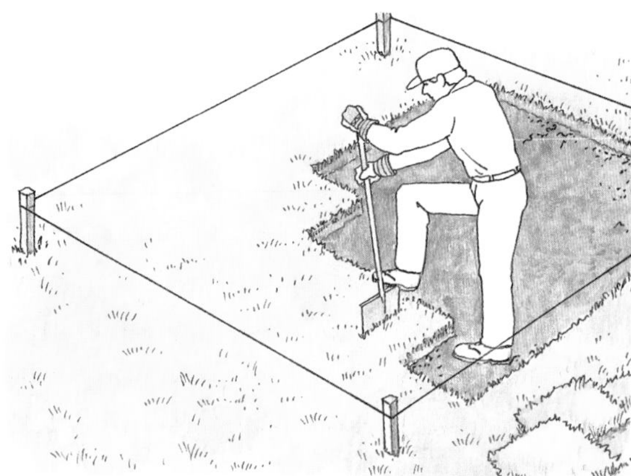

1 Outline the site with stakes and string. Make sure you can reach comfortably into the center to plant or weed. For best sunlight, position the bed with its longer sides running from north to south. Dig away all the turf from the enclosed area.

2 The ground on which you set the frame should be level. Set the first course of timbers slightly below the surface, and check to make sure they are level. If necessary, excavate a bit more earth underneath any higher sides.

3 As you add extra courses of timbers, overlap the ends as shown, pinning them in place with 12-in (30-cm) galvanized spikes. You can build the frame as high as you want — a height of 1 ft (30 cm) should provide for ample drainage.

4 Dig out the soil to a depth of 10 in (25 cm), mix it with an equal quantity of organic matter, and return it to the frame. Top up the bed with a mixture of equal parts topsoil and organic matter; add more after the soil has settled.

WATER CONSERVATION

In many places too little, not too much, water is a major problem. But you can conserve this essential resource with some simple techniques.

In many regions of North America, gardeners face not an overabundance of water but a chronic shortage. Many of the continent's fastest-growing cities are in arid or even desert regions, places where rainstorms are rare and water must be brought in from hundreds of miles away. Water shortages are even occurring in many areas of abundant precipitation as populations outgrow the existing water-supply systems. Learning to use water wisely is now considered an essential skill for all gardeners.

On the following page is an example of a water-saving garden — one that uses many of the techniques listed here, yet still provides variety, interest, and color.

Improving your soil

More than any other factor, the quality of your soil determines how often you must water your garden. Water that drains through sandy soil, for instance, is lost to the plants growing there. Adding organic matter to any type of soil is the best way to conserve water. It creates humus, which acts as a sponge to hold water. Furthermore, by enhancing the porosity of the soil, breaking it up into loose crumbs, humus increases the rate at which soil can soak up rainwater or melting snow. Likewise, water that runs away across the surface of a heavy, slick clay will soak in once the clay has been mixed with humus.

In a hot, humid climate, decay eats up humus almost as fast as you can add it. Any supplemental humus you provide, however, will enhance your garden's ability to thrive on existing rainfall, and it will also increase the efficiency with which it makes use of any additional irrigation water.

Irrigation

New technologies, such as drip irrigation systems and microsprinklers, release water slowly and under low pressure. They can deliver the same amount of water to plants as conventional sprinklers, but they consume only half as much water. This is because much of the water that leaves traditional sprinkler heads evaporates before it reaches the ground — and the plants.

Drip systems, by contrast, bring the water right to the root zone of the plants so that there is virtually no waste. Soaker and sprinkler hoses can also cut water use, especially on a slope where much of a sprinkler's water simply runs off the surface.

Harvesting water

Designing your garden to capture water runoff after a rainstorm can also provide a source of water for irrigation. Whenever possible, pave walks and patios with permeable, rain-absorbent surfaces, such as bricks set in sand.

Place plants that need extra moisture, such as deciduous shade trees, at the bottom of a broad, shallow basin. A depression only 3-4 in (7.5-10 cm) deep but 2-3 yd/m in width will collect a considerable quantity of rainwater and hold it until the ground at the plants' base is soaked. In very arid regions, feeding water from your home's downspouts into a series of linked basins often furnishes all the supplemental moisture needed by deep-rooted desert plants.

Choosing adapted plants

Another key to water conservation is selecting plants that are adapted to your soil and climate. If you move to an arid or semiarid climate, you may have to sacrifice a blue-green lawn — or you'll find yourself watering all the time. If you live on the Great Plains, you would be much better advised to plant a lawn of native buffalo grass, which will flourish with no more than one monthly soak. Studying the native plants of your region is a great help in learning which plants will thrive locally with a minimum of care. Botanical gardens, arboretums, and your local Cooperative Extension or Agricultural Service can recommend appropriate regional plants. Your public library can direct you to local wildflower and native plant societies.

However, native plants are not always the best for water conservation. Many need a very specific set of environmental conditions, and do not prosper in the average suburban yard. Often, so-called exotic plants — species of foreign origin — will prove better adapted to garden conditions. Zoysia, for example, an Asian species, makes the toughest, least thirsty grass in many areas of the central South. A good source of information about exotic plants adapted to your area is the local water company; often it provides free booklets, source lists, and advice.

Landscaping for conservation

The way in which you arrange your plants affects the amount of water you need. Always plan to put plants with similar watering needs close to one another. This layout ensures that you don't overwater one plant while leaving its companion thirsty.

You can create a lush effect while reducing the garden's water needs by placing luxuriant plantings — finer turf and flower beds — near your house, arranging them around the windows or seating areas where you spend most of your outdoor time. Though limited in size, these spaces of intense green and color will be the dominant feature in the garden.

Fill the periphery of the garden with plantings that, while attractive, require less irrigation: a lawn of rougher grasses; a wildflower meadow; or configurations of shrubs, trees, and ground covers.

Wind evaporates water from leaf surfaces, forcing plants to draw more water from the soil. Redirecting the wind reduces such water loss. Set a windbreak — a fence or hedge — along the property line that faces into the prevailing wind. Covering the soil with a blanket of mulch also helps to limit the amount of water lost through evaporation.

A WATER-SAVING GARDEN

Create zones in the landscape, with manicured, lusher plantings in the high-use areas adjacent to the house. Place beds of self-reliant trees and shrubs at the periphery.

Plant a windbreak of evergreen trees and shrubs. They protect plants within the yard from dehydration, thereby reducing their water needs. A fence or wall serves the same purpose.

A microclimate that is cooler and moister exists beneath shade trees. It provides a refuge for people, and protection for tender plants from the burning heat of the summer sun.

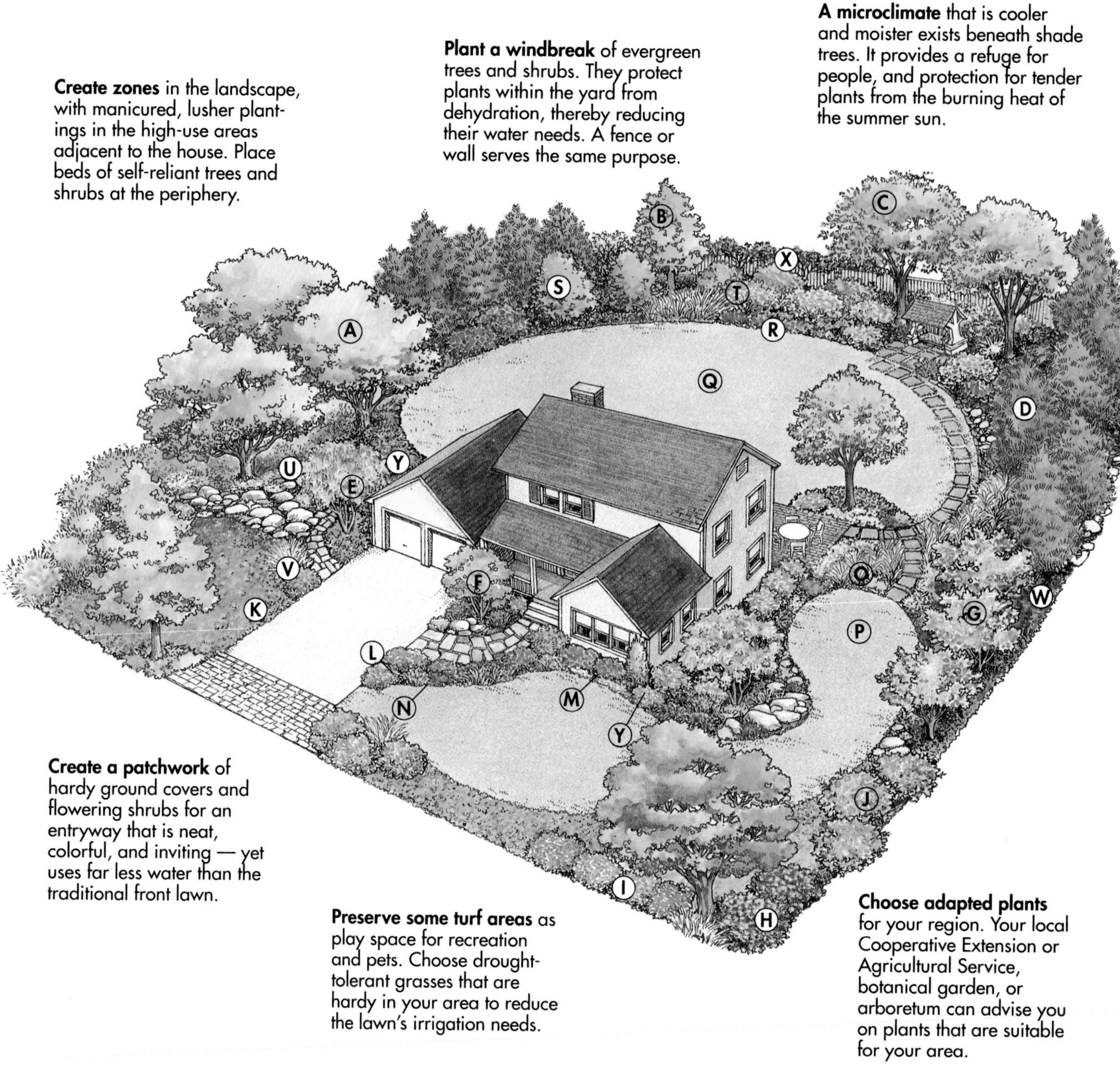

Create a patchwork of hardy ground covers and flowering shrubs for an entryway that is neat, colorful, and inviting — yet uses far less water than the traditional front lawn.

Preserve some turf areas as play space for recreation and pets. Choose drought-tolerant grasses that are hardy in your area to reduce the lawn's irrigation needs.

Choose adapted plants for your region. Your local Cooperative Extension or Agricultural Service, botanical garden, or arboretum can advise you on plants that are suitable for your area.

Plant Key:

A Coast live oak *(Quercus agrifolia)*
B American sweet gum *(Liquidambar styraciflua)*
C Black locust *(Robinia pseudoacacia)*
D Aleppo pine *(Pinus halepensis)*
E Goldenrain tree *(Koelreuteria paniculata)*
F Western redbud *(Cercis occidentalis)*
G Crepe myrtle *(Lagerstroemia indica)*
H Oregon grape holly *(Mahonia aquifolium)*
I California lilac *(Ceanothus* species)
J Dwarf oleander *(Nerium oleander)*
K Creeping mahonia *(Mahonia repens)*
L Indian hawthorn *(Rhaphiolepsis indica)*
M Rockrose *(Cistus* species)
N Iris *(Iris douglasiana)*
O Lily of the Nile and Day lilies *(Agapanthus and Hemerocallis)*
P Tall turf fescue *(Festuca elatior)*
Q Hybrid Bermuda grass *(Cynodon dactylon)*
R Autumn sage *(Salvia greggii)*
S Toyon *(Heteromeles arbutifolia)*
T Evergreen currant *(Ribes viburnifolium)*
U Juniper *(Juniperus* species)
V Eulalia grass *(Miscanthus sinensis)*
W Organic mulch
X Blood trumpet vine *(Distictis buccinatoria)*
Y Cotoneaster species

USING FERTILIZERS

Plants, like people, thrive on a balanced diet — the soil they grow in must be enriched with all the foods needed for healthy development.

Several of the essential nutrients for plants are readily obtainable from water and the soil, and do not need supplementing under normal conditions — these are carbon, hydrogen, and oxygen. Plants manufacture their own food from these nutrients and from raw materials in the soil — weathered rock and humus.

Other major nutrients, dissolved in water, are taken up by hairs growing near the tips of plants' roots. The three principal elements on which plant life depends — nitrogen (N), phosphorus (P), and potassium (K) — are absorbed in this way. A well-tended soil will be rich in all three, together with the so-called "trace elements." The latter are required in very small quantities only — or a trace — but are just as important as the other three. Atmospheric nitrogen is "fixed" in the soil, and rendered available to plants as it is broken down by different soil-borne bacteria.

In time, plants use up the available nutrients in the surrounding soil, so gardeners need to supply extra food if their plants are to thrive. In addition, nitrogen is likely to be leached from the soil by the action of water drainage following rainfall or excessive waterings.

All the complex needs of a plant could be met by constantly enriching the soil with farmyard or stable manure — animal droppings mixed with straw. However, this simple method of maintaining fertility is no longer practical for most gardeners, who must supplement whatever organic material is present in the soil.

So-called "chemical" fertilizers feed plants directly, supplying nutrients that can be absorbed immediately. However, they do nothing to improve soil structure and may even deplete its reserves of organic material. You should aim to strike a balance, adding as much organic material as possible, and using fertilizers to remedy known deficiencies or meet special needs.

Another alternative is to use "organic" fertilizers, which are now available at most garden centers and through many gardening catalogs. Although there is no standard definition of what constitutes an organic fertilizer, it relies mainly on materials that come from once-living sources. Chemical fertilizers, on the other hand, are manufactured by controlled chemical processes. Organic fertilizers provide the same nutrients as nonorganic ones, but often in lower concentrations. The nutrients may not be as readily available to plants and need to be broken down by soil microorganisms before plants can use them.

Fertilizer types

Each of the essential nutrients — nitrogen, phosphorus (in phosphate), and potassium (in potash) — can be purchased separately as so-called "straight," or "incomplete," fertilizers, or in balanced mixtures known as "complete" fertilizers. The latter type generally also contains the most important trace elements.

Nitrogen sources Some organic fertilizers derived from animal products, such as dried blood, are rich in nitrogen. But they are expensive and are normally used only in special circumstances, such as when sowing grass or using potting soil mixtures.

Less expensive sources of nitrogen are the inorganic fertilizers — the cheapest being ammonium sulfate, which can acidify soil and has the potential to burn plants. More expensive are calcium nitrate, ammonium nitrate, and sodium nitrate. Again, the ammonium form can acidify the soil.

When plants need to have quick stimulation, nitrogen is often

◀ **Organic fertilizers** Bone meal is a slow-release general fertilizer that can be worked into the soil around perennials and shrubs at planting time. It supplies nitrogen and phosphorus.

PLANT NUTRITION

SOIL NUTRIENT	NEEDED BY	REQUIREMENTS
Nitrogen (N)	All plants, especially leafy vegetables and grasses	For leaf and stem growth. Soon washed out of the soil by rain, especially on sandy soils. Replenish every year.
Phosphorus (P) (as phosphate)	Root crops and all young plants; also flowering, fruiting, and seeding plants	For root growth and the production of flowers and seeds. Remains fixed in the soil for 2 or 3 years after application; less so in sandy soils.
Potassium (K) (as potash)	Flowering and fruiting plants	For flower and fruit formation, maintaining general growth and providing resistance to disease. Remains in the soil for 2 or 3 years after application; less so in sandy soils.
Calcium (Ca)	All plants	For general plant growth; encourages the growth of soil bacteria that are responsible for producing certain plant foods. Deficient in acid and potassium-rich soils.
Magnesium (Mg)	All plants, especially tomatoes and roses	For the production of the green pigment chlorophyll. Deficient in well-drained or potassium-rich soils.
Trace elements: Iron (Fe), Boron (B), Cobalt (Co), Copper (Cu), Sulfur (S), Manganese (Mn), Zinc (Zn), Molybdenum (Mo)	All plants	For general plant growth. Rarely deficient in well-tended soils. Certain plants have higher demands for trace elements, which can be supplied by specially formulated fertilizers, such as rhododendron feed that has added iron and manganese. Sulfur is more likely to be deficient in rural areas than in urban ones. Soil type may affect the availability of certain elements — the calcium in lime may render iron and manganese unusable by plants, for instance.

APPLYING FERTILIZERS

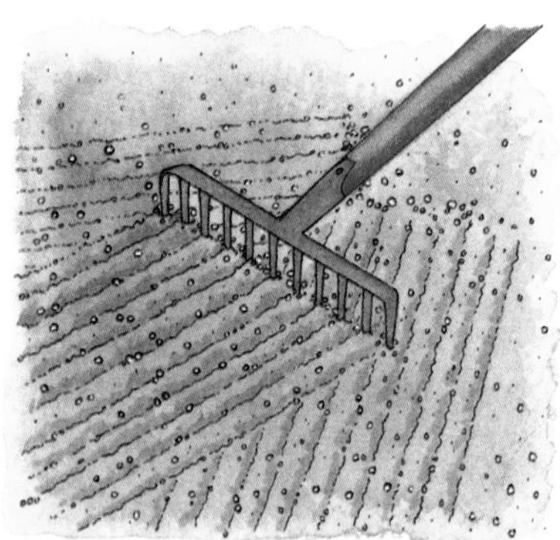

1 Broadcast preplanting or preseeding fertilizers at an even rate over the bed, then rake in. Follow manufacturer's instructions carefully for application rates — use sticks to mark out 1-sq-yd/m areas as a guide.

2 When planting shrubs in soil that has not been well cultivated, prepare a planting mix consisting of good garden soil with a couple of handfuls per bucketful of a slow-release general fertilizer.

3 Topdressing fertilizers are scattered evenly on the ground. Sprinkle them around the roots of growing plants to promote flowering or a high fruit yield. Water in granules if the soil is dry, or if it does not rain soon after application.

4 Special fertilizer blocks are available to meet the needs of every plant group. These are put into a dissolver canister attached to a garden hose — a precise way of applying liquid fertilizer to leaves and roots.

5 Liquid fertilizers can be applied to moist soil using an ordinary watering can with the sprinkler head removed. It is the best way to give garden plants and crops a feed during dry weather, after initial watering.

6 Liquid foliar feeds should be applied to the leaves using a garden sprayer. This is an excellent way to give a rapid boost to plants, and is ideal for applying trace-element plant tonics. Do not spray in hot weather.

applied alone. Overwintered vegetables need nitrogen in spring to replace that lost from the soil by winter rains and snows or not yet made available by bacteria activated by the warming spring soil.

Most fruit crops require a dressing of ammonium sulfate in spring. Liquid fertilizers containing nitrogen can also be sprayed onto the foliage of starved fruit trees and bushes in the spring. Special high-nitrogen feeds or urea can be bought from a garden center, but be sure to follow the manufacturer's instructions carefully to avoid excess application.

Phosphorus sources Phosphorus, in the form of soluble phosphates, is particularly important to a plant in the seedling stage and as it forms a root system. When the soil has too little phosphorus, the leaves may turn dull purple, and are smaller than normal. In addition, the overall growth of the plant slows down. Too much phosphorus will cause premature ripening.

Good sources of phosphorus include slow-release bone meal, which is organic and easy to find, and nonorganic superphosphate.

Potassium sources Potassium, in the form of potash, heightens the intensity of flower color; it is sometimes given as a topdressing to improve the formation of flowers and the ripening of fruits. It also increases a plant's resistance to pests and diseases, and hardens the tissues. Potassium is especially important for fruit crops, tomatoes, and potatoes.

Sandy soils, in particular, are likely to need added potassium, and the most suitable form for the gardener is potassium sulfate.

Complete fertilizers These are generally identified by a ratio of three numbers, for example, "5–10–5." This ratio means that the particular product contains (by weight) 5 percent nitrogen, 10 percent phosphorus, and 5 percent potassium. Learning to read the ratios will ensure that you get your money's worth. A 25-pound bag of 20–20–20, for example, delivers several times the nutrients of a 20-pound bag of 5–10–5, so that the more concentrated product may be a better buy.

Fertilizers are also available in packaged formulations for special purposes. For instance, there are quick-absorption liquid feeds for potassium-loving tomatoes.

NUTRIENT-DEFICIENCY SYMPTOMS

1 Nitrogen deficiency is indicated by poor, stunted growth with pale leaves and weak stems. Leaves often turn orange, red, or purplish and may fall prematurely. Fruit trees and vegetables are most commonly affected.

2 Potassium deficiency is indicated by brown scorching around the edges of the leaves. Flowers may be dull and sparse, and fruit yield may be low and of poor quality. Tissues are soft and more prone to pests and diseases.

3 Magnesium deficiency is indicated by yellow patches between the leaf veins that later turn brown. The affected leaves may wither. Roses and tomatoes are often affected. Magnesium sulfate (Epsom salts) spray is the best cure.

4 Manganese deficiency is indicated by yellowing between the veins of older leaves. Leaf edges may curl in and turn brown. Many types of plants may be affected. Lower soil pH; apply fertilizer with trace elements.

Slow-release fertilizers These are coated or contain compounds that prevent them from breaking down quickly. They are often used for feeding trees and shrubs.

Liquid fertilizers Concentrated complete fertilizers are sold in both solid and liquid form, and must be diluted with water before use. They are easy to apply and are quickly absorbed by plants.

Some liquid fertilizers are derived from seaweed and humus extracts; others are made solely from chemicals. They are mixed in various proportions to suit the needs of different plants and soils.

Foliar feeds Plants take several days to make use of nutrients absorbed through their roots. However, if their leaves are sprayed with dilute solutions of fertilizers, they benefit almost immediately. Special fertilizers for foliar feeding are available: some are based on soluble, inorganic fertilizers; others are all-organic preparations with a seaweed base. All types are quickly absorbed.

Foliar feeds should be regarded as supplemental to other organic or inorganic fertilizers rather than as the sole means of feeding your plants. They are particularly useful, however, if the plants have poorly developed root systems or if a dry spell occurs, because then plants have difficulty drawing nutrients from the soil.

Applying fertilizers

Do an annual soil test to find out the nutritional content of your soil. Use the results as a guide to determine the fertilizing needs of your plants. The soil type and the climate also dictate the type of fertilizers to use. A light, sandy soil, for example, needs more potassium than heavier soils. In areas with a heavy rainfall, nitrogen washes out of the soil quickly and must be replaced.

Roughly measure the area to be fertilized. Then calculate the required amount of fertilizer and measure it in a cup kept for this purpose (if instructions are given by weight, use an old kitchen scale covered with waxed paper).

About 2 weeks before sowing seeds, spread a complete fertilizer evenly over the soil and hoe or rake — don't dig — it into the surface. Do not scatter fertilizer along a seed row, as it can injure germinating seedlings. Sprinkle topdressings — those applied to the ground's surface — around the base of plants and lightly hoe them in. Do not allow inorganic fertilizers — except foliar feeds — to touch any plant's foliage or flowers. In dry weather, water immediately after fertilizing.

Caution: Always follow manufacturer's instructions for applying fertilizers and wash your hands after use. Store fertilizers in a dry place, out of the reach of children or animals. If you transfer a fertilizer to a new container, label the container clearly.

FERTILIZER TYPES AND THEIR CONTENT

FERTILIZER	NUTRIENT CONTENT (approximate)	APPLICATION METHOD	SPECIAL FEATURES
INORGANIC			
Magnesium sulfate (Epsom salts)	10% magnesium; sulfur	Topdressing	Effective against chlorosis (chlorophyll depletion that causes the plant to lose color).
Ammonium nitrate	35% nitrogen	Liquid feed	Do not mix with lime.
Sodium nitrate	16% nitrogen; trace elements	Topdressing	Fast-acting but quickly washed out of the soil. Keep off foliage.
Calcium nitrate	16% nitrogen; calcium	Topdressing	Contains 48% lime. Long-lasting, fast-acting; useful on acid soils. Can be used to aid rotting of compost.
Potassium nitrate	12%-14% nitrogen; 44%-46% potash	Topdressing/ liquid feed	A general spring fertilizer. Impure Chilean potassium nitrate contains only 15% potash.
Ammonium sulfate	20% nitrogen; sulfur	Topdressing	Best source of N, but makes soil more acid. Do not mix with lime. Fast-acting.
Ferrous sulfate	Iron; sulfur	Topdressing	Effective against iron-induced chlorosis. Acidifies the soil.
Potassium sulfate	48% potash	Base or top-dressing	Best general source of potassium. Fast-acting for flowers and fruit. Acidifies the soil.
Superphosphate	13%-20% phosphorus	Base dressing	Best source of phosphates. Keep off delicate leaves. Do not mix with sodium nitrate.
Urea	46% nitrogen	Liquid/foliar feed	Very rich source of N. Not available in all areas.
ORGANIC			
Bone meal	2%-5% nitrogen; 20%-30% phosphorus; calcium	Base or top-dressing	Slow-release fertilizer; apply in spring or fall. Contains lime. Ensure it is sterilized.
Dried blood	9%-14% nitrogen	Topdressing/ liquid feed	Fairly fast-acting. Apply in late spring or summer. Ideal for leaf vegetables.
Fish meal	4%-9% nitrogen; 7% phosphorus; 1%-2% potash	Base dressing	Fairly slow-release; apply during spring cultivation, one spade's depth.
Seaweed extract	2% nitrogen; 1% phosphorus; 4%-13% potash	Liquid/foliar feed	Gentle, fairly quick-acting, neutral pH; good source of trace elements, enhances winter hardiness.
Wood ash	5%-10% potash	Topdressing	Must be kept dry to retain potassium. Young wood produces the richest ash. Keep off foliage, as it can scorch badly.
COMPOUND			
Broad-leaved evergreen fertilizer	4% nitrogen; 6% phosphorus; 4% potash	Base or top-dressing	Balance of fast-acting inorganics and slow release organics. Acidifying action to lower soil pH.
Bulb fertilizer	4% nitrogen; 10% phosphorus; 6% potash	Base or top-dressing	Rich in slow-release organics. Applied at planting in fall and as topdressing in midspring to late spring.
Rose fertilizer	6% nitrogen; 6% phosphate; 4% potash; iron; magnesium	Topdressing	Fairly fast-acting. Apply in summer. Specially formulated for roses, but suitable for other flowering shrubs.
Iron tonic	6% chelated iron, 4% sulfur	Liquid feed	Cures yellowing caused by iron deficiency or alkaline soil.
Tomato fertilizer	8% nitrogen; 24% phosphate; 8% potash	Base or top-dressing	Incorporated into soil around base of seedling at time of transplanting; also as topdressing as fruiting begins.

COMPOST AND MANURES

All plants, especially fruits and vegetables, benefit from regular applications of organic material, in addition to fertilizers, to promote strong growth.

The requirements for organic matter go hand in hand with those for fertilizers. Organic material breaks down in the soil to become humus — a dark, gummy, fibrous substance that binds the soil particles into small groups, leaving gaps in between for air and water to circulate. The bacteria in the soil convert humus into chemical salts, which in turn become dissolved in water and are taken up by the roots of the plants for food.

If a heavily planted garden is supplied with ample fertilizer but no organic matter, it will deteriorate as the soil's existing humus is used up. In sandy soil, there will eventually be no material to contain water or to hold the soil particles together. The soil will dry out rapidly and could be eroded seriously. Clay soil will become harder as the humus becomes depleted, because there will be nothing left to hold the minute particles apart.

Soil that is supplied only with limited amounts of organic material but no fertilizer may lack the nutrients needed for healthy vegetables and good flower growth. In particular, soil bacteria consume a lot of nitrogen, which must be replenished.

Bulky organic manures for the garden can be difficult to obtain, especially for urban and suburban dwellers. A convenient alternative is compost, which you can buy at garden centers, or make yourself with vegetable waste matter from your garden and kitchen. (Do not confuse garden compost with potting soils, which may also be referred to as composts.)

◄ **PVC compost bins** These ready-made bins provide a convenient means of containing garden compost while it is decomposing. Several weeks or months need to elapse before waste from the garden is fully converted by soil bacteria into a usable, dark brown, crumbly, manurelike substance. With this type of bin, the rotted compost can be extracted from the bottom while new waste is being added continually to the top.

Making a compost pile

The material in a compost pile is broken down by bacteria and other microorganisms, which will thrive only if given air, water, nitrogen, nonacid conditions, and a high temperature. Unfortunately, the average suburban garden seldom yields enough material to create the necessary conditions to produce rapid fermentation and decay in a compost pile. However, there are many ways to improve the situation; the easiest is to build up the compost pile with extra material such as straw, grass clippings, or fallen leaves.

Even under ideal conditions, there are limits to the rapid breakdown powers of microorganisms, so do not put woody material — not even Brussels sprout stems — on the pile. Chop any tough stems into small pieces before adding them.

Never use obviously diseased or pest-infested plant material in the compost pile, as the rest of the compost can be infected. Don't add the roots of perennial weeds, such as quack grass, oxalis, or bindweed. Also, avoid seed-carrying annual weeds.

The best compost is made from soft rubbish, such as dead leaves, lettuces that have bolted, pea stalks and leaves, beet leaves, dead flowers, leafy hedge clippings, hay, straw, and grass clippings, along with material from your kitchen.

MAKING GARDEN COMPOST

1 Begin the compost pile on bare garden soil to allow excess water to drain away freely. Spread the first layer about 1 ft (30 cm) deep and about 5 x 5 ft (1.5 x 1.5 m) wide.

2 Press down the garden waste and soak it with water. Sprinkle ammonium sulfate at the rate of 2½ teaspoons per sq yd/m to speed up decomposition, then cover with a 2-in (5-cm) layer of soil.

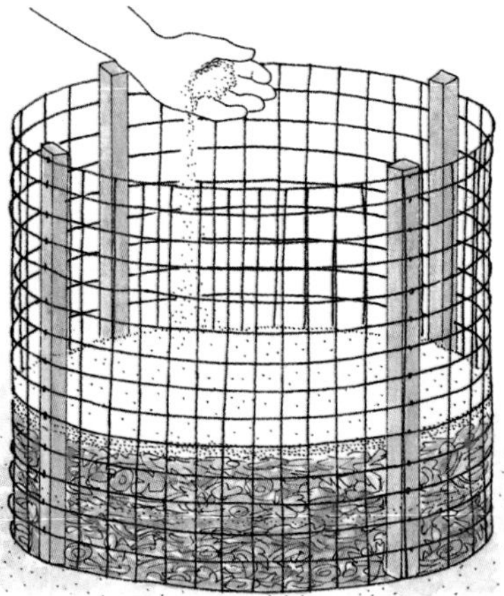

3 As you build up the pile, contain it within wire netting secured on wooden stakes. If your soil is acid, add a little lime to every alternate layer. Keep the top covered with plastic or burlap.

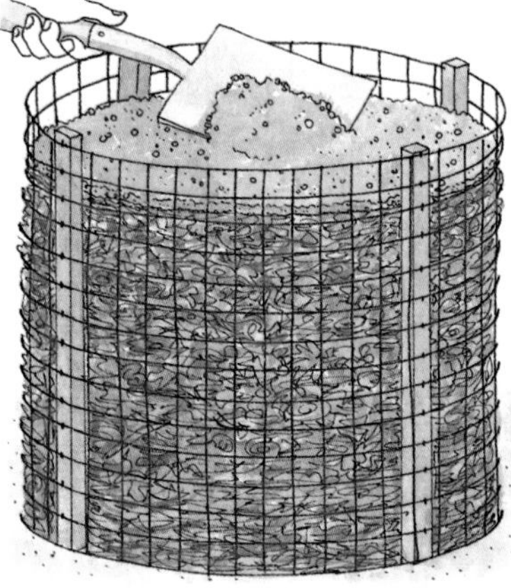

4 As garden waste becomes available, continue building the pile in 9- to12-in (23- to 30-cm) layers up to a height of about 4 ft (1.2 m). Sprinkle each layer with complete organic fertilizer.

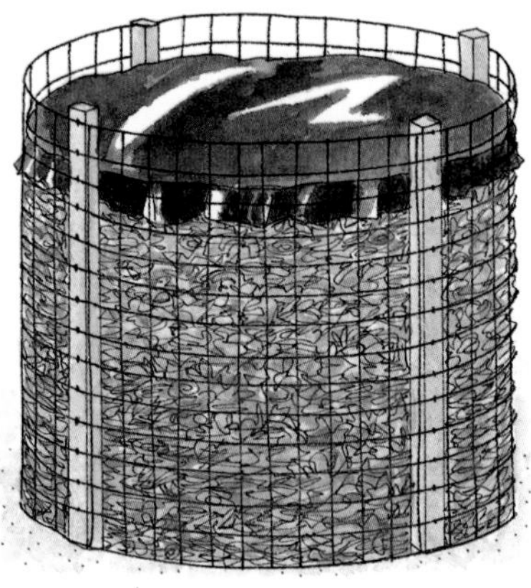

5 Cover with a final layer of garden soil. In dry areas, moisten the pile with water every 2 weeks. Heat will build up in the pile quite rapidly at first, but it will cool down as it decomposes.

6 After several weeks the pile will have shrunk to about one-third its original size. At this stage, turn the pile so that the outer material, which is slower to rot, can be placed on the inside.

You can collect compost from the kitchen. However, do not use any kitchen scraps — cooked or uncooked — that contain meat, poultry, fish, grease, dairy products, or protein of any kind. These can attract vermin or neighborhood animals, including dogs, cats, and raccoons to your compost pile. Mice, too, are sometimes lured by the heat of a compost pile. If you discover that animals are getting into your compost, try putting a fine mesh net around any open spaces or investing in one of the enclosed compost bins shown on the facing page. Insects and worms will find their way into the compost; they do not pose a problem and often contribute to the process of decomposition.

Situate the pile directly on the soil, so that any excess water can drain away. The soil beneath, however, should be well drained. Build the pile into a neat, regular shape, so that it is less likely to become dry around the edges. For quick results you will need a pile approximately 6 ft x 6 ft x 4 ft high (2 m x 2 m x 1.2 m). In a small garden, set up a closure of wire netting and posts. The dimensions must depend on the size of the garden, but 5 ft x 5 ft x 4 ft high (1.5 m x 1.5 m x 1.2 m) is about right for an average garden.

You can also buy ready-made compost bins or make an open-topped wooden box, leaving spaces between the side boards to let air through. Brick constructions are equally suitable, as long as you omit a few bricks from the sides for aeration. If one side of the box is removable, it will give easier access to the compost.

Try to build the pile a layer at a time, with each layer about 1 ft (30 cm) thick. Tread down each layer and then give it a good soaking with a hose. To each layer, add ammonium sulfate at about ½ oz (15 g) — 2½ teaspoons — per sq yd/m to act as an accelerator for the decomposition process. Cover the pile with 2 in (5 cm) of ordinary garden soil and then with plastic or burlap to keep in the heat until the last layer has been added.

For a free-standing compost pile, build it up to the desired height and gently slope the sides. If your soil is naturally alkaline, there is no need to add any amendments to the pile. If the soil is acid, sprinkle pulverized lime at the rate of 4 oz per sq yd (120 g per sq m) over every other layer, and again over the finished pile before covering with a final layer of garden soil. The lime will keep the pile sweet. In dry weather, hose the pile with water as soon as it shows signs of drying out.

Heat will build up rapidly when the pile is first made, but will cool down after about a month, when the pile will have shrunk to about one-third its original size.

To speed up decomposition, turn the pile every 6 weeks, moving the material on the outside of the pile into the center. At the same time, water any dry areas. If you use compost bins, simply transfer the contents to a second bin, mixing the contents thoroughly as you do so.

However, turning is not essential, and in 3 months (or more if the pile was made at the beginning of the winter) the pile will turn into a crumbly, dark brown, manurelike material that can be dug into the vegetable garden or spread thickly around border plants, including perennials, shrubs, and trees.

The normal application rate for garden compost is one 2½-gallon (10-liter) bucketful per sq yd/m. It can also be used as a topdressing or as a surface mulch.

If the pile is to remain undisturbed over winter, protect it by covering with plastic held down by bricks or stones, or tucked down between the compost and the rails of the bin.

Sources of organic matter

Many types of bulky organic waste can be dug in as a soil amendment. Some types are rich in plant nutrients while others have little immediate food value, but all add to the soil's humus content and improve its condition. Organic matter needs to be used in fairly large quantities. A good dressing would be a 2½-gallon (10 liter) bucketful per sq yd/m.

Farmyard manure, also called

COMPOST ENCLOSURES AND BINS

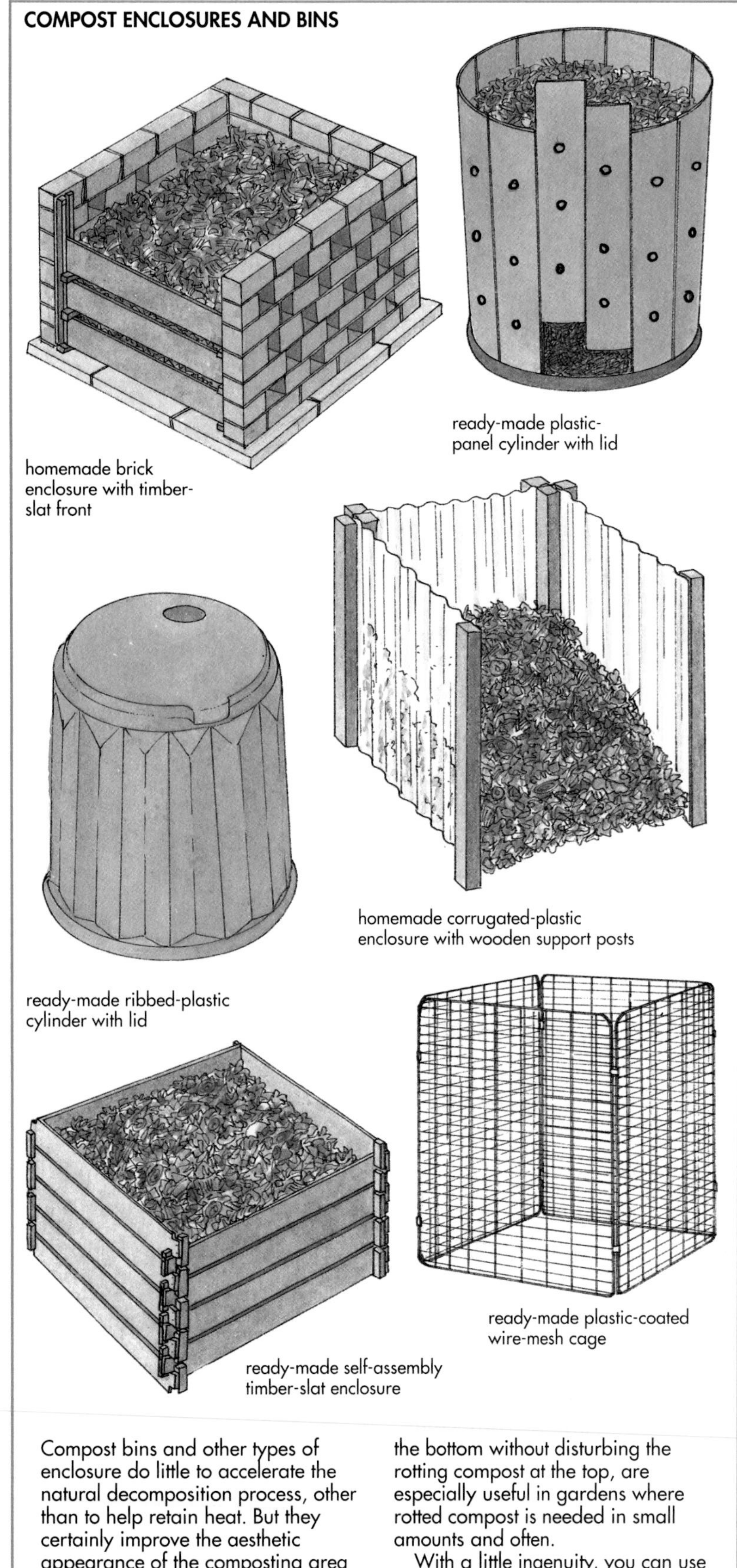

Compost bins and other types of enclosure do little to accelerate the natural decomposition process, other than to help retain heat. But they certainly improve the aesthetic appearance of the composting area — free-standing piles can look very unsightly in a small garden.

Specially designed bins, which allow compost to be extracted from the bottom without disturbing the rotting compost at the top, are especially useful in gardens where rotted compost is needed in small amounts and often.

With a little ingenuity, you can use bricks, corrugated plastic or iron, wire or plastic netting, chicken wire or timber to build an improvised compost enclosure.

stable manure, includes the animals' straw bedding, and is one of the best forms of organic manure. Its ammonia content may damage plants, however, so do not apply it until it has been composted. Composted manure is available at most garden centers.

Horse manure is "hot" — that is, it ferments rapidly — and so was traditionally used to warm hotbeds for raising early food crops. Although horse manure is one of the richest and driest manures, that sold by riding stables often contains mainly urine-soaked straw and a few droppings. It can decay rapidly into a disappointingly small pile.

Pig manure is slow to ferment and, when fresh, tends to be caustic and to burn the roots of young plants. It is best composted with straw and left for at least 3 months before use.

Cattle manure containing straw from the yards is wetter and lower in nutrients than horse manure; it decomposes slowly into the soil, and is therefore ideal for sandy soils.

Poultry litter may be bought in bulk from poultry farmers. This partly rotted mixture of droppings and straw or wood shavings is usually dry and dusty, and must be composted before use. It takes many weeks for the wood shavings or straw to break down. During this time the compost pile may develop an offensive smell, so it should be placed as far as possible from your house. When composted with soil, poultry litter is rich in nitrogen but deficient in potassium and phosphorus.

Spent mushroom compost may be available from mushroom nurseries. Mushrooms are grown commercially on a compost based mainly on horse manure. When all the mushrooms have been harvested, the compost is sold — either in bulk or in prepacked bags. It is a good garden manure or mulch, containing humus and plant foods. It also has lime, which makes it less suitable for soils that are already alkaline, though it won't do much harm unless applied every year.

Spent hops, sold direct by breweries, help to improve the physical condition of the soil, but they are low in plant nutrients. This deficiency can be remedied by composting them in conjunction with a complete fertilizer.

A THREE-COMPARTMENT BIN

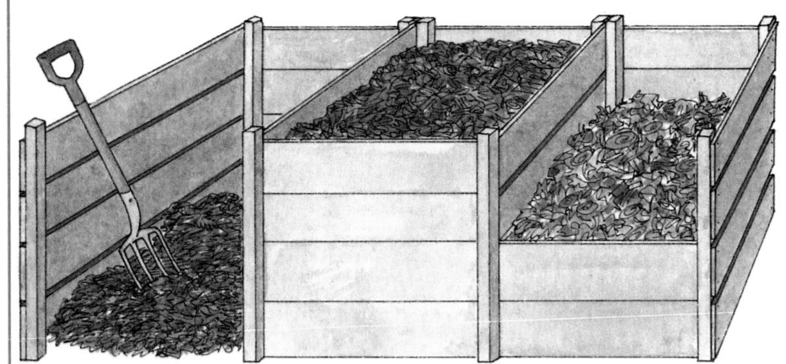

If you have enough space, a three-compartment timber bin is ideal. Construct it so that the front boards can be slipped into position as the boxes are filled. The left box contains compost being used; the middle box holds compost in the process of decomposing; and the right box is being filled. Fork the compost from one box to another to aerate it.

Sewage sludge, which is processed by some municipalities, is a well-balanced manure. Despite its unpleasant origin, this material is generally inoffensive to handle. It may also be available locally without cost; inquire at the Sanitation Department in your community. Before buying sewage sludge, make sure that it is free of toxic heavy metals.

Seaweed is rich in plant foods, especially nitrogen and potash, and breaks down quickly into humus. Stack seaweed for a month or two to allow rain to wash out most of the salt, then dig it in at the rate of about 12 lb per sq yd (5.5 kg per sq m).

Leaf mold is made by composting any fallen leaves, though oak and beech leaves are the most satisfactory, despite their acidity. (Do not use conifer needles.) To make leaf mold, pile up alternate layers of leaves and soil, each about 2 in (5 cm) deep. A sprinkling of complete fertilizer on each layer of leaves will assist decomposition. Do not make the pile more than 3 ft (1 m) high. Turn it at two- or three-month intervals.

Leaf-mold compost will be ready in about a year. Apply 5-6 lb per sq yd (2.5-3 kg per sq m).

Peat substitutes Peat products have long been used by gardeners, but the bogs from which peat is harvested do not renew themselves for many years. Peat adds nothing to soil fertility, and you may prefer to use alternatives from renewable natural resources. Composted bark is a by-product from the softwood timber industry and is sold at garden centers. Sawdust in its raw state is often available for free at lumberyards and mills. (Do not use sawdust from woods that have been pressure-treated with toxic chemicals.)

Once composted, both materials can be employed in much the same way as peat to improve the soil. They do, however, tend to deplete nitrates in the earth, so their use as soil amendments must be accompanied by extra doses of nitrogen fertilizers.

Green-manure crops are plants grown for the sole purpose of supplementing the soil. As they break down, they supply organic matter that enriches the soil structure. These crops are particularly valuable on heavy clay and light sandy soils. Plants you can grow for green manure include clover, buckwheat, comfrey, fenugreek, alfalfa, lupines, mustard, canola, and ryegrass.

After clearing away all current growth, plant the green-manure crop and allow it to grow for the amount of time specified by the supplier — usually for the winter months. Then cut the crop down and turn it into the soil. Ideally, wait for several months after the green manure has been dug in before you plant again.

Finally, local industries often provide sources of free or inexpensive organic materials, such as wool waste, peanut shells, feathers, tobacco stalks and stems, leather dust, and cottonseed hulls. Add these to your compost pile.

USING MULCHES

A surface dressing of a bulky organic or inorganic material reduces moisture loss from the soil, keeps roots cool in summer, and suppresses weed growth.

Soil is a natural reservoir for water, which is needed in varying degrees by all plants. The only natural source of water in most gardens is rain — and to a lesser extent snow — though moisture can seep in from adjacent streams and permanently boggy soil, especially in low-lying sites.

In addition to surplus rainwater that drains away, soil loses moisture in two ways — by direct evaporation from the surface and through the action of plants, which take up water in their roots and keep cool by transpiring it through their leaves.

During hot, dry spells the moisture content of soil needs to be supplemented by watering, but it can also be conserved by mulching. This technique entails placing a physical barrier between the moisture-holding soil and the air.

Mulches can be made from many materials — both organic and inorganic — but wood chips, shredded bark, garden compost, composted manure, and sheets of plastic or other material are the most commonly used types.

In some regions, other organic materials may be readily available for use as a mulch — spent mushroom compost from mushroom farms, spent hops and brewery waste, seaweed, straw, waste from cotton mills, and sawdust or wood shavings from sawmills.

In the long term, mulches of organic material, such as manure or compost, have an additional value — they ultimately add to the humus content of the soil.

Advantages of mulching

In addition to moisture conservation, placing a good mulch on the soil surface has other useful functions in the garden, around both crop plants and ornamentals.

❑ Weed seedlings are suffocated and shaded from light, so they mostly die soon after germinating. Continual use of sheet material, such as plastic, prevents weed seeds from establishing themselves in the soil. Annual weeds in particular are suppressed by mulches.

❑ Surface capping — crusting of the soil's surface — is prevented and good soil structure is maintained.

❑ Excessive fluctuations in surface-soil temperature — which can scorch delicate young roots — are reduced. Mulches also delay the risk of the soil freezing in areas where winters are cold.

❑ The decorative value of the ground around ornamental plants is increased by the use of some mulches — such as wood chips, or even gravel — especially where new beds or borders have a lot of space between young developing plants.

❑ Worms are attracted by the extra protection offered by surface mulches, and these creatures, in turn, improve the aeration of the soil.

❑ Grass clippings (provided they

◀ **Straw mulch** makes a useful surface dressing around these artichokes, helping to conserve soil moisture, keep roots cool, and suffocate weed seedlings as they emerge.

have not been treated with a chemical herbicide) can be used as a moisture- and nitrogen-retaining mulch around peas and bean beds.

❑ Alkaline-mulching materials, such as spent mushroom compost, composted seaweed, or limestone chips, work to prevent acid soils from becoming even more acid — they are unlikely to make an acid soil alkaline.

❑ Organic mulches, such as well-rotted manure or garden compost, add plant nutrients to the soil and increase its fertility.

❑ Sheet materials, such as plastic, and straw can be used to keep strawberries and other low-growing soft-fruit crops clean. Without mulch, rain often splashes soil and debris onto the fruits.

❑ With the improved soil conditions, vegetable crops frequently produce a higher yield, and ornamental plants grow faster, with better foliage and flowers.

Disadvantages of mulching

As with all good things, mulching has its disadvantages in certain situations, though many of these can be overcome.

❑ The roots of perennial weeds left in the soil before the mulch is applied can grow into new plants. They are not easy to eradicate by hand weeding or hoeing without disturbing the mulch.

❑ Some mulching materials, such as wood chips, can deplete the soil of nitrogen.

❑ It may be more difficult to apply fertilizers — especially granular forms — once the mulch is in place.

❑ Sheet plastic and other watertight materials prevent rainwater from reaching the plant roots under the mulch. Absorbent organic materials soak up light showers of water, keeping plant roots dry.

❑ All mulches can harbor pests, especially slugs, snails, and wireworms.

❑ If moist organic mulches smother the bases of plant stems, they can cause rotting.

Preparing the soil

The addition of a mulch to the surface of the soil will impede subsequent cultivation of the ground, so it is important to prepare the site thoroughly. Dig over the soil and eliminate all perennial weeds, either by hand weed-

ORGANIC MULCHES

▲ **Wood chips** make a decorative and long-lasting mulch. The large and relatively heavy particles don't blow away in the wind, and they prevent rain from splashing onto low plants. Rot-resistant cedar is a good choice.

▲ **Garden compost,** provided it is well rotted, can be applied as a combined mulch and soil conditioner — as it decomposes further, nutrients and humus are mixed into the soil. Renew it every year.

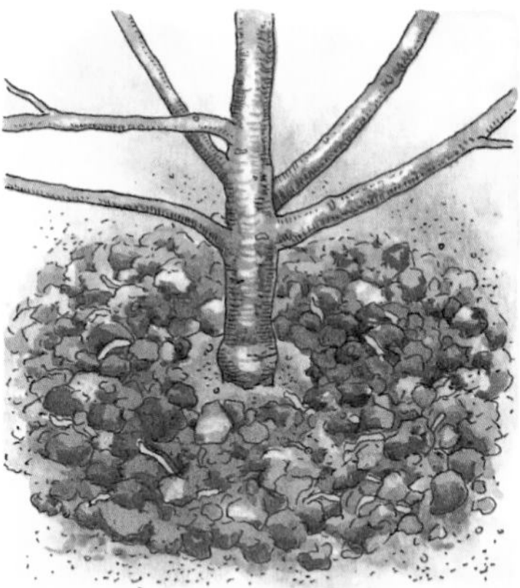

▲ **Stable manure** should be well composted; otherwise, it will scorch delicate roots and smell unpleasant. Don't pile it up around the base of plants. Undesirable grass weed seeds may be mixed with the straw.

▲ **Composted bark** is used as a mulch and can also be dug into the ground as a soil conditioner. It is good for acid-loving plants, and its dark color provides an excellent visual foil for decorative plants.

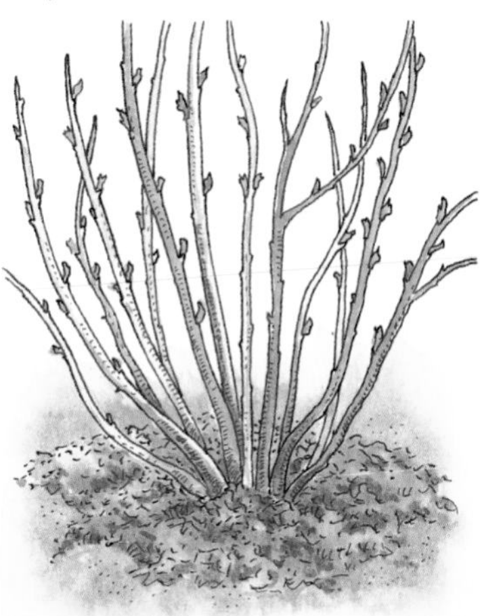

▲ **Grass clippings** can be used as a mulch, but compost them first. Avoid clippings from a lawn treated with chemical herbicide, and keep the mulch to a maximum of ½ in (1 cm).

▲ **Straw** makes a soft, open-textured mulch for strawberries and other low-growing soft fruit crops, helping to keep the ripening fruits clean. It is too obtrusive for use among ornamentals.

ing or by applying a selective herbicide, since even broken segments of root can grow into new plants and penetrate the mulch. At the same time, remove as many annual weeds as possible.

Rake in a general-purpose slow-release fertilizer that will feed your plants for several months after laying the mulch. Later feeding can be achieved by using liquid fertilizers applied to the foliage or to the ground, but it will be impossible to mix granular types with the soil.

If you plan to use organic material that has not been composted, it will deplete nitrogen from the soil as it decomposes. Rake in an extra dressing of nitrogenous fertilizer at the rate of about a handful per sq yd/m before mulching. If the reason for laying a mulch is to conserve moisture, ensure that the soil is saturated with water before covering it. Either wait for a heavy downpour of rain or water the site by hand. The water in the soil will still be depleted by the plants and by evaporation, and you will need to water during dry periods, but not as often as you would if the soil had no mulch.

Using mulches

When and how to apply a mulch will depend on your choice of material and its main purpose.

Midspring is generally the best time to use a mulch — at this point in the year weeds are rarely established and the ground is moist. Don't mulch any earlier, because it is also important for the ground to be warmed up by the sun. Once applied, a mulch acts as an insulating blanket.

The plants that will profit most from a regular yearly mulch are your garden's long-term residents — the shrubs, roses, fruit trees and bushes, especially the surface-rooting raspberries, and strawberries. All these plants remain in the same place year

A LIVING MULCH

Certain shallow-rooted low-growing plants can themselves be used as a living mulch around the roots of larger plants that like their roots to be cool and moist. Here, golden creeping Jenny *(Lysimachia nummularia* 'Aurea') provides the right cool soil conditions for a large-flowered clematis hybrid, without competing significantly for water or nutrients. It's also a very decorative feature in its own right.

INORGANIC MULCHES

▲ **Circles of roofing felt** eliminate the need for grass trimming around trees. Cover with a layer of bark mulch for an attractive effect.

▲ **Black plastic** is a good mulch for conserving soil moisture and suppressing weeds, especially around thirsty salad crops such as tomatoes.

▲ **Fabric mulches** of woven or spun plastics let air and water pass to strawberry roots but suppress the growth of weeds. They also help to keep fruits clean and free of soil-borne pests.

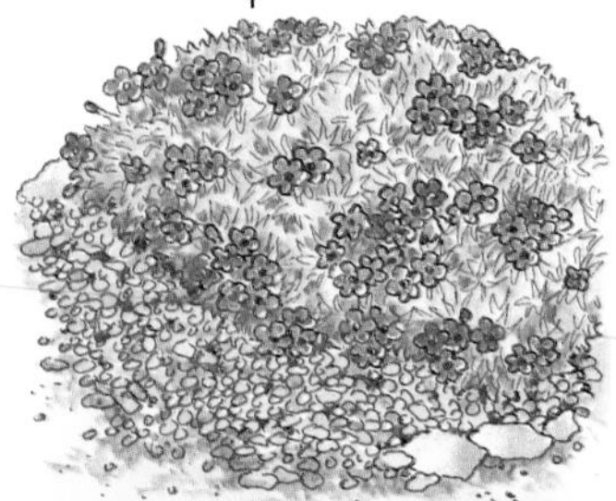

▲ **Crushed rock** or coarse gravel makes a natural-looking, free-draining mulch around alpines. It keeps the collars of the plants dry and rot-free.

LAYING A BLACK PLASTIC MULCH

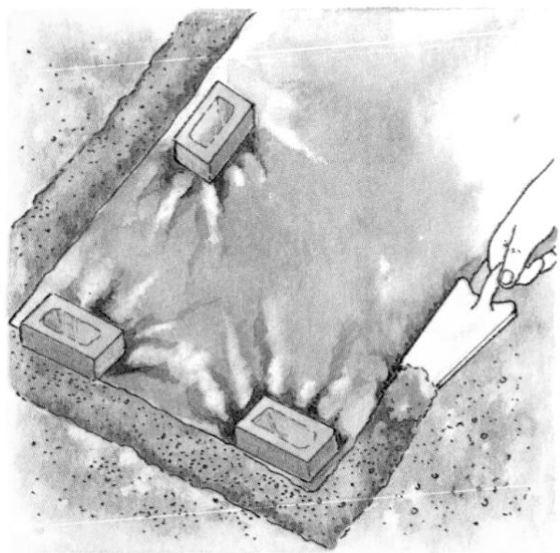

1 Prepare the planting bed as usual. Then lay the plastic sheeting over the entire area, allowing a little overhang at the edges. Using a hand trowel, make a shallow trench all around the perimeter of the bed.

2 Tuck the edges of the plastic into the trench, then anchor them by refilling the trench with soil. The surface of the plastic should be flat but not too taut. Don't tread on the mulch — work at all times from the edges.

3 Using a sharp knife or scissors, cut crossed slits at the required spacings to act as planting and watering holes. Then dig planting holes in the soil below the slits, using a hand trowel or bulb planter.

4 Insert young plants through the slits, patting the soil down underneath the mulch. Water well through the slits and make sure that the plastic is smoothed back around each plant stem.

after year, and there is usually room to work around them. Herbaceous borders and vegetable gardens also benefit from a spring mulch.

If possible, mulch all bare soil in your garden, except around annual seedlings or tiny, newly planted rock garden plants until they are well established.

As a general rule, leave a gap of 1-2 in (2.5-5 cm) around plant stems. Most young ornamentals and vegetable plants are liable to suffer if an organic mulch, such as compost or manure, is in direct contact with them. They may become infected if the mulch contains any disease. Incompletely rotted compost could also burn the stems and basal leaves.

Any plant that is grown as a grafted variety on a rootstock — most roses and fruit trees, for instance — is further threatened if any mulch is piled up against its stem. The covering can induce the grafted variety to develop its own roots above the union with the rootstock. These roots can change the nature of the plant — on a fruit tree, for instance, the new roots will overpower any dwarfing effect of the rootstock, and so the tree will grow larger.

Thickness When using bulky organic or inorganic mulches around herbaceous plants, roses, and other established plants, apply an evenly forked layer that is 2-3 in (5-7.5 cm) deep. Both smaller plants and young plants require a thinner layer — 1 in (2.5 cm) is usually adequate. Straw or salt-marsh hay mulches around raspberry canes and berry bushes are most effective in a layer 3-4 in (7.5-10 cm) deep.

If you haven't got enough mulching material for all your needs, spread the appropriate depth around each individual plant. Leave the rest of the garden uncovered rather than applying too thin a layer over it.

At the other extreme, don't be too generous with the mulch. If it is spread too thickly, the mulch becomes just another rooting zone for weeds and will cut down on the amount of air and water able to get through to the soil and the roots beneath.

Special uses

Black or clear plastic sheeting can serve as a surface covering to protect a newly prepared bed from the elements — keeping it in prime condition until sowing or planting. This mulch is excellent if you garden only a day or two per week or you are ruled by the weather. Secure the plastic in place with a few bricks or stones.

Reduce weeds in a seed bed by using a clear plastic mulch to promote the germination of weed seeds. After initial preparations of the bed, anchor the plastic with a few bricks until weed seedlings appear. Remove the plastic and hoe off the weed seedlings. Then sow your vegetable or flower seeds without disturbing the surface of the seed bed any further.

Weed-free salt marsh hay can be used to protect the crowns of perennial plants that are not reliably frost-hardy. Lay the hay over the crowns in late fall and cover this with a sheet of plastic anchored with a few bricks or large stones. Remove the plastic covering in spring.

Try clear plastic sheeting as a surface mulch to warm up the soil in spring and early summer. Grow early crops — potatoes, tomatoes, zucchini, and sweet corn, for instance — through the plastic, and their roots will be kept several degrees warmer than normal, speeding growth.

Shallow-rooted plants that hug the ground, such as pachysandra, provide a decorative soil cover beneath taller growing plants. At the same time, they form a living, weed-smothering mulch for adjoining plants.

Lawns and hedges

In terms of garden design, lawns are the carpets, and hedges are the walls, of an outdoor living space. As with interior design, careful thought should go into the choice and placement of lawns and hedges since they are both permanent features and provide a constant, soothing green setting for short-lived seasonal displays of flower color. Usually the aim is to create a large, often flat surface that contrasts with the livelier shapes of flowers, trees and shrubs, garden furniture and ornaments.

Choosing the right lawn grasses and hedge plants for your garden depends largely on their intended use. Soil, aspect, and climate must also be considered, along with your taste, budget, and style.Hedges, for example, can create security, shelter and privacy, or be purely decorative. They can be evergreen or deciduous; flowering or foliage only; formal or informal; and plain or ornate (even incorporating topiary and arches). Lawns can be started from sod or seed; be low- or high-maintenance; and range from golf-course perfect to all-purpose family areas, and even rough, wild meadows.

Site and soil preparation, leveling for lawns, and planting or sowing techniques are important, as is early care, while the young lawn or hedge becomes established. But the overall garden picture can be perfected only with regular maintenance. Feeding, watering, and seasonal mowing or trimming keep lawns and hedges healthy and attractive. Any lawn troubles or areas needing repair should be dealt with quickly and effectively to minimize damage and maintain a consistently lush appearance.

Green carpets Closely cut, neatly trimmed lawns are the hallmark of good gardening.

GRASS IN THE GARDEN

A beautiful lawn, as smooth and dense as a golf course, is many gardeners' dream. It can come true if you create the best conditions possible.

Lawns are one of the garden's most popular features, and for good reasons. A lawn can draw together your garden's other elements into a harmonious whole. An established, well-tended lawn provides a background of green that — in many parts of North America — can last all year round. It offers cool, restful relief next to the brighter colors of flowers and contributes textural contrast to the bolder forms of branches and foliage.

An uninterrupted stretch of grass is a marvelous surface for recreation, be it throwing a football or sunbathing. Lawns are also particularly suitable for toddlers, allowing them to be adventurous without suffering cuts or grazed knees from hard surfaces.

However, there are also some drawbacks. If you are starting a lawn from scratch, it takes a lot of preparation — leveling, removing debris and weeds, and improving the condition of the soil, then seeding or laying sod. Unlike most trees and shrubs, which, once established, more or less look after themselves, lawns require careful watering, mowing, and fertilizing to keep them looking healthy. However, don't despair if you've inherited a neglected lawn. There are solutions to most lawn problems (pp. 45–48).

Where to put the lawn

Some grasses are more capable of growing in shade than others, but no lawn will thrive in deep shade, especially under trees, where roots and the overhanging canopy of leaves can make the soil bone-dry and starved of nutrients. Nor will lawns prosper in waterlogged

▼**Lawn design** A well-planned lawn is more than a stretch of grass — it draws together the various components of a garden, while providing greenery that acts as a foil to foliage and brightly colored flowers.

The addition of elegant brick-edged terraces has made this lawn a central feature of the garden.

▲ **Grassy banks** A slope can be used to link two different lawn levels as long as it doesn't take heavy use. Make sure that the slope isn't too steep, or cutting the grass can be a problem.

◀ **Ground covers** in place of grass Chamomile is less hard wearing than lawn grass. Use stepping-stones to save it from wear and tear.

soil, although some grass is more tolerant of damp soil than others.

Lawns can also be sloped, or even sunken, to form a sheltered seating area and create a feeling of intimacy. Raised lawns add interest, while providing informal seating on the retaining wall. Small raised lawns, however, look odd and dry out quickly in hot areas. With raised and sunken lawns, easy access for a mower is important.

Shaping a lawn

A formal square or rectangular lawn surrounded by borders is one of the most popular garden layouts. Such a lawn usually echoes the property's boundaries. But the shape of a lawn can also differ from that of the garden.

Interestingly shaped areas of lawn — those that extend partway across the yard — can add a sense of mystery as to what lies beyond. As a general rule, though, the simpler the shape, the better a lawn looks and the easier it is to maintain. Avoid small, fussy curves and lots of small island beds. Both of these work against a lawn's soothing quality and make mowing difficult. With an island flower bed, see that there is at least a mower's width of lawn between this bed and any others.

Whatever a lawn's shape, a strip of edging, such as a single row of bricks, wooden timbers, or paving stones, between lawn and flower or vegetable beds makes mowing much more convenient.

Types of lawn

There are over 10,000 species of grass. Many have been developed from European grasses, adapted for the different climate zones of North America. Grasses are usually categorized as either Southern (generally warm-season) or Northern (more commonly cool-season), but there is a large transitional zone that stretches from southern California to the District of Columbia. Southern grasses flourish during the hot, humid months of summer. Northern grasses are able to survive through winter months as well as summer.

Most turf grasses are sold as blends of different grass types. For instance, a typical Northern seed blend might contain grasses that grow in bunches, such as the fescues (*Festuca*), and sod-forming types, such as Kentucky bluegrasses (*Poa pratensis*), which have leafy shoots that creep along the ground. Typical Southern grasses include Bermuda, zoysia, centipede, and Bahia. The blend you choose should be suitable for your climate, soil type, and rainfall. Consult your local Cooperative Extension or Agricultural Service to find out which type to plant in your area.

Beautiful velvety lawns are made up of named cultivars of such fine-leaved grasses as bent grass. These tend to be demanding grasses that require a lot of water and fertilizer to look their best. Many of these grasses are also relatively delicate and do not stand up to heavy wear or periods of neglect. In addition, they tend to be vulnerable to invasion by stronger, coarser grasses, such as common tall fescue (*Festuca arundinacea*) — close mowing is needed to discourage them from gaining a foothold. Any coarse grasses or lawn weeds that do become established stick out like a sore thumb. Furthermore, any small bump, hollow, or awkward level change is immediately noticeable because the lawn hugs the ground so closely.

Ordinary, hard-wearing lawns often include relatives of these finer cultivars — grasses of the same species but not of any special cultivar. They give the lawn a healthy diversity and make the seed more economical. For extra durability, a lawn may include broad-leaved bunch-type grasses, such as turf-type tall fescues or turf-type perennial ryegrasses (*Lolium perenne*). These grasses

▼ **Formal layouts** In this split-level garden, the sharply trimmed lawn edges, flower beds, pathways, and hedges create a formal geometric design.

▲ **Grass paths** Beneath pergolas and archways, grass paths look inviting and intimate. Use a hard-wearing grass mixture that will also tolerate light shade.

Alternatives to grass

Grass tolerates heavier wear than any other plant, and is self-renewing once established. But there are alternatives. Many ground covers require less water and little care. Before planting a ground cover, however, make sure it is suitable for your zone and that you can meet its watering needs.

Chamomile (*Chamaemelum nobile*) was a favorite lawn with the Elizabethans because of its sweet scent when bruised. Though short lived, it does not need to be cut and it is softer and springier to walk on than grass. Creeping thyme (*Thymus serpyllum*) is another possibility for small areas. It, too, is sweetly scented, but can also become thin and uneven. Both need full sun and free-draining, sandy soil.

Paths of pennyroyal (*Mentha pulegium*) and Corsican mint (*M. requienii*) are lovely, but they tend to be invasive.

► **Semiwild corners** Meadow grass cuts maintenance to a minimum, as it needs mowing only twice a year. Wildflowers and garden flowers can flourish undisturbed among the long grass.

are slow to knit into a turf, but very tough once established. However, broad-leaved grasses need frequent mowing, especially in spring and summer.

Meadow areas, spaces of coarser grass that you allow to grow long, can be placed at the periphery of large gardens to create a rustic feel. They are ideal for naturalizing bulbs, such as daffodils and bluebells, and concealing their unsightly foliage as it fades. Selected wildflowers, such as coneflowers, bee balms, coreopsis, and butterfly weeds, can be encouraged, particularly those that attract butterflies.

Coarse grass needs cutting only twice a year — once after the bulbs have died down completely and again in the fall. Weeding can be a problem, though, since ground elder, ragwort, thistles, plantains, and brambles quickly establish themselves. Apply a selective lawn herbicide once the bulbs have completely died down.

LAWN MAKING

For a pleasing end result, plan your lawn first, if only in your mind's eye — and prepare the site thoroughly.

▲ **Lawn stripes** Use a sharp reel mower to maintain regular stripes in closely cut grass.

▼ **Stepping-stones** Prime-quality lawns don't tolerate a lot of hard wear. Lay paths of paving stones, stepping-stones, or wooden logs on the routes most often followed through the garden.

A prime-quality lawn — fine-textured, even, and with a short pile — makes a wonderfully cooling and refreshing visual impact. Such perfection is achieved through sowing fine-leaved grasses of compact growth, mowing frequently to prevent coarser grasses from becoming dominant, constant maintenance, and minimum wear. But what most people need is a lawn that is hard wearing, long lasting, and easy to maintain. A lawn that will stand up to reasonable wear and can tolerate a certain degree of neglect contains grasses that are coarser and broader-leaved than a prime-quality lawn. It won't have a luxuriant, close texture — although a sharp mower will help to improve the finish — but will present a pleasing contrast to the color and leaf shapes of flower beds and shrubs, while allowing you and your family to enjoy it as an outdoor recreation area.

Preparing the site

The optimum time to sow depends on the type of seed. Northern grasses, such as Kentucky bluegrass, germinate best from late summer through early

PREPARING THE BED

1 Break down clods using a roller or by trampling systematically with your feet over the surface. Then rake the bed carefully, removing stones and debris.

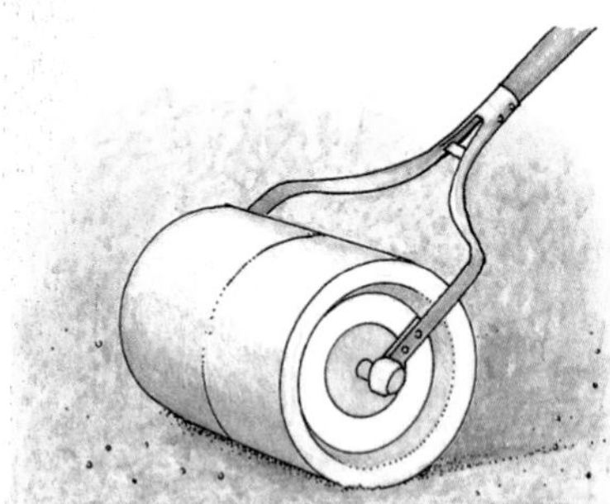

2 Once you have made a level bed with an even, stone-free surface, roll over the area again with a lawn roller to make sure it is quite firm. Work in two directions at right angles to each other.

3 A week later, firm the bed again by trampling across it, putting all your weight on your heels. Rake, then repeat both procedures until the bed is even, firm, and absolutely level.

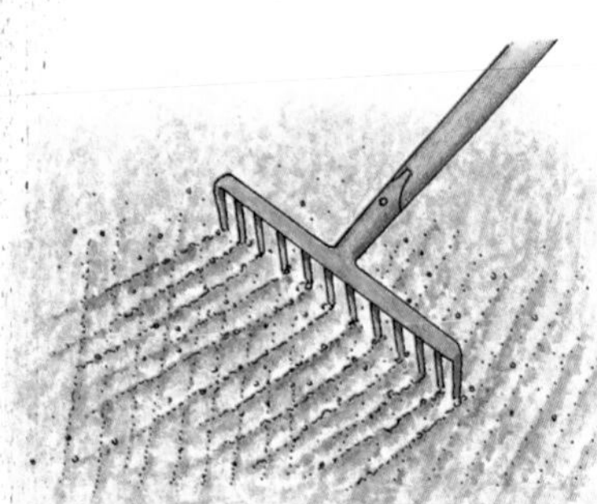

4 Lastly, rake in a general-purpose fertilizer and leave the bed untouched for a further week before sowing seed or laying sod. Have the sod delivered as close to the laying time as possible.

fall, while Southern species, such as Bermuda grass, grow at their best from late spring through early summer. Sod may be laid anytime the soil is not frozen and the weather is not excessively hot. Whenever you plan to sow seed or lay sod, you must start preparing the ground at least 3 to 4 months in advance.

Leveling Begin by clearing the site of all debris, then you can concentrate on adjusting levels and dealing with any drainage problems. A gentle slope can be an advantage and, on a large area, slight undulations are not a problem. But no lawn should have abrupt bumps and hollows.

Small-scale irregularities can easily be adjusted if you first lay out stakes and string at an equal height across the site — you can use the level string as a guide. You may need to bring in some topsoil to fill hollows; even when you take soil from bumps, you should leave an absolute minimum of 6 in (15 cm) of topsoil. A lawn roller is the best tool for leveling a site; they are available at many tool-rental suppliers.

Drainage On most sites, improving the soil texture by adding bulky organic matter or inorganic matter, such as sharp sand, will give the free drainage that a lawn needs. On heavy clay soils you may have to construct drainage holes at the end of sloping sites (p.13). Having a professional install drainage tiles bedded in gravel in the subsoil is an effective but costly solution that should be considered only if other attempts to improve drainage fail.

Weeding Dig the area or work it over with a power tiller about 3 months before sowing or sodding to allow weed seeds to germinate and the soil to be broken down by weathering. Avoid bringing subsoil to the surface, and remove stones and dig out the roots of perennial weeds as you go along.

Hoe out weeds that grow during the weathering process or treat them with a selective herbicide. A final treatment is useful just before preparation of the surface.

Preparing the bed Success in establishing a lawn depends on having a well-leveled, firm bed. The worked surface, or tilth, should be finer for sowing seed than for sodding. Break down clods using a roller, if you have one, or trample over the surface. Choose a day when the soil is reasonably dry to do this activity. Next, rake across the bed, removing any stones or debris.

About a week later, firm the ground by working your way systematically across it, treading very closely and putting your weight on your heels. Rake and then repeat both procedures, this time moving at right angles to the direction you first took.

Repeat until there are no soft patches and no bumps and depressions. The top layer of soil should have a crumbly texture. At this stage, rake in a small handful of complete fertilizer per sq yd (sq m) and leave the soil to settle for about a week before sowing seed or laying sod.

Buying sod

Buy sod from a reputable supplier and ask to see a sample first. Enough sod to fill the average yard is a substantial investment, and you should shop carefully.

Sod is cut in various sizes, but there is rarely a choice from any one supplier. Most are cut to a width of 2 ft (60 cm). Lengths

SOD OR SEED?

Sod

- ❑ Gives instant cover and color, and can be walked on quite soon.
- ❑ Not prone to seedling troubles.
- ❑ Planting bed doesn't have to be as finely prepared as for seed sowing, but sod is very heavy to lay.
- ❑ May be laid anytime the ground is not frozen and the weather not excessively hot.
- ❑ Should contain virtually no coarse grasses or weeds.
- ❑ Deteriorates quickly if not laid within a few days of delivery.
- ❑ An expensive option, especially prime-quality and seeded sod.

Seed

- ❑ Less physically demanding to "lay," but requires a finely prepared bed.
- ❑ Doesn't deteriorate quickly after purchase.
- ❑ The cheapest option.
- ❑ Contains no introduced weeds.
- ❑ Best sown in late summer to fall or late spring to early summer — a busy period in the garden.
- ❑ Takes a year to reach maturity, during which time the lawn cannot be used and needs close attention.
- ❑ Seed frequently eaten by birds.
- ❑ Seedlings prone to damping-off and competition from weeds.

LAYING SOD

1 Lay the first row at one edge; adjust level as you go. Press it down firmly.

2 Standing on a plank, lay the next row with sod staggered like brickwork.

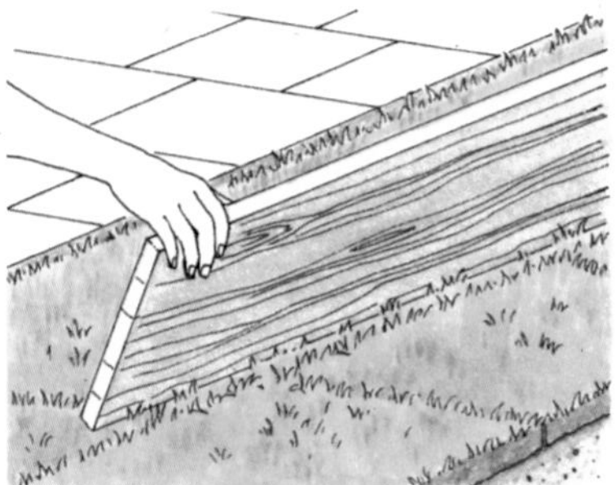

3 Roll over the plank onto the second row, then lay the third row, and so on.

4 Lightly roll the lawn twice, first in one direction, then the other.

5 Lift the flattened grass and remove any debris, using a rake.

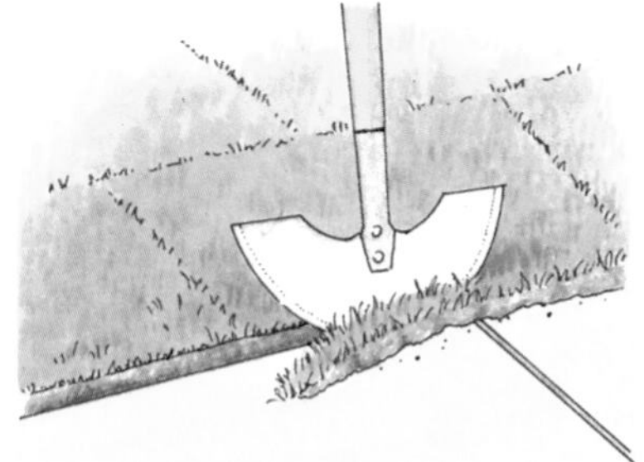

6 Once the lawn is fully laid, trim all the edges with an outward sloping cut.

greater than 3 ft (1 m) can be difficult to handle.

The grass should be healthy looking, with no weeds — these can be hidden from view if the grass is not cut reasonably short. Check that the sod is of uniform depth — about $^{3}/_{4}$-1 in (2-2.5 cm) thick — and that the soil is of satisfactory quality. The roots should be well developed, so that the strips show no tendency to fall apart. The rolled-up or folded strips should be neither soggy nor dry, but evenly moist. Don't buy any sod whose leaf blades are of poor, pale color or that show any signs of yellowing.

Also make sure that the sod originated at a good sod farm and that it is, in fact, composed of the species or variety advertised. If in doubt about whether to buy an advertised grass type, contact your local Cooperative Extension or Agricultural Service.

Laying sod

When the sod is delivered, it can be left stacked for a couple of days; if you have to wait any longer before laying it, spread it out in a shady place. Do not lay sod when the ground is frozen. Lay the sod a row at a time, with the first row slightly overhanging the edge of the lawn area. Remove any weeds that you find in the sod as you lay it and discard any strips that have a lot of weeds. Keep the strips uniformly level by adding or removing soil underneath the sod.

Press the first row down firmly before starting the next one. Work across the rows you have already laid, using a plank to stand on. Stagger rows like brickwork, but never have less than half-sized pieces of sod at the end of a row. Do not try to bend sod to fit curving edges; lay it in straight lines and trim off the excess later.

When all the sod has been laid, fill any cracks with a topdressing consisting of half sharp sand and equal quantities of organic material and good soil. Using a half-moon edging tool, or the edge of a flat-bladed spade, trim edges with an outward sloping cut. Brush the lawn with a garden rake to lift flattened grass and to remove debris, then water thoroughly.

Some experts recommend rolling a new lawn lightly about a week after the sod is laid. This procedure is not essential, but, if you are going to do it, roll first one way and then at right angles.

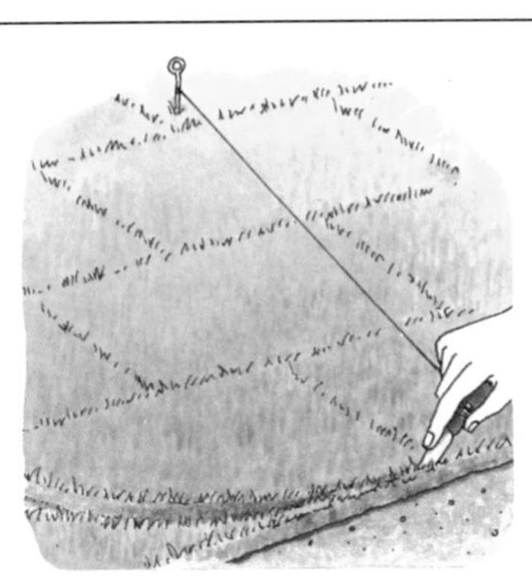

To cut a curved edge, first mark out the desired curve with a piece of string firmly attached to a peg. Cut an arc with a large, sharp knife held at the end of the taut string. Using a half-moon edging tool or a flat-bladed spade, sever the sod with a sloping cut.

Aftercare of newly laid sod

The new lawn may need watering to help it get established and to prevent the sod from shrinking. If any cracks do open up, fill these with the same mixture of sand, organic material, and good soil that you used before. When lawn growth starts in spring, begin your mowing regime with the mower blades set high; they can be gradually lowered as the lawn becomes established.

SOWING SEED

1 Hoe out any weeds that have germinated on the prepared seedbed. Then rake over the surface for a final time to make sure it is free of lumps and very even.

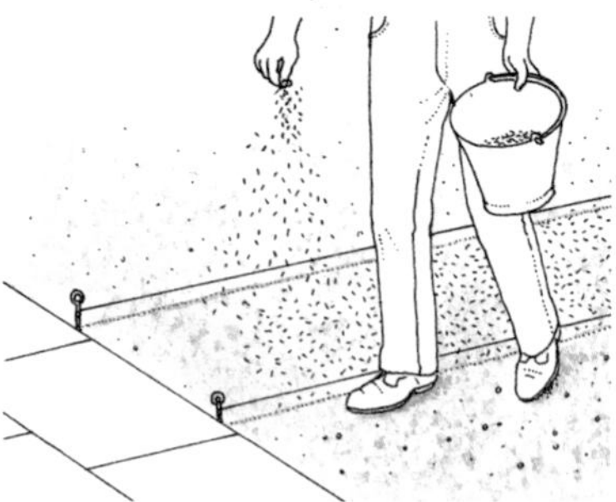

2 If sowing by hand, mark out strips about 3 ft (1 m) wide. Measure out the exact quantity of seed for a strip, then sow half the amount as you walk in one direction and half in the other.

Choosing a seed mixture

If you opt for seed, either buy a prepared seed mixture suitable for your particular region and conditions, or make up one with seed of several species. For most gardeners, especially those with a relatively small lawn area, it's easier to buy a mixture.

Each grass species has its own particular merits — some are good on light soils or in shady areas (though no lawn prospers under heavy shade), others resist dry conditions or extreme winter cold, or heavy use.

Special seed mixtures are available for particular soil types — there are selections for sandy soils, for example. Other mixtures give better results than the standard grades when grown in shaded areas. A shaded lawn, no matter which grass types it contains, should never be subjected to close cutting.

The highest-quality lawn-seed mixtures are composed of only the fine-leaved compact-grass types — and include mainly seed of named cultivars such as 'Merion' Kentucky bluegrass or 'Pennlawn' fine fescue. Mixtures for utility lawns may consist largely of named cultivars of coarser but tough bunch-forming grasses, such as the turf-type tall fescues. These tolerate heavy wear, withstand some neglect, and camouflage the infiltration of native grasses that would stand out as weeds on a high-quality lawn.

Less expensive mixtures include perennial ryegrass, old varieties of which, although quick to establish, tended to grow too vigorously and to die out when close cut. Recently developed fine-leaved ryegrasses are a great improvement and can be a useful addition to a utility lawn mixture.

Sowing seed

Choose a rain-free, still day for sowing, ideally when the soil is dry on top but moist just underneath. Begin by raking over the surface one last time, making sure it's free of lumps and rocks. Shake the seed and thoroughly mix it before dividing it up for sowing. Most seed should be sown at a rate of a small handful per sq yd (sq m) or 3 lbs per 1,000 sq ft (1.4 kg per 100 sq m), but check the supplier's instructions. Allow for additional seed that may be lost when sowing along the edges.

A mechanical spreader is fast and will help distribute the seed evenly — one type has a whirling disk that throws the seed out, covering the edges of each row as well as the center. If sowing by hand, mark out strips about 3 ft (1 m) wide to get an even distribution and to prevent double sowing. Always sow half the appropriate quantity in one direction and half in the other. After covering the entire area, lightly rake the seed into the soil.

A light scattering of mulch — it should be thin enough to show some of the soil — will speed germination by keeping the soil moist. Mulch will also prevent water from washing seed and soil down slopes. Don't use straw or hay, which contain weed seeds; salt-marsh hay is a better choice.

Aftercare of a new lawn

Lawn seed takes one to three weeks to germinate, depending on the seed type, humidity, and soil temperature. Immediately after sowing, water the ground thoroughly and give it three or four gentle sprayings daily thereafter until the grass sprouts. Ideally, use a lawn sprinkler adjusted to give a fine spray that will not dislodge the seeds or emerging young seedlings. Remove any weeds that appear at this stage by hand, taking care not to disturb the delicate young grass seedlings. It is important not to use chemical herbicides on newly sown lawns.

Watch for damping-off, which will show as yellowing and collapse of the young seedlings. Promptly spray the affected area with an appropriate fungicide. If necessary, reseed the area with a seed mixture that has been treated with fungicide.

When it stands 2½ – 3 in (6-7 cm) high, cut it for the first time. Take off about ½ in (1.2 cm). In subsequent cuttings, the mower blades can be gradually adjusted until they are set to the height recommended on page 41. Avoid too much wear and tear on the lawn for the first year.

Sprigs and plugs

For gardeners in the Southern states, there is one more option: starting a new lawn from sprigs or plugs. This is, in fact, the regular approach for such standard Southern turfs as the hybrid Bermuda grasses, St. Augustine grass, and zoysia grass, and is often used with carpet grass and centipede grass.

Sprigs may be bought by the bushel, and should have roots at the time of delivery, or at least two to four nodes each from which roots can develop. If you cannot plant the sprigs immediately, keep them cool and moist. Plugs — which are small circles or squares of living sod — are less perishable, but also respond best to prompt planting.

To plant sprigs, use a hoe to cut furrows 2-3 in (5-7.5 cm) deep — at intervals 4-12 in (10-30 cm) apart — across the lawn area. Lay the sprigs in the furrows at 12-in (30-cm) intervals, taking care to run any tips with leaves up over the furrow's top. Then pull the soil back to fill the furrows, leaving only leaves exposed.

When planting plugs, simply set them into holes of the same size and depth at intervals 6-12 in (15-30 cm) apart. After planting sprigs or plugs, roll the lawn lightly and then water it immediately.

ALL-SEASON LAWN CARE

A lawn needs regular care — especially mowing and feeding — if it is to become and remain first-class turf in both appearance and texture.

The basis of a really good lawn is careful preparation of the site before sowing or sodding. Adequate drainage is essential, although the soil itself must be moisture-retentive and not be shaded by a dense overhead tree canopy. By judicious fertilizing, eliminating weeds, and regular watering in dry weather, the grass will soon become established. But even an existing lawn can quickly deteriorate if it does not receive proper attention.

To maintain healthy growth, color, and texture, a lawn should be cut and aerated routinely, raked, topdressed with fertilizer, weeded, and kept free of fungi (such as blight or pink snow mold) and pests (such as beetle grubs or chinch bugs).

Regular mowing is the most important requirement — an operation similar in effect to pruning. If it is carried out frequently in late spring, when growth is at its most vigorous, it will encourage a thick, firm but resilient turf to develop, which will be resistant to drought, diseases, and insects, as well as invasion by weeds and moss. If cut infrequently, the coarser grasses become dominant, and will sometimes smother the finer, more desirable grasses completely.

Fertilizing is another essential spring activity. As the grass begins to grow again, its vigor must be maintained. A lawn that is well supplied with the correct nutrients will also recover quickly from any environmental setback, such as drought or heavy use.

Nor should the lawn be forgotten in fall. You must try to correct conditions that may have developed during the summer, such as compaction, wear, thin patches, thatch (a layer of grass roots, runners, and stems that builds up between the grass and the soil), or emerging fungal diseases.

Mowing

A lawn must be cut in order to preserve its attractive appearance, but a balance between visual charm and plant health must also be maintained. In general, the grass should be kept tall enough to prevent it from being starved of energy, but short enough to look tidy. How often you should mow depends on how rapidly your grass grows. It can be as often as once a week in the height of the growing season (late spring and early summer) but twice a month should be adequate at other times. If the lawn is cut frequently, the job is neither very strenuous nor time consuming. The mowing season is from early spring to midfall, but an occasional light topping may be needed in southern areas where winters are fairly mild.

Do not mow when the grass is very wet, since you will damage the surface both with the mower and with your feet. You will also clog the mower with mud and clippings. Riding mowers should be used only when the soil immediately below the surface is fairly dry; otherwise, the wheels will sink in, leaving deep tracks.

◀ **Pleasing green** A neat lawn, rich in color, with an even texture and free of weeds and bare patches, is every gardener's dream. Regular maintenance — mowing, trimming, watering, raking, fertilizing, and aerating — will give you a healthy lawn.

Before mowing the grass, remove debris with a spring lawn rake. If you have a lot of debris on the lawn, it will form uneven humps, rot the grass, and cake mower blades. How high you cut your lawn depends primarily on the type of grass; bent grass should be cut to a height of ½ in (1.2 cm) for example, while turf-type tall fescues should be left to grow to 3-4 in (7-10 cm). Leave the grass slightly longer in hot, dry weather; cut it shorter in early spring and fall.

Mowing in parallel strips gives a lawn the best appearance, but you should change direction at successive mowings so that the new mowing is made at right angles to the previous one. This method prevents the lawn from forming ridges. Push the mower at a constant speed in a forward direction, completing each strip in one nonstop pass — moving a reel mower back and forth creates an uneven surface.

CHOOSING A LAWN MOWER

push-reel mower

electric-powered rotary mower

gasoline-powered reel mower

gasoline-powered rotary mower

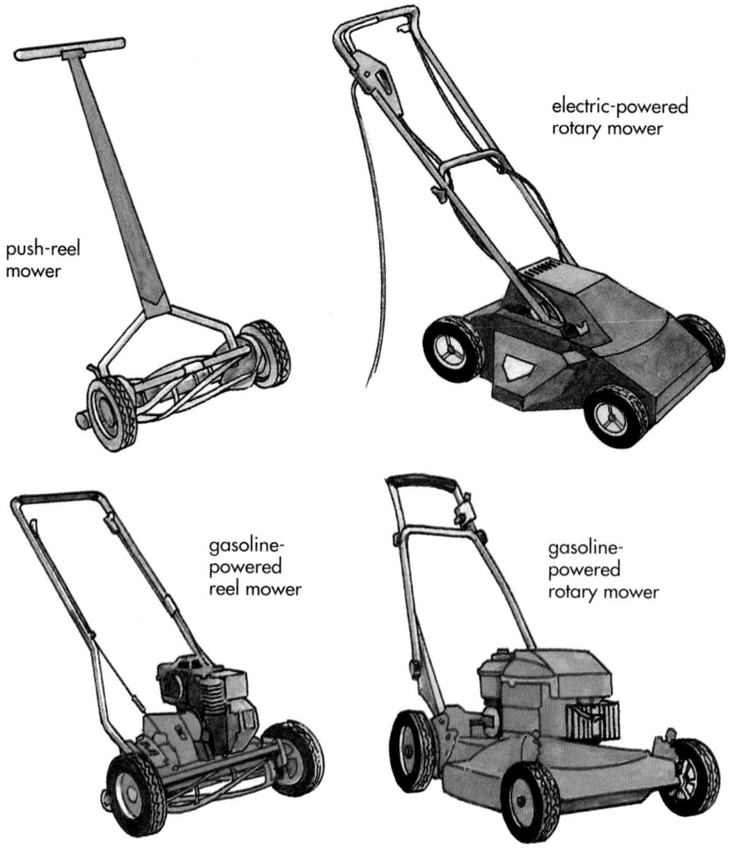

There are a multitude of lawn mowers on the market, including those that are powered by hand, electricity, or gasoline. For small gardens, the hand-driven or electric types are adequate — both demand far less maintenance than a gasoline-powered mower. The more powerful gas mowers will ease the task of cutting larger lawns — and with a really large yard, a riding mower is both a labor- and time-saver. But for a lawn of a half acre or less, especially one interrupted with trees, shrubs, and other obstacles, a riding mower is hard to maneuver and unnecessary.

Reel mowers have blades arranged in a spiral that cut with a scissorlike action, producing a particularly neat surface. The cutting height can be set to various levels by raising or lowering the back roller. Reel mowers are less suitable for coarse grass since wiry flower stalks remain intact and tufts are often flattened rather than cut.

Rotary mowers cut with a slashing action — one or more blades rotate at high speed — which makes them better for cutting long grass or going over bumpy surfaces. However, the quality of cut is coarser than that of a reel mower.

Both rotary and reel mowers may come equipped with a grass catcher designed to collect clippings for easy disposal. "Mulching" mowers have blades that shred grass clippings before dropping them back onto the lawn so that the operator is spared the task of removal. This type not only saves work, it reduces the lawn's need for fertilizer.

Caution: Follow the safety precautions listed below and by the manufacturer whenever using an electric- or gas-powered mower.

Creative mowing

Parallel-striped lawns, with alternating bands of light and dark grass, give a garden a formal appearance. You can achieve a striped finish on a lawn by mowing each strip in alternate directions. Reel mowers, which have their blades mounted on a roller, are the best tool for creating this effect, but rotary mowers can produce a similar look.

If a small lawn is striped lengthwise, it makes a garden seem longer. Similarly, a long, narrow lawn striped crosswise takes on an additional feeling of width.

Lawn mower safety

Accidents can, and do, happen frequently with lawn mowers. When using any power mower, keep pets away and do not allow children to play on the lawn while you are working. Do not leave electric mowers plugged in or gasoline-powered mowers running when unattended. Keep your fingers and feet away from the mower's blades unless you have cut off the power source.

If you have an electric mower, ensure that you use an extension cord of the right amperage rating and length — the manufacturer should provide this information. Keep the power cord well away from the cutting blades — you must be careful never to run over the power cord with your mower.

Do not run mowers over the edge of a lawn since the outer wheel may drop, causing the blade to scalp the surface. When cutting on a slope, wear shoes with good traction. Work from the top of the bank, in sweeping arcs, from side to side, not up and down.

If you have a rotary mower fitted with a grass catcher, clear the guide slot occasionally to ensure free passage of cuttings, especially when the grass is damp. But always switch off the mower before handling any parts near the cutting blades.

Use only clean fuel in a gasoline

engine, and drain and refill the oil crankcase regularly. In winter, drain the fuel from the tank, clean and lubricate the mower, and store it in a dry place.

Thoroughly clean and dry a mower after use — clearing off the blades with a stiff brush or a rag. Finish by wiping light oil over all bare metal, especially the blades. To ensure smooth operation, regularly lubricate all moving parts — such as wheels, cables, and any control levers. Although you will need to spend some time on this cleaning and lubricating routine, it will take much less effort than trying to operate a neglected machine, and your mower will last longer.

Check and adjust the cutting action of your mower's blades several times a year. Sharpen, balance, or replace the blades as necessary. Blunt and maladjusted blades will tear the grass rather than cut it, resulting in bruised, brown tips.

SETTING THE CUTTING HEIGHT

1 An advantage of rotary mowers is the ease with which the cutting height may be adjusted; often this change in position involves no more than moving a lever by each wheel. To adjust a reel mower, reset the roller behind the blades at a higher or lower level.

Turf-type tall fescue: cut to a height of 4 in (10 cm)

Perennial bluegrass and ryegrass, St. Augustine, fine and red fescues, buffalo grass: cut to a height of 2-3 in (5-7.5 cm)

Carpet grass, centipede grass, chewing fescue: cut to a height of 1-2 in (2.5-5 cm)

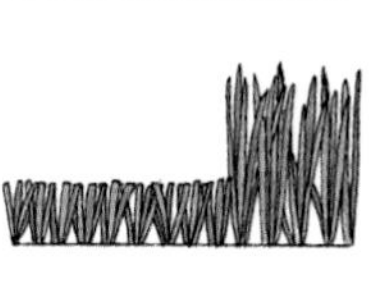

Zoysia grass, Bermuda grass, bent grass: cut to a height of 1/2-1 in (1.2-2.5 cm)

2 Adjust the cutting height to suit the species of grass, the time of year, and the weather conditions.

Dealing with lawn edges

A neat edge contributes as much to the overall attractiveness of a lawn as does the quality of the surface. However, no lawn mower can successfully trim the edges of a lawn — these must be treated separately, usually after the grass has been cut. There are a number of tools available that will help you, although for a small lawn the expense of some of the more elaborate models may outweigh their usefulness.

A rotary edger consists of a wheel with a disk of sharp-edged teeth that revolves as you push the tool along the edge of the lawn, cutting the grass against a fixed blade. Though slightly less tiring to use than other tools, such as shears, this edger may not make such a clean cut. Motor-powered edgers are also available — although this type helps to reduce the threat of backache, it can be difficult to maneuver.

Cut back the edges of the grass after the first mowing in spring and repeat frequently throughout the growing season — preferably after each mowing. The first time you edge, you will have to cut back some of the turf to get a straight or regular line of grass.

For a straight line, use a plank as a guide or mark the edge with a taut string line. Standing on the plank, make clean cuts with a half-moon edging tool, sloping slightly away from the lawn so that the edge does not crumble away. Alternatively, you can use a spade, but the slightly curving blade will not produce a sharp, straight edge, and it is harder to cut to a consistent depth.

During the rest of the year, use long-handled grass shears, a string trimmer, or a rotary edger to maintain the neat edge. Never use a half-moon edging tool to trim an edge that is already straight, since it is designed for cutting turf, not blades of grass.

If your soil is crumbly or the lawn receives a lot of wear, natural lawn edges may break away. To avoid this problem, lay an edging strip. Ready-made aluminum or plastic edging strip is available, or you can make your own from rot-resistant wood. Ensure that the edging strip lies slightly below the lawn surface so that you can mow right to the edge.

AN EFFICIENT MOWING PATTERN

For a pleasing visual effect and the most efficient cut, begin mowing a lawn by making two passes at both the top and bottom end. Then work up and down the lawn, overlapping slightly on each run.

Trimming around obstacles

Many lawns meander around trees, have beds with overhanging plants, or are edged with walls or steep banks. Lawn mowers work best on flat surfaces and cannot cut close to vertical barriers.

Various tools are available for trimming grass around obstacles — the choice depends on how much you are prepared to spend and on whether you prefer to stand up or bend down to do the cutting. Simple grass shears do an adequate job — provided they are sharpened regularly — but are suitable only for small areas since you must crouch to use them.

Applying the same cutting action as hedge shears, battery-

DEALING WITH EDGES

1 During the winter, lawn edges become ragged and often encroach on the flower beds. In spring, cut them to shape with a half-moon edging tool.

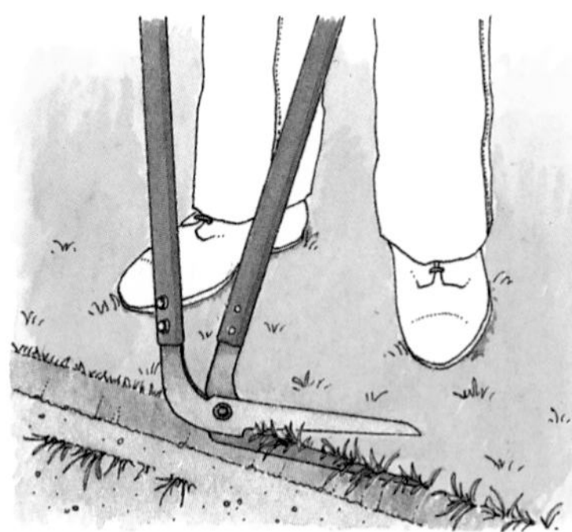

2 Throughout the rest of the growing season, use long-handled grass shears or a string trimmer to trim the edges after each mowing.

3 Rotary edging tools take much of the physical effort out of edge trimming, but they don't produce a neat edge, as do shears or an edging tool.

4 Aluminum edging strips keep the lawn in check. Make a slot, then press edging firmly in place, keeping the top edge just below the surface of the lawn.

THE LAWN-CARE YEAR

Midwinter to late winter Rake off fallen leaves and other debris.

Early spring As soon as the ground is firm, clear away surface debris. Roll when dry to consolidate ground lifted by frost. Rake thoroughly to lift up grass and weeds, and mow with blades set high.

Midspring Apply a fertilizer, followed a week or two later by a selective or preemergent lawn herbicide. Mow once or twice a week, removing no more than one-third of leaf blades each time.

Late spring Increase the frequency of mowing as necessary. Cut it close — with the mower blades set low (see table, page 41). Now is the best time to eradicate weeds.

Summer Mow at highest level; cut less frequently, perhaps twice a month. Water well — 1 in (2.5 cm) per week — during prolonged dry periods. Destroy isolated weeds with selective herbicide.

Early fall Resume more frequent mowing and lower the blade setting by ½ in (1.2 cm) below the highest level. Rake, aerate, and fertilize with a slow-release or organic fertilizer with a 3–2–1 ratio of nutrients.

Midfall Regular mowing comes to an end. Use low-blade setting for last cut — as much as 1 in (2.5 cm) shorter than highest level.

Late fall If the weather is not frosty or wet, and the surface is firm, mow once with the blades set high. Rake off any leaves.

Early winter Clear away the last of the fallen leaves, but keep off the lawn if it is very wet or frozen.

operated hand trimmers provide a less energetic means of cutting grass around obstacles. With a single charge, most batteries will last long enough to trim all of the edges in an average yard. However, you will have to stoop to use the hand trimmer.

The easiest of all to use, nylon cord, or string, trimmers have become very popular in recent years. These cut grass, weeds, and even quite coarse undergrowth by the whipping action of a nylon cord that rotates at high speed within a safety shield. The cut surface is not very neat, however, and this type of tool is most suitable for informal lawns. Although they will complete the job quickly, string trimmers pose a hazard from flying debris thrown up by the cord — wear safety glasses when operating the string trimmer — and they have a rather piercing noise generated by the motor and cord.

String trimmers can also pose a very serious threat to the health of trees and shrubs. When used to trim the grass around a woody plant's base, their whirling cord can bruise or slice into the bark. The result is a wound that leaves an unsightly scar or that may even cause the death of the plant.

Irrigating the lawn

If the lawn is not watered regularly during prolonged dry spells, it loses vigor, allowing tougher grasses and weeds to take over. Symptoms of water shortage include loss of springiness in the grass and fading of color from lush green to a rather grayish-green. Severe water shortage results in yellowing of the grass. However, grass is surprisingly resilient and usually recovers once water is applied.

Use your irrigation system, or a sprinkler, preferably an oscillating one, to obtain maximum coverage. In hot, sunny weather, soak the grass well at weekly intervals. Irrigate in early morning before the sun is high, however, or the water will evaporate as fast as you apply it. If you have sandy soil, water every 4 or 5 days.

The equivalent of about 1 in (2.5 cm) of rainfall is needed at each watering. To measure this amount approximately, position a straight-sided can underneath the sprinkler spray. Note the sprinkler setting and then see how long it takes to collect 1 in (2.5 cm) of water in the bottom of the can. Use the same setting and length of time for future waterings. Droughts may bring restrictions on watering in your community. If so, stop mowing to prevent serious damage to the lawn.

Should the lawn become neglected — while you are away on vacation, for instance — and looks parched, with a dry, cracked surface, it is best to prick the entire surface with a garden fork or aerator before applying water.

Feeding a lawn

The application of fertilizer to a lawn does not merely make the grass grow faster — something

TRIMMING GRASS AROUND OBSTACLES

1 If you don't mind stooping, grass shears will give the neatest trim to grass that the lawn mower cannot reach. For very best cut, sharpen blades before use.

2 Nylon cord trimmers, also known as string trimmers, are easy to use, but give a rougher cut. Keep them away from the bases of trees and shrubs.

3 Battery-operated hand trimmers are easy and convenient to use in a small garden, making a very clean cut with a scissorlike action.

that few people would want — but encourages more compact and greener growth that is better able to compete with weeds and coarser grasses. With constant mowing, the grass needs a regular supply of nutrients throughout the growing season to remain healthy.

Begin fertilizing in midspring when the soil is moist and the grass is dry. Apply a complete fertilizer with a nutrient ratio of 3–1–2; a typical formula on the fertilizer label might be 21–7–14, for example. Complete lawn fertilizers are available under many brand names — follow the manufacturer's instructions for application method and rate.

Distribute the fertilizer evenly so that the grass is not burned — too much fertilizer at one spot can kill the grass there. Mix powdered fertilizer with four to eight times its weight of sand before spreading it on the lawn. For even coverage, divide the mixture and apply half up and down the lawn, and the other half, working across the lawn, from side to side.

Granular fertilizer is easy to disperse with a wheeled mechanical spreader that distributes it at the correct rate. If dispensed by hand, use pegs and string, or garden canes, to mark out the site into 1-sq-yd/m sections. Water in granular fertilizers with a garden sprinkler to reduce the risk of burning the grass and to feed the roots as quickly as possible. Apply liquid fertilizers with a hose-end sprayer. Avoid overlapping or double application, which may burn the grass.

Give the lawn a fall feeding with an organic or slow-release chemical fertilizer; use a fertilizer with a 3–2–1 ratio of nutrients and a high percentage of WIN (water-insoluble nitrogen).

Aerating and topdressing

Aerating the lawn in early fall is essential on heavy soils with poor drainage. It is also necessary where soils have been compacted

APPLYING FERTILIZERS AND TOPDRESSING

1 Fertilizers must be spread very evenly; otherwise you will get random patches of untreated or overtreated (burned) grass. Mark out 1-sq-yd/m areas with canes or pegs and taut string, then treat them separately.

2 To ensure an even distribution of granular fertilizer, use a mechanical spreader. Work systematically in back-and-forth strips, as for lawn mowing, but don't overlap each run by more than the thickness of the spreader's wheels.

3 Apply a topdressing — a mixture of screened loam, leaf mold, garden compost, and sharp sand that has been left to mature for at least a year — by raking half a bucketful of dressing over each sq yd/m of lawn.

AERATING A LAWN

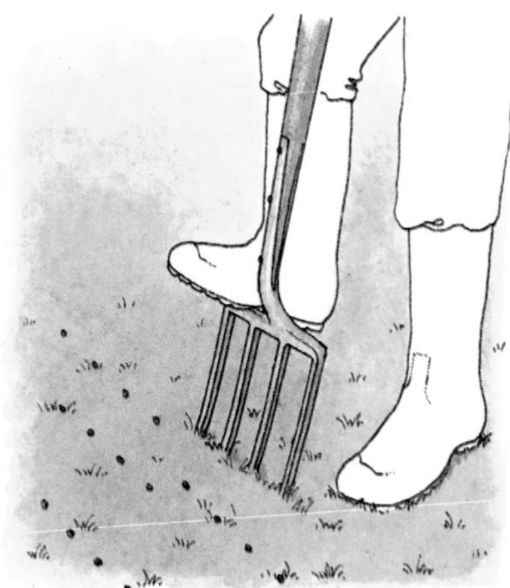

1 To aerate a lawn in early fall, spike it with a garden fork — making holes that are 3-4 in (7.5-10 cm) deep. This process will assist drainage and allow air to penetrate down to plant roots.

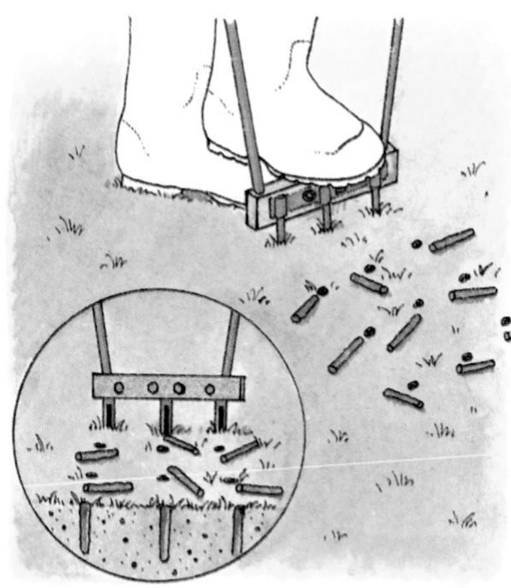

2 The hollow tines of a sod coring aerator open up the soil more than a garden fork because they remove plugs of soil. Sweep up the plugs and sprinkle a sand-and-soil mixture into the holes.

3 Spiked-wheel cultivators do the job more quickly and with much less effort — they are ideal for large lawns. Interchangeable tines are available. Weigh down the tool with rocks.

by heavy use and wear. Aerating also assists root growth.

On small areas and lighter soils use a garden fork. Push it in at intervals 3-4 in (7.5-10 cm) apart to a depth of 3-4 in (7.5-10 cm). Use a straight, in-and-out action with the fork — do not pull back on the handle because this motion will make a ridge.

There are also specially designed aerators that have interchangeable tines. They are easier to use than a garden fork and give better aeration on all types of soils. The solid tines can be replaced by hollow ones, which remove a core of earth — these are best on heavy soil. When you have finished, sweep up the cores of earth and sprinkle a topdressing of soil and sand into the holes.

In fall, after aerating the lawn, apply a light topdressing. This addition will smooth out slight surface irregularities and will form a layer of moisture-retaining material. Make the topdressing in advance by piling alternate layers of good garden soil, 6 in (15 cm) thick, and composted manure, 4 in (10 cm) thick. Let the pile stand for a year, and then screen the mixture. Add sharp sand to this dressing when using it for heavy clay soil, but leave it as is for sandy soil. Apply it at the rate of half a bucketful per sq yd/m.

Raking

In spring, lightly rake the lawn with a lawn rake to remove winter debris, particularly before mowing for the first time. Avoid dispersing any moss. In late spring and summer, rake the lawn occasionally before mowing it. This activity helps to remove any thatch that has built up under the surface and — by lifting flattened grass or weed stems — ensures a more even cut.

In early fall to midfall, scarify, or rake thoroughly and vigorously, to clear away all debris. In addition, remove leaves from the lawn once a week in the fall; a leaf blower makes this task easy.

RAKING, ROLLING, AND SWEEPING

1 A rake made of bamboo, plastic, or wire is the best tool for removing winter debris before the first spring mowing. It is also excellent for scarifying (raking thoroughly) in fall.

2 Use a roller to consolidate the turf in spring — winter frosts often lift the soil surface. Never use a roller to try and smooth out bumps in summer — you will merely accentuate them.

3 A leaf blower makes clearing leaves easy. While many types simply blow air, some models also vacuum up leaves and then shred them, storing them in a bag for later use as a mulch.

LAWN REPAIRS

A patchy, uneven, or badly worn lawn is unattractive and difficult to mow. However, neglected lawns can be repaired quite effectively.

The lawn in most gardens often receives far more wear and tear than is good for it, and many types of damage can occur:

❑ Bumps and hollows caused by poor initial laying, or later heaving or settling.

❑ Bare patches caused by wear, poor drainage, shade, burning by pet urine, excess fertilizer doses, weed removal, or continuous drips from overhead foliage.

❑ Broken or dead edges caused during cultivation of beds, or by overhanging plants.

❑ Surface breakup caused by shrub suckers and tree roots.

Some are only minor and, if left alone, may repair themselves. Others, however, need careful treatment to restore the natural beauty of the lawn.

Leveling bumps and hollows

Bumps show up especially when the lawn is closely cut in summer. The raised areas tend to get scalped, leaving brown patches. Hollows, on the other hand, show as areas of much lusher grass.

Simple leveling work is best carried out when the grass is dormant but the ground is not frozen — anytime from late fall through early spring.

Level small hollows by scattering a thin layer of soil over the area and brushing it in. Make up a mixture of half finely screened good soil and half sharp sand. Apply no more than ½ in (1.2 cm) at a time, repeating every couple of weeks. The soil will settle in after each application and eventually level the site.

To reduce a small bump, prick it over with a sod coring aerator to remove small plugs of soil. As the remaining soil settles, the level drops slightly. Begin in fall and repeat every month or so (when the ground is not frozen) until the bump has leveled out.

Larger hollows and bumps need different treatment. Peel back the turf over the affected area and add or remove soil until the right level is reached.

▼ **Lawn discoloration** Unsightly yellow patches on an otherwise healthy lawn may result from urine burning — especially that of a female dog. Reseeding or resodding the patches can resolve the problem, but make sure to remedy the cause.

BUMPS AND HOLLOWS

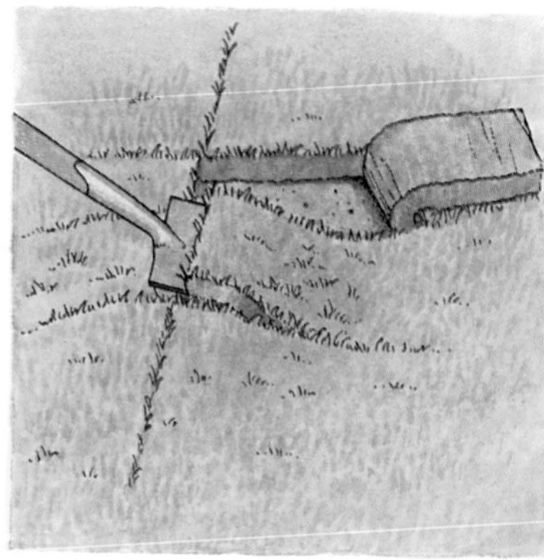

1 Using a spade or half-moon edging tool, cut a cross through the center of the bump or hollow, extending the cuts to the perimeter of the problem area. Make two or three parallel cuts on each side of one line of the cross. Undercut the pieces of turf and peel them back.

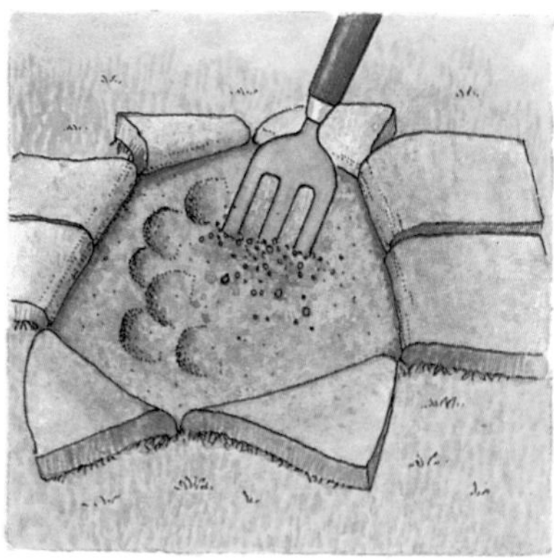

2 Taking care not to tread on the rolled-back pieces of turf, fork over the exposed soil to a depth of 3-4 in (8-10 cm) — it may be solid, so break it up well. If the surface was too high, remove some soil, then press it down firmly and rake level. If the surface was too low, add fresh soil, then firm and level it.

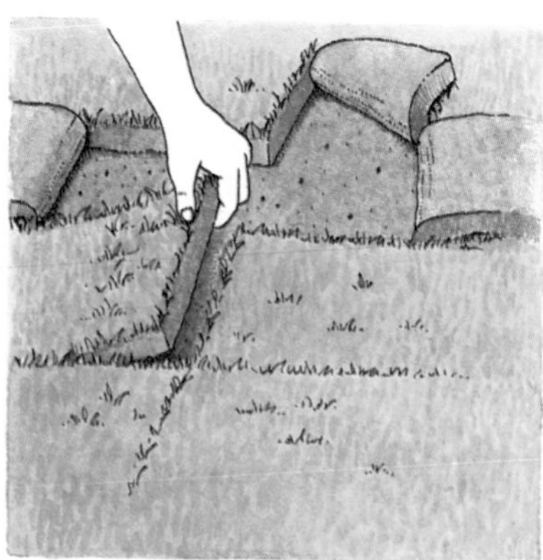

3 Finally, fold back the pieces of turf over the leveled soil and press them down well with a roller, or by treading systematically over the area. Fill any cracks with screened soil — sprinkle it by hand, then brush in lightly. Water in gently and keep the area moist.

Filling bare patches

If you have bare patches, try to determine why the grass has died out. Some causes, such as weed removal, chemical spillage, or pet-urine burning, may not recur on the same spot. Others, such as poor drainage or wear, are likely to be long-term persistent problems. Learn to recognize the symptoms:

❑ Excessive wear — muddy, compacted footprints.
❑ Drought — yellow and eventually dead, brown grass.
❑ Weed/moss removal — irregular areas of dead or depleted grass.
❑ Pet urine — regular, circular brown patches surrounded by a narrow ring of unusually deep green grass.
❑ Chemical/oil/gasoline spillage — brown patches, often with an irregular outline.
❑ Buried builder's debris — brown or yellow patches on a new site.

Before starting the repair, remedy the cause, if possible. Worn patches generally reflect routes of maximum use. Consider replacing these areas with a path or stepping-stones. Train pets — especially female dogs — to use a spot away from the lawn. Repair and maintain the lawn mower in the garage, not on the grass.

Reseeding This method is the easiest way to repair a bare patch. The optimum time to reseed is spring or fall, during reasonably good weather, but wait at least 6 weeks after applying a selective hormone herbicide to the lawn. First, loosen the surface with a hand fork. Work in a sprinkling of granular fertilizer, then rake the soil to a fine, even tilth. (Add a little fresh, screened soil if the site isn't level or the soil is poor.)

Select a seed mixture that matches your existing lawn type. Some suppliers also offer special reseeding mixtures that germinate more quickly than standard mixtures and produce acceptable turf within just a few weeks.

Sow general-purpose grass seed, containing ryegrass, at a rate of 1 oz per sq yd (25 g per sq m). Spread fine-quality lawn seed a little more thickly, at about $1^1/_2$ oz per sq yd (40 g per sq m). Rake the seed in and firm down lightly. Water gently but frequently in warm, dry weather. If you have a sprinkler, leave it running for about 15 minutes in the morning.

Also, protect seed from birds. Stretch bird netting or burlap over the area, pinning it down with stakes. Alternatively, in areas where the spring sun isn't too hot, lay a sheet of clear plastic over the patch and secure it with pegs. This method will also conserve some moisture. Remove the plastic as soon as the seedlings start to emerge.

Resodding may be more appropriate where deep digging is necessary to eliminate the cause of the problem — for example, if you are removing buried debris or improving drainage. If the bare patch lies in a prominent spot, replace it with sod taken from a less noticeable part of the lawn, then reseed this area later. If you have several bare patches, however, it's wiser to buy new sod.

TREE ROOTS AND SUCKERS

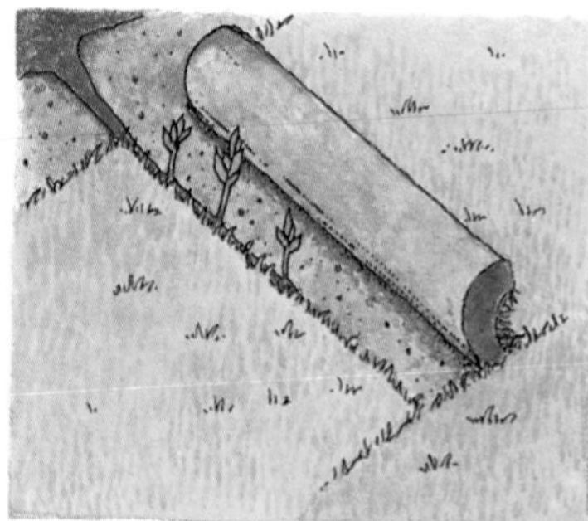

As trees and shrubs age, their roots swell and may lift grass into a hump. Many of these plants also produce suckers — a hazard when mowing. Cut and peel back the turf, then chop off the offending root.

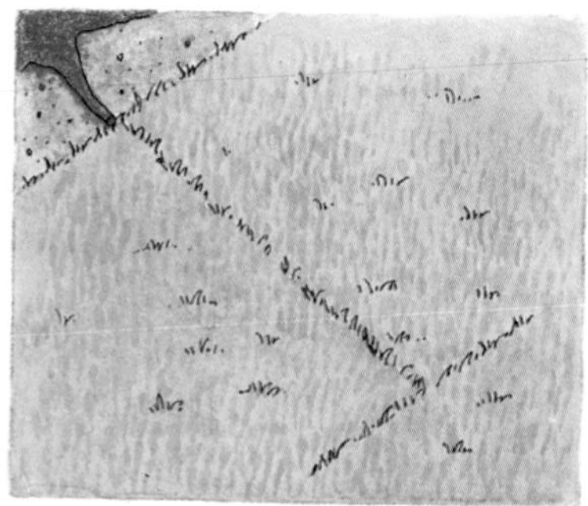

Fork over the soil and relevel. Roll back the turf and press it down firmly. Where bulky tree roots break through, it may be best to reshape the lawn around the root and grow ground cover plants instead.

RESODDING A BARE PATCH

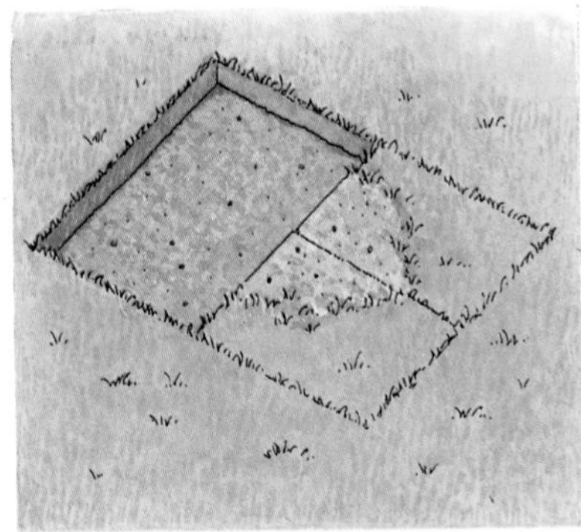

1 Cut out any dead or diseased grass, together with any other debris from the bare patch. Where chemical or oil spillage has occurred, dig out all the polluted soil and replace it. Square off the area with a spade.

2 If you intend to replace the damaged area with commercial sod, cut out a patch equal in size to the sod you have bought. Otherwise, make the patch as small as possible. Turn over the soil with a garden fork and level it.

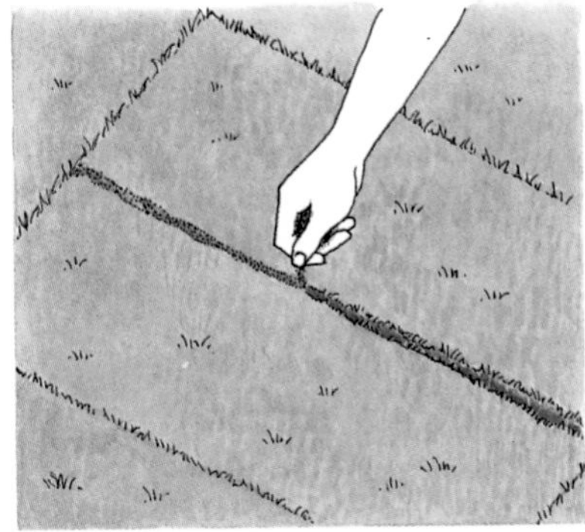

3 Lay the replacement sod in position, making sure it is level with the lawn. If not, take it out and add more soil or remove some, as necessary. Press in the sod firmly, then fill cracks with screened soil and sand.

RESEEDING A BARE PATCH

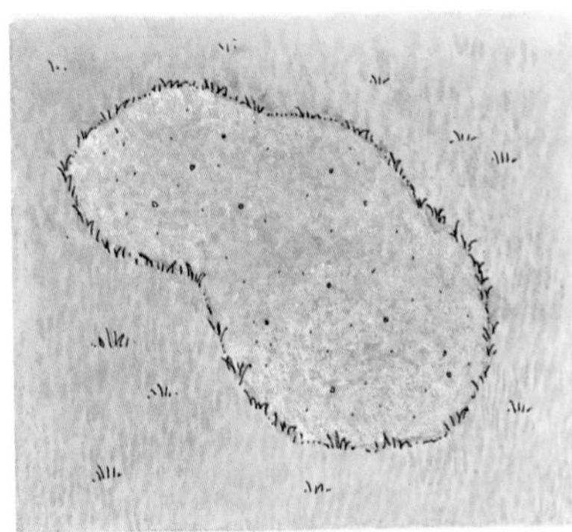

1 Prepare the patch by forking up any dead or diseased grass, together with weeds or any other debris. Gently loosen the soil to a depth of about 3 in (7.5 cm), using a hand fork, but don't loosen the surrounding grass.

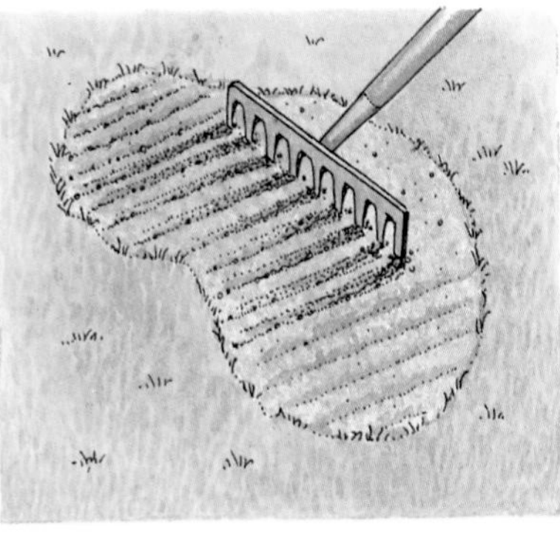

2 Sprinkle some general-purpose fertilizer — about a handful per sq yd/m — over the patch and rake it in, leaving a level, even surface. Scatter grass seed and rake in. Press down the earth with the back of the rake or tread in lightly.

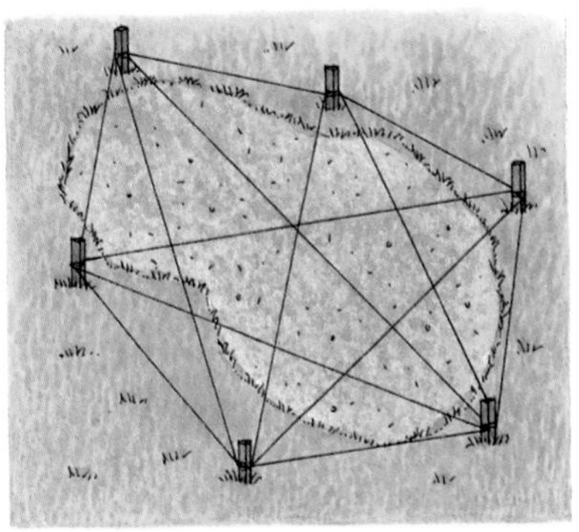

3 Keep animals off until new grass is well established. Bird netting or burlap stretched between pegs deters birds. Or, lay clear plastic over the patch — secured with pegs — until seedlings grow. Keep well watered.

Begin by digging out the dead patch with a hand fork. If deep digging is necessary, use a garden fork or spade. Remove all polluted soil and debris. Once the full extent of the problem has been exposed, square off the area by making shallow cuts with a spade or half-moon edging tool. If you intend to replace the damaged spot with sod, make sure you buy the same type of grass, and that it is in good condition.

Loosen and relevel the exposed soil, adding fresh soil if necessary, before bedding the replacement sod. Lastly, press down the new sod firmly, fill in the cracks with a 50:50 mix of screened soil and sand, and water in well.

Water reseeded and resodded areas if they show signs of drying out. Remove weeds by hand and delay mowing until the repaired patches are properly integrated in the established lawn, usually a few weeks later, or when the blades are 3 in (7.5 cm) high.

Renovating a sparse lawn

A lawn that has been treated with herbicide can become sparse. If growing conditions are perfect, the lawn may fill in on its own, but you can speed up the process. The best time to do so is spring or fall. Once the herbicide is inactive (generally allow at least 6 weeks), mow the grass and then rake it over to loosen the soil surface. Spread grass seed evenly over the entire area at a rate of $^{1}/_{2}$ oz per sq yd (15 g per sq m). Sprinkle a fine layer of good screened garden soil over the seed. Lightly roll the surface or use the back of a spade to pat down the soil. Keep the lawn well watered.

Repairing broken edges

Lawn edges can be damaged in a variety of ways. Overhanging plants often smother the grass, and soon it dies out. When the offending plants are cut back, the lawn must be repaired. Certain lawn mowers — particularly the rotary type — can also spoil an edge, or sometimes the heel of your shoe can accidentally break an edge while you are cultivating an adjoining flower bed.

To repair an edge, cut out a rectangle of sod around the broken edge, using a sharp spade or half-moon edging tool. Make sure that it can be lifted out without breaking into pieces. You may need to make several cuts along a badly damaged edge. Trim away any dead roots or bare soil from the broken edge. Lift out the sod with a spade, turn it around so that the undamaged inner edge forms the new outer edge, and relay it. Lastly, reseed or resod the bare patch.

Aerating stagnant areas

Poor drainage, especially under an old or neglected lawn, is a common cause of poor grass growth. The surface may become very compacted with constant wear, yet soil just below remains constantly wet. Using a sod coring aerator, remove small plugs of soil all across the stagnant area. Sprinkle sharp sand over and brush it into the holes. In this way, dozens of tiny drain holes will be made that will allow the trapped water to seep away.

A drought-stricken lawn

Grass is surprisingly resilient to drought — in most northern areas, a well-established, deep-rooted turf can survive a month or more without rainfall or irrigation, especially if the soil was well enriched before planting. Sandy, free-draining soils are most susceptible to drought damage. For the best protection against drought, incorporate plenty of organic matter to increase water retention before making a lawn.

Without moisture, grass does, however, become almost dormant, allowing the growth of certain weeds — such as yarrow and clover — which are better adapted to dry conditions. Also, annual meadow grasses may die out more quickly than coarser grasses.

If the surface is baked and hard, spike it with a fork or aerator. Turn on a sprinkler for an hour or so during early evening or morning — in the hot sun water evaporates faster than it soaks in. (If the use of hoses and sprinklers has been restricted by your community, apply bath water with a watering can.) Water two or three times per week during very hot spells, but never do it more than once a week during normal summer weather — you will encourage weeds and reduce the vigor of grass roots.

REPAIRING A DAMAGED EDGE

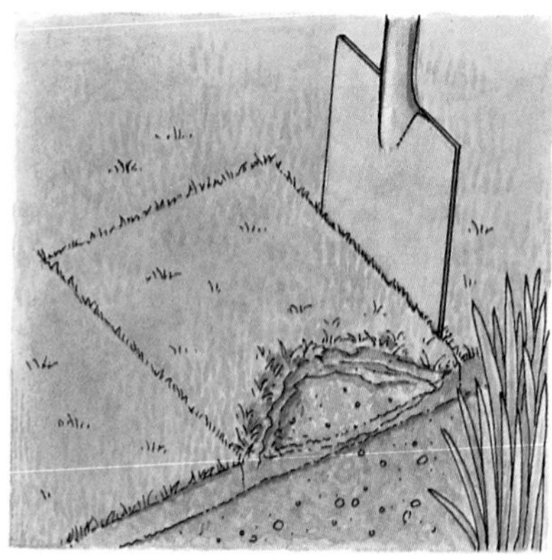

1 Using a spade or half-moon edging tool, cut a rectangular section around the damaged edge — large enough to incorporate a good chunk of healthy grass, but small enough to lift with the spade without breaking. If the damaged area is large, you may have to cut out more than one section of sod.

2 Undercut the severed section with a spade and lift it carefully. Remove loose old soil and any dead grass — you can do this work before lifting, if you prefer. Turn the sod around and reposition it with the ragged edge innermost. You can now appreciate the importance of cutting a perfect rectangle or square.

3 Press the sod down firmly. Fill the remaining hole with screened soil, then sow with grass seed, as shown for reseeding a bare patch. Keep well watered and deter birds and pets with bird netting or burlap.

RENOVATING A NEGLECTED LAWN

Begin the process by examining the grass and weeds covering the lawn. If the dominant plants are coarse grasses, mosses, and persistent weeds, the best solution is to lay a new lawn. If, however, good-quality grasses make up the main part of the lawn, they can be made to recolonize the whole lawn area.

Start renovating in spring before the grass begins to grow actively. Cut down tall grass and weeds to 2 in (5 cm) above the ground. Use a rotary lawn mower, a string trimmer, or a pair of shears, depending on the height of the growth.

Remove all dead vegetation, using a rake or blower, and move large sticks and stones. Mow the grass with the lawn mower blades set as high as possible. Subsequent mowings should be carried out regularly, with the blades set highest in summer. Remove the clippings or leave them in place (which reduces the need to fertilize).

Fertilize the lawn in late spring or summer, using a general lawn fertilizer first. Then apply a selective herbicide about 2 weeks later. Some manufacturers supply a mix of fertilizer and herbicide that does the job more quickly and easily. If a test indicates that soil pH is much below 6.8, apply lime in the amounts recommended by the testing kit or report — lime will also help to rid the lawn of moss. Place the lime in a fertilizer spreader or sprinkle it by hand over the affected area. If, after 6 weeks, some persistent weeds remain, use a selective liquid herbicide containing mecoprop.

In fall, apply a fertilizer rich in slow-release nitrogen, and a fungicide, if needed. (These may be available in a combined form.) Remove coarse grass with a selective application of glyphosate.

A week or two later, aerate the surface all over with a sod coring aerator to improve drainage and aeration. Apply a good topdressing of screened soil and sand, or scatter composted manure, garden compost, or leaf mold over the surface at a rate of about 10 handfuls per sq yd/m. Work it well into the surface with the back of a rake.

If the lawn is thin, mix in grass seed with the topdressing at a rate of ½ oz per sq yd (15 g per sq m). Rake off fallen leaves, which can shade young grass seedlings.

Reseed or resod any bare patches that appear after the herbicide applications have taken effect. The lawn should be in a satisfactory condition by the following spring, when you can resume normal lawn maintenance.

LAWN TROUBLES

Weeds, pests, and diseases will more readily find a home in a neglected lawn. Treat problems before they become serious.

Prevention is better than cure when it comes to lawn weeds, pests, and diseases, since a thick covering of healthy grass with few bare patches will resist the onset of such infestations. It is also more resistant to prolonged drought. If your lawn looks more like a highway median, however, with weeds, mushrooms, mole hills, and moss patches, there are still many ways of renovating it to a golf-course finish.

Controlling lawn weeds

A weed is any plant that grows where it's not wanted. Identify weeds first, then choose the best method to remove them.

Check surface-creeping weeds, such as clover and yarrow, by raking them upright before each mowing. This technique ensures that their leaves and stems are cut off by the mower blades. Some annual weeds, such as trefoil and mouse-ear chickweed, may also be controlled by this treatment.

If the lawn is very weedy, use a grass catcher when mowing and discard the clippings, as they will contain weed seeds and fungal spores. Isolated weeds can be uprooted with a dandelion weeder or small hand fork; lift out as much of the root system intact as possible, since broken sections of root often regrow, especially those of dandelions and thistles.

Selective herbicides in the form of powders or liquids are effective against most weeds. They are best applied in late spring to midsummer, but can be used until early fall. To give the grass an extra boost before using the herbicide, apply a complete lawn fertilizer 2 weeks in advance and then cut the grass 2 or 3 days beforehand. If possible, pick a warm, still day for application, when the grass is dry and the soil below it is moist.

Chemicals frequently used to kill lawn weeds include 2,4-D, dicamba, dichlorprop, and mecoprop. Often two or more of these chemicals are combined to give a more thorough weed-killing action. You can buy them in different forms, including concentrated liquids, soluble powders, granules, or ready-mixed in spray bottles.

Selective herbicides are based on a hormone substance that overstimulates weed growth, causing the leaves to twist and curl. Finally, the weeds die and rot away. The amount of hormone absorbed by the grass is not enough to do any harm — grass leaves are narrow, with a waxy surface and a longitudinal channellike midvein, so liquids tend to run off the surface before they are absorbed.

Do not mow the lawn for at least

▼ **Lawn weeds** Daisies and dandelions commonly infest lawns. While they have individual charms — and look attractive in a wild meadow — such weeds destroy the appearance of the lawn and compete with the grass for light, water, and nutrients. Once established, these weeds may spread with ever-increasing speed by means of seeds or runners; you should eradicate them quickly and permanently, if possible.

ELIMINATING LAWN WEEDS

1 Isolated weeds can be removed by hand, taking care to lift out as much of the root system as possible. Use a dandelion weeder (above) or a small hand fork for daisies and other rosette-forming weeds.

2 For widespread weeds, apply a lawn herbicide with a hose-end sprayer. A selective hormone herbicide, if used carefully according to the manufacturer's instructions, will kill weeds but not grass.

3 days after using a herbicide. Discard the clippings from the first cutting — they may contain chemical residues.

Timing is important when using hormone herbicides. Since they kill by disrupting the weeds' growth, apply them only when the weeds are in a period of active growth — typically during the mid-to-late spring and early fall.

Herbicides can be bought as combined formulations with lawn fertilizers, though the effect on weeds may be slightly less than when applied after a fertilizer.

Spot herbicides can be used to treat isolated weeds in a lawn. Among the most convenient spot herbicides are those packaged as foam sprays. Aim the spray directly onto the crown of each weed. The active ingredient is usually 2,4-D mixed with dicamba.

Among the most useful weapons against weeds are the preemergent herbicides — those that kill weeds as they are germinating, such as benefin, siduron, and DCPA. If spread in early spring, these prevent all seeds from germinating for as long as 4 months. That makes it impossible for annual weeds (such as purslane and chickweed) and weedy annual grasses (such as crabgrass) to sprout during that period, and thus gives a head start to the turf.

Preemergent herbicides may also affect the growth of grass seedlings, so these products should never be applied to newly seeded lawns. In addition, benefin must never be spread on mature bent grass, as it is liable to cause damage.

For particularly persistent weeds, glyphosate may be the best product. Though nonselective — it kills desirable grasses just as readily as it kills weeds — glyphosate is absorbed only through a plant's leaves; it doesn't spread through the soil to act on roots. It is, however, systemic. Once absorbed by the leaves, glyphosate is transported throughout the plant, killing it right down to the root tips. As a result, it offers the most effective response to weeds with spreading underground stems, such as quack grass.

Caution: Whatever herbicide you select, make sure to use, mix, store, and dispose of it with care. These chemicals affect more than just vegetation and "bad" plants. Herbicides can be harmful to people and animals, too. In addition, if applied carelessly or excessively, herbicides can pose a very serious environmental hazard.

Always follow the instructions on the product label exactly. If instructed to do so by the manufacturer, wear goggles, gloves, and even a respirator. Take care to apply herbicides only on a windless day — otherwise, the wind may carry the spray or dust considerable distances to damage plants other than the intended target, and possibly wildlife, too.

Always keep children and pets out of the way when you spray, and do not allow them back on the lawn until after the interval specified by the manufacturer. After use, dispose of any leftover herbicide according to your local environmental regulations, or store them in the original container in a secure cupboard or toolshed. Herbicides are a very useful tool, but they can cause serious injury if misused.

Other lawn troubles

Broad-leaved weeds are not the only causes of lawn problems. Certain pests and diseases attack even the best-kept lawns.

Algae may appear in damp grass. These simple plants are usually black, slippery, and jellylike. Aerate the lawn to improve drainage, and if you have clay soil, apply lime or gypsum to improve its texture (p.12). Fertilize the lawn to build up its strength.

Ants make small hills of soil as part of their nest-building activities; these may be merely an unsightly nuisance, or in the case of fire ants in the Southern states, a serious health hazard. Ant hills are mostly found on sandy soils and generally appear in summer. Brush off the soil hills before mowing. Sprinkle the affected area with an ant killer or place baits around the nests.

Beetle grubs may kill small patches of turf by gnawing at the roots in spring and summer. The grass turns brown in color and breaks away from the surface. Treat with diazinon and water heavily to wash the insecticide down into the soil where the grubs hide.

If Japanese beetles are living in the lawn, you can achieve long-term control without poisoning your yard by inoculating your soil with their enemy, milky spore disease. These fungal spores are ultimately fatal to Japanese beetles but harmless to other forms of animal and plant life. Once sprinkled throughout the lawn, the spores persist for years, usually providing effective control of the pest even if they do not eliminate it altogether.

Another organic control that can work well over small areas is an application of beneficial nematodes mixed with water. Milky spore and beneficial nematodes are both sold through catalogs and at some garden centers.

Dogs, especially females, urinate on lawns, causing the grass to turn yellow, then brown. Once

IDENTIFYING MAJOR LAWN WEEDS

SPECIES	FEATURES
Annual bluegrass *(Poa annua)*	Low-growing, broad-leaved annual grass forming unsightly clumps in closely cut turf.
Bird's-foot trefoil *(Lotus corniculatus)*	Creeping plant, often forming large clumps; each leaf made up of three oval, pointed leaflets, with two leaflike growths at the base of their stalk; clusters of red-marked bright yellow pea flowers in late spring to late summer.
Buttercup, bulbous *(Ranunculus bulbosus)*	Bulbous-rooted plant; deeply toothed and finely hairy, 3-lobed, dark green leaves; golden-yellow, cup-shaped flowers in early spring to early summer.
Buttercup, creeping *(Ranunculus repens)*	Creeping stems rooting frequently; deeply toothed and finely hairy, 3-lobed, rich green leaves; golden-yellow, cup-shaped flowers in late spring to late summer.
Cat's-ear *(Hypochaeris radicata)*	Similar to dandelion, but leaves hairy, with less jagged teeth; flower stalks branched.
Chickweed, mouse-ear *(Cerastium vulgatum)*	Creeping stems; small oval leaves covered with silvery hairs; tiny white starry flowers in midspring to early fall.
Clover, white *(Trifolium repens)*	Creeping plant rooting frequently; each leaf made up of three rounded leaflets; white or pinkish globular flower heads from late spring to fall.
Crabgrass, smooth *(Digitaria ischaemum)*	Broad, bluish-green leaves; stems erect and prostrate, often rooting at lower nodes to form dense mats.
Crowfoot *(Ranunculus acris)*	Clump-forming plant of the buttercup family; deeply lobed, rich green leaves with coarse teeth; golden-yellow, cup-shaped flowers in late spring to late summer.
Daisy, English *(Bellis perennis)*	Rosette-forming plant with a very spreading habit; spoon-shaped leaves with scalloped edges; prominent yellow-centered white flowers from early spring to fall.
Dandelion *(Taraxacum officinale)*	Rosette-forming plant; lance-shaped leaves with deep, jagged teeth; stems and leaves exude a milky sap when broken; many-petaled bright yellow flowers.
Ground Ivy *(Glechoma hederacea)*	Creeping plant; square stems that root at joints; nearly round, scalloped leaves; purplish-blue, trumpet-shaped flowers.
Heal-All *(Prunella vulgaris)*	Creeping plant rooting at intervals; oval, pointed leaves; clusters of purple-hooded flowers in early summer to early fall.
Medic, black *(Medicago lupulina)*	Creeping plant; cloverlike leaves; small, yellowish, cloverlike flowers from midspring to late summer.
Nut grass, yellow *(Cyperus esculentus)*	Triangular stems with clasping, yellow-green leaves; nut-like tubers at end of underground shoots.
Pearlwort *(Sagina procumbens)*	Tufted plant with radiating, creeping stems, often forming a dense mat; tiny, narrowly lance-shaped leaves; diminutive white flowers in late spring to early fall.
Plantain, broad-leaved *(Plantago major)*; hoary plantain *(P. media)*	Rosette-forming plants; large, coarse-textured leaves with prominent parallel ribs; greenish flowers from late spring onward, in slender, upright spikes in *P. major*, and with compact, oval heads in *P. media*.
Plantain, buckthorn *(Plantago lanceolata)*	Rosette-forming plant; very large, lance-shaped leaves with prominent parallel ribs; flowers similar to those of hoary plantain.
Purslane *(Portulaca oleracea)*	Bright green, fleshy, thick but small oval leaves; thick, reddish stems; tiny yellow flowers borne only by plants growing in sunny areas.
Sheep sorrel *(Rumex acetosella)*	Slender, wiry plant with somewhat creeping stems; deep green, narrow, arrow-shaped leaves, turning reddish with age; spikes of green to red flowers in late spring to late summer.
Small hop clover *(Trifolium dubium)*	Similar to white clover, but with smaller flowers that are yellow to brownish.
Speedwell, creeping *(Veronica filiformis)*	Slender trailing stems rooting frequently; small, rounded leaves with scalloped edges; tiny mauve-blue flowers in midspring to summer.
Yarrow *(Achillea millefolium)*	Creeping plant rooting at intervals; long, feathery leaves; flattish clusters of small cream-white flowers in summer.

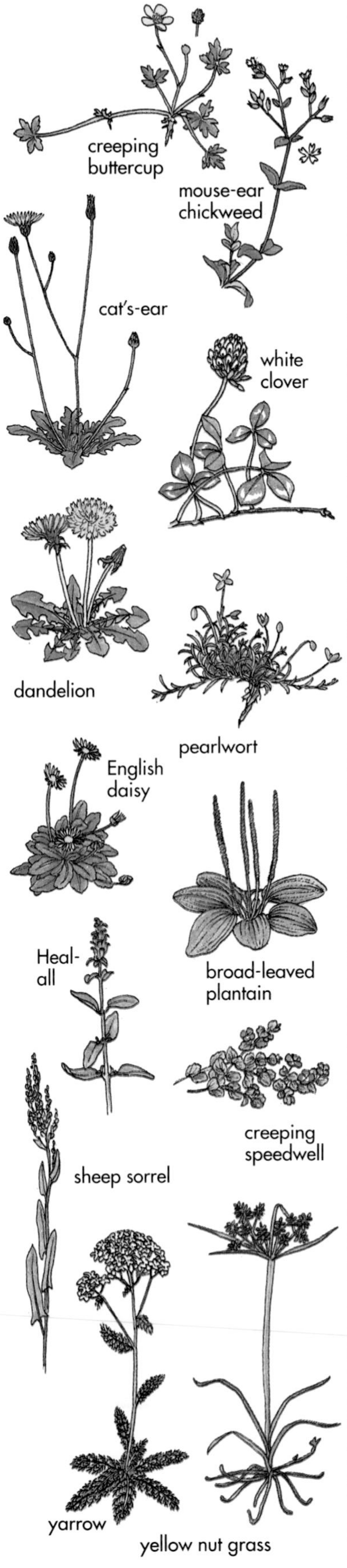

SPECIAL LAWN DISORDERS

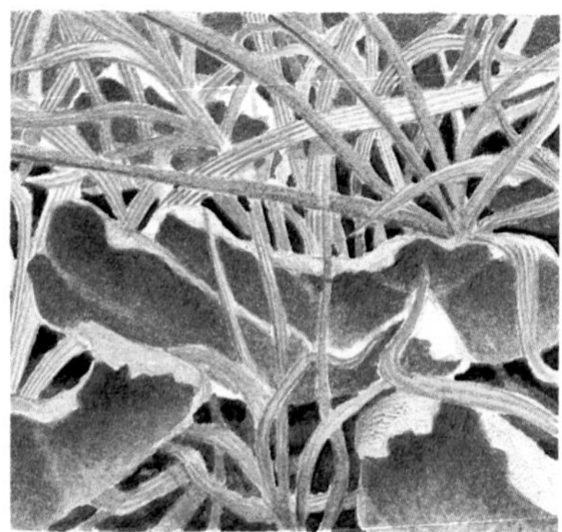

1 Lichens are composed of horizontal overlapping leafy structures. They are deep green-black when moist and gray-green or brown when dry. They may appear at any time of year. Rake out the growths, aerate the lawn, and improve drainage by adding gypsum or lime to the soil. Topdress with mixture of sand and leaf mold.

2 Snow mold, or fusarium wilt, is a fungal disease that creates dead patches of turf about 1 ft (30 cm) across, covered with white, cottonlike growths. These are most obvious in moist weather and after snow. Treat affected areas as for red thread disease (**3**), but do not apply too much nitrogenous fertilizer, especially after late summer and fall applications.

3 Red thread, or corticium, disease shows as dead patches of turf bearing red, threadlike fungus growths. The danger period is in fall, after rain. Apply a complete lawn-care compound containing herbicide and fertilizer in fall. Or, apply chlorothalonil or mancozeb fungicides. Aerate the soil and use a nitrogenous fertilizer in spring.

killed, the turf must be replaced with sod or by reseeding. Isolated incidents can be treated by immediately flooding the affected area with water.

Chinch bugs form a distinct circle of yellowing grass. Grubs feed on grass roots, while adults prefer the stems. Apply grub control in June; in Southern areas, repeat if necessary in late summer.

Moles can ruin a lawn by excavating large heaps of loose soil and building long, interlinking tunnels just underneath the surface. These tunnels sometimes collapse, causing sunken channels across the lawn.

Eradication of moles is rarely successful unless carried out by a professional exterminator. Traps and poisons are the most effective means, but smoke pellets placed in the runs may deter some moles.

Moss is a common enemy. It is a symptom of run-down turf, primarily associated with overcompacted soil, poor drainage, excess shade, and underfeeding. Moss infestations frequently take over entire areas of the lawn. Better maintenance will eventually solve this problem. Regular applications of lime or gypsum on clay soils, when combined with aeration and topdressing, will gradually improve their drainage. Rake out dead moss and reseed any bare patches of grass. Keep the remaining grass in good condition and don't cut it too short.

▲ **Grass invasion** Fairy rings of small mushrooms can appear at any time of year. The grass around the ring may become darker green and look unsightly, though the mushrooms themselves do no harm. Conceal this effect by applying a high-nitrogen fertilizer to the rest of the lawn. There is no effective chemical treatment for fairy rings. For serious cases, the remedy is quite drastic: Dig up and burn diseased turf to a depth of 1 ft (30 cm) and at least 1 ft (30 cm) on either side of the ring. Remove all the soil, ensuring that it does not fall onto the healthy turf alongside. Replace with fresh topsoil and reseed.

CHOOSING HEDGES

Hedges provide shelter and privacy, and — with their foliage, flowers, or berries — they can be beautiful as well as practical garden features.

Hedges are as much a part of a garden landscape as flower beds and lawns, and can range in size from huge walls of greenery made of yew or beech to decorative edgings of lavender or dwarf box. They can demarcate boundaries, make a garden private and sheltered, create a series of separate spaces within a design, or form a backdrop for focal points.

Boundary hedges

Hedges are a traditional way of defining land ownership. Large, thick, and thorny types, such as hawthorn, physically deter intruders and animals. (For more thorough protection, reinforce this type of hedge with chain link fencing through the center.)

Smaller hedges can act as boundary markers, though dwarf hedges are liable to be trampled, especially in corners or in areas used as shortcuts. Some people prefer low boundary hedges so that their homes and yards are visible from the street.

If you are considering a shared boundary hedge, it is courteous to discuss your plans with the neighbors whose property borders yours. Legally, you may have to plant the hedge within your garden so that it doesn't encroach on the adjoining property. In addition, some communities have bylaws that restrict the height and placement of hedges. However, a cooperative neighbor might allow the hedge to be planted on the boundary line, and may even be willing to share the cost. It is also a good idea to discuss the hedge's height and shape in order to avoid future disagreements.

Hedges for shelter

Hedges act as windbreaks, and because they filter wind rather than block it, they can cause less turbulence on their leeward side than more solid walls. Plants benefit from the shelter created by a

▼ **Boundary hedges** A beech hedge forms a nearly impenetrable barrier and can be maintained at the desired height with a light annual trimming. The brown leaves remain attractive through fall and winter, and complement the berries of the wall-trained *Cotoneaster horizontalis*.

than they really are when seen from the lower level.

Within the garden, hedges can be used to screen eyesores, such as a trash-barrel area, compost pile, or shed. Hedges offer minimal protection against noise, although they are psychologically soothing. They also cut down the glare of car headlights at night.

Hedges as features

Ornamental dwarf hedges are excellent for creating interlocking geometric designs, known as "knot and parterre" patterns, and the spaces between can be filled with colorful flowers and paths. These are particularly effective when seen from a raised patio or an upstairs window.

Large hedges can be combined with topiary, with shrubs allowed to grow out at regular intervals, then clipped into geometric or ani-

◀ **Flowering hedges** Compact growth and even shape are the main considerations in choosing an informal hedge. The yellow-flowered shrub *Hypericum* 'Hidcote' grows to a maximum height of 5 ft (1.5 m) and flowers throughout summer and fall.

hedge. Fierce winds have a drying effect on plants, especially newly installed evergreens, and can prove fatal over time.

On sloping land, hedges can be used to redirect frost, which flows like water, away from the garden. Hedges also block dust, and their roots help to check soil erosion. The higher the hedge, the more shelter it creates, but it also produces more shade. Generally, the larger the hedge, the more water and nutrients it requires.

Hedges for privacy

Hedges for general privacy should be at least 5 ft (1.5 m) high, although those that are 4 ft (1.2 m) high will supply privacy for a seating area. Enormously tall hedges, especially in small gardens, can be overbearing and not worth the extra seclusion provided. Hedges planted next to a level change, such as along the top of a retaining wall, seem much higher

▶ **Formal hedging** The small-leaved evergreen box *(Buxus sempervirens)* comes in a number of varieties. Dwarf varieties can be planted as formal borders; large varieties can be used in topiary or for a boundary hedge.

mal shapes. Arches, buttresses, and alcoves for seats or statues can be formed out of hedging, given time, space, and patience.

Formal or informal?

In old-fashioned formal hedges, usually composed of a single species, each plant's individual character is sacrificed to create an overall geometric shape. The lines of a formal hedge can complement the rough-and-tumble of a mixed flower bed, or an area of long grass and naturalized spring bulbs. Formal hedges are particularly suitable for edging small, square- or rectangular-shaped gardens, but they require regular pruning, up to four times a year. As a result, they tend to be dense and nonflowering, because you remove the young flowering wood.

In informal hedges, a plant's natural shape and habit of growth are the main features to consider. Plants grown in such hedges tend to produce more flowers and berries than rigorously clipped formal hedges, since less new wood is removed. Escallonia, shrub roses, hydrangea, and spirea make excellent informal hedges. Traditional hedging plants, such as yew and privet, can look as attractive in informal gardens as in formal ones. However, an informal selection of mixed shrubs can lose its "architectural" quality, and look simply like a bed of shrubs. In addition, too many different types of shrub in one hedge may result in an uneven barrier that lacks visual effect.

Dwarf hedges, ideal for edging flower beds or dividing up areas within a garden, can be formal or informal, depending on the choice of plant and how you prune it. Box, for example, makes a formal dwarf edging; lightly pruned cotton lavender, an informal one.

The chart on page 58 gives a selection of formal, informal, and dwarf hedges.

Evergreen versus deciduous

Evergreen hedges offer year-round color and more privacy than deciduous hedges, but, with a few exceptions, they do not produce flowers. Deciduous hedging plants, on the other hand, not only produce flowers in season, but many also have colored spring foliage as well as handsome fall

▲ **Conifer screens** The vigorous Leyland cypress (x *Cupressocyparis leylandii)* is ideal for screening. A fast-growing conifer of dense columnar form, it withstands high winds.

▼ **Color and protection** The firethorn *(Pyracantha* 'Buisson Ardent') makes an impenetrable hedge, its thorny branches deterring intruders. Colorful, with cream-white flowers in spring and berries in fall, it grows to a height of some 6 ft (1.8 m).

tints and berries. Several, like the hornbeams and beeches, are effective visual screens, even in winter when their foliage is brown.

You can combine two or three types of deciduous plants for an interesting, formal tapestry effect. Try variegated and green-leaved forms of holly or privet, or purple- and green-leaved forms of beech. Combining deciduous and evergreen plants makes for winter interest. The proportions can vary, but if the plants are not equal in vigor or growth rate, be prepared to give the weaker ones a helping hand with extra water and fertilizer.

Flower and berry hedges

If you choose hedges that flower or produce berries, keep in mind the amount of time during the year that the hedges will not have flowers or berries, and try to choose plants that also have attractive foliage or form. *Rosa rugosa* varieties make excellent flowering hedges, and their tangle of prickly canes are dog- and child-proof. The flowers, which range from white in 'Blanc Double de Coubert' to rose-pink in 'Fru Dagmar Hastrup' and wine-red in 'Roseraie de l'Hay,' can be single, semidouble, or double. They bloom in summer and fall, often followed by attractive hips.

Hedge cotoneaster *(Cotoneaster lucidus)* exhibits brilliant berries and richly colored fall foliage, and stands hard pruning. There are even some hedges that provide fragrance from their foliage, such as rosemary or lavender.

Practicalities

Quick-growing evergreen hedging, such as Leyland cypress, is tempting, but it can grow too tall unless cut back vigorously. Single plants sometimes die off, creating unattractive gaps. The faster a formal hedge grows, the more often it needs pruning — three times a year for privet and shrubby honeysuckle *(Lonicera nitida)*, for example. Yew is often thought of as slow growing, but can add 9-12 in (23-30 cm) annual growth and may need clipping only once a year, depending on the cultivar.

When buying hedging plants, keep in mind that small shrubs are cheaper, less risky to establish, and grow more strongly than larger specimens. Always choose plants that are well furnished

▲ **Hedge tapestry** The deciduous cherry plum *(Prunus cerasifera)* makes a dense windbreak and is highly decorative when mixed with the purple-leaved variety 'Atropurpurea.'

► **Informal hedges** Yellow- and red-flowered varieties of broom *(Cytisus)* create vivid splashes of late-spring color on the edge of a lawn.

▼ **Mixed hedges** Evergreen and deciduous shrubs, clipped into rounded shapes, form an ornamental hedge suitable for a small front garden that would seem overpowered by a high hedge.

with branches down to ground level. Make sure you select the right species or variety for the desired height. For example, *Buxus sempervirens* 'Suffruticosa' is a dwarf edging box while *B.s.* 'Handsworthiensis' grows to a height of 8 ft (2.4 m).

Hedges can be planted in single or double rows. Single rows are considered better for the ultimate health of the plants, which have more space. However, they take longer to make effective screening. Double rows are more expensive and crowd the plants, but they quickly provide privacy. Space plants 2-3 ft (60 cm-1 m) apart, according to size and growth rate; leave about 18 in (45 cm) between double rows, staggering the plants.

Pruning regimes are varied (pp.127–150), but formal hedging must be cut back hard, by up to half, in the first year after planting to encourage compact growth. Concentrate on the rough shape and proportions first.

Formal hedges should be more narrow at the top to allow light to

► **Hedge decoration** Privet is one of the most popular hedging plants. A quick-growing evergreen, it responds well to trimming and is ideal for ornamental topiary work and unusual decoration.

◄ **Internal hedges** Foliage shrubs don't have to be confined to the boundaries but can be ornamental features in their own right. This meandering design of low-growing *prunus* attracts the eye without inhibiting the view.

reach the lower branches. Large-leaved hedging plants, such as Portugal laurel *(Prunus lusitanica)*, look best trimmed branch by branch; a once-over is fine for others. Established formal hedges should be pruned as often as is needed to keep them neat, usually in the summer.

Informal hedges will always need light pruning to remove old, dead, or diseased wood, to keep the hedge within bounds, and to encourage flowering. As a general rule, prune flowering shrubs that produce their flowers on new wood in winter or early spring and prune those that flower on one-year-old wood immediately after they have finished flowering. Those hedges that produce flowers on old wood should be pruned very lightly.

HEDGING PLANTS				
NAME	**DESCRIPTION**	**HEIGHT & SPREAD**	**FOLIAGE**	**GROWTH RATE**
FORMAL HEDGES				
Beech *(Fagus sylvatica* 'Riversii')	Purple leaves; foliage turns golden-brown over winter	8 x 3 ft (2.4 x 1 m)	Deciduous	Moderate
Box *(Buxus sempervirens* 'Handsworthiensis')	Dark green leaves; erect and robust	8 x 3 ft (2.4 x 1m)	Evergreen	Slow
Cherry laurel *(Prunus laurocerasus)*	Leathery dark green leaves; purple-black berries	8 x 4 ft (2.4 x 1.2 m)	Evergreen	Moderate
Cockspur thorn *(Crataegus crus-galli)*	Tough; thorny, white flowers, red fruit	8 x 3 ft (2.4 x 1 m)	Deciduous	Moderate
Cotoneaster *(Cotoneaster lucidus)*	Oval, glossy dark green leaves, black berries	6 x 3 ft (1.8 x 1 m)	Deciduous	Moderate
Holly *(Ilex* x *altaclarensis* 'Camelliifolia') *(Ilex aquifolium* 'Aureo-Marginata')	Moderately spiny dark green leaves; purple stems Dark, glossy, spiny leaves with gold edges, red berries	8 x 3 ft (2.4 x 1 m) 8 x 3 ft (2.4 x 1 m)	Evergreen Evergreen	Moderate Moderate
Hornbeam, European *(Carpinus betulus)*	Pointed leaves, gold-brown in fall/winter	8 x 3 ft (2.4 x 1 m)	Deciduous	Moderate
Leyland cypress (x *Cupressocyparis leylandii)*	Drooping sprays of gray-green leaves	10 x 4 ft (3 x 1.2 m)	Evergreen	Very fast
Portugal laurel *(Prunus lusitanica)*	Bushy, glossy dark green leaves; reddish stalks	8 x 4 ft (2.4 x 1.2 m)	Evergreen	Slow
Privet *(Ligustrum ovalifolium* 'Aureum')	Oval glossy midgreen leaves, edged with wide yellow borders	3 x 4 ft (1 x 1.2 m)	Evergreen	Fast
Yew *(Taxus* x *media* cvs)	Densely bushy, with narrow green leaves	8 x 3 ft (2.4 x 1 m)	Evergreen	Slow
INFORMAL HEDGES				
Wintergreen barberry *(Berberis julianae)*	Lustrous dark green leaves; profuse yellow flowers, blue-black fruits	6 x 4 ft (2 x 1.2 m)	Evergreen	Moderate
Escallonia *(Escallonia* x *langleyensis)*	Dense and luxuriant growth, with glossy leaves; pale pink flowers	6 x 4 ft (2 x 1.2 m)	Evergreen	Moderate
Firethorn *(Pyracantha coccinea)*	Bright green leaves; golden-yellow to reddish-orange berries	8 x 6 ft (2.4 x 2 m)	Semievergreen — Evergreen	Moderate
European cranberrybush *(Viburnum opulus)*	Dark green leaves; white flowers, red fruits	8 x 6 ft (2.4 x 2 m)	Deciduous	Moderate
Mock orange *(Philadelphus* x *lemoinei* 'Belle Etoile')	Fragrant single white flowers; oval green leaves	4 x 3 ft (1.2 x 1 m)	Deciduous	Moderate
Potentilla *(Potentilla fruticosa* 'Katherine Dykes')	Bushy, with lobed midgreen leaves and bright yellow flowers	4 x 4 ft (1.2 x 1.2 m)	Deciduous	Moderate
Rose *(Rosa rugosa)*	White, pink, or red flowers; red hips	4 x 4 ft (1.2 x 1.2 m)	Deciduous	Moderate
Spirea *(Spiraea* x *vanhouttei)*	Arching habit; profuse white flowers in early summer	6 x 4 ft (2 x 1.2 m)	Deciduous	Moderate
DWARF HEDGES				
Barberry *(Berberis thunbergii* 'Atropurpurea Nana')	Oval red-purple leaves, redder in fall; red berries	1.5 x 1 ft (45 x 30 cm)	Deciduous	Moderate
Box *(Buxus sempervirens* 'Suffruticosa')	Dense; leathery, glossy bright green leaves	1.5 x 1 ft (45 x 30 cm)	Evergreen	Slow
Lavender cotton *(Santolina chamaecyparissus)*	Silver-gray leaves, with button-sized yellow flowers	2 x 3 ft (60 cm x 1 m)	Evergreen	Fast
Lavender *(Lavandula angustifolia)*	Aromatic; narrow gray-green leaves, mauve to purple flowers	3 x 3 ft (1 x 1 m)	Evergreen	Moderate
Rosemary *(Rosmarinus officinalis)*	Bushy and spreading; narrow, aromatic leaves and lilac-blue flowers	4 x 3 ft (1.2 x 1 m)	Evergreen	Moderate
Sand cherry *(Prunus* x *cistena)*	Bushy, with reddish-purple leaves, white flowers, and black-purple fruits	3 x 3 ft (1 x 1 m)	Deciduous	Moderate

PLANTING HEDGES

Thorough preparation of the site and regular aftercare are essential if a new hedge is to remain healthy and attractive for many years to come.

All hedges, whether formal or informal, should be even and compact in growth so that they retain their shape over a long period. For a formal effect, they must be able to withstand regular trimming. In particular, hedges should not die out at the bottom or develop patches with age.

To grow hedges successfully, you must pay great attention to site planning and preparation, since a hedge is a permanent feature. It will be difficult to attend to soil conditions once the hedge is established.

Landscaping considerations

A hedge must be tended regularly, and so access to both sides is essential. If it is to form a boundary between your property and that of your neighbors, you may leave half the job to them, if they agree. Elsewhere, you should be able to walk freely around both sides. A tall hedge may need trimming from a stepladder, and so firm, level ground to a width of at least 3 ft (1 m) on either side is required. For safety, power trimming tools should not be used in confined spaces — never overreach when using a power tool.

Ideally, the site should be consistent from end to end in terms of sun and shade, soil drainage, soil type, and wind exposure — uneven conditions invariably produce an uneven hedge.

Preparing the site

For best results, the planting strip should be about 3 ft (1 m) wide. Narrow sites encourage competition from weeds, neighboring plants, or grass during the hedge's early years, causing poor or erratic establishment.

For spring planting, which is recommended for most evergreens, prepare the ground in fall and winter. Sites for deciduous hedges to be planted in fall are best prepared in spring and kept weed-free during the summer.

Soil condition along an old boundary is often poor, especially where a wall or fence has been removed. If there is a lot of rubble, poor soil, or drainage problems, dig out the site to at least one spade's depth and replace with new topsoil — bought or transferred from elsewhere in the garden. Other sites may be grassy or occupied by weeds or ornamental plants, which must be cleared. A garden tiller provides a quick means of turning over the soil, but the roots of perennials will be sliced up and turned in, creating a

▼ **Ubiquitous privet** The golden-leaved *Ligustrum ovalifolium* is a common hedging plant. It is inexpensive, tolerates polluted air, and is ideal for clipping into almost any shape.

PREPARING THE SITE

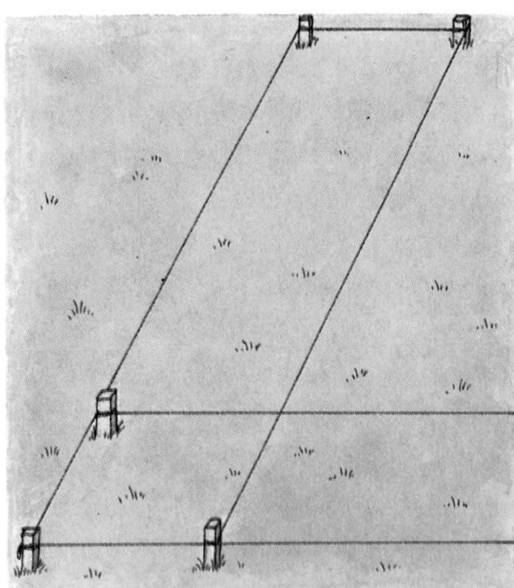

1 Plan and mark out the planting site with wooden pegs and strings. A mature hedge will have roots that grow 3 ft (1 m) or more in all directions, so prepare a planting area of at least that size.

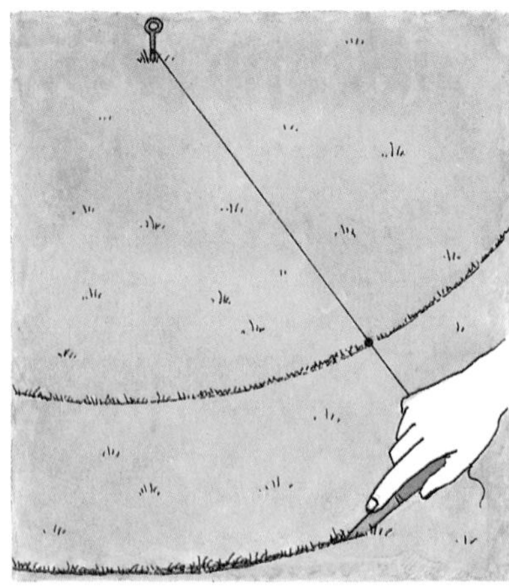

2 To mark out a curved site, insert a peg at the center of the area and knot string around it. Make two guide knots 3 ft (1 m) apart, corresponding to the position of the hedge. Pull the string taut and cut against the knots.

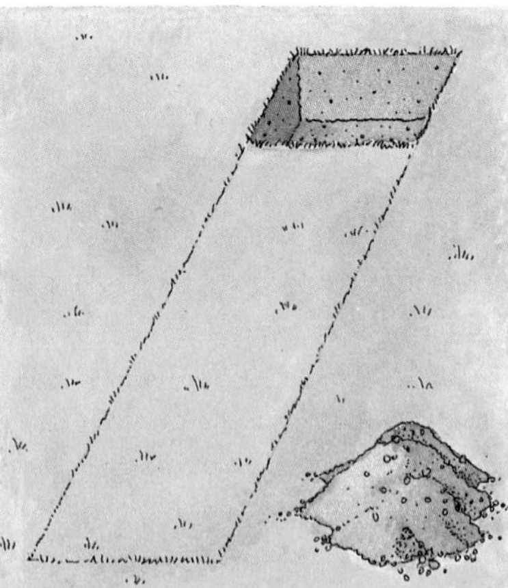

3 Begin preparing a grassy planting site by digging out one spade's depth of soil, starting at one end. Pile this soil at the other end of the site — it will be used to fill in the last hole. Fork over the earth in the bottom of the hole.

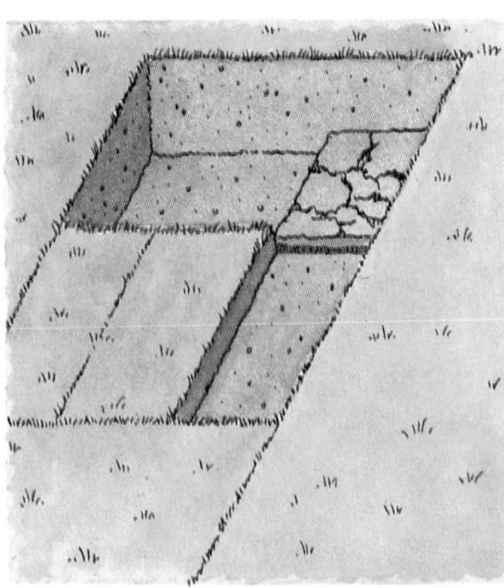

4 Skim off the turf from the next 1 ft (30 cm) or so of the site, using a spade, and turn it upside down into the bottom of the previous hole. If the soil is heavy, break it up slightly with a garden fork and remove any tough roots.

5 Add a layer of organic material, then turn in the soil from the newly exposed area. Now you have another hole adjacent to the first. Fill it as before. Repeat the procedure until the site is complete.

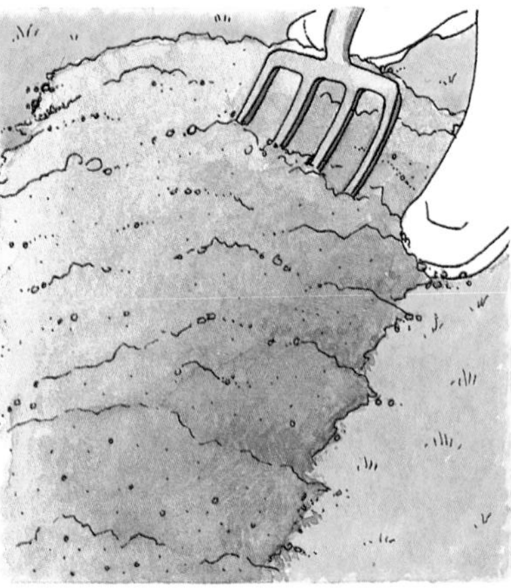

6 Keep the site weed-free until ready for planting. Shortly before planting, fork over the soil again, at the same time time incorporating a complete fertilizer. If the site is very wet, raise the soil into a slight ridge.

persistent weed problem. Manual cultivation, using a hand fork or trowel, gives better results. Alternatively, apply a nonselective but nonpersistent herbicide, allowing plenty of time for the chemical to disintegrate in the soil before planting the hedge.

If no perennial weeds are present, turf can be turned upside down and buried one spade's depth in the bottom of the planting trench. This method preserves the valuable topsoil and improves the organic content of the soil.

Begin by marking out the site with pegs and string lines. Regular arcs and semicircles can be plotted using string pulled taut from a peg inserted at the center of the curve. Gauge the desired radius by knotting the string, then slicing the curve with a knife held against the knot.

Turn over the soil throughout the site to one spade's depth and fork in a layer of organic material — about one full wheelbarrow for every 2-yd/m run. Shortly before planting, fork a complete fertilizer, such as 5–10–5, at one handful per yd/m run, into the soil over an area 1 ft (30 cm) wide along the hedge line.

Planting the hedge

Deciduous hedges can be planted when weather and soil conditions permit, between midfall and early spring, but preferably in fall. Evergreen hedges are best planted in spring when transpiration loss will be smallest. Set the plants $1^1/_2$-2 ft (45-60 cm) apart, depending on vigor; 10-12 in (25-30 cm) apart between dwarf types.

The ideal age of hedging specimens for planting varies, but, as a general rule, they should be small enough to make handling easy and staking unnecessary. Plant in a single row against a garden line to ensure a straight hedge. When making a curved hedge, use a length of wood marked or notched in the center as a gauge to determine the planting position.

Set the plants at the same depth as they were in the nursery, indicated by a dark soil mark at the base of each stem. Ease soil around the roots and press it in firmly — more hedging plants die from loose planting than any other cause.

Trim all plants to a standard height, using a string stretched between two tall stakes as a guide. This type of pruning ensures that they all have the same start. If plants aren't very bushy, encourage growth by cutting them back by one-half or two-thirds, either when you plant or in spring.

Water young plants during dry spells in spring and early summer. Allow at least 2½ gallons (10 liters) to soak in around each plant daily until it is established. Sprinkling, preferably with rainwater in a watering can fitted with a fine sprinkler head, is also beneficial.

Aftercare

Keep the base of the hedge free of weeds and do not allow any other plants to grow within 1 ft (30 cm) on either side of a new hedge.

Regular applications of fertilizer are not needed, but all young hedges benefit from a dressing of complete fertilizer in late winter, one year after spring planting or 18 months after a fall planting. Apply a handful per each sq-yd/m run on each side of the hedge. Repeat the following year, if growth is poor.

Staking is usually not required

HEELING-IN

If hedging plants are delivered too early, heel them in temporarily in spare ground. Lay them close together in a trench, angling away from prevailing winds. Lightly press down the soil over the roots.

PLANTING THE HEDGE

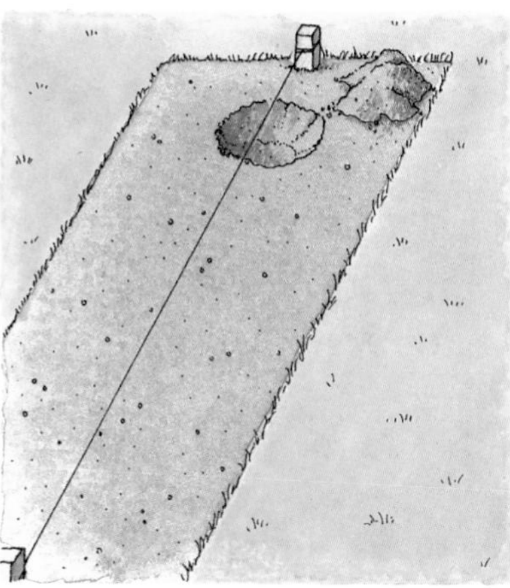

1 Mark out the center of the planting area with pegs and string. Keep the string in place throughout the planting operation, making sure it remains taut — it's essential to plant the hedge in a perfectly straight line.

2 Use a length of wood with a notch cut at its center to gauge the planting position when making a curved hedge. If the edges of the site are tidy and parallel, this method can also be applied to straight plantings.

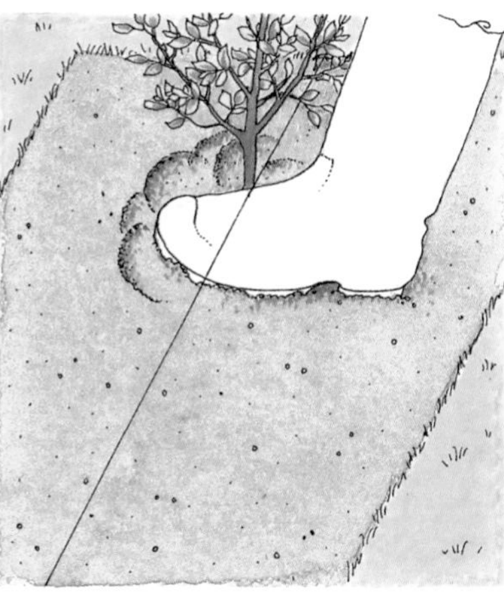

3 Dig the first planting hole, making it slightly larger than the plant's root mass. Bury roots to the same depth as they were in the nursery — the stem will be darker at soil level.

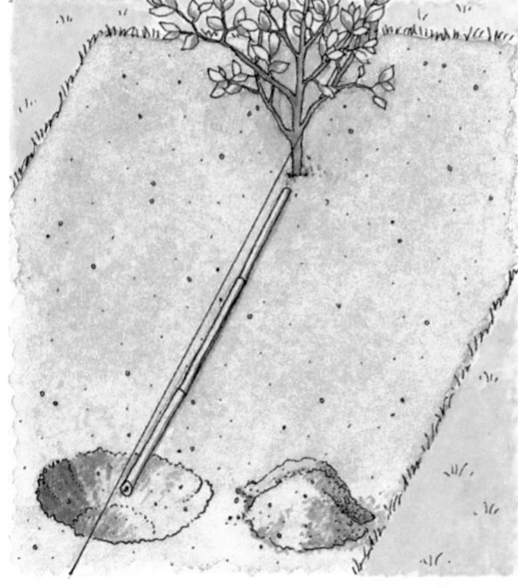

4 After pressing down the soil around the first plant very securely with your heel and toe, mark the position of the next plant. Use a cane cut to the required length as a gauge. Plant as before.

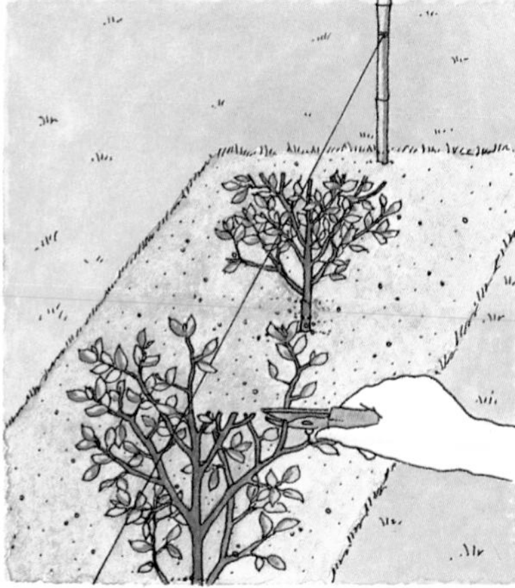

5 Trim the plants to a standard height. Insert stakes and stretch string between them at a height equal to that of the strongest growth on the shortest plant. Prune to the level of the string.

6 Water in well if the soil is dry and repeat daily, as necessary. Give enough water to soak the soil thoroughly over the whole planting area — at least 2½ gallons (10 liters) per plant.

MAKING A SPIRAL CONE

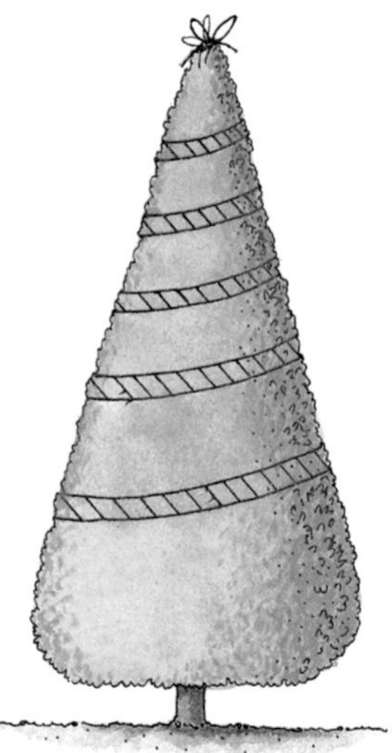

1 To make a spiral from a mature cone-shaped bush or small tree, begin by marking out the spiral with strings, attaching them to branch tips at regular intervals. Step back to check the pattern.

2 Using shears or a hand pruner, cut into the plant following the string lines. Remove all stems and leaves back to the main stem or trunk. With time, foliage will grow in to hide the bare surfaces (as below).

for most hedges (except in the case of free-standing topiary), but on exposed sites a new hedge may need the shelter of a temporary fence or screen until established. Alternatively, support each plant individually or erect a line of stakes with wires or strings stretched between, tying in as required with string.

For all hedges, early training is important. Aim to make the hedge widest at the bottom, with a rounded or broadly sloping top. This practice produces better growth of the low branches and gives the best wind shelter.

To promote this thick, bushy growth from the base to the top, side branching must be encouraged. Start to prune a hedge before it reaches the height you desire it to be; otherwise, it will become thin and straggly at the base. Allow formal hedges to reach the desired height only in stages. Prune the leading shoots regularly when they are 9-12 in (23-30 cm) long.

Informal, flowering hedges may be left to grow freely after the initial pruning at planting time. If branches are growing poorly, however, sacrifice the second year's flowers by pruning again.

Decorative hedge trimming

Many free-standing hedging plants can be trimmed into decorative shapes when they are mature, or they can be trained to shape from young plants. The former method is suitable for simple topiary designs, such as cones, globes, and pyramids.

Make use of a shrub's normal growth shape — for example, a naturally conical shrub is much easier to train into a cone than a spreading species. Privet, yew, and the accommodating box lend themselves to topiary designs.

See that the plant is well staked and securely tied so that wind action cannot separate and disfigure the branches. Bind the branches with string or thin rope over winter to prevent snow loads from breaking them.

Specimen topiary shrubs can look effective in large tubs. Choose a container to complement the shape of the topiary, ensuring that it is large enough to accommodate the expanding root ball — the shrub will be growing for many years, ideally without being disturbed.

HEDGE MAINTENANCE

All hedges need regular trimming to promote a dense, impenetrable screen and to maintain their shape and beauty.

The first few years of a hedge's life are very important. Most plants will develop into a bushy or upright shape without any assistance, but these characteristics alone do not ensure a good hedge. Each plant must have a dense, uniform growth habit and a shape that suits the desired height and width of the hedge. Regular, careful pruning and trimming from the year of planting onward is the only way to achieve these features; a neglected hedge is very difficult to restore.

In general, formal hedges should be trimmed two or three times during the growing season, and informal ones after flowering. If a formal hedge grows densely enough, there is no need for it to exceed 2 ft (60 cm) in width. To be most stable and resistant to wind and snow damage, all hedges should be wider at the base than across the top. Informal hedges, on the other hand, don't need to be so dense or regular in outline, and require less pruning and care than free-standing shrubs.

Trimming and pruning tools

For a couple of years after planting, the only tool you will need for hedge trimming is a sharp pair of pruning shears. In subsequent years, manual hedge shears or a power hedge trimmer (pp.161–172) will be essential for all small-leaved, formal hedges.

Species with large leaves, however, such as cherry laurel, should be trimmed throughout their life with pruning shears — hedge trimmers slice leaves as well as stems, and the damaged edges later turn yellow and brown, creating a very unsightly effect. Pruning shears are also best for trimming all informal hedges.

Caution: Choose and use power hedge trimmers with care — though they can save time and labor, many are potentially quite hazardous. Look for models with as many safety features as possible. Blade extensions are very useful; they prevent any object larger than about 3/8 in (1 cm) in diameter — equivalent to the size of the largest stems of most hedging plants — from coming into contact with the cutting blades. The blades should also be fitted with an automatic shutoff system that

▼ **Hedge shears** The traditional tool for trimming small-leaved hedges has handles offset to the blades. This position gives a good cutting angle for both the sides and top of a hedge, according to how you hold the shears.

TRIMMING UPRIGHT HEDGING PLANTS

1 In the second winter after planting — preferably in late winter — prune back the previous year's stems by half and trim any remaining lateral shoots to within an inch or two (2.5-5 cm) of the structural framework stems.

2 During the following summer, trim back all lateral shoots whenever they reach about 8-12 in (20-30 cm) in length. Maintain the desired hedge shape; ensure that the sides taper toward the top of the hedge.

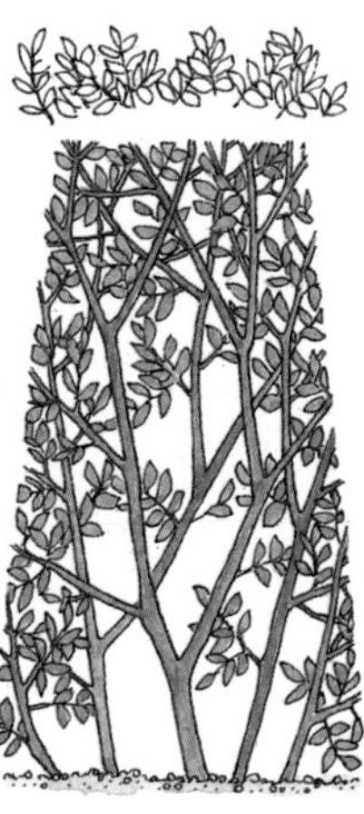

3 In the third winter, cut back any leaders that are developing an uneven height. This procedure must be repeated yearly until the desired height is reached — never let a new hedge gain height too quickly.

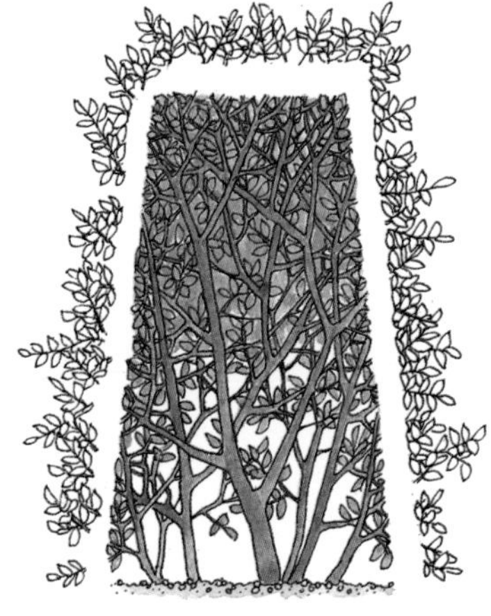

4 Once the hedge is established, summer trimming is all that's necessary. Using hedge shears or a power trimmer, trim the side and top growth to maintain the desired shape, repeating every 6 to 8 weeks.

TRIMMING CONIFER HEDGES

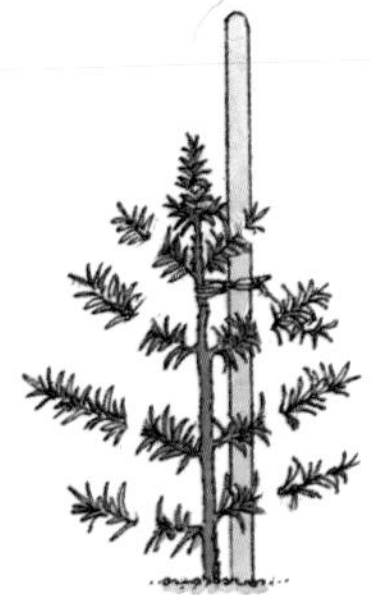

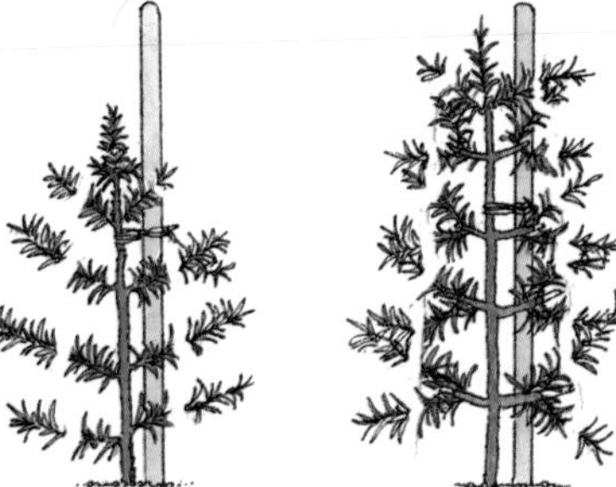

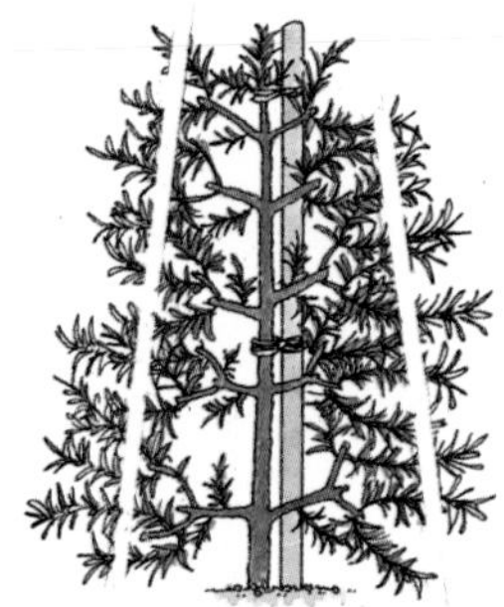

1 Securely tie all conifers to stakes or bamboo canes at planting time. Trim all straggly side shoots to encourage even branch development.
2 In the following summer, tie in the leaders and trim back the side shoots, maintaining tapering sides.
3 Pinch out the leaders when they reach the desired height. Trim back any side and top growth every summer.

functions within a fraction of a second of the power switch being released. Wear safety goggles and gloves when using a hedge trimmer, and grip the trimmer with two hands at all times, since most accidents occur when the operator lets go of the handle with one hand to clear debris or move the power cord of an electric model. Some trimmers cannot be used until you grip both handles and activate both switches. Before clearing jammed blades of debris, unplug the trimmer.

Always plug an electric trimmer's cord into a GFCI outlet. It will ensure that the power is switched off immediately if the cord is cut or if a short circuit occurs, saving you from serious electric shock or burns in an accident. The safest place to keep the extension cord while working with an electric trimmer is across your shoulder, where it is least likely to come into contact with the blades.

Pruning and trimming

Hedging plants fall into three categories: those with a naturally upright growth habit, which must be encouraged to thicken at their base; those with a naturally low and bushy growth habit, which must be induced to gain height and density at their top; and the conifers, which need only minimal training to establish their shape.

Upright hedging plants, such as privet, hawthorn, snowberry, and buckthorn, must be cut back hard throughout their early years to promote strong basal growth. Left inadequately pruned, these plants become bare at their base.

At planting time, they should be cut back to about 6 in (15 cm) from the ground. During the following summer, lightly trim all branches to promote active growth of as many new shoots as possible. The cutting pattern must reflect the desired final shape of the hedge. Cut back new growth again by half during the second winter to produce further bushiness. At the same time, prune back all other branches close to the main structural stems. Above all, discourage the leaders — the shoots by which the main stems extend themselves — from reaching their final height too quickly.

Pruning during the next year will depend on how dense the

hedge has become. If further thickening is desired, repeat the winter pruning once more, as you did the second year. If you are satisfied with the density of the hedge, trimming in subsequent years can be restricted to the growing season. How often you trim during any one year will depend on the climate and on the species concerned, but every 6 to 8 weeks from midspring to early fall is usual. Aim to keep the plants neat and within the confines of the desired overall hedge shape, and ensure that the sides of the hedge taper toward the top.

Bushy hedging plants, such as beech, hazel, and hornbeam, need less severe pruning in the early formative years.

At planting time, trim back the major side branches and the leaders by about one-third. Allow the plants to develop naturally throughout the first summer. During the second winter, repeat the pruning as you did the first year and cut off straggly growth.

As with upright hedging plants, trim only during the growing season in every subsequent year, maintaining a tapered outline. Ideally, trim twice in each season: in early summer, then again — most importantly — in late summer or very early fall.

Coniferous hedging plants, such as Lawson and Leyland cypresses, and arborvitaes, need different treatment. Don't remove the leaders at planting time. Slightly trim only the straggly side branches to promote the formation of well-balanced laterals.

For arborvitae hedges, trim all plants to 6 in (15 cm) below the height of the shortest plant to encourage lateral growth.

The main stem of most young conifers is not rigid enough to withstand strong winds or snow loads, and must therefore be staked and tied loosely but securely. As the conifers get older and stronger, remove the stakes.

Allow the leaders to develop unhindered until they reach the desired final height. During the second and subsequent years after planting, trim only the side branches in the course of the growing season. Most species require only one trim in late summer. If vigorous species become too overgrown by midsummer, you can overcome this problem in subsequent years by giving an extra trim in early summer.

Flowering formal hedges, such as forsythia, should be trimmed in the growing season, immediately after the flowers have faded. A second trim in late summer may be necessary to maintain a neat shape, but do not remove too

NEGLECTED HEDGES

Overgrown hedges can be renovated, though replanting with a new hedge may be better. Cut all branches back to the main stems — in winter, for deciduous hedges; in spring, for evergreens. Cut one side back hard, leaving the other side until the next year.

TRIMMING THE ENTIRE HEDGE

1 To ensure a perfectly straight top edge when trimming a small-leaved hedge, always use a taut string line stretched between a solid stake inserted at each end of the hedge. For a patterned top edge, construct a template made from stiff cardboard or rope. A regular wavy top can be gauged by draping string from a tight line positioned across the top of the hedge.

2 Never use shears or a power trimmer to cut a large-leaved hedge, such as laurel — you will slice many of the remaining leaves, and these will later turn yellow and brown, creating an unattractive effect. Instead, use a pair of pruning shears and trim in the same way as for a free-standing shrub. Though more laborious and time-consuming, it will pay off in the long run.

3 Using pruning shears or loppers, cut out deadwood from a hedge in summer, when healthy wood is clearly visible. Make a clean, downward-sloping cut through healthy wood a little below the dead material. To avoid damaging surrounding healthy stems, cut large dead branches into several pieces before extracting them from the hedge. Train surrounding stems into the bare patch.

AVOIDING SNOW DAMAGE

Heavy accumulations of snow can cause considerable physical damage to all hedges, especially those with weak stems, such as conifers, or those with large leaves, such as laurel. Using the head of a soft broom, gently shake the branches after each snowfall to dislodge the snow — once branches have been allowed to sag for more than a few hours, it can be difficult to train them back into position. In areas where heavy snowfalls are common, bind hedges with string or rope throughout winter to prevent snow-laden branches from breaking.

HEDGE-TRIMMING TIMES

Arborvitae *(Thuja occidentalis)*: late summer
Beech *(Fagus sylvatica)*: midsummer to late summer
Barberry *(Berberis* x *stenophylla)*: late spring to early summer
(Berberis thunbergii 'Atropurpurea Nana'): late summer
Box *(Buxus sempervirens)*: early summer
Cherry plum (*Prunus cerasifera*): midsummer
Shrubby honeysuckle *(Lonicera nitida)*: midspring to early fall
Cotoneaster lucidus: midsummer
Escallonia x *langleyensis:* early summer
Firethorn *(Pyracantha coccinea)*: early summer
Forsythia x *intermedia:* immediately after flowering and late summer
Hawthorn *(Crataegus monogyna)*: early summer to late summer
Holly *(Ilex* species): midsummer
Hornbeam *(Carpinus betulus)*: midsummer to late summer
Hydrangea macrophylla: late spring
Laurel *(Prunus laurocerasus)*: midsummer to late summer
Laurustinus *(Viburnum tinus)*: after flowering
Lavender *(Lavandula angustifolia)*: early fall
Lavender cotton *(Santolina chamaecyparissus)*: spring
Lawson cypress *(Chamaecyparis lawsoniana)*: early summer or fall
Leyland cypress (x *Cupressocyparis leylandii)*: early summer
Mock orange (*Philadelphus* hybrids); immediately after flowering
Portugal laurel *(Prunus lusitanica)*: early summer to midsummer
Potentilla fruticosa 'Katherine Dykes': after flowering
Privet *(Ligustrum ovalifolium)*: late spring to early summer, and midsummer to late summer
Rose *(Rosa rugosa* varieties): early spring or fall
Rosemary *(Rosmarinus officinalis)*: midsummer to late summer
Sand cherry *(Prunus* x *cistena)*: midsummer to late summer
Spiraea x *vanhouttei:* immediately after flowering
Western red cedar (*Thuja plicata*): early summer to midsummer

much growth or next year's developing flower buds will be lost.

Flowering informal hedges, such as *Rosa rugosa,* are pruned according to the age of wood on which they flower. If they flower on old wood, trim them to shape right after flowering; if they flower on the current season's wood, trim them in early spring.

Fruiting hedging plants, which develop attractive fruits after the flowers have faded, such as pyracantha and spirea, should have their young growth trimmed in midsummer to late summer, leaving most of the fruiting wood intact. This selective trimming must be done with pruning shears. Alternatively, leave trimming until the fruits have gone.

Other routine care

To succeed, hedges need more than just annual trimming. If they are to remain healthy and attractive, you must pay attention to watering and fertilizing, and to the control of pests, diseases, and disorders.

Watering is necessary during dry spells in the growing season — hedging plants are generally spaced much closer than other garden plants, and so their roots compete heavily for water. You can use a garden hose or sprinkler, but the most effective method is to lay a soaker hose along the base of the hedge. Leave the hose on until there is enough water to saturate the top 6 in (15 cm) of soil — equivalent to 1 in (2.5 cm) of rainfall — at each application and repeat whenever the top 1 in (2.5 cm) of soil is dry.

Applying a 2-in (5-cm)-thick layer of mulch annually around the roots of a hedge will help to prevent water loss from the soil.

Fertilizing should be carried out regularly. In spring, apply a mulch of organic material, or a side-dressing of granular 5–10–5 fertilizer at the rate 5-10 lbs per 100 feet (2.2-4.5 kg per 30 meters) of hedge. Treat a strip up to 3 ft (90 cm) wide from the base of the hedge and hoe the fertilizer into the surface 1 in (2.5 cm). Water it in if the soil is dry.

If the roots of the hedge are growing under sod or pavement, apply nutrients as a foliar feed from a garden sprayer. Use a liquid fertilizer that is rich in nitrogen for leaf growth. Repeat whenever the foliage appears dull and lacking vigor. Foliar sprays can also be applied as a midseason backup to the main spring application of fertilizer to the soil.

Weeding should be done at the base of a hedge with a hoe, by hand, or with herbicides. Weeds compete with the hedge for nutrients, water, and light, so remove them before they accumulate.

Glyphosate is an effective herbicide for use against even persistent perennial and annual weeds. Because it kills on contact, and does not move through the soil to injure roots, this product will not harm the hedge as long as you are careful not to wet its leaves.

Cutting out deadwood is another vital task. Branches often die out in the center of an established hedge. These should be pruned away, as should damaged or weak branches. With pruning shears, make clean cuts back to healthy wood. This work is best done during the growing season, when the difference between live wood and deadwood is obvious.

If a whole plant dies out within a hedge, dig it out. Prepare the soil as you would for planting a new shrub, and replace the dead plant with a new specimen.

Pests and diseases found on hedges should be treated like those that attack other garden shrubs and trees. Healthy plants are naturally resistant; use chemicals with care and discretion.

Planting and sowing

Buying plants is one of the most pleasurable aspects of gardening. A thoughtful choice, based on sound knowledge of the conditions in your garden, the space available, and the plant in question, is far better than an impulse buy, which rarely works out well. Doing your homework beforehand, so that you know exactly what you want and what a healthy specimen should look like, helps to prevent disappointment or problems. Garden-center staff may not always be as helpful or knowledgeable as you would like, and labels may be inadequate or misplaced.

Knowing where to buy is also important. It is usually best to purchase your plants at reputable garden centers and nurseries, which have access to the most reliable sources. You will also find a huge selection of cultivars — seeds, bulbs, and grown plants — in the catalogs of mail-order suppliers.

To give new plants a healthy start, they must be planted in the right position, at a suitable depth, and at the correct distance apart. Annuals, bulbs, shrubs, and trees vary slightly in their planting requirements, and, of course, planting in containers demands a different technique. Since new plants are vulnerable until they have become established, aftercare, such as watering, weeding, and staking, is vital. With shrubs and trees — the most permanent and expensive plants — this initial care is doubly important.

Plants grown from seed are the cheapest option, and seed catalogs offer the greatest choice, especially of annuals. Using the right techniques for preparing your seed flats, for sowing, and for caring for the seedlings after germination can make the difference between success and failure. Home-saved seed, especially of hybrids, however, doesn't always breed true to type; fresh replacement seed is best.

Balled-root shrubs Newly lifted shrubs have their root balls wrapped in burlap for sale at garden centers.

BUYING THE BEST PLANTS

Start gardening with young, healthy, and vigorous plants and you're well on the way to success. Knowing how to select the top quality means you won't be wasting money on weak plants, and it also avoids the risk of spreading disease and pests.

It is sometimes difficult to imagine how gardeners managed before there were garden centers. The latter are certainly not the only source of plants, however, and you may do just as well — or sometimes better — if you look elsewhere. For instance, many general and specialized nurseries sell direct to the public, on site as well as by mail order. Large supermarkets and department stores often sell plants, too. But always put quality before economy, and make sure that the plants you buy are clearly labeled so that you know exactly what they are. Even when your stock comes to you through a network of gardening friends, be choosy about the plants you accept.

Bedding plants
Since annual plants complete their life cycle in just one year, and biennials in two, they can readily be grown from seed. There are, however, good reasons for buying young plants.

One packet contains a large quantity of seeds, and you may need only a few plants for window boxes or containers; alternatively, you may want just a small sample of a new vegetable. Or, the plants you choose may be particularly susceptible to cold weather — such as marigolds, petunias, pepper plants, and tomatoes — and need protection from frost as seedlings. It is an easy shortcut to let the garden center deal with the delicate, early stages of these

▲ **Annual bedding plants** These are strong, healthy, disease-free specimens.

▼ **Garden centers** A wide selection of plants can be bewildering. Follow the guidelines suggested here to help you make your selection.

plants' lives. Buy them only when all danger of frost is past and the soil is ready for planting.

Space is another factor, since biennials, such as hollyhocks and sweet Williams, take two years to produce flowers, and they need to be sown outdoors in late spring the year before flowering. For the small garden, at least, it makes sense to occupy that space with other plants and buy already-growing biennials in the fall for flowering the following year.

Packs, flats, and small pots

The most common containers in which small bedding plants are sold are flats and individual plastic cell packs. When buying, look at the soil and the overall appearance of the plants, particularly their leaves and flowers, if any.

Plants should be compact and sturdy. Uneven, lanky growth is a sign of badly lit and perhaps overheated conditions, or of plants that have outgrown their containers and soil. No matter how good the conditions are that you provide for the plants, they will never recover completely.

If the plants are in cell packs, they should be fairly uniform in size. Where seed has been distributed unevenly, you may get one or two robust specimens and many straggly ones that have been choked out by the competition.

Check that the leaves are a good, healthy color and that there is evidence of emerging strong growth. Yellowing or discolored leaves or, worse still, the presence of pests are all signs of disease, inadequate nutrients, light, or water, and general neglect.

Touch the soil to see if it is moist. Plants that are allowed to dry out suffer delays in their growth that they never make up. When buying plants in cell packs, pop one out of its cell and make sure that the roots aren't spiraled around the ball of soil, since that is a sign that the plant has been in its container too long. For the same reason, avoid specimens with roots growing through the bottoms of pots and flats.

Ornamentals in full flower have probably exhausted the nutrients in their soil. In the case of plants grown in individual containers, a few open flowers are not serious, but bypass any with dead flower heads or that show evidence of deadheads having been removed.

▲ **Healthy bedding plants** Select plants with bushy, well-proportioned growth and healthy, fresh green leaves (left). Discolored foliage, lank stems, and full blooms (right) are signs that plants have exhausted the soil.

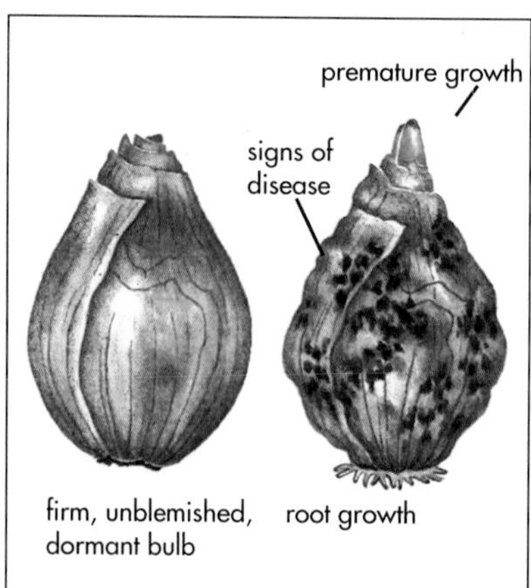

◀ **Dormant bulbs** Best buys are firm and rounded, with no premature sprouting (left); avoid any with shriveled, moldy skins, which can indicate the presence of disease (right).

Bulbs and corms

Bulbs and corms are available at different times of the year, according to when they flower. Most benefit from early planting, so the sooner you buy supplies after they arrive at the nursery, the better.

Some corms and tubers, like those of cyclamens and winter aconites, are naturally hard and woody. But most dry bulbs should be plump and firm, and show no sign of gray or blackish molds, which indicate pest damage or fungal attack.

Others, — lilies, for example — do not settle down well if the bulbs are allowed to dry out. They are therefore often kept in damp soil. Look for fleshy bulbs that show no sign of shriveling. Take extra care to buy lilies from a reliable nursery or supplier, as virus diseases are a major problem and are difficult to detect in lily bulbs.

Avoid the "specials" of bulk, low-priced bulbs advertised on the garden page of local newspapers, since they may be the growers' second-quality product. Undersized, less vigorous bulbs bear smaller flowers, or worse, do not flower at all.

Container plants

Shrubs, roses, and conifers are often sold in plastic or fiber pots or even metal containers. These containers allow you to plant when you choose, particularly for trees and shrubs — in the past, the general pattern was to plant only in the fall or early spring.

Look for young stock of well-balanced growth. Large, older shrubs are frequently slow to establish and are quickly overtaken by younger, more vigorous ones. Check that grafted plants

▲ **Container-grown roses** Choose plants with robust growth from the base (left). Reject weak specimens or any that have dried out (right).

(where the stem or bud of one plant is united to the root of another) have a sound joint, and that leaves, branches, and roots are healthy. The joint should not be higher than 12 in (30 cm) above the ground, or a strong wind could snap off the new stem; nor should it be so low that suckers can grow from the rootstock.

Large bedding plants and perennials — such as delphiniums, dicentras, and hostas — are also good container buys, saving several years of waiting if you plant them from seed. The time it takes for perennials to mature from seed can be frustrating when you are longing for the yearly display of flowers and foliage. Some perennials, too, need to be reared from cuttings or by division — again, a slow process that is best left to the nursery if you would like color in your garden sooner.

When you are buying container plants in full growth, select ones that are well proportioned and vigorous, with no straggly or wilting stems. The foliage should show no sign of disease or pest infection — black spot is a particular problem with roses.

Some weed growth on the surface of the soil is a good sign — an indication that the plant has not been dug out of the ground and dropped into a container shortly before sale. (Plants loose in pots

▲ **Signs of good health** A compact shape (left) is proof of a strong root system and overall health. Do not buy plants with thin, straggly growth (right), as these have had a poor start in life.

Container-grown shrubs Choose young and vigorous specimens (left). Wilting foliage or damaged branches (right) are a bad sign.

WHY BUY READY-GROWN PLANTS?

Sowing seed is the cheapest and easiest method of creating bedding plants; perennials are easily propagated by division; and cuttings are the most economical way of propagating trees and shrubs. So what are the pros and cons of buying ready-grown plants?

Bulbs
- ❑ Seeds of bulbous plants take years to grow and develop a bulb that will produce flowers.
- ❑ Seeds of some bulbous plants are not readily available.

Bedding plants
- ❑ Only a few plants are needed.
- ❑ Delicate seedlings receive protection in nursery greenhouse.
- ❑ Space is saved on biennials that will not flower for a year.

Perennials
- ❑ Mature plants offer a quicker, showier display of flowers.
- ❑ Cuttings and division take up time and space that can be saved.
- ❑ Provides an "instant" garden.

Container shrubs and trees
- ❑ Cuttings take time to mature.
- ❑ More flexibility for planting times.
- ❑ Best chance of healthy specimens.
- ❑ Container-grown plants may be expensive.

Bare-root and balled-root shrubs and trees
- ❑ Cuttings take time to mature.
- ❑ Bare-root plants are cheaper than balled-root and container plants.
- ❑ Restricted to planting in late fall through early spring, depending on zone.
- ❑ Plants packaged this way can be difficult to check for health and are prone to being damaged or started into premature growth.
- ❑ Convenient for mail order, but sometimes delayed or damaged.

▲ **Balled-root evergreens** When selecting, ensure that the ball has not broken (right), although a light growth of weeds is a healthy sign. The ideal stock has balanced growth and plenty of flourishing leaves (left).

▲ **Balled-root trees** These trees have spent their formative years in open ground, as proved in this case by the abundance of annual seedlings. When you buy them, the soil ball is wrapped in burlap or a similar material.

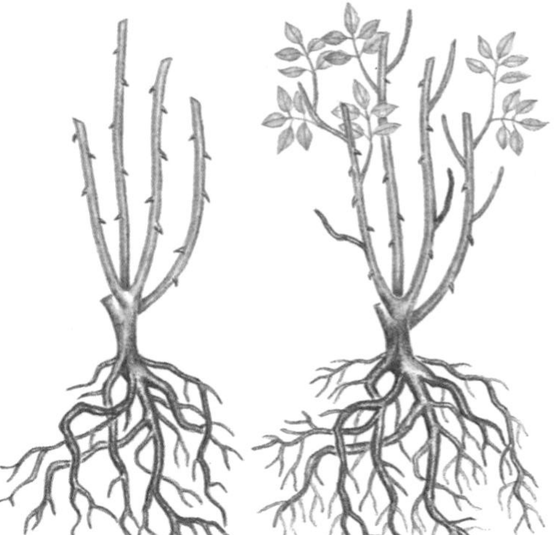

◀ **Bare-root roses** Healthy plants should have a well-developed root system spreading in all directions (left). Opening leaf buds are a sign of too much early growth (right); avoid plants with white roots and damaged stems.

signal that they have only recently been lifted from open ground.) Strong weed growth means, however, that the plant has had to fight for water and nutrients.

The plant should have a sturdy root system, growing in moist soil, but discard any specimens with thick roots escaping through the base of the container or with matted roots at the surface. In the case of hardy perennials bought in spring and fall, you should be able to see healthy growth buds.

Balled-root plants

Evergreen trees and many shrubs are sold in balled-root form — they are lifted from the ground, and the soil around the roots is kept in place by a wrapping of burlap (they are also known as balled-and-burlapped plants).

Choose well-proportioned specimens with a good framework of stems and healthy foliage. Feel through the burlap to make sure that no roots have developed outside the soil ball, indicating that the plant has been balled for too long. Discard any stock that has penetrated the burlap; it is likely that the soil inside has dried out.

Bare-root plants

Many deciduous shrubs, roses, and perennials, such as day lilies and summer phloxes, are sold as bare-root plants. They are taken out of the ground in the fall or during early spring to be sold and planted before they begin growing again.

In addition to being sold through nurseries and garden centers, bare-root plants are also specially packaged for supermarkets and department stores in a box or plastic bag, with a moist potting mixture around the roots. The packaging often obscures the condition of the plant, and so it is difficult to tell whether the building's heating has caused drying out, shriveling, or premature development. As a general rule, therefore, buy stock as soon as possible after it becomes available.

Any bare-root stock delivered through the mail should be moist but not soggy when opened. It should show no bruising of roots, stems, and leaves. All plants should be completely dormant when bought, exhibiting no premature growth of rootlets and no sign of leaf buds opening. But they must have sturdy, well-ripened stems (at least two in the case of roses) and an evenly developed root system, with no sign of damage from pests or diseases.

Reputable nurseries and mail-order suppliers should replace plants that have arrived in a damaged or unhealthy condition.

PLANTING IN BEDS

Annuals and herbaceous perennials give the best performance of color if planted with minimum root disturbance in well-prepared beds and borders.

A garden can be filled quickly with color from annuals and biennials — they flower longer than most other plants and are excellent for filling gaps in a bed or for creating an entire summer landscape. Herbaceous perennials, which spring up again year after year, can be grown exclusively in a border or island bed, but do equally well as attractive companions to mixed shrub planting.

A good-looking border or bed depends to a great extent on how the plants are arranged. Later-flowering or foliage plants should conceal gaps left by earlier flowers, colors should blend, and everything should be in scale. Seed and nursery catalogs provide inspiration and are available in good time for you to plan a selection and design the layout.

MARKING OUT THE SITE

1 If your plan has a regular design, use a wooden plank to mark out the planting positions, setting plants inside the squares or at intersections.

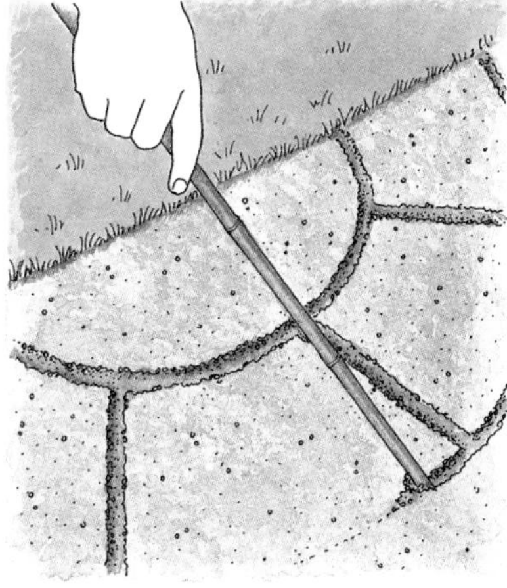

2 For less regular designs, draw the planting areas with the tip of a cane or stick, varying the size and shape of each section.

◀ **Planting beds** Mark out the site with trails of sand if there is a chance of rain before planting is begun — they will remain visible, whereas scratched lines may get washed away.

Preparing for annuals

Begin soil preparations in early fall to midfall. Pull this season's faded and dead plants from the soil, using a garden fork to loosen stubborn ones. Once all the old vegetation has been removed, apply 1-2 in (2.5-5 cm) of organic material — composted manure or regular garden compost — to the surface of the soil. This amendment will give body to light, dry soil and help it to retain moisture; it will also improve the aeration and drainage of heavy soils as well as provide nutrients.

Turn over the soil and organic material together with a garden fork. Leave it lumpy, since a better soil surface is produced if winter frosts are allowed to penetrate deeply and break down the soil naturally. It is easier to turn over soil when it's moist — if the ground is hard, water it thoroughly the day before. However, if the soil is too sticky after rain, leave it for a few days before digging.

In spring, as soon as the soil is dry enough, loosen up the top 6-8 in (15-20 cm) — slightly deeper, if winter brought severe frosts — with a fork. Just before planting, add some general-purpose fertilizer, such as 5–10–10, to the soil. Scatter the fertilizer evenly at a rate of 5 lbs per 100 square feet (2.2 kg per 9 sq m) of bed, then rake it into the top 1 in (2.5 cm) of soil to produce a fine tilth.

Planting annuals

The best time for planting in cold climates is between late spring and very early summer. Planting of most annuals can begin as soon as the risk of local frost has passed. (The plant label will indicate specific planting times.) In mild-winter climates, you can set out plants in the fall — then they will be established in time for summer's stresses.

In addition to purchasing seedlings from a garden center or nursery, you can grow annuals indoors in various containers — plastic flats or cell packs, wooden seed trays, or individual plastic, clay, or compressed peat pots. Some hardy annuals get a better start if they are sown in flats the previous fall. The type of container determines the best planting technique you should use.

If you have raised plants from seed, harden them off (accustom them to the harsher outdoor climate) before planting them in a sheltered outdoor site. (Seedlings from a garden center should have been hardened off there.) Water flats and packs an hour or two before planting — this step ensures that the potting soil adheres to the root ball, reducing root damage during planting.

At the planting site, the soil should be moist, and it's best to plant during the cool morning or evening. Mark out the planting site, according to your plan, using a garden stake, a stick, the edge of a wooden plank, or trails of sand.

Plants grown in individual pots or cell packs can be set out with almost no root disturbance, but with other types you will have to carefully separate individual plants, and so some root damage is inevitable, though not fatal.

Take plants out of wooden or plastic flats with as much root as possible. Ideally, remove the whole mass of seedlings, roots, and potting soil intact. Loosen the soil and root mass by bumping the flat gently, then with the flat on the ground, tilt it to almost 90°, until the root mass begins to flop out of the flat. Quickly insert the palm of one hand under the root mass, let go of the flat with the other hand, and maneuver the plants gently onto the ground. If the potting soil is moist and the plants are well rooted, this step is less difficult than it sounds.

Separate the plants grown in flats by cutting them apart with a knife or the edge of a hand trowel. Less root damage may be caused by easing the plants apart with your fingers, but be careful not to squash and break up the soil around the roots in so doing. Ensure that each plant has a well-developed root system.

If your annual seedlings are in peat pots, you can plant them pot and all. But before setting them in the ground, rip off the pot's upper lip. Otherwise, this lip may emerge above ground level as the soil settles and act as a wick to draw moisture up and away from plant roots.

Spacing The species usually determines the correct spacing between plants. However, a good general rule is to space plants half their eventual height apart, except for those with a spreading growth habit; these should be

▼ **Planting annuals** Before setting bedding plants in the ground, space them out within the planting plan, then step back and assess the overall balance. Adjust the spacing if you feel it is necessary.

spaced the equivalent of their fully grown height apart.

When planting a lot of annuals, work in batches. To prevent their roots from drying out, remove from their containers only the number of annuals that you can set out in a couple of minutes, especially on a warm day.

Dig a planting hole with a hand trowel, making it wide and deep enough to accommodate a plant's entire root system but not so deep that air spaces are left beneath the roots. Remove any stones or other obstacles that may impede root penetration. Insert the plant so that the base of its stem is level with the surface of the soil. Fill the hole and press the plant in firmly with your fingers. When you have finished a bed, water in well with a fine spray. Apply a liberal amount of water, since a light sprinkling will not penetrate to the roots. Instead, it will encourage roots to grow near the surface, where they will be more vulnerable to damage.

Alternatively, insert the plant, then wash the soil into the hole and around the roots by "puddling" with water from an open-spouted watering can or a hose. Let the water soak in, then fill any remaining small holes around the plant with soil.

Soon after planting, encourage plants that are not normally bushy to develop branching side shoots and more blooms by pinching off their growing tips.

Planting biennials

It is essential for biennials to be planted out in their beds by midfall — whether they come from a nursery, garden center, or greenhouse — otherwise, they may not establish themselves before the onset of severe weather.

Before planting, dig over the soil and work in a light dressing of organic material, together with a generous handful of bone meal or a small handful of superphosphate for each sq yd/m.

Lift the plants from their nursery bed or container, easing them out with a hand fork, with as many roots attached as possible. If the soil is very dry, water it first to ease lifting and to lessen damage to the roots.

After lifting, put them into their permanent positions as soon as possible, before their roots can dry out. In cold areas, plants put out in exposed positions may need winter protection — lay light evergreen branches or straw mulch around them.

To replace plants lost through winter cold, it is wise to keep aside a few plants. In spring, they can be used to fill in any gaps in a bed caused by dying plants.

Preparing for perennials

Perennials are best planted in early fall, when the soil is still warm. Or, you can plant them during spring — container-grown perennials are widely available from nurseries then and, in fact, can be set out at any time of year, weather and climate permitting.

PLANTING ANNUALS

1 It is easier to separate plants if the whole mass of soil and roots is first removed. Having loosened the roots by bumping the flat on the ground, hold the flat at an angle and ease out the entire plant mass.

2 Separate the plants by slicing through the root mass with the edge of a hand trowel or with a knife. Or, ease the plants apart with your fingers — but do not break away too much soil from around the roots.

3 After arranging the plants in position to get a balanced layout, dig holes sufficiently deep for the roots and set the plants in place. Ease soil around the roots until filled in.

4 Instead of pressing plants in by hand, they can be settled in by "puddling" with water from an open-spouted watering can — wash soil from the sides of the holes onto the roots and leave to drain.

▲ **Firming in** All annuals, biennials, and perennials should be pressed in firmly, by hand or by "puddling" with water, to ensure that no air spaces are left and that roots make contact with the soil.

For fall planting, dig the bed thoroughly in the early part of the season to give the soil a week or two to settle, adding a bucketful of organic material per sq yd/m. Just before planting, break up any large clods of soil and level the surface of the bed. Finally, sprinkle a couple of handfuls of a general-purpose fertilizer onto each sq yd/m and rake it into the top 1 in (2.5 cm).

For spring planting, use the same technique, but prepare the soil in early fall and leave the final preparations until spring.

Planting perennials

Like other seedlings, perennials are best planted in the evening or morning, or on a sunless, windless day. The soil should be wet but not soaking. Begin by marking out the planting area. Then, working from the center of the bed outward, lay out the plants one section at a time. Space them evenly, allowing room for their foliage to spread as they grow.

For plants with a small root system, use a trowel to dig circular planting holes; for larger ones, use a spade. The hole should be large enough to accommodate the spread-out roots of bare-root plants, or the entire root ball of container- grown plants.

Insert the plant upright and fill in around the roots with fine soil until the hole is level. Press the soil down firmly with your fingers, if it is moist and lumpy, or with your heel, if it is fairly loose and dry. Make sure that the plant is no more than 1 in (2.5 cm) deeper than it was in its original nursery bed or container.

When setting out container-grown plants, check that the root ball is not tight and spirally congested — ease away long roots by hand and spread them out in the planting hole before filling it with soil. Container-grown plants not treated in this way won't grow well and may show leaf browning a month or so after planting. If these symptoms do appear, lift the plants, loosen the soil around the roots, and replant immediately.

Plant prostrate perennials, such as artemisia and thyme, which are intended for spreading ground cover, in groups of three or four. Bunch the roots and stems together to form one plant and insert them as a clump. This arrangement will encourage the stems to grow out in all directions, and so produce a more even coverage of the soil surface.

After the bed has been planted, prick the soil with a garden fork (using only the tips of the tines) to aerate trodden areas.

Some perennials planted in the fall will show no signs of growth until well into the following spring. If you have not made a plan on paper showing the position and name of each plant, label them clearly. Use plastic, metal, or wooden plant labels and write names in black carbon pencil or indelible ink. Metal plant labels, on which names can be scratched or etched, are available from catalogs and garden centers.

PLANTING PERENNIALS

1 For small perennial plants, dig the planting hole with a hand trowel. Use a spade to dig holes for larger plants. Make the hole deep and wide enough to accommodate the spread-out roots. Try not to step on the planting area — work off a wooden plank if the site is large.

2 Hold the plant upright and set it in the center of the hole, spread out the roots, and replace the soil between and over the roots until the hole is filled. Prostrate perennials can be inserted in clumps of three or four to give rapid and more even ground cover.

3 When planting container-grown perennials, make the hole large enough for the root ball to sit level with, or slightly lower than, the surrounding soil. If roots are coiled around the ball, gently ease away the largest ones and spread them out in the hole.

4 After planting, press the soil down well around the roots so that no pockets of air are trapped — use your fingers if the soil is moist or lumpy. Loose plants won't be able to take up water or nutrients from the surrounding soil fast enough and may wither or die.

5 On soil that is loose or dry, firm in plants with your foot, or "puddle" in, using an open-spouted watering can. Label all plants, especially when set in the ground in the fall — they may be almost invisible until the late spring.

PLANTING BULBS OUTDOORS

To get the best results from hardy bulbs, they need careful and correct planting at the right time of year.

Bulbs provide some of the most attractive and undemanding garden plants. They vary tremendously in size, color, and scent, as well as in flowering season. They adapt well to different conditions and garden types, whether they are planted in flower beds or containers, or "naturalized" — grown randomly for a casual effect. With a little planning, you can have bulbs in bloom from early spring to late fall — year after year.

The term "bulb" is generally used to describe not only true bulbs, such as daffodils and tulips, but also the corms of crocuses and gladioli and the tubers of dahlias and begonias. Rhizomatous plants, such as lilies of the valley, are also often grouped with true bulbs.

When to plant

When you should plant depends on the hardiness and flowering

► **Planting bulbs** Clumps of flowers look better than straight rows.

▼ **Spring bulbs** A fall planting of anemones, daffodils, and tulips bursts into glorious spring color.

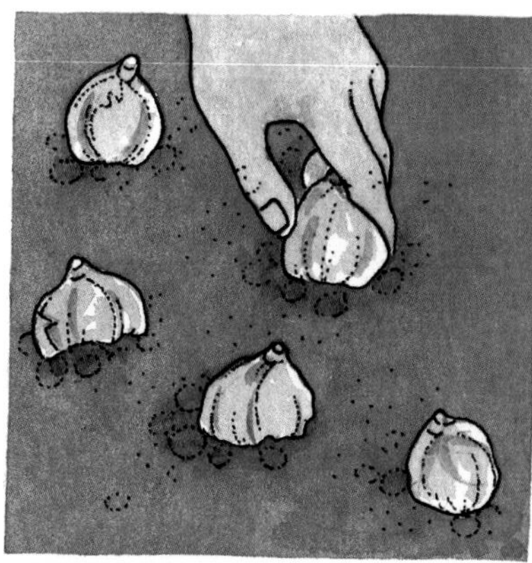

PLANTING IN GROUPS
1 Place the bulbs, with their pointed tip up, throughout the planting area, spacing them at regular intervals.

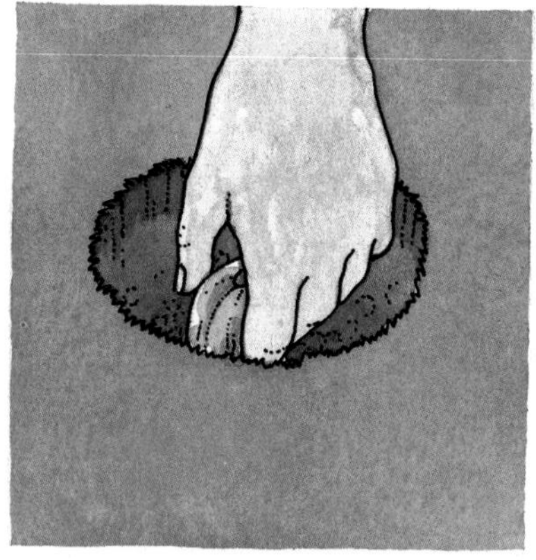

2 Using a narrow trowel, dig a hole three times the depth of the bulb (or use a bulb planter). Put the bulb in firmly — don't trap air beneath it.

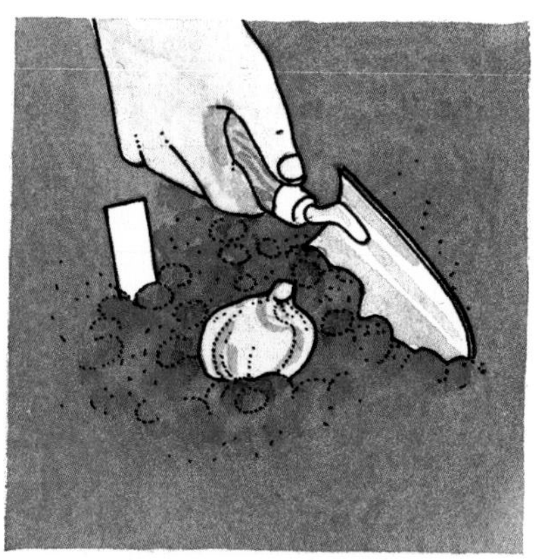

3 Cover the bulb with soil and press it down firmly with your foot. Water the area thoroughly after planting to encourage immediate growth.

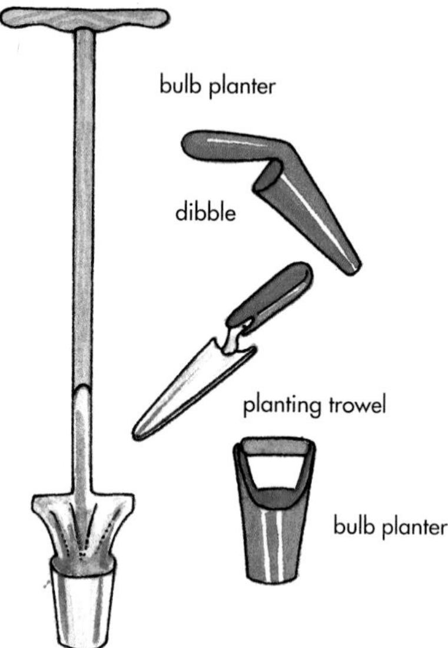

▲ **Planting equipment** Bulb planters (particularly long-handled ones) save you time and effort when naturalizing large numbers of bulbs. They take out and hold the plug of turf while you plant.

time of the particular type of bulb. **Hardy spring-flowering** types, such as crocus corms, are planted in fall. Snowdrops are an exception, however. You can plant them in fall, but they also do well if planted "in the green" — immediately after flowering in early spring, if you can find a garden center that sells them like this.

Plant daffodil bulbs as soon as they become available — late summer, if possible — so that they have the chance to develop a good root system before sending up shoots.

Don't begin planting tulip bulbs until late fall or the beginning of winter. This delay reduces the risk of tulip fire disease.

Hardy summer-flowering bulbs, such as lilies, can be planted between fall and early spring, even in Northern areas during winter thaws, provided the ground is unfrozen. (*Lilium candidum,* however, *must* be planted in fall.) But wait until early spring or midspring to plant the more tender ones — gladiolus corms, for example — or frost may damage growing shoots. A good plan is to stagger the planting of gladioli over several weeks so that you extend the display of blooms.

Fall and winter-flowering bulbs provide color when it's most wanted. Colchicum corms, with their crocuslike blooms, settle down well if planted in late summer, even when they're on the point of flowering.

Planting depth

As a general guideline, plant bulbs in a hole three times their depth — for example, a bulb that is 2 in (5 cm) high should be planted 6 in (15 cm) deep. Do not set the bulbs as deeply in heavy soils, but put them in even deeper in sandy soils, where winters are cold, or where you want bulbs naturalized in grass. There are, of course, exceptions — namely lilies and cyclamens.

Lilies Many lilies produce roots on the stem above the bulb, and so need to be planted to a depth about four times the height of the bulb. If you are not sure whether the lilies are stem rooting, cover them with 5 in (12 cm) of soil and add a 2-in (5-cm) layer of leaf mold on top. However, plant the Madonna lily (*Lilium candidum*) just below the soil surface.

Cyclamen corms should be planted just below the surface — *Cyclamen hederifolium* should be set so that the tips are just above the soil level.

Which way is up?

Always plant a bulb with its pointed tip up and its base (where the roots grow from) down. It is usually easy to distinguish between the two — if not, do not worry. Plant the bulb on edge and it will probably grow in the correct way. The woody tuberous roots of anemones and winter aconites, for instance, have no obvious top and bottom, but they will pull themselves around in the soil to face upright. Cyclamen corms can present a particular problem: If you are in doubt, look carefully for signs of old or new roots from the base.

Spacing bulbs

How you space bulbs depends on the effect you want to create. In containers, place bulbs close together without actually touching. In beds, natural-looking groups or boldly planted clumps are most striking — don't scatter bulbs about. Small bulbs, such as miniature daffodils, are best set quite close together, about 2 in (5 cm) apart. Larger bulbs, for example daffodils and tulips, need about 6 in (15 cm) between plants, and lilies require even more space — about 10 in (25 cm) between them. For naturalized planting, space bulbs randomly.

Massed bulbs

The stunning effects of massed spring bedding schemes — a

familiar sight in public parks — rely on bulbs that flower at more or less the same time. Even in a relatively small garden, you can achieve a similar result. Tulips and hyacinths are among the best spring-flowering bulbs for this purpose. They look wonderful combined with other plants, for example, tulips with forget-me-nots or hyacinths with pansies.

For large mass plantings, prepare a sunny bed well in advance, adding a layer of organic material if the soil is poor. As a further boost to growth, apply a light sprinkling of bone meal at planting time. Allow the bed to settle for at least a week before planting. If you're mixing the bulbs with other plants, put the other plants in beforehand.

Planting in borders

Smaller bulb plantings make an appealing feature in borders, rock gardens, and raised beds.

Bulbs grow best in beds containing a mixture of shrubs and perennials — they do not thrive in pure herbaceous borders because the rich, moist soil there can be harmful to the bulbs, causing them to rot. Prepare the ground as you would for massed bulbs, and plant them in clusters of at least five bulbs at a time.

▼ **Container planting** Plant bulbs close together in containers, but do not allow them to touch. They can be mixed with other plants, such as pansies and azaleas (right); in a shallow container, it is better to use small bulbs, such as crocuses (below).

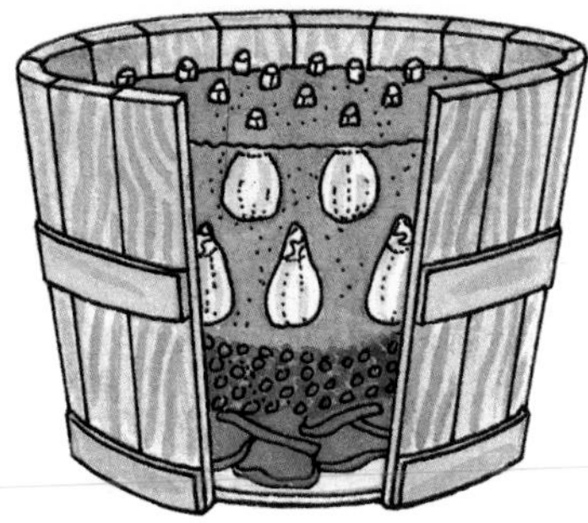

▲ **Bulb layers** For a spectacular effect, plant bulbs in two layers in a deep container. Plant the first layer not less than 4 in (10 cm) deep and add potting soil, leaving the tips exposed. Set the second layer above the gaps in the lower layer. Cover with soil. Three-tier planting is also possible — place daffodils at the bottom, tulips in the middle; and grape hyacinths on the top.

▲ **Naturalized planting** Daffodils and grape hyacinths are ideal for rough grass. Scatter the bulbs at random; they will eventually form colonies.

Bulbs in containers

Window boxes, wooden barrels, and earthenware pots are all excellent containers for outdoor bulbs. They do need adequate drainage holes, however. A layer of broken clay or terra-cotta pots, stones, or gravel at the bottom prevents the soil from sifting out. The best mixture is one part good garden soil, one part peat, and one part perlite or vermiculite.

Space the bulbs evenly at the right depth (three times their height) on a layer of the planting mixture. Cover them to within about 1 in (2.5 cm) of the top of the pot. If you are growing a large number of small bulbs, a shallow layer of sharp builder's sand on top of the mixture reduces weed growth. However, bulbs will not overwinter in containers in zones where winter temperatures fall below -15°F (-25°C).

Naturalized bulbs

For an informal display, few effects can match a colony of bulbs growing in grass. Crocuses and daffodils are the outstanding choices for naturalizing, but others are equally striking. It is best to group colors separately.

Most bulbs appropriate for naturalization prefer some sun. Many flower before the foliage of deciduous trees is fully developed, while others do better in woodland fringes, where they are protected from direct sunlight. Yet others, such as cyclamens and lilies of the valley, will thrive only in shady spots.

For a truly natural effect, scatter a handful of bulbs and plant them where they fall. If you are naturalizing more than a few, use a bulb planter. For large areas, cut and peel back the turf with a spade; turn over the soil and plant the bulbs. Fill in with organic material and fold back the turf.

Lifting and storing

Although many bulbs can be left in the ground from year to year, lift tender bulbs — for example, freesias, gladioli, acidantheras, ranunculuses, and tigridias — at the end of the growing season.

When leaves and stems have shriveled, use a hand fork to lift the bulbs, taking care not to pierce them. Remove dead leaves, stems, and old roots, and detach bulblets — small bulbs that spring from the parent bulb. (You can use them for starting new stock for the next season.) Make sure that the bulbs are thoroughly dry before storing them in a cool, frost-free, dry place until it is time to plant them again the next year.

BULBS FOR NATURALIZING

Daffodils
'Actaea'
white, with small orange-red cup
'Carlton'
golden, large-cupped
'Fortune'
yellow, with large orange-red cup
'Mount Hood'
ivory, large trumpet
'Van Sion'
golden, double

Bulbs under trees
Anemone
(Anemone nemerosa)
Bluebell
(Scilla non-scriptus)
Colchicum
(Colchicum speciosum)
Crocus
(Crocus tomasinianus)
Cyclamen
(Cyclamen hederifolium)
Dogtooth violet
(Erythronium dens-canis)
Glory-of-the-snow
(Chionodoxa luciliae)
Lily
(Lilium martagon)
Lily of the valley
(Convallaria majalis)
Scilla
(Scilla sibirica)
Snowdrop
(Galanthus nivalis)
Snowflake
(Leucojum aestivum 'Gravetye Giant')
Winter aconite
(Eranthis hyemalis)

PLANTING SHRUBS AND TREES

Shrubs and trees form the backbone of the garden. Many create stunning focal points, and if planted correctly, they will flourish for years.

Shrubs are long-lived and prefer to stay in one position. They will form the permanent plantings around which other plantings, such as annuals and bulbs, are arranged. Consider where shrubs and trees will look their best — then plant them with care to give them the best chance of survival.

Preplanting care and methods of planting differ according to the type of shrub. You can buy shrubs in three different ways:

❑ Growing in a container
❑ With their roots wrapped in burlap, known as "balled-root" or "balled-and-burlapped" shrubs
❑ Dormant, with their roots bare.

Container-grown shrubs are established plants growing in plastic, fiber, or metal containers filled with potting soil. You can plant these at any time of year, as long as the ground is workable.

Balled-root shrubs have some soil around the roots, kept in place by a wrapping of burlap. Plants that may have difficulty establishing themselves after being lifted from the nursery bed are treated this way to keep the root ball intact, as are evergreens (including conifers) when their root systems have grown too big for containers.

Bare-root shrubs are sold without any soil — a system generally reserved for shrubs that transport easily, such as roses and hedging plants. Damp potting soil is some-

▼ **Mixed shrub arrangement** With container-grown shrubs, a bed can be created in a day. Keep the soil moist until the plants are established.

Container-grown shrub

Balled-root shrub

Bare-root shrub

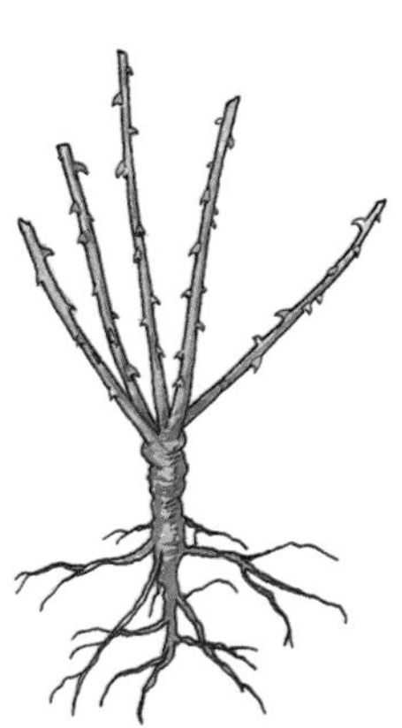

Container-grown shrubs These are clean and easy to handle, and can be kept until planting conditions are perfect.

Balled-root shrubs Large shrubs and conifers with long roots suffer from root disturbance, and are sold with the roots wrapped in burlap. They can be heavy and need careful handling to keep the root ball intact.

Bare-root shrubs Dormant deciduous shrubs are sold with bare roots from late fall through early spring. Care is needed because the roots are easily broken.

times packed around the roots to prevent them from drying out. They are cheaper than container-grown and balled-root types, but may occasionally be difficult to establish — particularly if the roots have dried out.

Planning and preparation

Timing is crucial when planting shrubs. Of equal importance is the condition of the soil. It must not be frozen or waterlogged, and must be well dug and fertilized.

Container-grown shrubs can be planted at any time of the year, except during Northern winters. If you plant in summer, keep the soil constantly moist until fall — newly planted shrubs will die if their soil dries out. Should you be unable to plant a container-grown shrub for several weeks after you purchase it, make sure that the soil stays moist (but not waterlogged) until you're ready to put it in the ground. Also, protect the shrub from high winds, staking the stem after you have planted it, if necessary.

Balled-root shrubs Plant evergreen shrubs and conifers in mid-spring and deciduous shrubs during the dormant season, from fall through early spring, depending on your zone. Balled-root shrubs can be left unplanted for several weeks as long as the soil ball is kept moist. Do not remove the burlap covering before the plant is set in the planting hole.

Bare-root shrubs are planted during the dormant season, and must be in the ground before their leaf buds burst. Plant from

PLANTING CONTAINER-GROWN AND BALLED-ROOT SHRUBS

1 Check that the stem base of the shrub will be at or just above soil level when the shrub is planted and the soil settled.

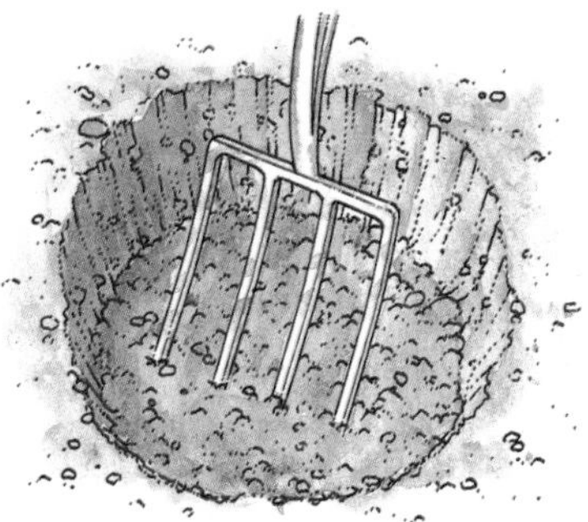

2 Break up the soil at the base of the hole, then add a layer of the prepared planting-soil mixture.

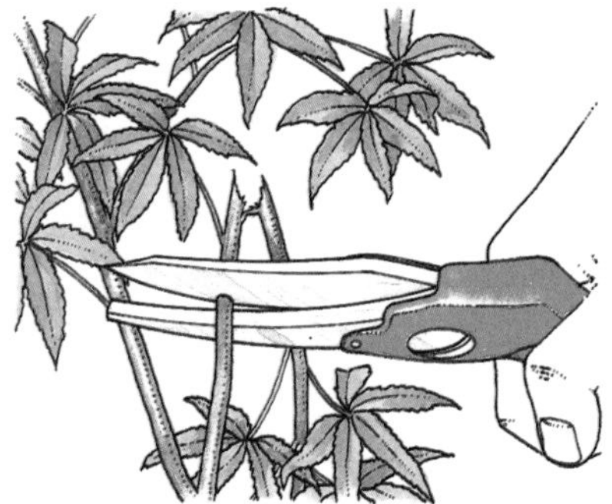

3 Remove damaged or diseased wood, cutting the stem just above a healthy bud. Also remove stumps of old wood.

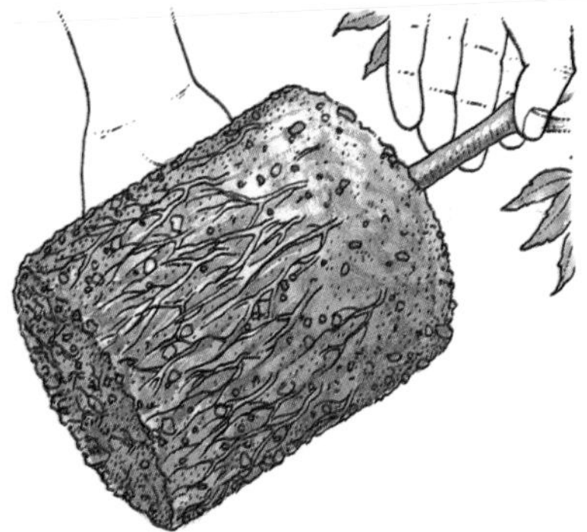

4 See if the shrub has a good, healthy root system. Cut away any tangled or encircling roots.

5 Place the plant in the hole, fill in with the soil mixture, and press down firmly, ensuring that the shrub remains upright.

6 After planting, leave a shallow basin around the shrub for water retention. Water thoroughly but gently.

late fall through early spring, depending on your zone.

Ideally, bare-root shrubs should be planted as soon as they arrive. If necessary, they can be stored for a couple of days in a frost-free place, with the roots kept moist. Alternatively, heel them in outdoors in a trench (p.61) and cover them firmly with soil until they can be replanted.

Preparing for planting

Dig over the soil thoroughly to one spade's depth, removing perennial weeds. Add bone meal into the topsoil at the rate of 4 oz per sq yd (130 g per sq m), then allow the soil to settle for about 2 weeks. Just before planting, press down the soil thoroughly by treading over the entire bed.

Mark out with sticks where the shrubs are to go. The space between two shrubs should be at least half the width of their combined mature spreads. Next, remove one of the markers and dig a hole as deep as, and slightly wider than, the shrub's container or root ball; don't make the hole too deep or too narrow.

Prepare a planting-soil mixture: In a wheelbarrow, mix the soil you removed from the hole with some organic material, such as garden compost or composted manure. (An ideal ratio is two parts soil to one part organic material.) Backfill the hole with this mixture. Finally, water container-grown plants thoroughly just before planting.

Planting shrubs

Check the hole for depth by inserting the container or root ball. With a container shrub, the surface of the planting soil should be level with that of the surrounding soil, or just above it. With a balled-root or bare-root shrub, the mark indicating the old soil level on the stem should be level with the surface of the surrounding soil; set a wooden plank or stake across the top of the hole to gauge the correct planting depth. Ensure that the hole is wide enough to allow the roots to spread out evenly. Break up the soil at the base of the hole with a fork, then add 3-4 in (7.5-10 cm) of the soil mixture you prepared.

Examine the plant for damaged or diseased top growth. Trim back any such stems, cutting just above a bud with pruning shears.

PLANTING DOS AND DON'TS

- ❑ Do choose shrubs carefully, noting eventual maximum height and width.
- ❑ Do handle plants with care.
- ❑ Do check planting times.
- ❑ Do use a good soil mixture to encourage roots to establish.
- ❑ Do dig a big enough hole — condemning a plant to live in a tiny hole is a recipe for disaster.
- ❑ Do make sure the shrub sits at the correct level in the soil.
- ❑ Do water container-grown plants thoroughly before planting and soak all shrubs well after planting.

- ❑ Don't buy diseased or damaged shrubs.
- ❑ Don't damage plants when handling or planting them.
- ❑ Don't rely on existing soil.
- ❑ Don't allow shrubs to dry out at any time during their first season.

Remove the container or loosen the burlap from the shrub and inspect the root system — be very careful not to break up the soil ball. If a container-grown shrub has a poor root system, return it to the supplier; if the roots are tangled or if they encircle the soil, carefully cut them away, but do not break up the soil ball.

Holding the plant by the base of its stem, put it into the hole. With a balled-root shrub, insert the burlap into the ground and start to fill in the hole. Fold the burlap back over the soil when the hole is about half filled (the burlap will break down in the ground). Press the soil down firmly with your heel, add more soil, and press down again. When the hole is full, shape the soil around the stem into a shallow basin to hold water.

With a bare-root shrub, put the plant in the hole and work in a couple of trowels of prepared-soil mixture around the roots. Shake the roots gently so that the soil settles around them. Continue to fill up around the roots with more soil and keep pressing the soil down firmly to eliminate air pockets. Lastly, build up the soil slightly around the stem and shape the remainder like a shallow basin that will retain water.

Planting between shrubs

Avoid the unattractive bare patches left between correctly spaced new shrub plants by filling in the open area with annuals. The flowers can be moved when the shrubs grow and spread.

PLANTING BARE-ROOT SHRUBS

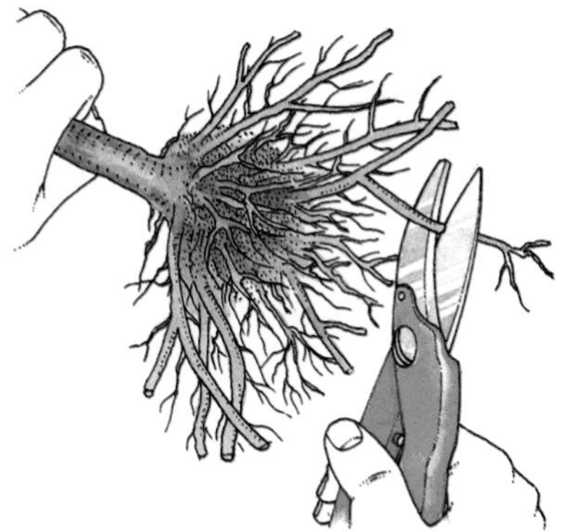

1 Dig and prepare the hole as for container-grown shrubs. Cut back damaged roots to healthy growth.

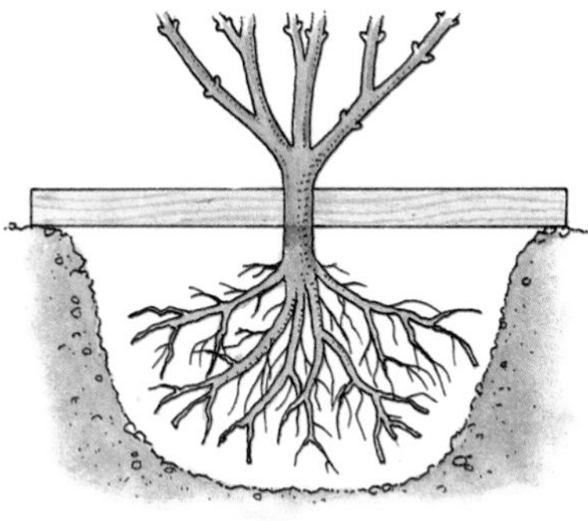

2 The old soil mark on the stem should be level with the new soil surface.

3 Once the hole is dug to size, set the shrub in place and work soil between the roots; shake it gently to settle the soil. Add more soil and press down firmly.

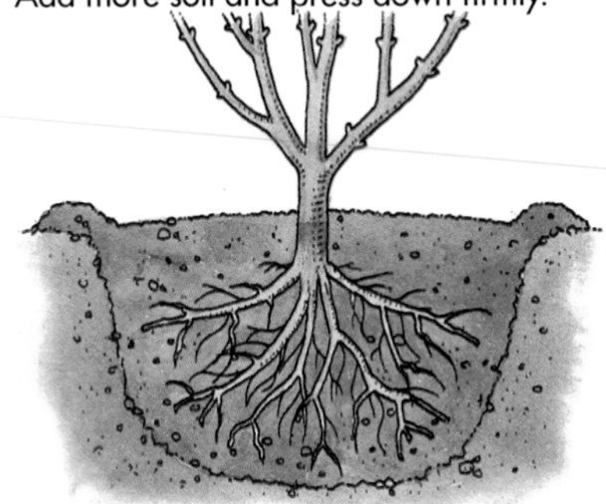

4 Build a shallow ring of soil around the area. Water thoroughly but gently.

PLANTING TREES IN GRASS

1 For a lawn-specimen tree, mark out a circle 4 to 5 times the width of the root ball, using string stretched between two pegs. Cut through the grass.

2 Cut out sections of the grass with a sharp spade and set the sod aside, then dig out the hole within the marked area to the depth of the root ball.

3 Drive a strong, rot-resistant stake into the center of the hole. On clay soils, fill the bottom of the planting hole with gravel to aid drainage.

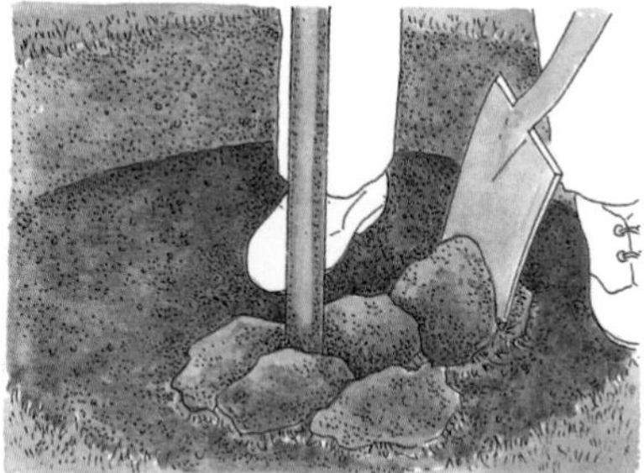

4 Chop the sod into pieces and place in the hole, grass side down. Top with a mixture of organic material and the excavated soil until the hole is half filled.

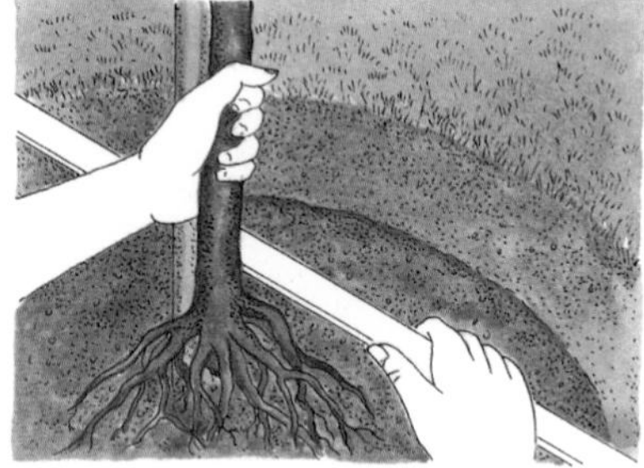

5 Tread firmly over the soil, then line up the tree against the stake, using a wooden plank to ensure that the old soil mark is level with the surface.

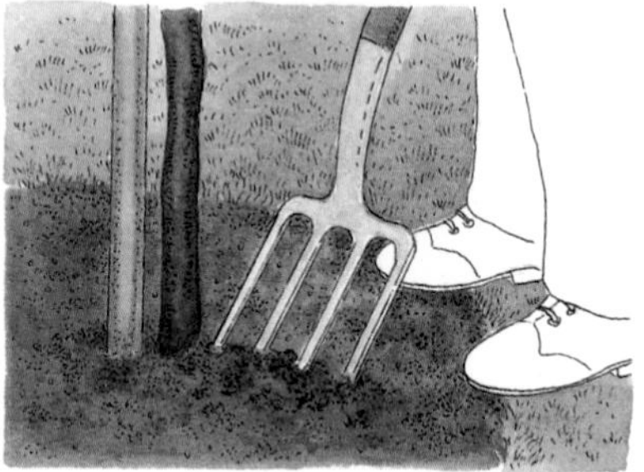

6 Fill in the hole, pressing the soil down firmly, and adding diluted fertilizer when the roots are completely covered. Tie the tree to the stake. Water thoroughly.

Planting trees

Most ornamental trees are sold when they are three to four years old. Ideally, plant deciduous types in late fall to early spring, depending on your zone, and plant evergreens, including conifers, in midspring. Container-grown trees can be planted at any time that the climate permits.

Plant trees like shrubs, but make the planting hole the depth of the root ball and 4 to 5 times its width. If you plant the tree in the lawn, remember that you will have to keep the area around the base free of grass for a few years.

A young tree needs staking until its roots take hold. Drive a strong wooden stake into the hole before planting. When the hole has been filled in, tie the tree to the stake, using a tree strap made from plastic or webbing and with rubber buffers that act as a cushion between tree and stake. Fasten the strap against the stake.

► **Tree ties** A stake should reach just below the first branches of the tree. Secure the new tree to the stake with a plastic strap or burlap wound first around the stake, then around the stem and the stake together.

PLANTING IN CONTAINERS

Plant-filled containers brighten up a window, deck, patio, or yard. With careful preparation and selection, they can provide year-round interest.

There is such a wide choice of plant containers — from the heavily ornate to the starkly plain — that you can always find one suitable for any site in your garden. Chiefly thought of as additions to patios and terraces, containers also make a welcome sight alongside a front door or they can be positioned to conceal an ugly drain cover. Both pots and hanging baskets can break up the vertical plane of a blank house wall and can be used to great effect as a home for outdoor plants. Containers come in a range of types and sizes, from plastic tubs, baskets, and troughs to wooden and stone planters.

Preparing the container

All containers must have adequate drainage holes in their bases — waterlogging is the most common cause of plant ill-health in containers, especially when they are exposed to rain.

Most manufactured pots have drainage holes already made. If necessary, however, you can drill holes quite easily into wood, fiber glass, plastic, and even concrete containers — tubs, troughs, and window boxes, for instance. Use a ¼-in (6-mm) drill bit, or larger — be sure to select a masonry bit for concrete — and drill at a slow speed to avoid cracking fragile materials. When drilling through a smooth surface, crisscross masking tape over the spot in order to prevent the drill bit from slipping and splintering the surface.

Clean the container so that it is thoroughly free from any pests and diseases. Scrub old pots and troughs with a mild detergent, then wash with a mixture of 1 part household bleach to 10 parts water and rinse well — pieces of dead roots clinging to the sides, in particular, can harbor disease.

To increase the life of containers made of wood that is not rot-resistant, treat them with a wood preservative recommended for horticultural use. (Never use creosote, as it is toxic to plants.) Naturally rot-resistant woods, such as cedar or redwood, require no preservative. Old whiskey barrels that come with their interiors charred need only be washed with detergent and water. Cover the metal bands around these barrels with rustproof paint.

Before filling a window box, ensure that it is standing firmly or is fastened securely to a wall by metal brackets (again, cover the bands with rust-resistant paint). Use wooden wedges to prop a win-

▼ **Potted annuals** Begonias, petunias, small-flowered tagetes, and trailing lobelias provide a riot of color throughout the summer months. They flourish in the confines of containers as long as they have good soil, adequate watering, and regular fertilizing.

HANGING BASKET LINERS

Modern liners make hanging baskets easy and neat. Preformed liners — made from coconut fiber (coir) shaped into a bowl — are the simplest of all and give a natural effect. Place the liner in the basket, fill with sterilized potting soil, plant, and water well — no drainage material is required because the liner is porous.

Use trailing and cascading plants — such as fuchsias or nasturtiums — around the edge of the basket and add a single upright plant — such as geranium or impatiens — to give height to the center.

With a porous liner, the soil in the basket will dry more quickly than that in a plastic basket. Coir-lined baskets require more frequent watering, but the humidity they generate benefits the plants.

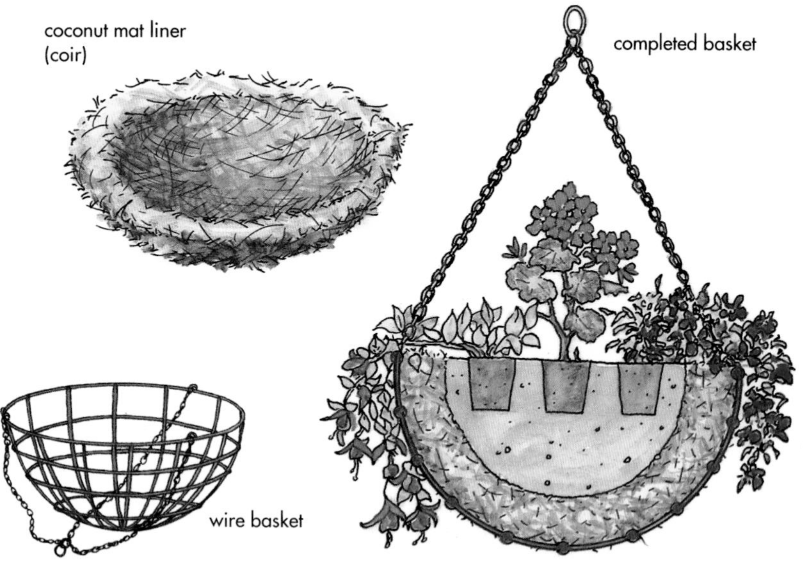

dow box level on a sloping sill, and to raise it off the sill to allow free drainage from the bottom. Or, position a window tray underneath the box to prevent waterlogging and to keep water from running down the wall.

Similarly, with a hanging basket, check that the supporting bracket is very secure — if it is at all corroded, replace it.

Filling the container

There are many fine premixed potting soils available, but be sure that the one you buy has been sterilized. To keep your container lighter, you may wish to use a commercial soilless, peat-based potting mixture. In any case, avoid ordinary garden soil; it is not sterilized and may harbor weed spores, pests, and diseases that can quickly demolish the contents of a pot.

If you want to grow acid-loving plants, such as rhododendrons, azaleas, camellias, and some heathers, use a potting mix with an acidic (low) pH, or a peat-based potting mixture.

Before filling containers with soil, check that the drainage holes are not clogged. Broken shards of terra-cotta or old flowerpots placed over the drainage holes will ensure that they remain open. On top of the shards, place a layer of washed pebbles or coarse gravel. Both layers should, ideally, occupy about one-quarter of the container's depth, but if you want less weight, 2 in (5 cm) is usually adequate for a short-term planting.

▲ **Wall displays** Wall baskets and pottery faces make good planters. Line with black plastic to retain soil and prevent water from soaking the wall, but perforate the front for drainage.

To prevent soil from being washed into the drainage layer, cover it with a sheet of burlap or fiberglass screen. Or, place a thin layer of sod pieces — grass side down — on top. Finally, fill the container with the potting soil to just about 1-2 in (2.5-5 cm) below the rim; press the soil down gently with your hands.

Hanging baskets of the rigid plastic type are planted like any other container, but open wire baskets need different treatment. They should be lined with a layer of water-conserving material, such as coconut mat or moss, before you fill the basket.

The choice of plants

Window boxes 6-8 in (15-20 cm) deep are suitable for growing a large variety of plants. In spring, they can come alive with bulbs planted the previous fall — snowdrops (*Galanthus*), crocuses, dwarf daffodils, narcissus, tulips, hyacinths, scillas, and dwarf irises, for example.

Many summer bedding plants grow well in window boxes, but

avoid tall-growing types; they will spoil the proportions of the box. A charming effect can be created by mixing trailing plants — helichrysums, ivy-leaved geraniums, lobelias *(Lobelia erinus)*, nasturtiums *(Tropaeolum majus)*, and verbenas, for instance — with petunias, marigolds *(Calendula* and *Tagetes)*, fibrous and tuberous begonias, pansies *(Viola × wittrockiana)*, and salvias *(Salvia splendens)*. Do not overlook dwarf shrubs and conifers, which add form and permanency to a box — shrubby cinquefoils *(Potentilla hybrids)*, fuchsias, hebes, and dwarf conifers, such as the upright types of juniper.

In winter, dwarf conifers, especially the golden and blue forms, are excellent for window boxes. Grow them with early-blooming spring heaths *(Erica carnea)* and ivies *(Hedera helix* varieties). A few winter-flowering hardy cyclamens *(Cyclamen hederifolium)* lend a delicate touch.

Free-standing stone, concrete, and plastic tubs and troughs can hold the same plants as window boxes — and with very large containers, you have an even wider choice. Keep a good balance by setting tall plants in the center and low-growing and trailing ones around the edges. The evergreen foliage of variegated ivy and periwinkle makes a good foil for the bright colors of Busy Lizzies *(Impatiens)*, geraniums, sweet Williams *(Dianthus barbatus)*, and marigolds *(Calendula* and *Tagetes)*, as well as calceolarias and heliotropes.

Many houseplants look attractive mixed in with summer bedding plants. The arching leaves of spider plants *(Chlorophytum comosum)* complement agapanthus, while a cordyline set at the rear of a low container with bedding plants adds height and form. Also, the flaming colors of coleus provide an interesting contrast when paired with silver-leaved Dusty miller *(Senecio cineraria)* and either silver-gray or lemon-gray helichrysum.

Large tubs make perfect containers for lilies, hydrangeas, and standard fuchsias, both in sun and light shade. Bay trees *(Laurus nobilis)*, trained as standards, are favorites beside the front door. And for a less formal effect, consider winter jasmine *(Jasminum nudiflorum)* or forsythia. Roses, clematises, azaleas, camellias, and Japanese maples *(Acer palmatum* varieties) are also suitable for containers. In areas of deep shade, pieris, mahonias, hostas, brunneras, and hellebores do well.

Hanging baskets are usually viewed from below and look best when filled mainly with trailing plants — nasturtiums, tradescantias, fuchsias, creeping Jenny *(Lysimachia nummularia)*, petunias, lobelias, ivy-leaved geraniums, and pendulous begonias, for instance.

◄ **Moss liners** Hanging baskets look natural with a sphagnum moss liner, available from most garden centers. Choose a basket with a fairly close-woven framework so that the moss does not fall through.

Flowers tend to be produced more profusely if the plants are packed in tightly. Use a mixture of trailing and upright plants, such as fuchsias, geraniums, petunias, and pansies. Trailing lobelias are quite attractive planted through the base and sides of the basket.

MOSS-LINED HANGING BASKETS

1 Work on a table — not with the basket hanging up. Make a "nest" of fresh, moist moss inside the basket to a thickness of about 1 in (2.5 cm).

2 Line with a sheet of plastic to retain some water, but perforate it heavily to prevent waterlogging and also to keep the moss moist.

3 Fill in with sterilized potting soil or a soilless, peat-based potting mix to within 1 in (2.5 cm) of the top of the basket.

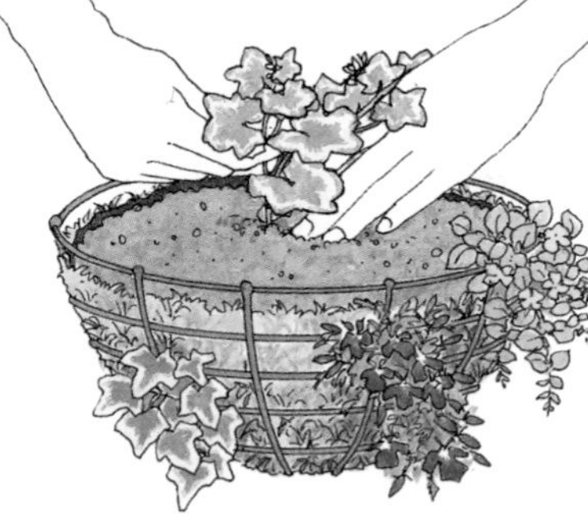

4 Insert trailing plants into the side after puncturing the lining with the tip of a small trowel or with a knife. Put upright plants in the center.

Planting containers

Water all plants a few hours before repotting them. Organize your design scheme by arranging the chosen plants on the surface of the soil. Put the largest in the center or toward the back of the container, and use dwarf or trail-

PLANTING A TUB

1 Cover the drainage holes with shards of terra-cotta or broken flowerpots to prevent them from becoming clogged, then add a thick layer of washed pebbles or coarse gravel for drainage.

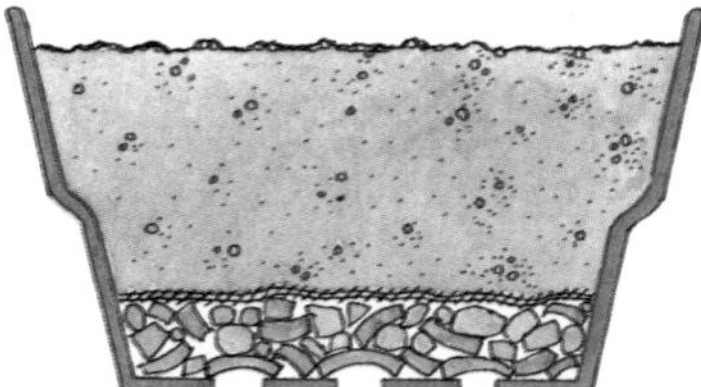

2 Put burlap or fiberglass screening over the drainage layer to prevent soil from washing into it, then fill the tub with sterilized potting soil.

3 Once you have planned the layout, set the tallest, upright plants in the center or toward the back, depending on the viewpoint.

4 Fill in with several low, bushy plants and add some trailing plants around the edges. Water in well immediately.

▲ **Summer window boxes** Bright colors provide a marvelous spectacle from both indoors and outdoors. The attractive foliage of zonal geraniums offers a lush foil for purple and brilliant white petunias. Ferny-leaved marguerites lend a delicate touch to the bold array, and yellow creeping Jenny softens the hard edges of the box.

ing types around the edges, and even peeking out of the sides of hanging baskets.

Once you have your design, set the plants aside. Using a hand trowel, dig holes for the largest ones first. Knock them out of their pots one at a time, and plant them so that they are slightly deeper than they were in the original pot. Press the soil in gently with your fingers and water lightly when all the plants are in place.

If the planting is permanent or semipermanent, a top layer of wood chips, gravel, or crushed rock can be sprinkled around the plants to improve the overall appearance and reduce moisture loss from the soil. A top layer of this kind also prevents soil-surface crusting, which can occur when hard tap water is applied regularly. For a seasonal planting, mulching is unnecessary.

Aftercare

Containers dry out quickly, so frequent watering is essential, especially when they are standing in full sun. Apply water to the soil — not over the leaves and flowers — preferably in the evening or early morning. Give enough water to moisten the soil thoroughly, then leave until the soil is almost dry before watering again — overwatering a container is as harmful as too little water. In hot areas, water may be needed twice a day.

For additional plant vigor, use a regular liquid fertilizer every 2 weeks — never apply fertilizer to dry soil. Deadhead all plants regularly (pp.119-122) and stake and tie tall species, if necessary.

Watch out for pests and diseases — dense plantings often encourage fungal diseases and many insect pests. Spray with a general-purpose insecticide and fungicide, if needed. Sprinkle slug bait to control slugs and snails — also check around the rim of a tub for snails hiding during the daytime. Clear away fallen leaves and other debris from the soil to discourage fungal growth and slugs.

With permanent plantings, scrape off the top 2-3 in (5-7.5 cm) of soil every spring and replace with fresh potting soil. Check the securing brackets of window boxes and hanging baskets too, replacing them when necessary.

SOWING SEEDS

Sowing seeds is the simplest and cheapest way of raising large numbers of plants, especially annual bedding plants and vegetables.

Seeds are embryo plants. Most produce plants of uniform appearance, virtually identical to their parents — these are said to be "true to type." They arise from natural self-pollination or else from the efforts of breeders who cross plants with similar features.

Nowadays, you will commonly find F1 hybrid seeds offered for sale. These are the result of crossing two purebred strains under controlled conditions. They are more vigorous and uniform, and often make better garden plants. But breeding and production costs increase the retail price.

Annual plants grow rapidly from seed, which is the only successful means of propagation. Although most perennials also do well from seed, cuttings or division often produce flowering plants sooner.

Shrubs and trees can be started from seed, but it takes many years for a good-sized plant to develop — for instance, a magnolia grown from seed may be just 5 ft (1.5 m) high after 10 years. Cuttings will usually give faster results, as do semimature plants bought from a nursery or garden center. Bulbs, corms, and tubers produce seeds, but bulblets or store-bought bulbs will increase your stock quicker.

Houseplants are frequently propagated by cuttings, layering, or division, but seed sowing is a perfectly good alternative. Many catalogs today offer houseplant seeds — even some rather exotic types. Cacti in particular can be successfully grown from seed.

Types of seed

Seeds vary greatly in shape and size. They may be as big as a Brazil nut or as fine as ground pepper; some have very hard coats, while others are soft and fleshy. A few have wings or barbed hooks that, under natural conditions, assist distribution. These differences largely determine their cultural needs.

Pelleted seeds are also available. Each seed is coated with a decomposable material, making it larger and easier to handle. With precise spacing possible, there's no need to thin seedlings — but the pellet does not improve germination, and can even slow it down.

For yet simpler sowing, buy a seed tape, which consists of a roll of tape with seeds stuck to it at precise intervals, and bury it in the seed drill. You can even find small containers with ready-sown seed in a soilless medium, such as vermiculite — you just add water

◀ **Plastic seed flats** Standard trays — "flats"- are ideal for germinating herb, flower, and vegetable seeds, and for pricking out seedlings. They are strong, and are stackable after use.

PEAT PELLETS

Peat pellets are perfect for raising species that suffer when roots are disturbed during replanting. Bought as dehydrated, compressed pellets, they consist of peat wrapped in a plastic netting. After soaking in water, they swell up ready for sowing. Just pop in a seed and press down. Plant out the whole thing — roots grow through the plastic netting.

SOWING IN A SEED FLAT

1 Fill the flat with screened, sterilized potting soil and press it down evenly to ½ in (1 cm) from the top. A wooden tamper, with a handle attached, will help you get a perfectly level surface.

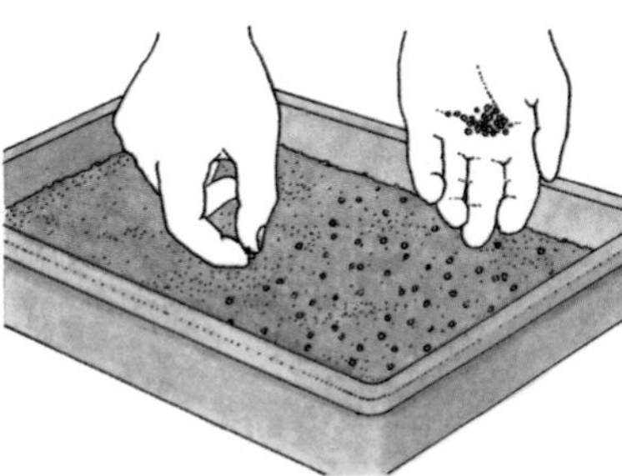

2 Scatter seeds thinly and evenly. Large ones can be placed individually, but tap smaller seeds directly from the packet. Mix dustlike seeds with a little sand to make them more visible and thus easier to get an even spread.

3 Cover the seeds with finely screened soil — not much deeper than the thickness of each seed. You can screen directly into the flat or sprinkle by hand. Fine seeds may need no covering — follow advice on the packet.

4 Water the soil, then cover the flat with a sheet of glass or plastic. An additional sheet of newspaper reduces condensation and shades tiny seeds that are not buried under soil.

to the medium and soon the seedlings will emerge.

Sowing depth

Generally, seeds should be sown at a depth equal to their thickness, although very large seeds can be planted deeper. Small seeds, such as petunias, need only a fine covering of soil. A few, such as begonias and celery, are best left uncovered, since light is essential to germination — most seed packets give instructions.

Raising seedlings indoors

Half-hardy annuals — those that cannot tolerate any frost — can be raised easily indoors. And with earlier sowing than is possible outdoors, these plants can be brought to flower sooner. Sow them between late winter and midspring, according to the instructions on the seed packet.

If you use old flats or pots, first scrub them in soapy water or detergent, then rinse thoroughly. Fill them with screened, sterilized potting soil (be sure to use one that doesn't contain any fertilizer, because it can burn delicate seedling roots) or a soilless, peat-based potting mix. Press the soil or potting medium down firmly to ¼-½ in (1-1.5 cm) from the top of the container.

Sow seeds thinly on the soil — open up the seed packet to make a spout, then, holding it over the soil, tap it onto a fingernail of the other hand to produce a slow but steady flow of seeds. Many suppliers seal seeds in plastic-lined foil pouches for freshness. Tear these open and tip the seeds into your hand, then either tap them off with a finger of the other hand or pinch a few between finger and thumb.

If the seeds are very fine, mix them with a little sand in a saucer before sowing — this technique makes it easier to see them and produces an even sowing. Cover large seeds with screened potting soil, sprinkling it carefully with your hand. Small seeds are best covered with fine sand.

Moisten the seeds by standing the flat or pot in water halfway up its sides in a sink or bowl. Remove it from the water when the surface of the soil appears wet — most soils darken when moist.

Label the container, using an indelible marker that won't wash off or fade. Cover with glass or plastic film, which must be wiped daily to remove excess condensation. You can drape the container with newspaper to prevent heat from building up and to reduce the amount of condensation.

Stand the container in a warm place — 60-75°F (15-24°C). Germination varies from a couple of days to three weeks after sowing, depending on the type of plant. The seedlings that appear generally consist of a pair of round or oval seed leaves. At this point, take off the cover and move the container to a bright windowsill. As soon as the first true leaves have developed, the seedlings are ready for pricking out.

If you use a commercial propagator, there's no need to cover the seed flat with glass or plastic. Once germination occurs, remove the top of the propagator during the day to allow a flow of fresh air over the container — damp, stagnant air promotes damping-off.

Pricking out seedlings

Fill a seed flat with moist, sterilized potting soil or a soilless potting mix. Press it in, as for seed sowing. Mark out the planting holes with a small dibble or ice-cream stick, spacing them 1-1½ in (2.5-3.5 cm) apart on each side.

Gently pry out a small clump of seedlings, with some of their soil, from the container — a plastic plant label makes a useful tool. Hold each seedling by one of its leaves and ease it away from the others. Never handle it by the stem — damage to this part is invariably fatal. Lower the

DAMPING-OFF

This common fungal disease turns the base of the seedling brown and kills it. Avoid sowing seeds too thickly and don't overwater them. Remove any dead seedlings immediately. Treat with a general-purpose systemic fungicide as soon as the disease strikes.

PRICKING OUT

1 Pricking out should be done once the seedlings have produced their first true leaves — the time it takes for these to appear varies according to species. Gently ease out a small clump of seedlings with some soil intact, using a plant label, ice-cream stick, or small dibble.

2 Make spaced holes in the potting soil with the tool. Gently ease away seedlings from the lifted clump and place them singly in each hole, holding the plant by a leaf, never the stem — damaged stems invariably result in death. Press in lightly and water.

◀ Young seedlings Prick out seedlings as soon as they have their first set of leaves. Crowded in a seed flat (far left), they become spindly and are starved of essential nutrients.

seedlings into their planting holes and press in the soil around each, again using a dibble or ice-cream stick. Don't damage the roots. Label the flat (include the date) and water with a fine spray or plant mister. Place the flat on a windowsill out of direct sun. A couple of days later, move the flat to a sunny spot or place it beneath grow lights. Keep the soil moist, but not wet.

Hardening off

Once established — 4 to 8 weeks after pricking out — harden off young plants. Begin by moving the flat to a sheltered spot outdoors in fine weather, bringing it back indoors at night. After a week or so, leave the plants outside permanently, but protect them from harsh weather and shelter them at night.

A glass- or plastic-covered cold frame is an ideal place to harden off plants. For the first few days, open the frame slightly, during the day only. Increase ventilation gradually so that by late spring the cold frame is completely open.

Sowing seeds outdoors

All hardy annuals and many half-hardy annuals, as well as biennials and certain perennials, shrubs, and trees, can be propagated from seed sown in the open ground — whether in a temporary seedbed

SOWING IN POTS

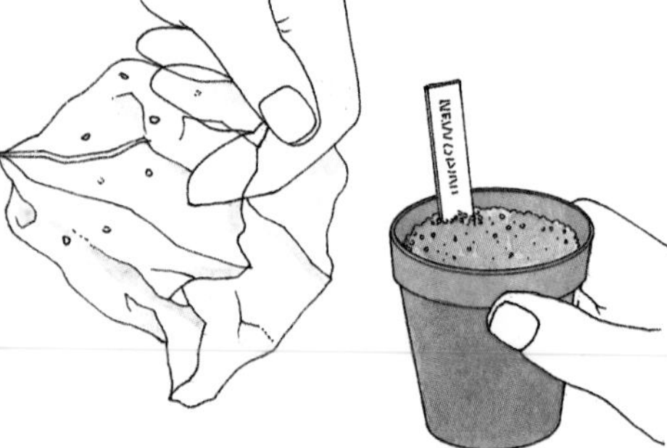

1 Small quantities of seeds can be sown in a 3-in (7.5-cm) pot. (Larger half pots or margarine containers are also suitable, but deep pots waste soil.) Fill with screened, sterilized potting soil and sow as for flats (facing page). Label it and keep the soil moist by putting the pot into a transparent plastic bag.

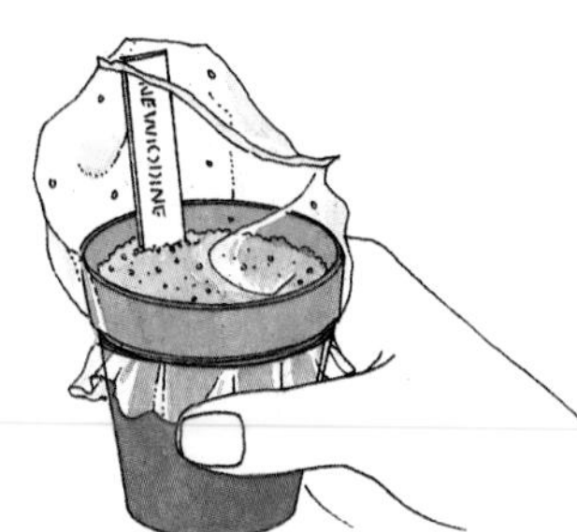

2 Prick a few holes in the bag for ventilation and secure it with an elastic band or twist tie. Stand the pot in a warm, sheltered place, such as a shaded windowsill, until the seeds have germinated. Look at the pot every day — some species germinate very quickly, others take more time.

3 If a lot of moisture forms on the inside of the bag, turn it inside out daily. After seedlings have emerged, remove the plastic bag and put the pot in a sunnier spot or under grow lights. If they are left in the dark, seedlings will grow very straggly and soon die. Watch out for damping-off.

MAKING A SEED DRILL

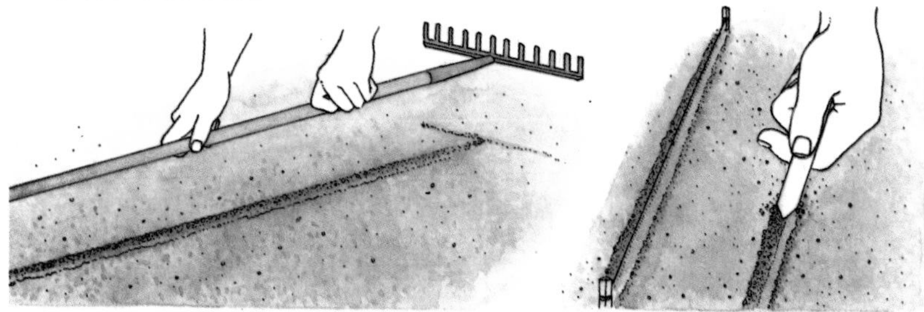

1 On light soils, make short drills by pressing the handle of a rake or hoe into the surface. (Do not use this technique on heavy soils.) Rows of vegetables get more even sunshine if you run the drill from north to south.

2 Short drills can also be scratched out using the pointed end of a plant label or a stick. Mark out the drills with a peg at each end, making them as straight as possible. Avoid standing on the sowing area, which compacts the soil.

3 For longer drills, use the corner of a draw hoe or the edge of a rake. Stretch a taut line between two pegs as a guide, then keep the hoe or rake against the line as you pull it toward you in short, gentle strokes.

SOWING SEEDS OUTDOORS

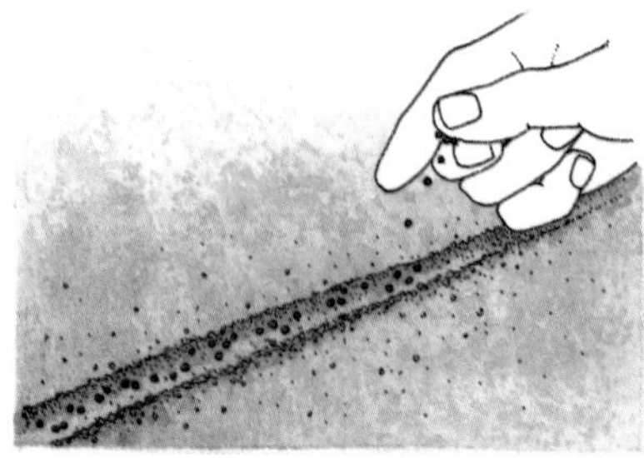

1 Sow seeds thinly to avoid the need for too much thinning later on. Tip a small quantity into the palm of your hand, then take some between the finger and thumb of your other hand and dribble them evenly into the row.

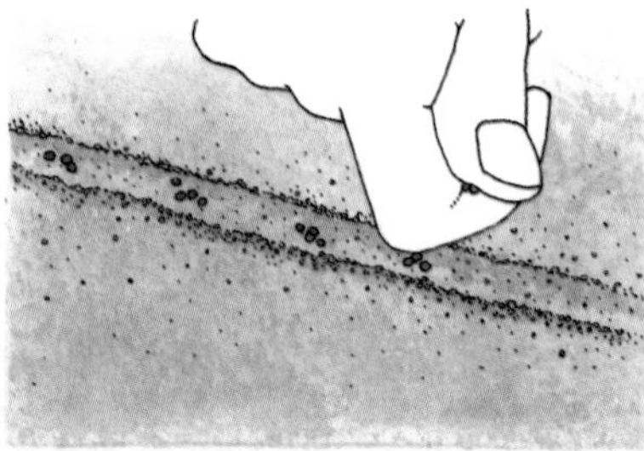

2 Another method is to sow three or four seeds at regular intervals — known as station sowing. The only thinning needed is to remove all but the strongest seedling plant at each of the stations.

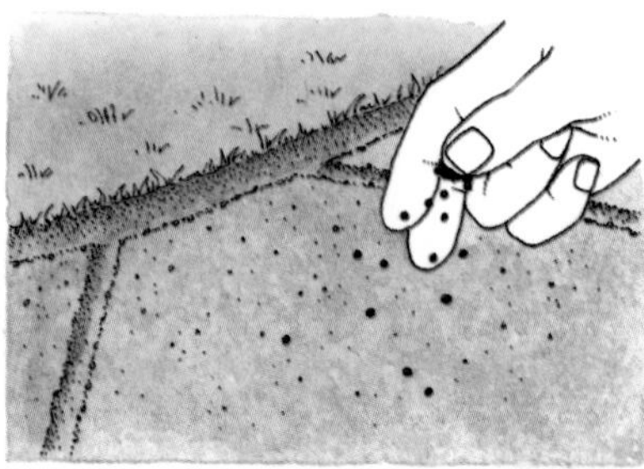

3 Informal drifts of hardy annuals can be broadcast sown. Mark the planting layout with furrows or trails of sand, then simply scatter seeds thinly over each section of the layout and rake in lightly.

or in their permanent positions. Sow only after the danger of frost has passed; in frost-free areas, you can sow in early spring, or even in fall for spring blooming. However, if you sow warm-weather seeds in cold, wet soil, they may rot before having a chance to germinate. And always check the seed packet's expiration date to ensure that seeds are still viable.

Soil preparation Dig the soil in the fall, allowing winter frosts to break up the clods. For vegetables — except root crops — work in some organic material. In spring, as soon as the soil is dry enough not to stick to your shoes, loosen the top 6-8 in (15-20 cm) with a fork. Apply a good handful of general-purpose fertilizer per sq yd/m, then rake it in. Just before sowing, rake the soil again to get a fine, crumbly tilth. Moisten the soil a day or so before sowing.

Sowing in a border Plan and mark out the sowing areas (p.73). Within each area, either sow seeds in shallow furrows (known as drills) or scatter the seeds over the whole surface and rake them into the soil — broadcast sowing. (The latter makes it more difficult to thin and weed later.)

Sowing in drills Make shallow drills, $\frac{1}{4}$-$\frac{1}{2}$ in (1-1.5 cm) deep. Space drills for upright species half the height of the plant apart; for dwarf or bushy types, the full height of the plant apart.

Cover seeds by running the tip of a hoe along the ridge of the drill, or by lightly drawing a rake along its length. Then tamp down with the flat side of the hoe or rake, or press the drill down lightly with your feet. Moisten the soil if it is dry, but don't overwater.

Thinning In general, thin spring-sown seedlings once, to 4-6 in (10-15 cm) apart; fall-sown seedlings of spring-blooming plants twice, to 2-3 in (5-7.5 cm) apart in fall, then 6-9 in (15-23 cm) apart in spring. Aim to keep the strongest seedlings. With mixed-color varieties, however, keep a selection of all sizes — small ones may bear unusual colors and will catch up in size later.

THINNING SEEDLINGS

When seedlings have two or three true leaves, thin them out while their roots are still small and removing them won't disturb adjacent seedlings. They come out more easily when soil is moist, so if dry, soak it the day before.

Pull out each weak or excess seedling with one hand while pressing the soil down on each side with the fingers of your other hand, holding remaining seedlings firm. Transplant thinnings to a spare area or discard them.

Propagation and plant care

Growing new plants from existing stock is both easy and inexpensive. The supply is potentially infinite, as each year's growth furnishes fresh new material for propagation. Since vegetative propagation from cuttings, division, or layering produces plants identical to the parent, you know just what you will get. No special equipment is needed, only simple techniques and the right timing. And success brings a sense of accomplishment, as you provide enough stock not only to fill your own garden but also to give to friends, and to exchange for other plants at your local garden club.

Keeping plants healthy is an ongoing challenge. It involves adequate watering in the growing season, ideally with equipment chosen to match your garden's size and needs. To prevent plants from becoming unwieldy or entangled with others, training and supporting weak or exposed plants must be done while they are still young. Healthy plants flower well, but you can easily extend the flowering season or add to the number or size of the blooms. Pinching the growing tips of plants such as zinnias increases the number of flowering side shoots. Disbudding, or removing unwanted buds, of plants such as dahlias encourages the remaining buds to grow to flower-show quality. Easiest of all, deadheading prevents flowers from setting seed and channels plants' energy into producing more blooms, as well as keeping them neat.

Some plants, especially young ones, need protection from the ravages of wind, rain, and snow; and from predators, such as birds, rabbits, mice, and deer, as well as pets. This chapter gives you the information you need to choose and create effective but unobtrusive barriers and deterrents.

Propagating for health New York asters should be divided every two or three years.

PROPAGATION BY DIVISION

Division is the easiest form of propagation for most perennial plants — you can increase your own stock or swap plants with friends.

Division is the process of lifting a clump of plants, complete with roots and growth buds, from the ground, pulling or cutting it into separate pieces, and then replanting each piece in freshly prepared soil.

Because these individual pieces will soon grow into new plants, each with characteristics identical to its parent, division is a very useful way of increasing the stock of a particularly desirable cultivar. The process is known as vegetative propagation. Growing from seed — sexual propagation — by comparison, introduces some genetic variation in the reproductive process — flower color, size, or growth habit, for instance, may tend to vary slightly among the offspring.

Herbaceous perennials — those that die down to ground level in winter — are the easiest to divide since they have a dormant period during which most can tolerate considerable root disturbance.

Evergreen perennials, including many houseplants, can also be increased by division, but you must be more careful when separating and replanting the roots, and spend more time on subsequent care.

To keep them healthy, most perennials should be divided every few years, regardless of whether you wish to increase your stock. Old, matted clumps frequently die out in the middle and develop unmanageable shapes. Staking and tying become difficult, and flower quality may be depleted.

The precise methods of division vary according to the size and type of rootstock. After removal from the ground, small clumps or fairly young plants can be pulled apart easily by hand. Older and overgrown plants, however, whose roots have formed a tangled mass, must be pried apart or severed with a sharp knife.

Woody plants, including some true shrubs, can be divided if they produce multiple stems or suckers from ground level, rather than a single stem or trunk.

Bulbs and corms can often be increased by offsets — a special type of division in which tiny bulblets or cormels are detached from the parent and grown to maturity. However, new plants obtained in this fashion may take several years to reach flowering size, whereas divisions are usually back to blooming within a year.

Lifting

The best time to lift perennials is in early fall to midfall, so that they have enough time to settle before the ground freezes. But they can also be lifted in early spring. Choose a day for lifting plants from open ground when the soil is neither frozen hard nor sticky — the soil should not stick to your boots.

To lift, push a garden fork into the ground alongside the clump of plants that you wish to remove. Gently pry the clump upward until you feel resistance. Repeat this procedure on the other side of the clump until all the roots are free. Lift the clump out of the ground — either by hand or with the garden fork.

Brush away as much soil from the roots as possible with your fingers, being careful not to damage any strong, fleshy roots or tubers. If growth buds are still concealed by soil, gently wash the clump by submerging it completely in a bucket of tepid water.

◀ **Overgrown perennials** Tough clumps are often difficult to split up once lifted, since their roots are tangled and woody. They can, however, be forced apart by inserting two garden forks, back to back, in the clump. Push the handles together to separate the roots, then apart to separate the crown.

DIVIDING YOUNG PERENNIALS

1 Lift the clump, using a garden fork. Pull the plants apart by hand or with a small hand fork. Each section should have healthy roots and strong growth buds.

2 With a knife, trim off any fibrous roots that are rotten, dead, or damaged. Try to keep the healthy root ball as intact as possible.

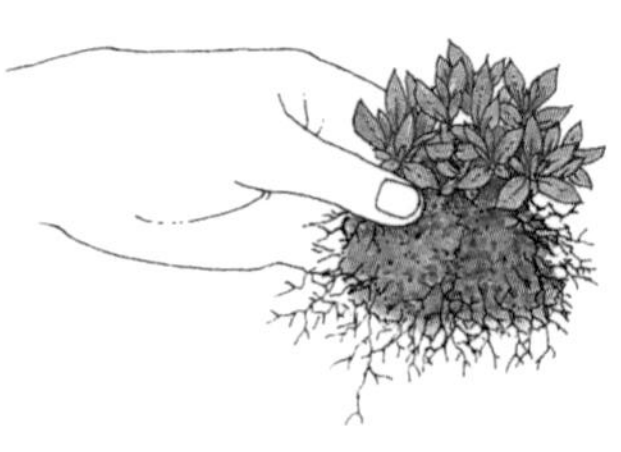

3 Replant the divisions right away. Put those with six strong shoots in their permanent position and smaller ones in nursery beds until they can be moved.

Dividing young perennials

Young, tufted perennials with fibrous roots, such as *Helianthus,* New York aster, and rudbeckia, are easily divided. Once lifted, they can be pulled apart by hand or with a small hand fork — each section should contain healthy roots and strong growth buds.

Cut off any dead roots and leaves and immediately replant the divisions in their permanent positions. Tiny divisions can be put out in a nursery bed (an area set aside to raise plants to maturity), in an out-of-the-way corner of the garden, or in individual pots until the following fall, when they can be moved.

Dividing mature perennials

Large, overgrown, fibrous-rooted perennials, such as helenium and phlox, are often difficult to divide because the crowns and shoots form a solid mass. Begin by lifting the clump — or part of it — as before. After lifting the clump, push the tines of two strong garden forks, back to back, into the center of the clump.

Most garden forks have curved tines, so that when put back to back they can be used as a lever. If you have only one fork, improvise by inserting a couple of stakes through the clump and into the soil below, then push the fork against them.

Pry the clump apart by pushing the handles of the forks together — thus forcing the tips of the tines apart. This action will separate the lower roots. Then push the handles of the forks away from each other. Repeat until the clump splits in half. Divide each half once again.

With a sharp knife, cut away and discard any dead or rotten roots, as well as the woody part of each portion that came from the center of the original clump. Separate the remainder into healthy pieces, each containing about six buds or shoots, then plant them. Water the divisions if the soil is dry.

Woody-crowned perennials, such as wild indigo and rhubarb, can't be split with garden forks. Instead, cut through the crowns with a sharp knife so that each severed portion has both root and growth buds. Replant the divisions immediately.

Fleshy-rooted plants, such as agapanthus and hosta, are best divided by hand in the same way as young perennials — it is easier to separate the roots, which can be brittle, without damaging them by this means than if you use forks.

Dividing tuberous plants

The method of dividing tuberous-rooted plants varies according to the type of tuber.

Dig up the clump as before and brush away the soil — be careful

DIVIDING MATURE PERENNIALS

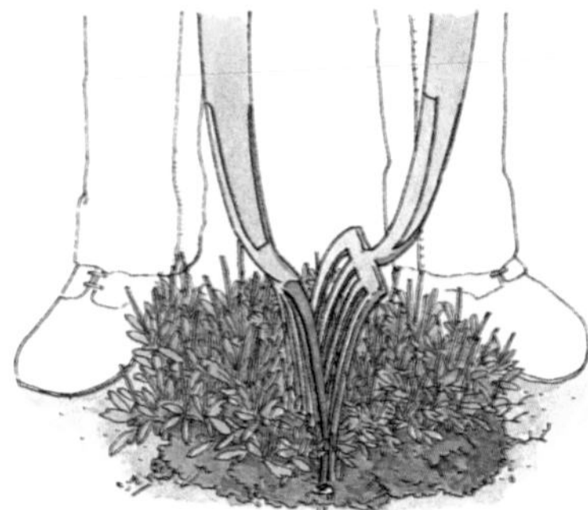

1 Mature clumps with matted roots can be split up by using two garden forks back to back. Insert the forks with their tines together into the center.

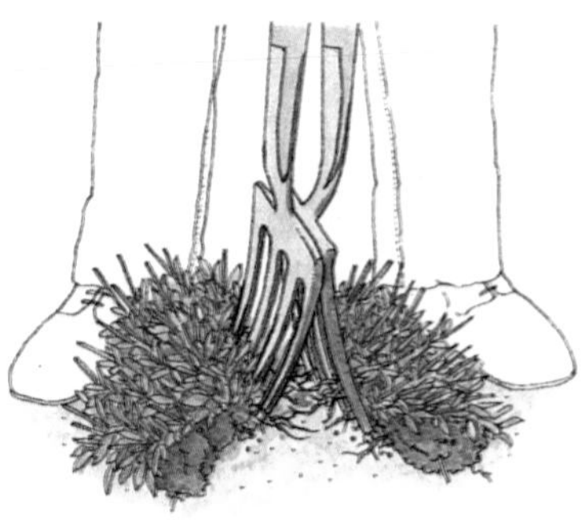

2 Push the fork handles together so that the tines are forced apart, thus separating the roots, then pull the handles apart to separate the crown.

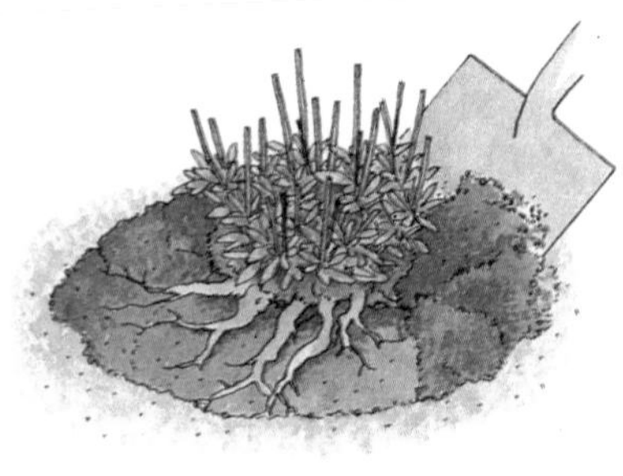

3 Having divided the clump into at least four parts, discard the old material that came from the center, then immediately plant each division.

▲ **Division of rhizomes** Perennials, such as bearded irises, once lifted, can be separated by hand. This method protects the fibrous roots from damage and the buds from being wounded.

not to damage the tubers. If the soil sticks to the tubers, immerse them in a bowl of water — the growth buds must be visible.

Root tubers, such as those of day lilies *(Hemerocallis)* and herbaceous peonies *(Paeonia)*, have growth buds in the crown, where the tubers join together. Using a knife, slice downward through the crown to divide the plant into several pieces, complete with tubers and growth buds. Immediately plant and water the divisions.

Generally, sections of single tubers with only one growth bud take longer to produce good-sized plants than those with three or four tubers and buds.

Herbaceous peonies need to grow new roots before winter comes. Divide them in late summer where winters are harsh, in early fall where winters are mild.

Small clawlike tubers, such as those of anemones and liatrises, can be pulled apart by hand. Large tubers may need to be cut into pieces with a knife. Make sure each piece has a strong growth bud before planting.

Dividing rhizomatous plants

Rhizomatous-rooted plants, such as bergenia, bee balm, ground cherry, and Solomon's seal, are easily lifted — their rootstocks, which are really swollen underground stems, grow just below the surface of the soil.

Lift the rootstock in early spring just as new growth buds begin to emerge. Brush away soil to expose the old main rhizome and the younger ones coming from it.

Choose side growths that have two or three strong growth buds or vigorous young shoots, as well as healthy roots. Any side shoot 2-3 in (5-7.5 cm) long is suitable for replanting. Remove these growths with a sharp knife, cutting through the rhizome and the roots.

Discard the old rhizome and trim the new growths back, cutting to just below a cluster of healthy fibrous roots. Remove any stump, rotten parts, dead leaves, and leaf stalks.

Plant each section immediately. Position it vertically in the soil, with the root cluster downward and fairly deep — the rhizome must be well anchored in the soil and at approximately the same depth as the original plant. Carefully label the plants and water them well.

DIVIDING BEARDED IRISES

1 Divide bearded irises every three years, in late summer. First, lift the clump with a garden fork.

2 Using a knife, cut off the younger rhizomes from the edge of the clump — each with one or two leaf fans. Some can be separated by hand.

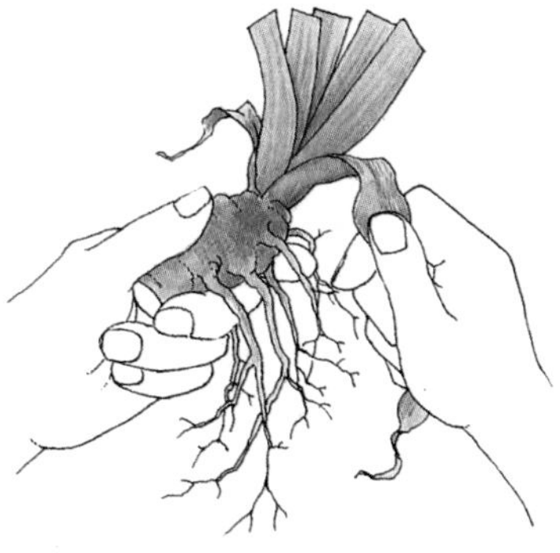

3 Using a knife or pruning shears, trim the fresh foliage into a small fan and peel any withered or dead leaves from the young rhizome.

4 Replant each rhizome in its permanent site — fill in with soil but leave the top of the rhizome barely exposed. Label and water the plants.

DIVIDING WOODY CROWNS AND TUBERS

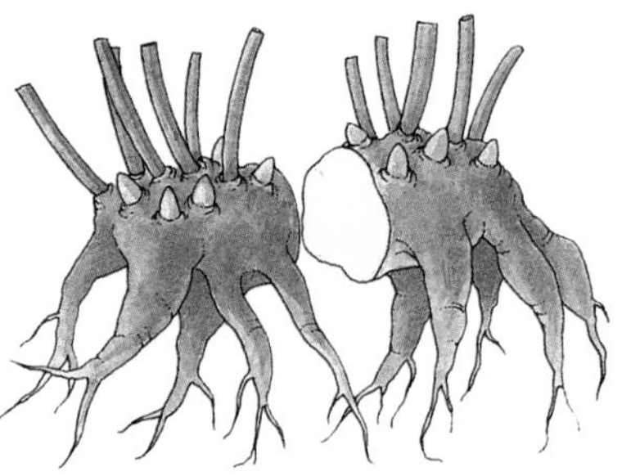

1 Tough, woody crowns of plants such as lupines should be cut with a knife, leaving roots and growth buds attached to each piece.

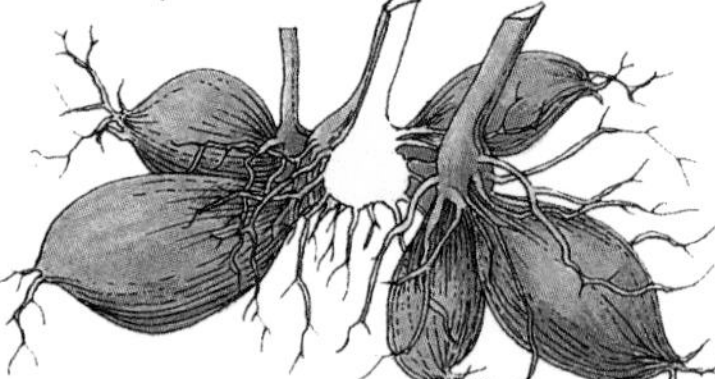

2 The swollen root tubers of dahlias don't bear buds. Split them by cutting downward through the stem — each piece must bear a portion of the stem with a growth "eye."

3 Divide shrubs that produce their main branches from below ground by cutting into equal-sized pieces with pruning shears; then replant.

Dividing shrubs

Many shrubs produce shoots from underground buds — including plumbago, clerodendron, California tree poppy, butcher's-broom, and kerria. The buried bases of the shoots sprout their own individual roots. Such shrubs can be divided in the same way as woody herbaceous perennials.

Lift the shrub in the spring — although, depending on your zone, any time between midfall and midspring may be successful. Using pruning shears or a small pruning saw, cut the woody base into several equal-sized pieces, each with plenty of roots and top growth attached. Immediately replant the divisions.

Many trees and shrubs also produce shoots from below ground — these are called suckers. They include ailanthus, deutzia, forsythia, mock orange, poison ivy, blackberry or raspberry, spirea, and weigela.

Suckers appearing from the base of grafted shrubs are not appropriate for use as propagation stock because they won't have the same characteristics as the parent and may be too vigorous. Additionally, suckers from grafted shrubs should always be taken off as soon as they appear.

Remove soil from the base of the sucker between midfall and early spring. If the sucker has roots, it is suitable for lifting. Using pruning shears, cut the sucker close to its point of origin with the stem or root.

Plant well-rooted suckers in a permanent site in the garden. Poorly rooted suckers should be set out in a nursery bed for a year or so until they mature.

Dividing bulbs and corms

All hardy bulbs and corms left to naturalize in the ground increase steadily from offsets. However, if left alone, they eventually form congested clumps with fewer or poor-quality flowers. Such clumps should be lifted and divided after the foliage has died. Dig them up with a garden fork, inserting the tines deep enough to avoid damaging the bulbs. Ease the soil away and separate the bulbs with your fingers. Cut away old and dead roots, discard any bulbs that show signs of disease, and separate the young bulblets that have formed at the sides of true bulbs, such as narcissus and tulips. Corms, including crocuses, form a new corm on top of the old and shriveled one, as well as many tiny cormels on top of and along the parent corm.

Narcissus, tulips, and crocuses don't need to be replanted right away, but can be left to dry off until the fall. Most other bulbs should be planted immediately after division; snowdrops are best split and replanted while the foliage is still green.

Discard very small offsets; larger ones can be raised in a nursery bed until they reach flowering size. In their first year, they will develop roots and leaves, but no flowers. Larger offsets will produce flowers in their second or third year. Young half-hardy gladiolus corms must be lifted or wintered in a frost-free place.

BULBLETS AND CORMELS

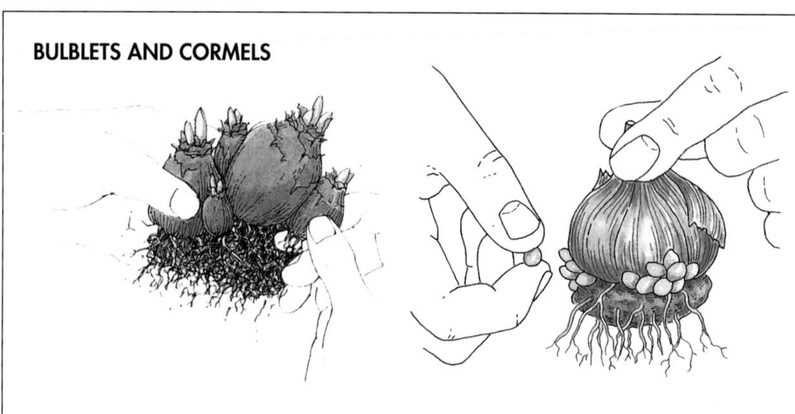

Small offset bulblets form at the side of most bulbs, especially those of narcissus and tulips. Such offsets can be removed by hand at lifting time or before planting (far left) and replanted in a different part of the garden to reach flowering size.

Gladioli produce cormels around the base of the new corm. When the corm has dried out, the cormels can be broken off gently for propagation and stored separately in paper bags in a cool, dry place. The old shriveled corm should be twisted off and discarded.

PROPAGATION BY LAYERING

Layering is a simple method of increasing plant stock without the need for an elaborate propagation box or a greenhouse.

Layering, another means of vegetative propagation, works best with plants that have long, flexible stems. If part of a stem's bark has been cut, scraped, or fractured, and this portion of the plant is then put in contact with soil or another rooting medium, roots are likely to grow from the wound. Once they do, the offspring can be detached and grown as a separate plant.

Often layering succeeds where cuttings fail; it is used principally for woody-stemmed plants — shrubs and trees, including some houseplants. Certain herbaceous plants, notably carnations and pinks, also respond to layering.

Many of the pendulous or lax-stemmed shrubs and trees, such as *Forsythia suspensa* and *Salix* × *chrysocoma,* layer themselves naturally when their stems touch the ground. The constant rubbing of the branch against the ground causes an injury to the bark, and roots develop from the callus formed over the wound, thus anchoring the branch.

Simple layering

Deciduous plants may be layered in early spring while the shoots are still dormant; for evergreens, such as rhododendrons or magnolias, wait until a new crop of shoots has emerged and begun to harden.

First, use a garden fork to turn over the surface of the soil that surrounds the base of the plant. Then choose a flexible, smooth young branch — a nonflowering one of the current season's growth for evergreens, a shoot not more than one year old for deciduous plants. Bend the branch down until it reaches the ground 9-12 in (23-30 cm) from its tip. Strip the leaves off the branch where it comes into contact with the soil.

Wound the underside of the branch to restrict the flow of sap, either by cutting a shallow tongue with a knife, slicing toward the

▼ **Layering shrubs** Flexible branches can be bent down to the ground and encouraged to produce roots by wounding the stem tissues. Buried in soil for several months, the rooted stem can then be cut and grown on its own.

LAYERING SHRUBS

1 Select a flexible branch that has grown in the current year, checking that it will bend to the ground 9-12 in (23-30 cm) from the tip without undue strain. Strip off the leaves where the shoot touches the ground.

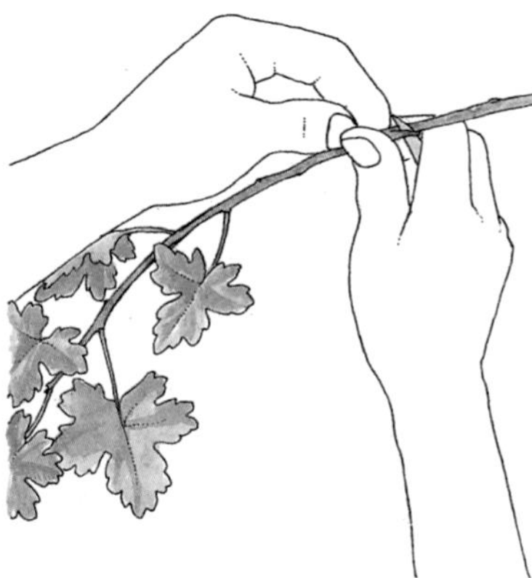

2 Using a sharp knife, wound the tissue at the point where it will come into contact with the soil. Cut a shallow tongue into the underside of the branch, slicing up toward the growing tip. Do not cut into the heartwood.

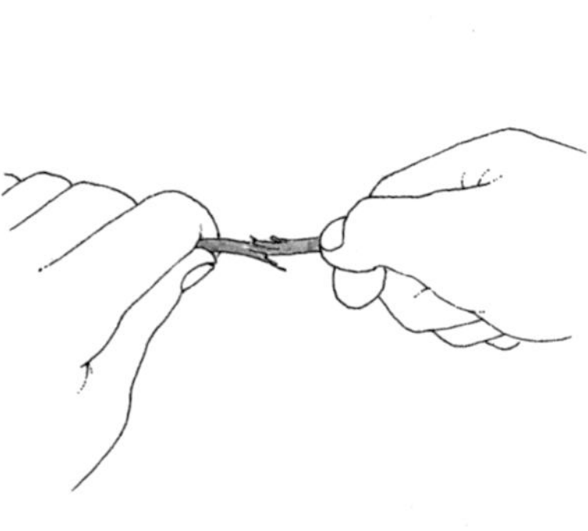

3 As an alternative to slicing a tongue out of the branch, especially where the wood is quite thin, twist the branch sharply to break or injure the surface tissue. The heartwood should remain uninjured.

4 Dig a small hole and partially fill it with a peat-based potting mixture. Bend the branch gently at the wound and peg it into the ground at the sides of the hole, using a piece of bent galvanized wire.

5 Stake the tip upright and cover the wound with more soil. Press in firmly. Anchor springy branches with a stone or brick. Keep the area watered thoroughly until the layer has rooted.

6 After about one year, check whether roots have grown successfully from the wounded tissue. If so, sever the branch with pruning shears and replant directly into the chosen site.

growing tip, or twisting the branch to injure the tissue. Dig a hole 3-4 in (7.5-10 cm) deep beneath the wound and partially fill it with a loose, peat-based potting mixture. A light dusting of a hormone rooting powder over the wound may encourage quicker rooting, but is not essential.

Push the wounded part of the branch into the hole, forming a right angle at the wound. Peg the branch to the ground with a bent piece of galvanized wire, 6-8 in (15-20 cm) long, and stake the upright tip. Fill the hole with more soil. Repeat with other branches. Water the area thoroughly and see that the soil never dries out.

Most ornamental shrubs take 6 to 12 months to root sufficiently, though magnolias and rhododendrons require up to two years before they can be severed from the parent plants. Carefully scrape away the soil and check the new roots. If they are well established, separate the new plant from the parent, lift with a good ball of soil, and plant elsewhere in the garden.

If the roots are not well grown, but the layer is healthy, replace the soil and let a few months elapse before reexamining the root formation.

Tip layering

Certain plants can be propagated simply by burying the tips of their shoots in the soil — brambles, such as blackberries and loganberries, in particular.

Toward the end of midsummer, bend down a new season's shoot and, where it touches the ground, dig a hole 6 in (15 cm) deep with a hand trowel. Plant the entire tip of the shoot in the hole and press it in firmly. Peg down the shoot if it is especially springy.

By midfall the tips will have rooted. Sever each new plant from its parent by cutting just above a bud. Do not move the plant yet. In late fall, transfer each new cane to its permanent bed. It will bear fruit in its second or third year.

Serpentine layering

A handy method of propagating woody plants with long, pliable stems — especially climbers, such as honeysuckle, clematis, and jasmine — is called serpentine layering. It should be done at the same time as ordinary layering. Use

TIP LAYERING BLACKBERRIES

1 In midsummer, bend down a current season's shoot and mark where its tip touches the ground at a convenient position for propagation. Using a hand trowel, dig a hole 6 in (15 cm) deep at this point. Plant the tip in the hole.

2 In midfall, when the blackberry tip should have rooted, cut the shoot from its parent just above a strong, healthy shoot bud. Use a sharp pair of pruning shears. Trim or retrain the remaining parent branch.

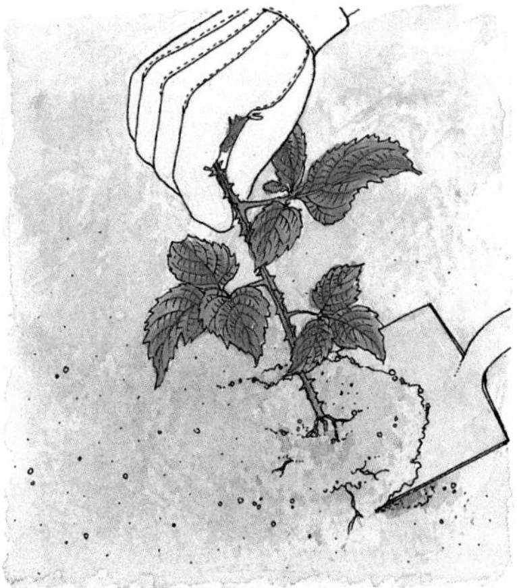

3 In late fall, lift the new plant, digging out a good-sized ball of soil and roots. Replant it in the garden immediately. It should bear good fruit in its second or third year. This method also works for boysenberries and loganberries.

long, trailing shoots that have grown during the current year.

Bend a shoot to the ground carefully and, where it first reaches the soil, dig a hole 2 in (5 cm) deep beneath it. Wound the shoot underneath, as for ordinary layering. Peg the wounded part of the shoot into the hole with a piece of bent galvanized wire. Fill in the hole with a loose, peat-based potting mixture.

Cover the shoot with soil and press it down firmly with your fingers. Leave the next two pairs of leaves above the ground and repeat the operation farther along the shoot. Continue working in this manner until the entire shoot is alternately buried and left exposed.

One year later, the serpentine layer should have rooted. Scrape the soil away from each buried section of the layer and, if you find that it is well rooted, sever it from the preceding section with pruning shears. (If it is not well rooted, bury the whole layer again and wait a few months before checking it again.) Each rooted section is now ready to be individually severed and planted separately in the normal way.

Another transplanting trick is to peg the shoots into pots of general-purpose potting soil sunk into the ground, instead of pegging them into the ground. When the layer has rooted, then you can sever it and move it for replanting without disturbing the new roots.

Growing from runners

A runner is an aerial or underground stem that, when it comes into contact with moist soil, puts down roots, forming new plantlets — a type of natural layering. The runners made by strawberry plants, and other ornamental members of the genus *Fragaria*, are easily propagated. In early summer, if the plants are growing in rows, pull the runners around to the unplanted areas between rows. Anchor the top of the runners firmly into the soil. When the runners have rooted into the soil, remove the remainder of the runners beyond the new plant.

If the plants are growing in wide rows or beds, select the strongest plantlets and peg each down into a pot of general-purpose potting soil that has been sunk to its rim in the ground. Water the pots frequently to aid root formation and remove all other runners as they form.

The plantlets should be separated from the parent in midsummer to late summer and planted out from their pots. If, for some reason, planting is delayed until the fall, the young strawberry plants should not be allowed to fruit the first season. To prevent it, pinch off the flowers as they appear.

Some houseplants, notably mother-of-thousands *(Saxifraga*

SERPENTINE LAYERING

1 Select a long, pliable stem and bend it down to the ground. Wound the shoot underneath. Using a piece of galvanized wire, peg the stem into a hole 2 in (5 cm) deep and fill the hole with potting soil.

2 Repeat the operation, leaving two pairs of leaves between each layer. Continue along the entire length of the shoot. When rooted, sever each section of stem and replant.

AIR LAYERING HARDY SHRUBS

1 Select a branch of the current year's growth and strip off a pair of leaves — any branch will do, however high or stiff, since it does not have to be bent down to the ground, as with the other methods of layering.

2 Using a sharp knife, cut off a shallow slice of wood. Ensure that the cut does not weaken the branch to such an extent that it will break. Dab a small amount of hormone rooting powder onto the wounded area.

3 Wrap plastic sheeting around the stem, just below the cut, and tie it with string or tape to form a funnel. Fill the funnel around the wound with a rooting mixture of peat, sharp sand, and sphagnum moss.

4 Moisten the rooting mixture, then fasten the top of the plastic with another piece of string to enclose it firmly around the wound. Leave the plant for at least 10 weeks before examining for roots.

5 When you see that the wounded tissue has grown a good ball of roots, remove the plastic wrapping. Using a pair of pruning shears, sever the new plant from the parent stem by cutting just below the roots.

6 Put the new plant into potting soil. Cover with a clear plastic bag and set it in a warm, shaded spot for a couple of weeks until new growth is obvious. Harden off the plant before replanting it the following spring.

stolonifera) and spider plants *(Chlorophytum comosum)*, also produce small plantlets, either on the flowering spikes or on thin runners from the parent plant.

With mother-of-thousands, detach the threadlike runners from the parent plant. Nip off the plantlet from the runner. Fill a pot with a peat-based potting soil.

Set the plantlet in a shallow depression in the surface. Press the soil down firmly around the plant. Place a plastic bag over the pot and secure it with an elastic band. Keep the pot out of direct sunlight and at a temperature of 64-70°F (18-21°C). If the soil dries out, water gently. After about 10 days, the plantlet should have rooted. Remove the bag and set the pot in a brighter, cooler place.

Spider plants often bear a number of plantlets on tough stalks. These can be layered into individual small pots and secured with paper clips. After about 3 weeks, the plantlets should have rooted enough to be severed.

Air layering

When branches are too stiff or too high to be layered at ground level, they may be "layered" in the air, sometimes known as Chinese layering. It can be done between late spring and midsummer. Air layering is particularly recommended for *Ficus* species, such as the common rubber plant, and for magnolias. After some years, houseplants such as dizygothecas and rubber plants may grow too tall, and will often lose their lower leaves. Instead of throwing out the plant, propagate it by air layering in spring to produce a new, shorter-stemmed version.

Select part of the branch from the current year's growth and strip off its middle leaves. Then cut off a shallow slice of wood and put rooting powder on the cut.

Wrap a sheet of black plastic around the cut and tie the bottom of it with string to form a funnel. Fill the funnel with a rooting soil mixture. Fasten the top of the plastic with more string or tape.

The conditions needed for rooting of the air layer are constant moisture, exclusion of sunlight, and restriction of the stem. Once the plastic is sealed, no further watering will be needed.

In 3 to 6 months, when rooted (check by unfastening the plastic), remove the plastic and cut off the new plants below the roots. Put the new plant into potting soil in a pot that is $4^1/_2$-6 in (11-15 cm).

Place the potted plant under a large, clear plastic bag in a warm, shaded spot. Leave it for 2 weeks, watering it just enough to keep it moist, then harden it off by puncturing holes in the bag to admit air. Gradually increase the number of holes until eventually the bag is removed entirely. Replant the following spring.

PROPAGATION BY CUTTINGS

A simple way of propagating most shrubs is by taking mature stem cuttings, while many perennials can be grown from tip or root cuttings.

Increasing plants by taking cuttings is probably the most widely practiced type of vegetative propagation. Either a section of stem — with or without leaves — a section of root, a single leaf, or a bud of a living plant is removed and treated in such a way that it develops into a new plant.

There are various types of cuttings, each with its own requirements, but certain general rules apply. For a cutting to strike — take root — it must have adequate light, warmth, and moisture. Except in special cases, very small cuttings should be avoided, as they tend to exhaust their food reserves before roots can be formed. Similarly, overlarge cuttings draw up too much water and soon wilt or suffer poor growth.

The rooting medium for cuttings must be free-draining yet capable of retaining sufficient moisture, and it must permit free passage of air. In addition, it must harbor no pests or diseases.

Tip cuttings

Some perennials, notably tender plants, such as *Centaurea gymnocarpa,* penstemon, and dimorphotheca, as well as foliage perennials, such as chamomile *(Anthemis)* and rue *(Ruta),* are best increased from tip cuttings. Take these from the ends of nonflowering lateral shoots during late summer and early fall. The rooted cuttings generally need protection — a cold frame or frost-free sun porch — during winter. Plants grown indoors can be increased from tip cuttings at any time of year.

Take the cuttings, 3-4 in (7.5-10 cm) long, from the tips of healthy, leafy stems, ensuring that each cutting has at least three leaf joints.

Fill a pot to just below the rim with a 1:1 mixture of screened peat moss and horticultural perlite. A 4-in (10-cm) pot will be able to fit about six cuttings.

Trim each cutting just below the lowest leaf node, slicing through it at a right angle to the stem. Make sure that you use a very sharp knife or a razor blade to make the cut. Pull off the lowest pair of leaves and dust the

▼ **Tip cuttings** Tender fuchsias, kept over winter in a heated greenhouse or sunny windowsill, are best increased from tip cuttings taken in spring and rooted in a pot or propagation box.

base of the cutting with hormone rooting powder.

Make shallow planting holes in the rooting medium with a dibble or ice-cream stick, far enough apart that they don't overlap each other. Insert the cuttings so that the base of each stem touches the bottom of the hole, without burying the leaves. Press the soil down firmly with your fingers.

Water the pot thoroughly and label the cuttings. Cover the pot with a plastic bag and secure with an elastic band. (To prevent the plastic from coming into contact with the cuttings, support it on a framework of sticks or wire hoops inserted in the soil.) Set each pot of cuttings in a protected spot out of the direct sun, such as a shaded cold frame. Alternatively, put the cuttings in a commercial propagation box with a regulated bottom heat of about 61°F (16°C).

After 4 to 6 weeks — about 3 weeks in a propagation box — the cuttings should have rooted. To check, tug them gently. If they don't yield, they have rooted. The plastic covering can be removed or the pots can be taken out of the propagation box. Leave the pots of cuttings in the cold frame for 4 or 5 days, then turn each pot upside down and carefully dislodge the rooting medium, with the rooted cuttings, in one piece.

Separate the rooted cuttings gently, then plant them individually in 3-in (7.5-cm) pots containing sterilized potting soil.

Press in the soil around each cutting and water thoroughly. Allow the pots to drain before returning them to the cold frame. After a week, pinch out — or remove — the growing tip of each plant to encourage the development of a strong root system, instead of excessive top growth.

Keep the cuttings in a closed cold frame or frost-free sun porch during winter. Plant them in their growing positions in spring, when all danger of frost is over.

Basal cuttings

Most clump-forming perennials, such as bugloss *(Anchusa)*, thrift *(Armeria)*, delphinium, helenium, lupine, and scabious *(Scabiosa)*, can be propagated not only by division but also from the young shoots appearing from the base of the plant in spring.

Cut off some of these basal shoots when they are 3-4 in (7.5-10 cm) long, at crown level or just below. Dust the bases with hormone rooting powder and insert the cuttings directly into the soil in a sheltered spot, or in 3-in (7.5-cm) pots of screened peat moss and horticultural perlite.

Keep cuttings well watered by sprinkling them from overhead with a watering can and make sure that they remain covered — cut off the bottoms from 2-liter plastic soft-drink bottles and set them over the cuttings or pots. As new growth starts to show, increase ventilation by removing the bottle caps.

After about 6 weeks, pot the cuttings individually in $3^1/_2$-in (9-cm) pots filled with sterilized potting soil. Do not plant them in their permanent positions in the

TIP CUTTINGS

1 Snip off nonflowering side shoots from perennial plants at any time during the summer. Each cutting should be 3-4 in (7.5-10 cm) in length and be free from all pests and diseases.

2 Trim each cutting straight across the stem, just below a leaf node — the point at which one or more leaf stalks join the main stem — then pull off or cut away the lowest pair of leaves.

3 Using a dibble, make planting holes in a 4-in (10-cm) pot containing a suitable rooting medium. Insert the cuttings, press in firmly with your fingers, and water gently from overhead.

4 Crisscross two galvanized wire hoops to make a framework and cover with a plastic bag. Make a few small breathing holes in the plastic and secure it with an elastic band.

5 After 4 to 6 weeks, remove the plastic and check for rooting — cuttings should not yield to a gentle tug. Plant each rooted cutting in a 3-in (7.5-cm) pot of potting soil.

6 About one week after potting individually, pinch the tip of each cutting to encourage side branching and a strong root system. Overwinter in a cold frame or frost-free sun porch.

SEMIHARDWOOD HEEL CUTTINGS

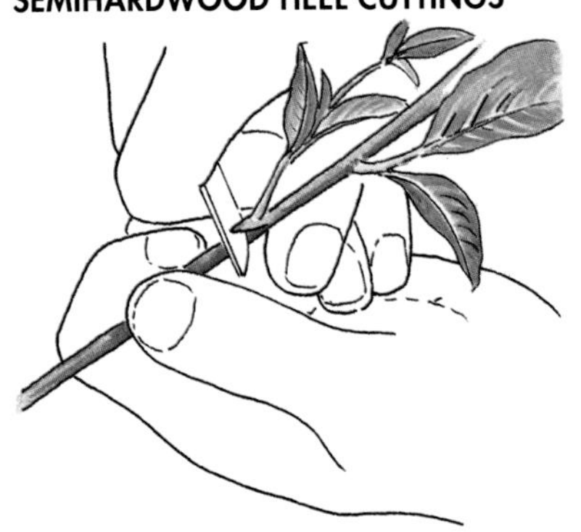

1 Most shrubs root more easily if taken with a heel — a sliver of wood from the main stem. Begin by making a slanting cut into the main stem below the joint with the side shoot.

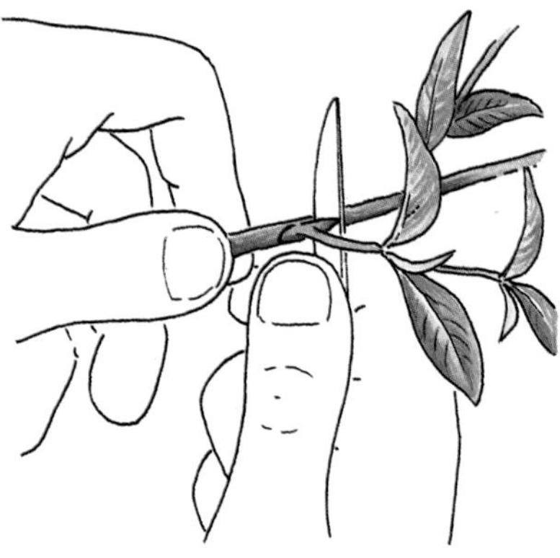

2 Next, make a similar cut in the opposite direction to remove the side shoot along with the heel. A very sharp, clean knife is essential for this operation.

3 Remove the leaves from the lowest part of the stem and also trim off the terminal soft tip just above a leaf joint. The final cutting should be about 2-4 in (5-10 cm) in length.

4 Insert the cuttings in pots of rooting medium and provide them with a warm, humid atmosphere by covering with a plastic bag or putting them in a propagation box.

fall until you have hardened them off — acclimatized them to the drier or colder conditions they will meet outside.

To harden off the cuttings, set them in a cool greenhouse or frame and raise the plastic (or pierce a few holes in it) to let in air. Keep the cuttings away from strong light. One week later, raise the plastic higher or make more holes in it. The next week, remove the plastic altogether. A week later, you can plant the cuttings.

If you do not have a greenhouse or frame, set the plants outside daily for increasing periods of time over several weeks.

Semihardwood cuttings
You can propagate many woody shrubs and trees from cuttings taken in midsummer to late summer. These include spotted laurel *(Aucuba)*, caryopteris, Mexican orange *(Choisya)*, and lavender *(Lavandula)*.

Semihardwood cuttings should be made from the current year's growth that has become moderately firm and woody toward the base but is still growing. The stem tips should still be soft. They require care from the time they are set out until they are rooted — their ideal position is in a cold frame, or a well-protected bed, and close attention should be paid to watering and shading from the sun. A year or two must elapse before the plants are ready for their permanent quarters.

Choose side shoots, 6-8 in (15-20 cm) in length, from the current season's wood — easily identified, as the shoots will have leaves growing on them. With a knife or pruning shears, cut off a shoot close to the main stem. Remove the leaves from the lower part of the shoot and sever it just below the lowest leaf node. Trim off the soft tip above a leaf so that the cutting is about 4 in (10 cm) long.

Heel cuttings Semihardwood cuttings often root more reliably if they are removed with a heellike sliver of the parent stem. Some species — including pyracantha and California lilac *(Ceanothus)* — will root very poorly, or not at all, without this sliver. The inclusion of a heel encourages roots to form, as it prevents the sap from draining away into the soil — the sap flows down from the leaves to help form the roots.

First, cut off a main shoot that carries several side shoots, preferably without flowers. With a sharp knife, make a slanting cut into the main shoot beneath the junction with the side shoot. Then cut in the opposite direction to remove the shoot. Heel cuttings should be 2-3 in (5-7.5 cm) long. If they are longer, trim from the tip. Take a few extra cuttings in case some fail to take root.

Once the cuttings have been

LEAF-BUD CUTTINGS

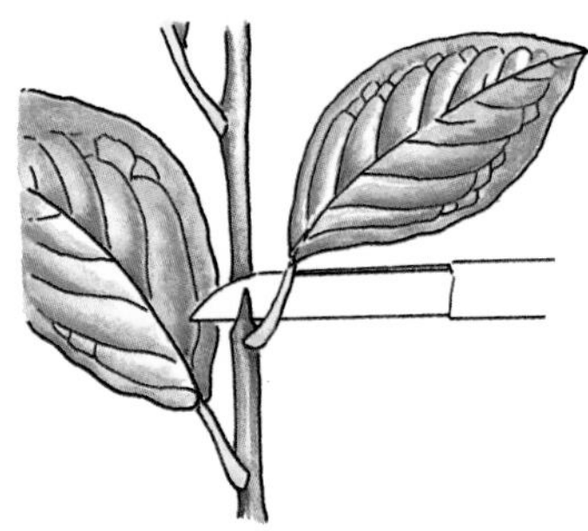

1 The method of making a leaf-bud cutting is much the same as for a heel cutting. Each cutting of a camellia should contain one tiny bud, one leaf, and just a sliver of wood from the stem.

2 Insert cuttings in the soil so that only the leaf shows on the surface. Leaf-bud cuttings of other shrubs usually include a short length of stem, rather than just a sliver of wood.

HARDWOOD CUTTINGS OF EVERGREENS

1 Make hardwood cuttings of evergreen shrubs, such as privet *(Ligustrum)*, by severing just below a leaf node. Strip off most of the lowest leaves, leaving no more than six.

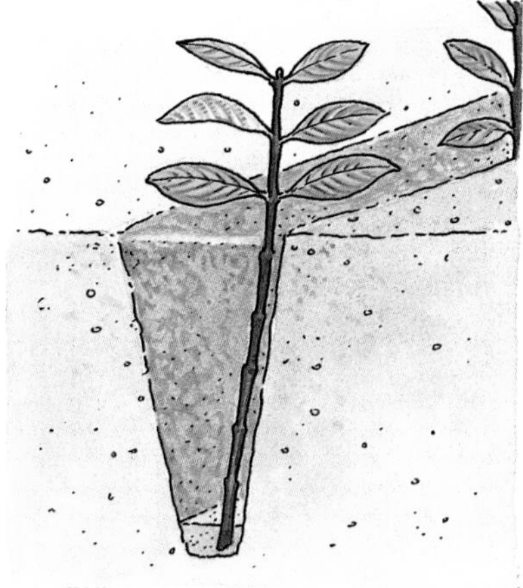

2 Insert the cuttings in the open ground in a V-shaped trench with a layer of sand at the bottom to assist drainage. Such cuttings will take about a year to root successfully.

taken — with or without a heel — fill a pot to just below the rim with a peat-and-perlite rooting medium. A 3-in (7.5-cm) pot will take up to five cuttings, and a 5-in (12-cm) pot will take up to ten.

Make a hole in the rooting medium, about one-third the length of the cutting. Insert the cutting and press it in with a dibble or ice-cream stick and your finger. Plant the other cuttings, then water them with a fine mist.

The cuttings need a humid atmosphere to prevent them from drying out. Bottomless soda bottles work well if you have only a few cuttings; for a large number of cuttings, however, cover a cardboard box with a wire frame and clear plastic film. Alternatively, use a propagation box.

For most hardy plants, the rooting medium should be maintained at a steady temperature of 60-65°F (15-19°C). A cold frame is suitable for most semihardwood cuttings, but better rooting conditions are created if a source of heat is provided from beneath, keeping the base of the cuttings slightly warmer than the top. Bottom heat can be supplied by placing the container over heating pipes or a radiator. You can also purchase propagation boxes with built-in heating elements or with separate heating cables.

After rooting, gently take the cuttings from the pot or box and ease them apart. Place potting soil in the bottom of a 3½-in (9-cm) pot. Stand the young plant on this layer and then fill the pot with soil to just below the lowest pair of leaves. Press the soil down firmly so that the surface is level and about ½ in (1.5 cm) below the rim, then water the cutting.
Keep the pot in a greenhouse or frame and do not allow the soil to dry out. In 3 weeks, the roots should have reached the outside of the soil. Put the plant into a larger pot and place it in a spot protected from excessive wind, heat, or cold. Any plants that are not fully hardy should remain in a frost-free sun porch or greenhouse for the winter. Replant in the spring when all danger of frost is past.

Leaf-bud cuttings

If you want to grow several new shrubs from a limited amount of propagating material, consider leaf-bud cuttings. Provided the material is taken at the right time, individual buds can root and break into growth more quickly than those on a traditional cutting. Camellias, black raspberries, lemons, and rhododendrons can all be propagated this way.

In late summer or early fall, take cuttings from semihard lateral shoots — those that began growing in the spring. Each shoot should have several leaves, with a growth bud in each leaf axil.

With pruning shears, cut off the shoot near its base. Then, with a sharp knife, make a clean cut through the shoot at an angle, about ¾ in (2 cm) below the lowest leaf. Sever the cutting cleanly just above the bud in the leaf axil. Three or four leaf-bud cuttings can be made in this way. Scrape off some bark from the cutting with a knife, then dip the end and the wounded part of the cutting into hormone rooting powder.

Fill a pot to just below the rim with the peat-and-perlite rooting

CHEMICAL AIDS FOR CUTTINGS

Cuttings generally root readily if you take them at the correct time of year. If your plants are having difficulty taking root, however, various rooting powders are available. The hormones in these products are present in the plants themselves, but often in such minute quantities that natural rooting is very slow. Rooting hormones speed the formation of a protective callus, a type of corklike scar tissue that forms at the base of a cutting and from which roots will develop.

You can buy rooting hormones in the form of a dry powder, which is dusted onto the base of the cutting, or as a diluted liquid into which the cutting is dipped. The powder types can be combined with a fungicide that helps to limit rotting of the stem base, and are available in different strengths — a weaker concentration for softwood and a stronger one for hardwood cuttings. There are also general-purpose compounds.

Hardwood cuttings of evergreen trees and shrubs, especially conifers, may die of dehydration due to rapid, excessive water loss through their leaves. This situation can be averted by spraying the cuttings with a liquid plastic, known correctly as an antidessicant, which is sold under a variety of trade names. This material comes either as a concentrate, which must be diluted and then applied with some sort of sprayer, or already mixed for use in a pump bottle.

When applied to the cutting's foliage (it is essential to thoroughly coat both tops and bottoms of the leaves or needles), an antidessicant temporarily seals the pores through which moisture normally escapes. Antidessicants can also be used on softwood or semihardwood cuttings of both deciduous and evergreen plants, particularly those with large leaves, which are especially susceptible to wilting.

medium. Insert the cuttings so that the bud just shows above the surface. Take about 12 cuttings for each 6-in (15-cm) pot.

With camellias, a leaf-bud cutting should contain only a small bud with a leaf and a sliver of wood attached — the sliver being scooped out of the parent stem with a sharp knife. Insert these cuttings in the rooting medium, pressing them in lightly until only the leaf shows on the surface.

Water both types of leaf-bud cuttings very lightly after insertion. Cover the pot with wires and a plastic hood, as for tip cuttings, to provide a humid atmosphere. Then place it in a greenhouse, cold frame, or sun porch.

Six months later, knock out the rooted cuttings from the pot and gently separate them. Place potting soil in the bottom of the necessary number of 3½-in (9-cm) pots — one for each cutting.

Stand the rooted cutting centrally in the pot, then top up with soil until the cutting is covered to just below the original leaf. Press the soil down firmly so that the surface is about ½ in (1.5 cm) below the rim, to allow for watering. Generously water the soil and keep the pot in a greenhouse or frame. Never let the soil dry out.

In 3 to 6 weeks, the roots should reach the outside of the soil. Hardy species can now be planted out in the open from zone 8 southward. Less hardy ones should be transplanted to a larger pot and kept in a greenhouse or frame during the following summer and winter before being planted outdoors in the spring.

HARDWOOD CUTTINGS OF DECIDUOUS SHRUBS

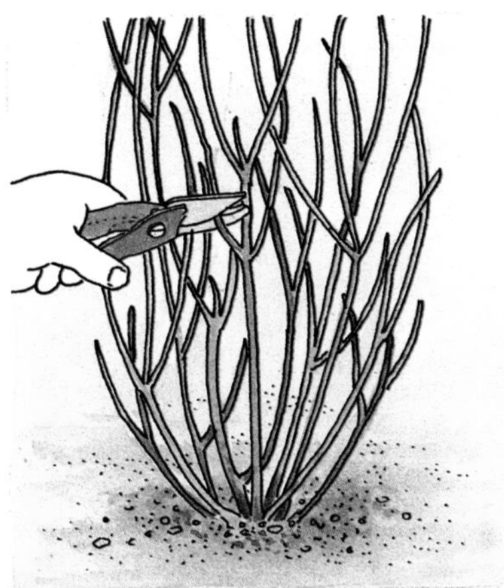

1 In midfall, choose a vigorous stem of the current year's growth — it should be hard and woody, and have small, dormant buds all along its length. Using pruning shears, cut the stem cleanly near its base.

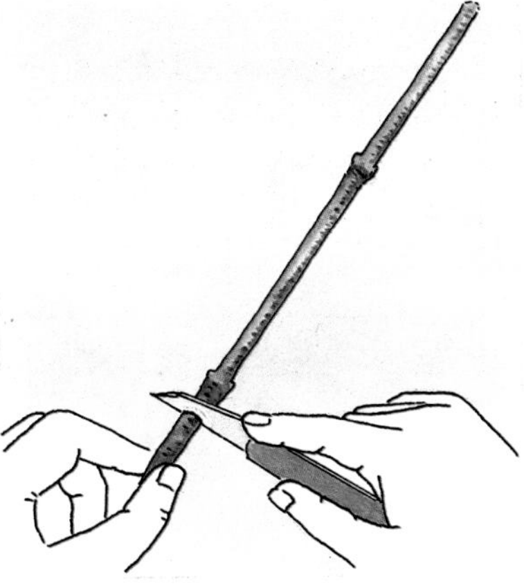

2 Using a sharp knife, trim the stem to 10-12 in (25-30 cm) in length, severing cleanly just below a bud or joint at the base and just above a bud at the top. Cut away from your fingers or lay the cutting on a board when trimming.

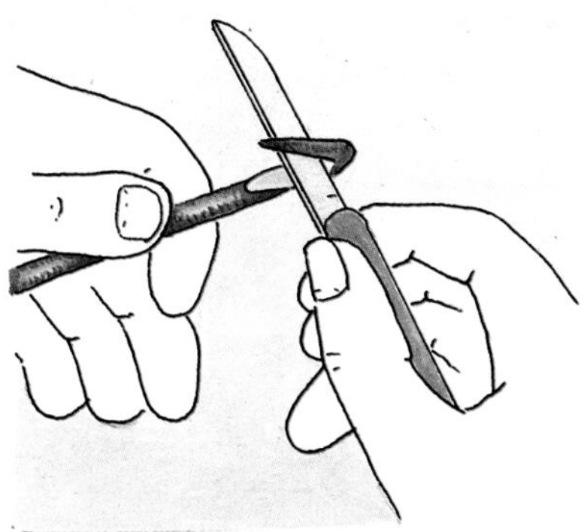

3 To aid rooting, slice off a thin sliver of bark and wood from near the base of each cutting, either on one side or opposite sides. A hormone rooting powder may also assist rooting.

4 Choose a site sheltered from north and east winds. Dig a V-shaped trench in open ground. Add a layer of sand to the bottom to aid drainage, and plant each cutting with its lower half below ground.

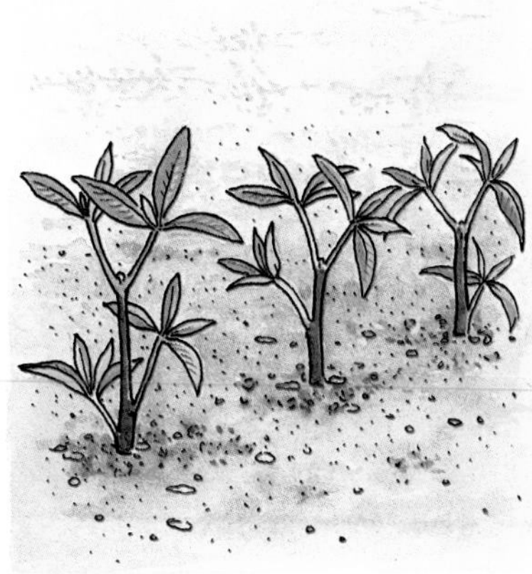

5 A year or two later, healthy shoots should have developed, and the rooted cuttings are then ready to be transplanted into their permanent positions in the garden.

Hardwood cuttings

These cuttings are vigorous stems that have just completed their first season's growth and have become hard and woody. They bear buds all along their length that will grow into new shoots the following spring.

The simplest way to propagate a large range of hardy shrubs and trees is to take hardwood cuttings in late fall and early winter. Except for watering in dry spells and weeding, no further attention is needed for one year. By then, the cuttings should have strong roots, and the young shrubs or trees can be planted in their permanent sites.

It is better to take the cuttings in midfall, when they have just stopped growing and are beginning their period of winter dormancy. There are some shrubs, however, that will grow from hardwood cuttings taken at any time in late fall or winter.

Before taking the cuttings, choose a site sheltered from north and east winds, and dig it thoroughly. If the soil is heavy, work in sharp sand or weathered ashes to help drainage and aeration. Make a narrow, V-shaped trench by pushing in a spade to its full blade depth and then pulling it forward for several inches. Place a layer of sharp sand, 1-2 in (2.5-5 cm) deep, in the bottom.

Use pruning shears to cut the stem near its base and then trim it to about 10-12 in (25-30 cm) in length. If the shoot is long, two or more cuttings may be made from it. Avoid using the soft, thin tip, as it may not root at all.

Sever each cutting cleanly just below a bud or joint at the base, and just above a bud at the top end. Cut evergreens below and above a leaf, and remove all the leaves on the lower half.

With large-leaved plants, such as cherry laurel (*Prunus laurocerasus*), reduce each leaf by half its surface area, using a razor blade or sharp scissors. This procedure curtails water loss until the cutting is rooted.

Cuttings from difficult-to-root shrub species often respond to wounding — removing a thin sliver of bark on one side or opposite sides near the base of the cutting. You can also encourage rooting by dipping the cutting's base into a hormone rooting powder, making sure to cover the wounded area. Shake off any excess powder.

Plant the cuttings 3-4 in (7.5-10 cm) apart with 2 ft (60 cm) between the rows. Stand the cuttings on the sand so that the lower half or two-thirds is below ground. Fill the trench with soil.

After severe frosts, cuttings can become loosened. Push each cutting down with your thumb or finger to ensure that the base is still in close contact with the soil.

In early spring, press the soil down again. One year later, all the easier-rooting cuttings will be ready for lifting and setting in their permanent quarters in the garden. Leave species that are slower to root, or slower to grow, in the ground for another year.

Root cuttings

Some plants, both herbaceous and woody, readily produce shoots direct from their roots as a natural process, particularly at a point where damage has occurred. Consequently, pieces of severed root can be used as cuttings. These require less attention than semi-hardwood or softwood cuttings.

Shrubs that grow well from root cuttings include sumac *(Rhus)*, smoke tree *(Cotinus)*, spirea, and ornamental brambles *(Rubus)*. Lift the entire plant in late winter or early spring, using a garden fork, or unearth part of a large root system. Then, with pruning shears, cut off the thicker roots close to the main stem or root.

Using a knife, cut pieces about 1½ in (4 cm) long from these roots. Cut each piece straight across the top (nearest to the main stem of root), and at an angle at the base — it will help you to remember which way up to plant them.

Perennials can be increased as well from root cuttings that have been taken during the plant's dormant season. Thick and fleshy rooted plants, such as bleeding heart *(Dicentra)*, Oriental poppy *(Papaver orientale)*, anchusa, and California tree poppy *(Romneya)*, are well suited to this method of propagation.

Lift the plants before the period of rapid spring growth and cut healthy roots into pieces 2-3 in (5-7.5 cm) long. Make a straight cut across the root close to the crown, and a slanted cut at the other end.

Fill pots to a level just below the rim with sterilized potting soil, and make small planting holes with a dibble or ice-cream stick to the same depth as the cuttings. Insert the cuttings, straight cut uppermost, so that the top is level with the surface of the soil. A 5-in (12-cm) pot will accommodate about six cuttings. Cover them with about ¼ in (6 mm) of sharp sand and spray them with water.

Fibrous-rooted herbaceous plants are often increased from root cuttings; it is a method used particularly for the perennial phlox to inhibit the spread of destructive stem nematodes.

Lift the plants during dormancy and cut the selected roots into short pieces, about 2 in (5 cm) long — it is not necessary to distinguish between the top and the bottom of the cuttings. Lay them flat on the surface of a box that has been filled with screened, peat-enriched potting soil and cover lightly with sand.

All types of root cuttings should be kept in a cold greenhouse or closed frame during the winter. By spring, the cuttings should have rooted well and begun to develop leaves. Knock them out of their box and separate them carefully before putting them in 3-in (7.5-cm) individual pots filled with sterilized potting soil. As an alternative, replant them in rows in an outdoor nursery bed.

By the following fall, the young plants should be sturdy enough to be moved to their permanent quarters in the garden.

ROOT CUTTINGS

1 Lift the entire plant or expose a section of the plant's root system. With pruning shears, cut off a thick root near the main stem, or close to a larger main root.

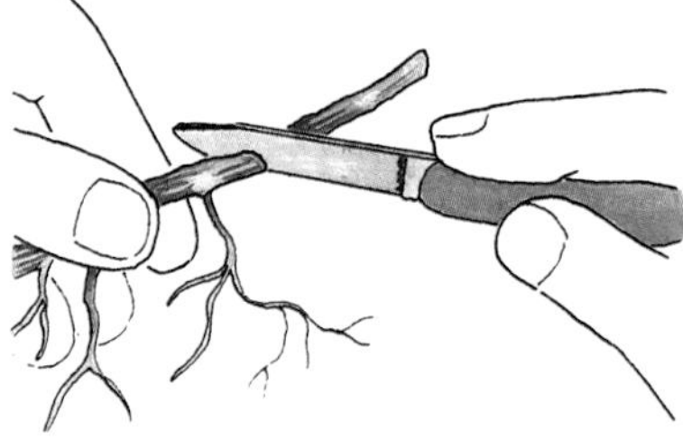

2 With a knife, cut pieces of root about 1½ in (4 cm) long — longer if the roots are thin — cutting straight across at the top but at an angle across the bottom.

3 Plant the root pieces in pots of rooting medium, angled end down, so that the tops are flush with the surface. Cover with a thin layer of sand.

4 Six months later, move the developing plants into individual 3½-in (9-cm) pots of sterilized, general-purpose potting soil. Press the soil down, then water.

IRRIGATING YOUR GARDEN

Rainfall is often insufficient to supply the garden with all the water it needs. To survive, plants depend on water.

Few plants survive for very long without water — even desert cacti and succulents, which store water in swollen stems and leaves, need a long drink from time to time. Temperature, soil condition, and wind also influence each plant's water requirements.

Not only must the frequency of watering be regulated to suit your plants, but the quantity supplied at any one time, together with the droplet size, should be correctly adjusted. Excess water causes waterlogging, which is as bad for plants as drought. Under waterlogged conditions, oxygen cannot reach the roots, which suffocate, killing the plant.

Insufficient water results in retarded growth. Plants can absorb nutrients from the soil only in solution with water, so they not only dehydrate in dry soils but starve as well. Without water, leaf pores close to restrict moisture loss from the plant. This action limits carbon dioxide intake; in turn, the plant is less able to manufacture the sugars that are their food. The plant's growth subsequently suffers.

Soil should be watered deeply enough to reach the plant roots. Frequent but insufficient watering merely dampens the soil surface — it does not penetrate to the soil layer where most roots are formed. It's better to water thoroughly once or twice a week than to give a little water several times a week. Even under drought conditions, a lot of water applied once a week is still the best remedy.

Before using water for your garden from the municipal supply system, check with your local water utility. There may be permanent restrictions on the times and days when you may irrigate, or temporary restrictions that are imposed during periods of water shortage or drought.

Susceptible plants

All plants, however deep their roots, can be adversely affected by drought. Those that have been recently put outdoors, as well as shallow-rooted plants, such as bedding annuals and vegetables, are at the greatest risk from water shortage. Plants grown

▼ **Oscillating sprinklers** Ideal for lawns, this sprinkler gives an even, gentle coverage of spray that moves automatically from side to side. The height and speed of the spray can be adjusted.

WATERING CANS AND HOSES

The choice of watering cans is huge; they are mostly made from plastic or galvanized metal. For garden use, cans that hold 1¾-2¼ gallons (7-9 liters)are ideal, but smaller ones are easier to handle, especially if you have back trouble or need to stretch up or across to reach the plants.
Choose a small can with a long spout for watering hanging baskets — some have a directional sprinkler head that can be turned downward for aiming into a high container, or upward to deliver a gently arching sprinkle onto seedlings at ground level.
Cassette hose reels are convenient to store — the hose squashes flat when not in use and rolls into an enclosed drum. They come complete with a faucet connector and a spray nozzle. It is sometimes difficult, however, to drain out all the water before rolling the hose back into the cassette.
Conventional hoses may be stored on a reel, which can be free-standing, on wheels, or fixed to a wall. Snap-on/snap-off connectors attach to any hose and eliminate the trouble of screwing accessories on and off as you move around to water the different areas of your garden.

COLLECTING RAINWATER

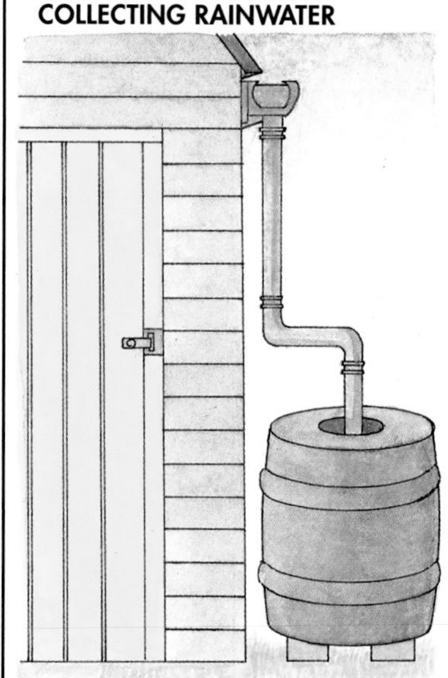

Rainwater is softer than most tap water, so it doesn't crust the soil — a common problem when watering pots from a faucet. Collect rainwater by directing the flow from a shed, garage, or house gutter via a downspout into a barrel. To allow room for a watering can to be placed under the barrel's tap, stand the barrel on bricks or concrete blocks. Always keep the top of the barrel covered.

close to a high wall — within 2 ft (60 cm) — are also vulnerable.

Slow-growing plants, such as many trees and shrubs, need regular watering during the growing season for a couple of years after planting. Some flowering plants, however, produce a better show of blooms when kept on the dry side — moist conditions encourage leaf growth, but few flowers. These include nasturtiums (*Tropaeolum majus*) and mesembryanthemums, or Livingstone daisies (*Mesembryanthemum criniflorum*).

Salad vegetables demand a lot of water to grow quickly and to be sweet and tender when picked. If lettuces or beets, for example, are too dry, they quickly "go to seed" — forming flowers and fibrous, tough growth. Excessive watering, however, can reduce the flavor of vegetables, so you must achieve a balance between the two.

Container plants require frequent watering. Hanging baskets are especially prone to dry out in sunny weather, and ceramic and terra-cotta pots lose water faster than plastic ones.

Soil types

Sandy soils and those that are low in organic content dry out fast, while clay soils retain the most water but quickly become waterlogged. Well-balanced loam holds a good quantity of water and is also open textured and more resistant to waterlogging.

The long-term use of inorganic fertilizers can also hinder water uptake from the soil. Where possible, use organic fertilizers (p.20).

When spraying water, large droplets or high pressure break down the soil surface. As it dries, a surface "crust" forms that blocks the entry of subsequent water and chokes out air. On a slope, large droplet size or rapid application of water also causes erosion — valuable topsoil washes to the bottom. With good watering equipment, it is possible to adjust the spray to suit the situation.

When to water

Should foliage become dull, it is an indication that water is needed. If you wait until leaves and stems wilt, the plant's growth will suffer. Check the soil's moisture content 2-4 in (5-10 cm) below the surface. Dig a small hole with a trowel — the soil at the bottom should be moist to the touch and darker than the surface soil.

The amount of water required to restore the correct soil-moisture level varies considerably. Small shrubs may need about 1 gallon (4 liters) per plant and a tree may need 4 gallons (15 liters) or more. Smaller plants are best given a watering that covers their entire planting area, about 2-4 gallons (8-15 liters) per sq yd/m.

When planting out delicate seedlings — including vegetables — set them in a shallow depression, rather than level with the surface, press in very gently, then water in with a watering can until a puddle forms in the "well."

Choosing watering equipment
You won't need a lot of expensive equipment for the average-sized garden. The simplest irrigation system is a watering can, but you will be surprised at how quickly a couple of bucketfuls of water can disappear into parched soil, necessitating several trips to and from the garden faucet. A can is best for localized watering of newly planted or specimen items.

A better solution for large areas is to use a garden hose, ideally one that is fitted with an on/off switch at the garden end so that you can regulate the supply as you work your way around the garden. But hand watering can be time consuming — it may take several hours to water a large garden properly, even with a hose.

Better still, you can connect your garden hose to a sprinkler — either a simple static type or one of the more sophisticated oscillating or pulsating types, some of which will also travel across lawns. The advantage of even the simplest type of sprinkler over hand watering is the volume of water it can deliver unattended, but there is the drawback of having to extend and rearrange the hose run as you water different parts of the garden.

A more efficient answer is a permanent in-ground system, which can be turned on and off as needed to deliver precisely the right amount of water exactly where it is required. Such systems are a common sight on golf courses and in public parks. If you are willing to take on the expense and work, you can install an irrigation system in your own garden.

Watering cans are available in many shapes, sizes, and colors,

SPRINKLER TYPES

1 The static sprinkler is the simplest of all. Water distribution is the same as with a standard hand-held nozzle — a circular pattern covering up to 35 ft (11 m) across — but this type has a spike for securing into the ground.

2 Revolving sprinklers have two or three rotating arms that produce a circular spray of fine water droplets up to 45 ft (13.5 m) across. Some models have a static vertical spray in the center to complete the area covered by the spray.

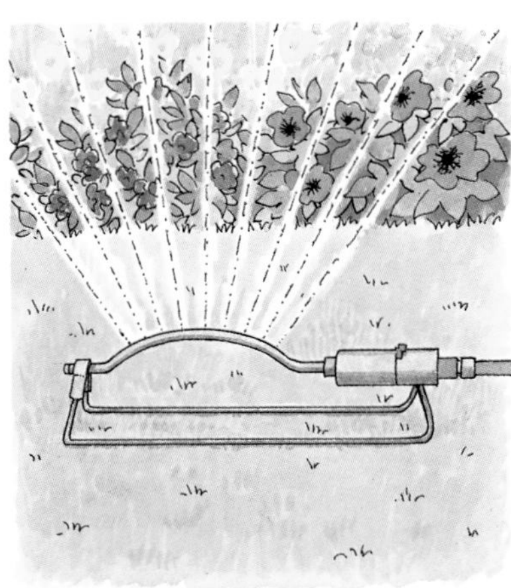

3 Oscillating sprinklers produce a rectangular spray coverage up to 55 x 40 ft (17 x 12 m). They have a tube or barrel bored with holes that oscillates slowly from side to side.

4 Impulse sprinklers give an even wider coverage by spraying in one direction only at any one time. The jet rotates through 360° in a series of strong automatic pulses.

5 This type of sprayer holds the nozzle high off the ground and gives a gentle "rain" of water — excellent for seedbeds and young vegetables. Several sprayers can be linked together in a chain.

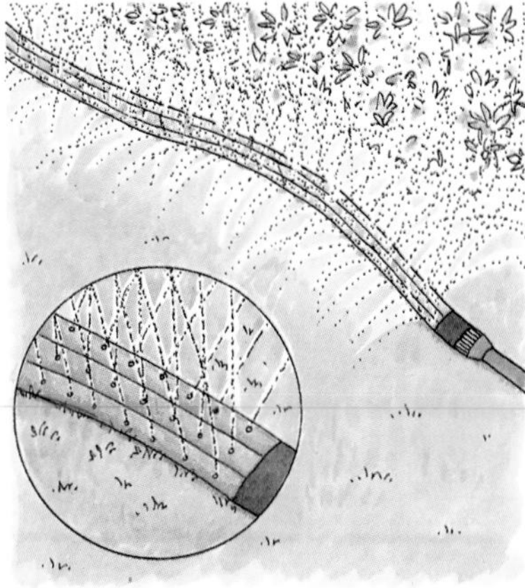

6 Soaker hoses give a gentle "rain" effect and can be woven easily through flower or vegetable beds. This type consists of a flat hose perforated on the upper surface with thousands of tiny holes.

and can be plastic or galvanized metal. Spouts, sprinkler heads, and handles vary according to brand. Some cans have detachable heads with alternative spray patterns — giving a fine, medium, or coarse spray. If you intend to use the can to apply herbicides, choose one with volumes marked on the side to help you dilute quantities accurately. Cans with two handles are easier to balance and maneuver. When watering-in large plants, remove the head and use the open-ended spout, holding it close to the planting hole.

Garden hoses provide a convenient means of applying a large amount of water to the garden with minimal effort. Hose is sold in various lengths — 25 ft (7.5 m), 50 ft (15 m), and 100 ft (30 m) are the most common — and in internal diameters of ½ in (13 mm), ⅝ in (16 mm), or ¾ in (19 mm). Though they may be made of rubber, vinyl, or plastic, what distinguishes a good hose is the number of "plys" (reinforcing layers) between the inner core and the outer skin. The best-quality types have two or more plys and will give years of service.

You can make do with a simple open-ended hose, using your thumb to regulate the flow of water. But you can greatly improve its effectiveness with a nozzle that can be adjusted to give various spray patterns or a single jet. Types giving a fine spray are best, since soil can absorb small droplets more quickly than large ones, and you are also less likely to damage delicate, young plants.

In addition, most nozzles and spray guns incorporate a trigger or on/off switch, which makes it easier to water selectively. The best nozzles are brass, but plastic ones can work equally well.

You can make it far easier to connect lengths of hose, or to secure attachments to the hose, by screwing a snap-on coupling into both the hose and accessory ends. This device makes it easy to unplug and reconnect individual sections of hose, change nozzles, or attach sprinklers of various patterns. Couplings come in male and female parts, like plumbing pipes. Once they are installed, it is simple to snap the female coupling at the end of the hose onto the male coupling on the faucet, and to snap the female coupling of the sprinkler onto the male coupling at the hose's other end. Some hose connectors incorporate what is known as a shutoff valve; it cuts off the flow of water through that section of hose if you disconnect the coupling.

To avoid dragging a hose inadvertently across plants, insert short stakes at the corners of flower and vegetable beds. Slip a length of plastic pipe over each stake to form a guide roller.

Soaker hoses wet the soil directly around them, losing little water through evaporation. Some soaker hoses are perforated with hundreds of tiny holes; others are made of recycled rubber and "sweat" water into the surrounding ground. Once positioned, soaker hoses can be left running until the irrigation is complete. But they tend not to provide uniform irrigation, since they deliver more water at the beginning of their run than at the end. Readjusting the position of the hose can solve that problem.

Sprinklers are available in many types. Attached to a garden hose, they water the garden while you engage in some other activity. By applying a fine spray over a long period, you can thoroughly moisten the soil without creating puddles and surface crusting. Use sprinklers in the evening or morning to reduce evaporation caused by the hot sun. Leave a sprinkler on until every area has had at least 1 in (2.5 cm) of water — stand empty cans in the spray area to check the amount. Lawns and vegetable plots in particular are best watered in this way.

Timer units are also available, though the price is high for the more accurate electronic ones. However, simple mechanical timers that work reasonably well may be found through catalogs or at garden centers. The mechanical types must be set before every watering; the electronic ones can

Soaker hoses Often made from recycled tires, these deliver water slowly and directly to the soil. Make a shallow depression in the soil and lay a soaker hose in it, snaking it around plants if necessary. Cover the hose with a light layer of mulch.

IN-LINE EMITTER

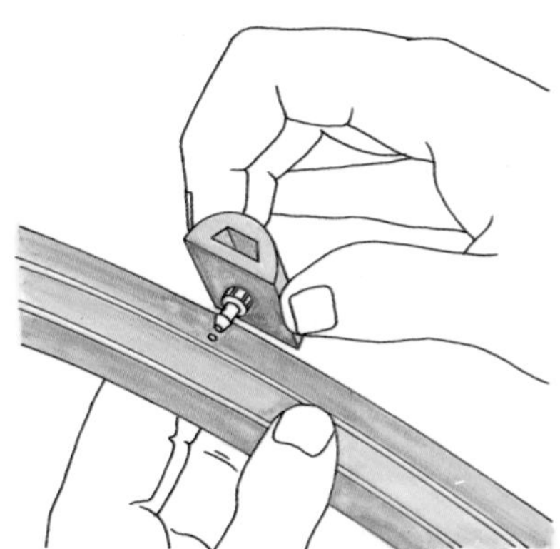

These emitters, which pop into a hole punched into a supply hose, make a drip irrigation system that is easy to install and take care of. Self-cleaning types cost a little more but do not get plugged up, simplifying maintenance.

be programmed to water for a full week. In either case, once set, the sprinkling is automatic, since the timer turns the water off when the irrigation is completed.

Simple static sprinklers are the cheapest; they can sometimes be mounted on a pole among tall plants, but their circular spray pattern makes it difficult to get even coverage on lawns. Rotating types generally cover a larger space, and can often be adjusted to vary the area watered, from a narrow wedge shape to a full circle. Oscillating types deliver water in a rectangular pattern, which may be preferable if you have a square or rectangular lawn.

Drip irrigation is an efficient system for watering a small area. Using a complex array of special plastic hoses or pipes connected by Y- or T-connectors, it feeds water, drop by drop, via special drip emitters to individual plants in the garden or greenhouse. The advantage of this system is that it virtually eliminates waste through evaporation. And because drip emitters deliver water so slowly — often no more than half a gallon (a few liters) per hour — they rarely generate runoff, even on heavy soils. Drip systems do require regular maintenance because the emitters plug easily. To prevent this problem, the lines must be flushed out at least once a month to cleanse them of accumulating grit.

Irrigation systems

The disadvantage of sprinklers and other movable irrigation devices is that you must change their positions, and turn them on and off. The ideal garden watering system is a permanent or semi-permanent installation that you can use as required.

There are two basic types of irrigation system you can install. One has flexible hoses laid on the surface, from which other hoses branch off via T-couplings to feed individual areas. You simply attach miniature spray and drip emitters along the feeder lines, turn on the water, and leave the system to water the garden. The other type consists of a network of underground pipes that feeds fixed spray heads and other watering devices positioned at intervals around the system.

Flexible systems

Flexible irrigation systems are a good choice if you redo your landscaping often, since you can easily adapt the irrigation layout accordingly. The main supply line — in reality, just special hose — is laid on or just below the soil surface, with T's connecting feeder lines as your layout demands. Then all you have to do is attach spray heads and drip emitters to the supply and feeder lines, either using special snap-on connectors or by screwing them into holes pierced in the wall of the hose.

Various types of spray heads are available, offering spray patterns of different sizes and shapes. Drip emitters can be connected to feeder lines, which are lengths of small-diameter plastic tubing that take water to individual plants some distance away from the main supply line. These lines are almost invisible if covered with a little soil.

The main difference between fixed and flexible systems is the water pressure; flexible systems

INSTALLING A FLEXIBLE IRRIGATION SYSTEM

1 A flexible watering system operates on low pressure, so fit a pressure regulator and water filter onto the main supply line just below the faucet to adjust for the correct pressure. An electronic timer can be attached to regulate watering times.

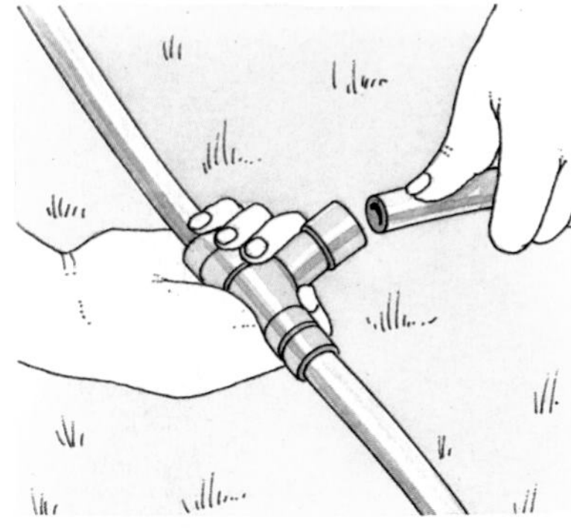

2 Lay out the feeder, or branch, lines and attach them to the main supply line, following the plan you drew up on paper. When the feeder lines are securely attached, run water through the system to flush out any debris.

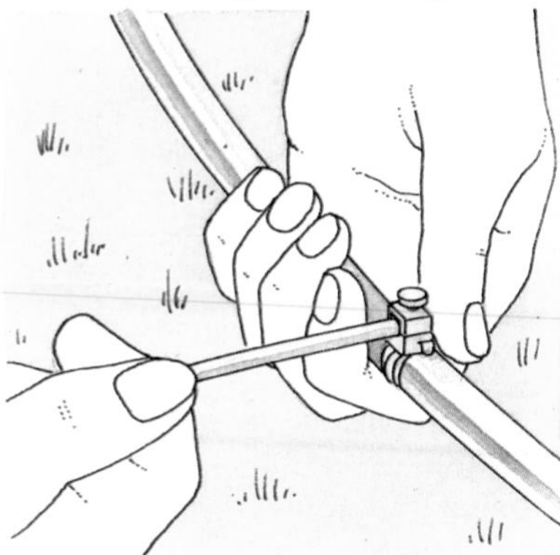

3 Drill holes in the main supply line and feeders lines, where needed. Attach drip emitter and spray connectors, taking into account the different watering requirements of your plants.

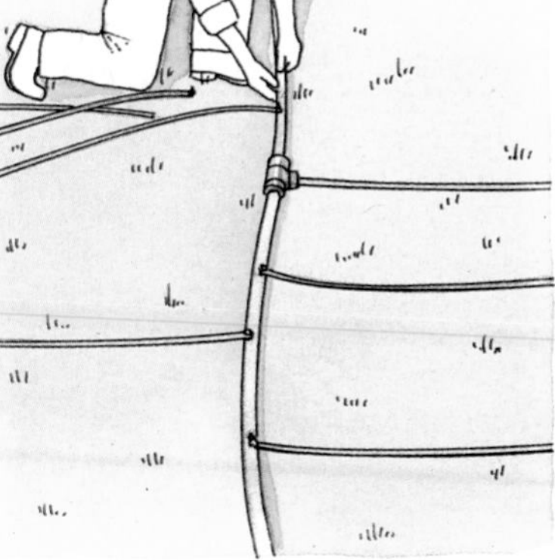

4 Complete the entire hose line, flush out the system a second time, ensuring that all connectors work. The system can be covered, but see that the ends of the feeder lines remain above the ground.

INSTALLING A FIXED IRRIGATION SYSTEM

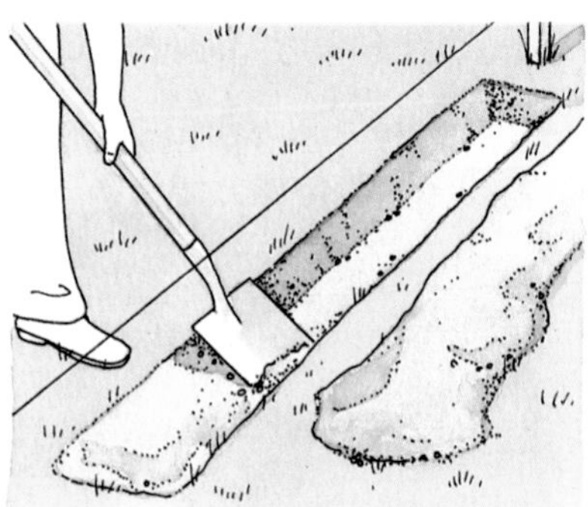

1 Mark out and stake the area of the garden you are irrigating, then dig a trench 8 in (20 cm) deep. Line the bottom of the trench with sand or screened soil, keeping it as level as possible. Remove stones and any pieces of root.

2 Lay the main supply line at the bottom of the trench, then fit the antisiphon device at the point where you are taking the supply off the main water source. It is important to ensure that the joint is watertight.

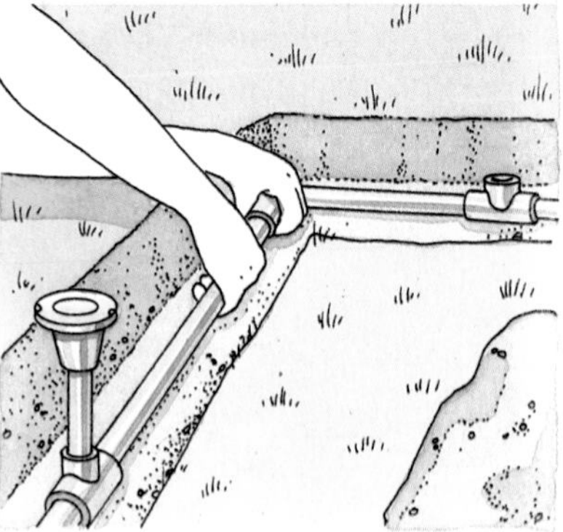

3 Attach the spray heads to the main supply line wherever they will be needed. Attach elbows and T's for the feeder lines. Allow the solvent-welded joints to dry for at least 6 hours, but for safety, preferably longer.

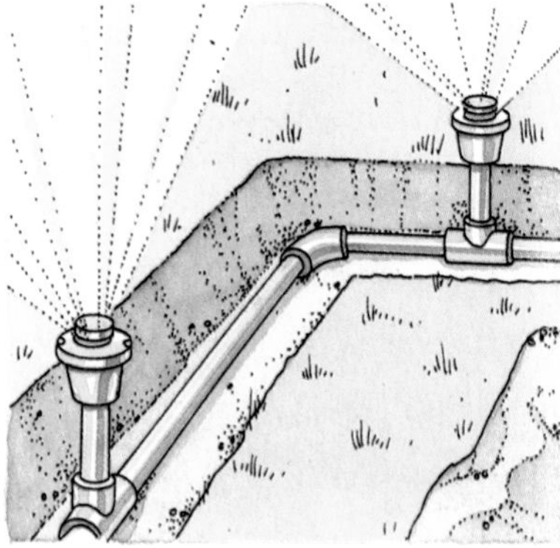

4 Once all the joints have set hard, turn on the water supply to test the antisiphon device, to flush out any debris that may have gotten into the pipes, and to check for any leaks that may exist in the system.

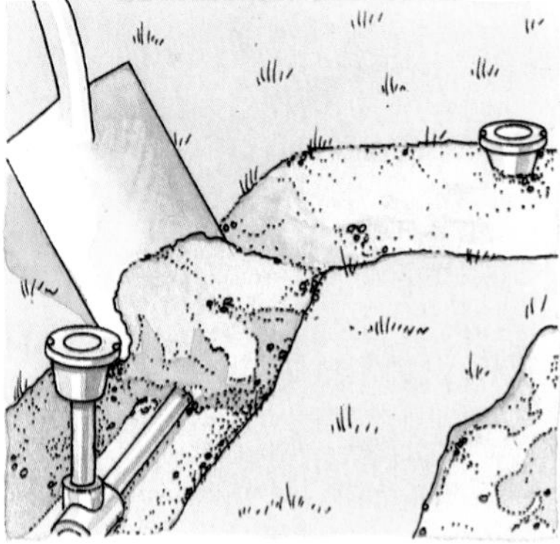

5 Once you are satisfied that everything is working well, and there are no leaks, backfill all the trenches with soil above ground level, taking care not to clog spray heads with loose earth — if you do, the system will not work.

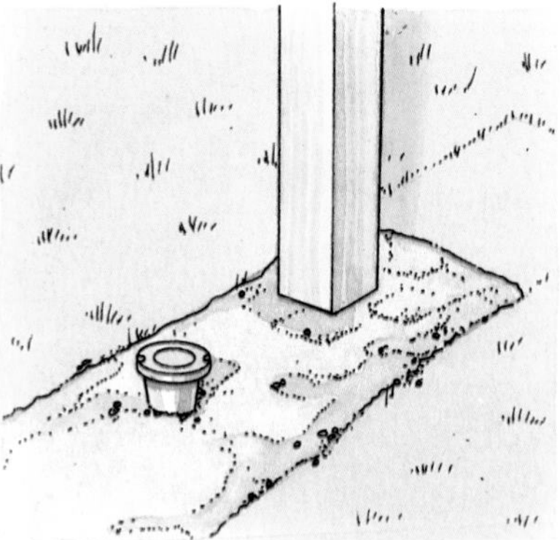

6 With a stiff board or some similar object, tamp and press the soil down around the spray heads, leaving them about 1 in (2.5 cm) above the surface. Take great care not to hit the heads as you do so.

operate on fairly low-pressure water — you fit a pressure regulator onto the main supply line just after it leaves the main water source, and adjust it to give the flow rates you require at the various connectors. The other difference is that the connectors in the flexible system can easily become blocked by particles of sand, soil, and other debris, so a water filter is usually fitted just after the pressure regulator. Clean this filter at regular intervals to reduce the risk of a blockage.

Fixed systems

A fixed underground system is the best choice if the basic layout and the positions of your flower beds and individual plants are unlikely to change in the near future. Several manufacturers provide spray heads, drip emitters, and other components; you supply and fit the system pipework, which is usually run in rigid PVC with fixed elbows and T's, just like solvent-welded indoor plumbing.

First of all, decide where the main supply lines will be needed. Draw a scale diagram of the garden on graph paper. Indicate where the main spray heads will be required — down each side of the lawn, for example, so their spray patterns overlap — and plan feeder lines where they are needed to supply water to individual areas or plants. Then you can work out how many spray heads, drip emitters, and other components you require, and also how much pipe and fittings to buy.

Your local plumbing codes may require you to fit an antisiphon device at the point where you take your supply off the main water outlet; otherwise, dirty or polluted water could siphon back into the household supply. Check the codes to find out about any requirements for the antisiphon device, for pipe dimensions, and whether you need a drain to empty the system during winter.

You will need trenches about 8 in (20 cm) deep. Begin at the point where the system is connected to the main water supply and work outward, laying the pipe in place on a bed of sand. Join elbows, pipe joints, and T-connectors as required. Add T's pointing upward where necessary to supply spray heads or drip emitters.

When all the joints are firmly connected, turn on the water supply and flush it through to clear out any debris in the pipes and to provide a visual check for any leaks. When you are sure that everything works, backfill all the trenches. Make sure all the spray heads are above the ground.

SUPPORTING AND TRAINING

Many plants need support, especially in exposed sites. Choose a kind of staking that is as unobtrusive as possible.

In exposed areas, prevailing winds can do a lot of damage to floppy or top-heavy plants — whether they are annuals, perennials, bulbs, shrubs, or trees. A few can't support themselves, even in the most secluded spot. Others give a longer-lasting and more pleasing appearance when propped up but can be left to sprawl, if you prefer.

In all cases, if you do have to support a plant, choose materials that are as inconspicuous as possible — you don't want to draw attention away from your planting scheme.

Simple ties

There is a range of ties available — make sure you select the correct one for the type of plant you want to support.

Soft green twine is an ideal tie for soft-stemmed plants. It can be cut to any length and is quite strong when new — though it generally rots after one season. The color also blends well with foliage. Rolls of twine usually contain about 100 ft (30 m).

Raffia is a good alternative to twine for tying indoor plants and small outdoor types, but it lacks the strength for supporting larger outdoor plants. Plastic raffia is also available; it is somewhat stronger than the natural raffia.

Wire-cored plastic ties are available in a continuous reel form or pieces suitable for tying individual stems to a stake. These ties are strong and durable, but can cut into soft stems.

Wire rings are useful for holding thin, woody stems to a cane. The rings can be pulled apart, looped around individual stems and supports, then squeezed back into their original shape. Because they can cut into the stem or pull open in windy conditions, they are appropriate only for indoor plants.

▼ **Staking border plants** Supports should be in place early in the year before tall growth has the opportunity of flopping. Galvanized wire ring supports, together with link stakes at the edge, keep many perennials upright but natural looking.

Bamboo canes

The most common supports for soft-stemmed border perennials, biennials, annuals, and the taller bulbs, corms, and tubers are bamboo canes. They are often dyed green, giving a natural appearance. They're also strong and long lasting. Moreover, they are readily available in various lengths and thicknesses from garden centers, and are inexpensive. Use them to support single stems or groups of plants from 2 ft (60 cm) to about 4-5 ft (1.2-1.5 m) in height.

Canes should be tall enough to reach just below the flower spikes, so check the ultimate height of each plant before staking. Remember that you will need an extra 6-12 in (15-30 cm) for anchoring it into the ground.

For a single-stemmed plant, insert one cane firmly in the ground as close to its base as possible without damaging the root or crown. Tie the stem to the cane with either raffia or twine. The tie should be tight enough not to slip down the stem or cane, but loose enough not to cut into the stem. As the plant grows, add further ties every 6-9 in (15-23 cm) along the cane.

For a group of stems, often produced by border perennials, insert three canes at equal distances around and close to the stems, tilting the canes slightly outward. Knot twine to one cane about 6-9 in (15-23 cm) above the ground, then loop the twine around the other two canes. Pull the twine taut and tie it again to the first cane. As the plants grow, tie additional lengths of twine around the canes at about 9-in (23-cm) intervals above the first.

Enclosure supports

Tall, floppy-stemmed plants can be supported by enclosing them in ready-made wire cages, or you can create a cylinder of wire mesh. Galvanized mesh is ideal for making cylinders; it can be bought in a green plastic-coated form for an unobtrusive appearance.

Cut enough mesh to make a cylinder just wide enough to enclose the whole group of plant stems. Insert three tall canes vertically in the soil, inside the cylinder. Tie each cane to the mesh at several points. Depending on the width of mesh used, as well as the ultimate height of the plant, you may need to add a second cylinder

SUPPORTS FOR BORDER PLANTS

1 Galvanized steel link stakes are ideal for supporting border perennials — herbaceous or evergreen — and annuals that are planted in an irregular pattern. They can be slotted together to make small enclosures or chains to suit any planting scheme.

2 Ring supports rest on a bamboo cane (about half the ultimate height of the plant) that is inserted close to the center of the plant. Push the wheellike support over the cane. Its height can be raised as the plant grows.

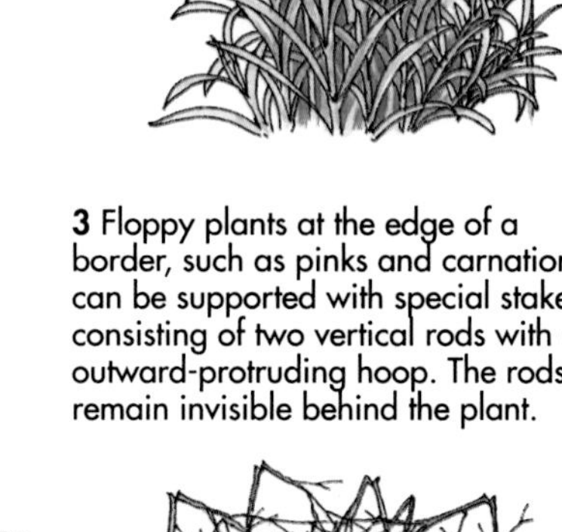

3 Floppy plants at the edge of a border, such as pinks and carnations, can be supported with special stakes consisting of two vertical rods with an outward-protruding hoop. The rods remain invisible behind the plant.

4 Cylinders made from galvanized wire mesh make good supports; install them early in the season so that stems and leaves have time to grow through and hide the structure.

5 Pea sticks are particularly suitable for wiry-stemmed plants that are difficult to tie individually. Interlace the upper twigs to make a close framework over the plants.

above the first; if so, ensure that the cylinders overlap and tie them together securely.

Link stakes made of galvanized metal are suitable for most border plants. They consist of a vertical rod topped with a hoop socket. With every upright comes a crossbar — which hooks into the socket. By hooking several together, you can construct chains — staggered or straight lines — rings, or combinations of the two to suit almost any planting scheme. Various heights are available; with some brands, it is possible to secure two or more rods on top of each other to add to their height.

Galvanized steel wire supports (plant props) are also available for single stems and for small groups of low, floppy stems, such as those of perennial pinks. They have a horizontal loop at the top that can be opened to allow stems to be slotted inside. Some types are adjustable in height in order to cradle heavy flowers such as those of tuberous begonias.

Metal or plastic ring supports are excellent for herbaceous border plants that send up new growths each year. One type slides onto a standard bamboo cane and is held in place by a clawlike clip, which maintains the ring in a horizontal position at almost any height. Others need three canes tied around the wheel edge for support. Rings should be inserted early in the season; as the stems and leaves grow, they will nicely conceal the rings.

THE CORRECT WAY TO TIE

First, loop a length of soft twine or raffia around the cane. Cross the ends between the stem and the cane, wrap them around the stem above a leaf joint, then knot the ends against the cane.

SUPPORTS FOR TREES AND STANDARD SHRUBS

1 Plastic strap ties, sold in various sizes, are suitable for standard roses or young trees. A spacing buffer prevents rubbing, and the buckle can be loosened as the trunk swells.

2 Also adjustable in length, ratchet-grip plastic cleats provide adequate support for thinner stems against a stake. However, they are difficult to release once in place.

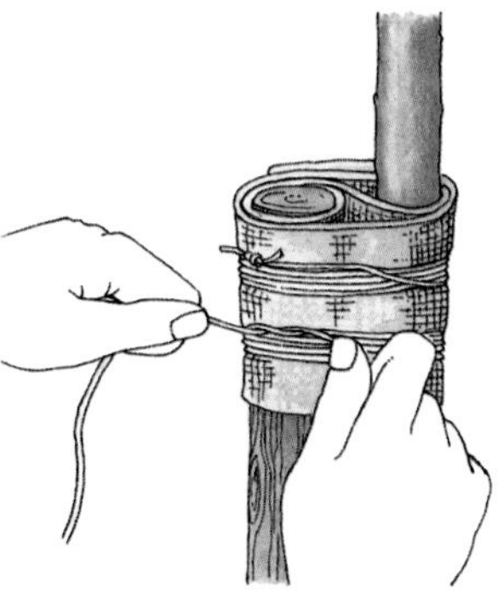

3 When using wire or strong string to tie a trunk to a stake, pad well with burlap; otherwise, the binder will cut into the bark. First, wrap the burlap around the stake, then around the stem and stake.

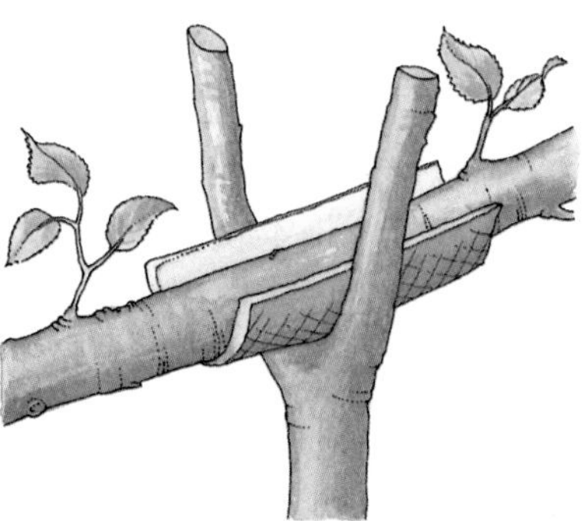

4 Prevent wide-spreading or old tree branches — or those heavily laden with fruit — from breaking by supporting them with a forked prop. Pad the prop with thick rubber or folded burlap.

Pea sticks

Traditionally used for supporting peas, these props are easy to make yourself. They are usually the trimmings from small trees and hedges that have been cut back. Almost any tree or shrub can provide good twigs — avoid those that are brittle and break clean with a sharp snap.

Use pea sticks to stake bushy plants up to 2 ft (60 cm) tall that may be exposed to wind damage — mainly annuals and herbaceous perennials. They must be inserted in spring while plants are small. Choose a day when the soil is fairly workable — pea sticks have to be pushed into the soil and cannot be hammered in. They will break if you have to apply too much pressure.

Insert two or three pea sticks as close to the center of the plant as possible, pushing them deep enough to remain firm. If the plant is of a type that has a tendency to sprawl, or flop badly after rain, insert a few extra pea sticks around the perimeter.

At the expected height of the base of the flowers, break the tops of the pea sticks and bend them inward. Intermesh them to form a firm top to the frame.

Wooden stakes

Upright shrubs, standard roses, and young trees need sturdy stakes, especially in exposed gardens. Bamboo canes are not strong enough; instead, use wooden stakes of at least 1½ in (4 cm) in diameter — preferably about 2½-3 in (6-7.5 cm) in diameter for trees. Choose stakes made of rot-resistant wood or wood that has been pressure-treated with a nontoxic preservative.

When planting a tree or standard rose, insert the stake at the back of the planting hole, using a sledge if necessary, before positioning the plant's root ball. Never knock a stake into the ground once the plant is pressed

SUPPORTING CLIMBERS AND WALL SHRUBS

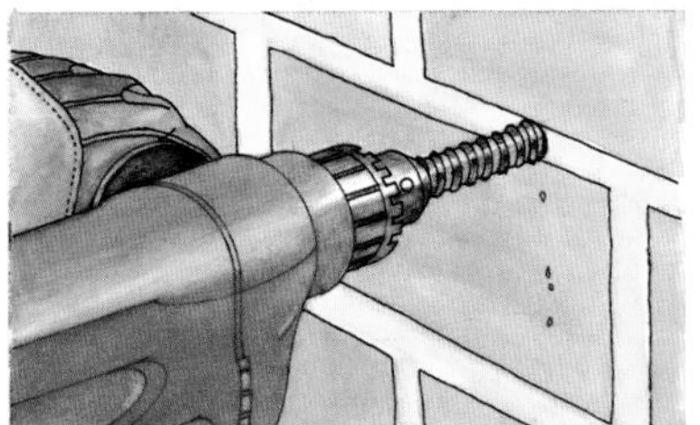

1 Horizontal wires stretched between screw eyes can provide the support needed to train woody-stemmed climbers up a masonry wall. To install screw eyes, first drill holes with a 5/16-in (8-mm) masonry bit.

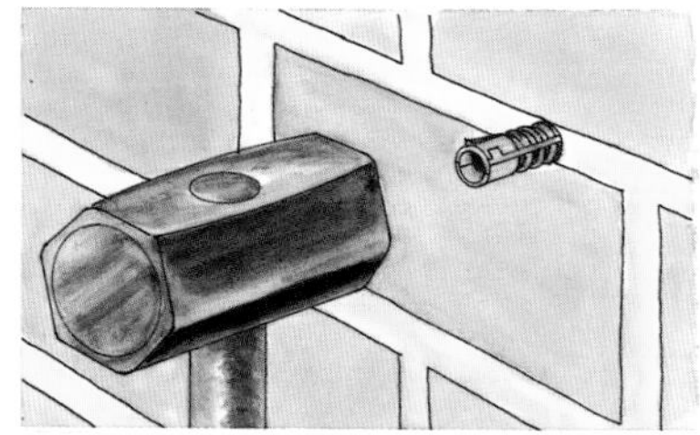

2 Drill the hole deep enough for a 5/16-in (8-mm) plastic anchor; clean out any debris and tap the anchor in with a hammer. For extraheavy climbers, such as an espaliered tree, substitute a lead sleeve for the anchor.

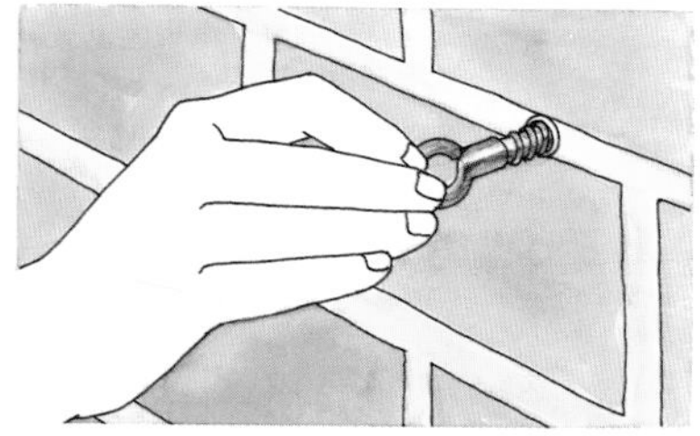

3 Twist a #12 screw eye into the anchor. Attach one end of braided wire to a screw eye with a bulldog clamp; cut to length and secure remaining end to other screw eye with a turnbuckle. Tighten turnbuckle to take up slack.

in — you may damage its roots. Select a stake that, once inserted into the ground, is long enough to stand level with the first horizontal branches.

The main stem or trunk must be tied firmly to the stake. There are several ready-made tree and rose ties available, the best being constructed of durable plastic or webbing straps with rubber sleeves. Loop the strap, at about 4 in (10 cm) below the branches, around the stem or trunk and through the buffer, which provides a cushion between the two. Pull the strap tight and fasten it against the stake, rather than fastening it against the tree.

Tall trunks, or those that are not very straight, may need two or more straps at intervals to prevent the trunk from rubbing against the stake.

Self-locking straps are also available. Design varies according to manufacturer, but most consist of a plastic chain or ratchet arrangement that can be pulled taut like a buckle, yet cannot easily slip undone.

An alternative method is to wrap burlap around the stake several times, and then wrap it around the trunk and stake so that there is a protective cushion between the two. Tie the girdle in place with one or two pieces of strong string or wire.

Straps should be checked frequently — at least twice a year, and always after wind storms. Retie any that have worked loose and slacken those that become too tight as the trunk swells with age.

Never tie a woody stem or trunk to a stake using wire alone — it will almost certainly cut into the bark, constricting the flow of nutrients up the wood from the roots and thus stunting growth.

Training wall plants

Support is necessary for all climbers and wall plants except ivy and Virginia creeper, which are self-clinging, but even these need help at first.

An inexpensive support for light plants can be made by stretching galvanized wire horizontally between screw eyes attached to a wall or fence. Place the first wire about 3 ft (1 m) above the ground and repeat every 9-12 in (23-30 cm) up the wall.

To support heavy wall plants, use stronger wire and tension bolts in conjunction with the screw eyes. Tie the plant to the wires using the same techniques as for tying to a cane.

Because of the siding, training wall plants up the side of a house may be a bit more complex. Vinyl and aluminum siding should not be pierced with any kind of hardware, and attaching screw eyes to wooden clapboards or shingles may encourage splitting. Instead, the best method is to affix panels of prefabricated wooden latticework to free-standing posts set next to the foundation.

In some areas, special masonry wall cleats are available. These consist of a toughened metal spike — which is hammered into a mortar joint — with a metal or plastic collar strap for bending or tying around the plant stem. They should be positioned at random wherever needed on the wall.

Other possible types of support include wooden trellises, panels of plastic-coated steel mesh, and all-plastic mesh. Fix these supports 1-2 in (2.5-5 cm) away from the wall on spacers to give twining plants room to weave in and out. Some plants, such as clematis, will cling by twisting their leaf stalks around the supports.

Many wall plants, however, must be tied to their supports. Any of the ties mentioned previously will be appropriate, depending on the diameter of the branches and the ultimate weight of the plant when it is fully grown.

Never plant close to a wall — the soil is usually too dry. Instead, set plants 1-1½ ft (30-45 cm) away from the wall and lead the young stems to the wall with one or more canes positioned in front of the stems to protect them from accidental damage.

WEEPING ROSE TRAINER

For a really unusual and pretty effect, a standard rose can be trained into a weeping umbrella-like shape. First, fix a special framework over the plant. Then tie in each branch to the underside of the frame; you may need to hard prune the rose to encourage new, malleable stems. Both flowers and foliage will grow through and around the trainer.

PINCHING AND DEADHEADING

To promote bushy growth with a magnificent show of flowers, many plants must be pinched, disbudded, or deadheaded, as well as cared for in other ways.

Left alone, the majority of soft-stemmed plants — annuals, biennials, bulbs, corms, tubers, and perennials — will develop a reasonable shape, with a good display of flowers. Woody plants, on the other hand, usually need some routine pruning in order to produce and maintain an attractive shape, and to retain vigor for subsequent growth.

However, all plants traditionally grown for exhibition — such as chrysanthemums, dahlias, and carnations — and many others besides, bring forth much better or larger individual flowers or heads of flowers if the growth of shoots and buds is carefully controlled from an early stage. Likewise, many foliage plants can be trained into a more pleasing shape when shoot growth is modified.

Pinching

The process of removing the growing tip of a plant to encourage the formation of side shoots and control the flowering habit is called pinching. For example, chrysanthemums and carnations are commonly treated in this way, both in the greenhouse and in garden cultivation. Some side shoots may require further pinching at a later date — known as the second pinching.

When setting out small, young plants in their final growing site — annuals and biennials in particular — pinch any that are not developing a compact, bushy shape naturally. Species that produce only one main stem, such as foxgloves and hollyhocks, do not require pinching.

When a young plant has become lanky through poor cultural conditions in the early stages of growth, it can often be

▼ **Deadheading annuals** Remove faded flowers regularly to keep plants neat and to prevent them from wasting energy in producing seeds. Deadhead with scissors or by hand.

PINCHING GARDEN PINKS

1 During the first growing season, young plants should be pinched once they develop 9 or 10 pairs of fully grown leaves.

2 At the sixth or seventh joint from the base, bend the stem sharply. If the stem does not snap cleanly, cut it as close to the joint as possible.

3 Side shoots will now emerge from each of the leaf joints. Their appearance delays flowering but creates much stronger growth.

4 The result is a bushy, shrublike plant, with a succession of flowers. Garden pinks should not be pinched again in subsequent years.

prompted to develop a better shape if the growing tip, together with one-third or more of the main stem, is pinched out. Don't be afraid to do so; soon the plant will respond with new bushiness. Restricting the plant's top growth may also redirect energy to the roots, enabling the transplanted specimen to anchor itself to the ground quicker.

Pinched plants produce new, soft side shoots immediately, and these shoots may be more susceptible to damage from cold or dampness than the rest of the plant. For this reason, don't pinch shoots any later than early fall — the new growths must have time to harden before the first frost. Plants should have several pairs of fully developed leaves before they are pinched. If they haven't reached this stage by early fall, postpone pruning until spring.

When buying plants from a nursery in the spring, check to see if the growing tips have already been pinched out. If they have not, wait for a damp morning so that the stems will be full of moisture and easier to break.

The growing tip will usually snap off cleanly — grasp the stem between finger and thumb at the base of a leaf joint, then place your other hand just above the joint and bend the stem sharply down. If it does not snap, bend the stem side to side at right angles. If this technique fails, do not pull at the stem; instead, cut it cleanly with a sharp knife as close above the joint as possible. It is better to remove the growing tip along with at least one pair of expanded leaves, or side shoots may appear only near the top.

Chrysanthemums must be pinched to get good flowers — when allowed to grow naturally, they develop into bushlike plants, with a mass of small flowers. Spray types normally produce side shoots on their own and don't require pinching.

Large-flowered dahlias send up strong center growths but exhibit little side growth until the center shoots develop flower buds. Two or three weeks after planting, pinch out the growing point — usually late spring or early summer. Six or more growing points will develop in the leaf axils during the next two weeks. Again, remove the top pair of shoots to promote vigorous growth in the lower side shoots.

The side shoots will each produce a bud at the tip — a terminal bud — with "wing" buds just below it. For large blooms, pinch off the wing buds when they are big enough to be removed without injuring the terminal bud. To encourage longer-stemmed side shoots and to stimulate growth in the upper part of a dahlia, cut off leaves that are on the main stem.

Pinching is also a useful technique for tomato growers in regions with shorter growing seasons. As soon as a plant has produced four trusses of fruit, cut off the growing point two leaves above the top truss. By forcing the plant to concentrate on fewer fruits, you increase the likelihood these fruits will ripen before the first frost strikes.

Disbudding

The procedure of removing unwanted buds so that all of a plant's energies can be directed into a few buds is known as disbudding. It is done to produce extra large sized blooms — particularly of carnations, chrysanthemums, dahlias, and roses grown for exhibition. As soon as they can be handled — when they are about the size of a pea — all the buds but one on each stem are taken off by rubbing them out between thumb and forefinger, or by cutting them off with a sharp knife.

When growing blooms for a specific date — an exhibition or a birthday, for instance — disbudding can be timed accordingly. To delay flowering of the main crown bud, allow side buds to grow on side shoots up to 2 in (5 cm) long before removing them. The time from securing the bud until the bloom is ready varies, according to the species and variety. With chrysanthemums, for example, this period is 6 to 9 weeks, depending on how often you fertilize them.

Plants that naturally produce sprays of flowers can be disbudded to ensure more uniform blooms. For example, with floribunda roses, remove the larger center buds and the smallest buds from each cluster.

Protecting blooms

When growing the highest-quality flowers for exhibition or cutting, it may be necessary to protect them from heavy rain, hail, and high winds. Staking early and correctly will help to minimize wind damage, as will a site sheltered from the prevailing wind.

To reduce wind damage further, plant or build windbreaks — hedging plants, wood, or plastic — around the growing area. Rigid plastic screens with a perforated or slatted construction give the best results, allowing air to pass through, but at a significantly slower speed. Solid structures, such as fences and walls, can create damaging turbulence around plants downwind of them.

For very valuable blooms, construct an open-sided wooden framework with a sloping roof around and over the plants. Cover the top with tough, clear plastic sheeting once the flower buds begin to show color — no earlier, or plants may develop weak, straggly stems because of the slightly reduced light.

Flowers rich in nectar can be destroyed by birds — especially spring-flowering crocuses. In most cases, the benefits the birds provide in devouring grubs, caterpillars, and other harmful insects will far outweigh any damage they may do. If the birds prove to be mainly herbivorous, you can discourage them by encircling the plants with unobtrusive sticks or canes, between which you stretch a web of black thread. Few birds risk getting trapped under the thread.

Deadheading

Dead flower heads should be removed from plants; otherwise, the plants' energy is diverted from producing more flowers to setting seeds. Deadheading flowers also gives a neater look to the garden and prevents the buildup of fungal spores in rotting material. Seed heads that are allowed to ripen can attract seed-eating birds, which can cause physical damage to other parts of the plant — African and French marigolds are frequently destroyed this way.

Deadheading of early-flowering perennials, such as delphiniums, lupines, and violas, will often encourage the plants to bloom a second time, later in the season.

Do not deadhead plants that are grown for decorative fruits or seed heads. If you want to save some seeds for the next season, allow one or two blooms to wither on each plant. Harvest the seeds when the pods are dry and ripe.

Soft-stemmed annuals and perennials can be deadheaded by hand. As soon as they fade, snap off flowers with a quick twisting motion. You will need scissors or pruning shears to deadhead those with tougher or wiry stems — do not tear the stem or loosen the roots by attempting to break stubborn stems by hand. Badly bruised or torn stems will die back and look unsightly, or kill the whole plant. Make all cuts diagonally, sloping away from a growth bud, so that water runs off.

Dead flower heads should not be put on the compost pile — any seeds that have ripened may remain dormant for up to several

PINCHING AND DISBUDDING CHRYSANTHEMUMS

1 To obtain the best blooms, pinch out the main stem above the top pair of fully developed leaves in late spring or very early summer.

2 New shoots appear from leaf axils on the stem. Pinch out unwanted shoots over several days, leaving six or eight to develop.

3 In early summer and midsummer, remove side shoots (which grow on the remaining side shoots) once they are about 1 in (2.5 cm) long.

4 By midsummer to late summer, a group of flower buds forms at the top of each side shoot. Pinch out the wing buds and their shoots to produce a bigger bloom on the central crown bud.

5 The result is an evenly branched, open plant, with earlier and bigger flowers. A chrysanthemum left to grow naturally produces a dense, bushy plant and many small flowers.

DEADHEADING

1 Lilies produce flowers on upright spikes that open from the base upward. Pinch faded blooms to improve appearance and stop seed formation, which weakens growth.

2 With annuals such as marigolds, either cut or snap off each flower as soon as it fades. This form of pruning encourages more blooms and increases plant vigor.

3 Regularly deadhead multiflowered roses, such as the shrub roses, climbers, and ramblers, by hand. Use a twisting action to maintain neatness, unless hips are desired in fall.

4 Hybrid tea roses and floribundas should be deadheaded with pruning shears. Cut just above a leaf that has an outward-facing bud in its axil, making a cut away from the bud.

5 With rhododendrons, break off the entire flower head once it has faded, gripping it between finger and thumb. Deadheading will help to produce the maximum number of flowers next year.

6 Perennial plants with bare flower stems, such as red-hot poker, should be deadheaded to ground level. If the stems bear foliage, however, trim to just below the top leaves.

years and germinate in unwanted places when the compost is spread around the garden. Instead, discard the "deadheads" with the trash.

The dead flower heads of certain plants can look attractive in fall or winter, and these can be left intact. The heads of many hydrangeas, for example, take on bronze and purple hues as the petals dry out. In addition, they provide some protection from winter frosts for sensitive, dormant growth buds — leave them on the plant until the following spring. The dead flower heads of summer heathers are also attractive.

Other factors

It is rich, fertile soil that generally produces the largest, lushest plants, but in some cases such soil can foster luxuriant foliage at the expense of flowers. Many annuals, including nasturtiums *(Tropaeolum majus),* can be disappointing on well-prepared soils. A sunny, dry spot with relatively poor soil can give much showier displays of flowers.

Succulent plants, such as stonecrops *(Sedum)* and mesembryanthemums, are reluctant to flower well when the soil is too moist — in nature, they may flower and subsequently set seeds only when the life of the plant is threatened by drought or intense heat. For the same reason, do not use fertilizers high in nitrogen on shy-flowering plants.

Recently, F1 hybrids — especially of annuals — have become popular. Many of these hybrids produce larger, showier flowers that may also be more resistant to rain, wind, and disease than open-pollinated flowers. For those annuals affected by any of these problems in previous years, switch to an F1 hybrid selection. It is pointless to save seed from such annuals; they do not breed true.

Siting is often very important in determining the display of flowers. A sun-loving plant grown in shade may exhibit a reasonable amount of healthy foliage, but few or no flowers. F2 hybrids — second-generation hybrids — also have improved flowering qualities over the open-pollinated varieties. They are not quite as spectacular as F1 hybrids, but the seeds are somewhat less expensive to buy.

PROTECTING GARDEN PLANTS

When you have spent time and money getting the garden in order, damage by bad weather or animals is disheartening. Prevent this harm with suitable protection.

Not only do fungal diseases and insects damage garden plants, but larger animal pests and adverse weather conditions are often equally destructive. When it comes to animals such as rabbits, deer, groundhogs, squirrels, cats, and dogs — even if they are ravenous pests — it is preferable to deter them from the garden rather than trap them. Similarly, we cannot control the weather, but can ward off its more harmful effects.

Plants may be damaged at any time during their life, from the seedling or cutting stage right through to maturity — even seeds can be unearthed or eaten by rodents before they germinate.

Each garden or regional area will, however, show certain trends in the type and cause of damage. For instance, rural gardens with adjacent fields may be troubled by groundhogs, but an urban garden will not. Similarly, pigeons may be a menace close to woodlands or in inner cities, but are an unfamiliar sight in open country. If you live in a mild region, severe frosts will not be a problem, but gardens in a frost pocket or sites exposed to biting winds will suffer losses unless precautions are taken.

The following pages show you how to prevent undue damage by each of the major animals and weather "pests," but you need to carry out measures against only those that are likely to appear in your garden. If you are new to a particular area, ask neighbors whether there are rabbits, deer, squirrels, and other garden mammals in the vicinity, or check for telltale droppings. Temperature zone maps and charts that show the extremes of weather you are likely to experience, based on data from previous years, may be available from regional meteorological offices or the U.S. Department of Agriculture.

◄Winter protection A wrapping of clear plastic, packed with straw and held in place with strong twine, can often protect plants growing at the edge of their temperature zone, and bring them through the winter.

Protection against frost

Some decorative shrubs and perennials, while not quite hardy enough to withstand severe weather during the winter months unprotected, can be grown successfully if they are sheltered from extreme cold. Freezing or very cold winds cause the most damage.

The ideal site for tender plants is on the south side of a wall or fence 6 ft (1.8 m) or higher. A dense evergreen hedge can also provide enough shelter. Plants that tolerate shade will usually be protected from the worst winds if planted among trees.

Shelter is not enough, however, during severe weather — further safeguards will be necessary. When a very cold spell strikes, wrap straw around the branches of bushy shrubs, binding it in place with sheets of burlap or clear plastic, tied with twine.

Wall shrubs and climbers can be shielded by "mats" made of straw or hay sandwiched between two sheets of fine chicken wire. Simply squeeze a layer of the material, 4-5 in (10-12 cm) thick, between two pieces of chicken wire, then connect the edges by twisting the wires together. Hang the mats in front of the plants in bad weather.

Free-standing shrubs — newly planted evergreens are especially

PROTECTING PLANTS FROM SEVERE WINTER WEATHER

1 Protect tender wall shrubs by screening them with straw sandwiched between two sheets of chicken wire and secured to canes.

2 Shield the crowns of tender herbaceous perennials by covering them with a 6- to 9-in (15- to 23-cm) layer of straw, leaves, or bark chips throughout the winter months. To keep the material in place, lay a few dead rhubarb or similar large leaves on top and weight them down.

3 Upright free-standing shrubs can be protected by wrapping them in a tent made from bamboo canes and burlap, stuffed with straw.

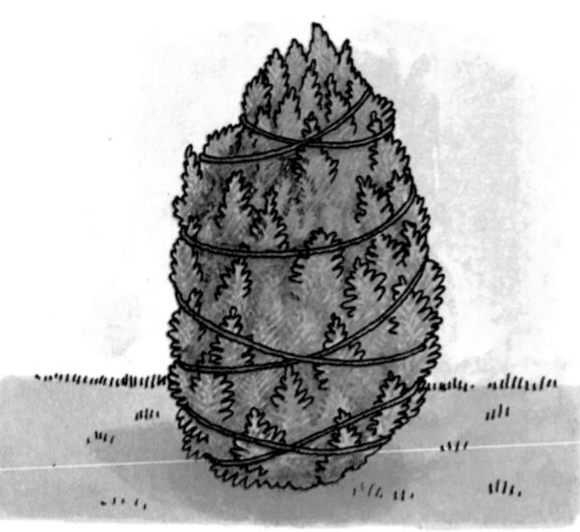

4 Bind dwarf conifers with twine or soft rope during snowy weather to prevent their branches from sagging or breaking under heavy loads of snow.

at risk — can be protected throughout the winter by using a strip of the same straw-matting construction. Stand it on end and wrap it around the plant like a collar. During the coldest weather, a lid of similar material can be put on top.

Bamboo canes and a plastic bag with the bottom slit open will also give some protection. Insert four canes around the plant in a square. Lower the bag over the canes to cover the plant.

An alternative is to use bamboo canes and straw. Form the canes into a tent by inserting about six at equal distances around the plant and tying them together with a string at the top. Also, loop string halfway down each cane, all around the tent. Stuff straw or even crumpled newspaper into this framework and, if necessary, tie it with more string. Cover this tent with a layer of burlap.

Plants that produce new shoots from the base each year — tender herbaceous perennials and certain shrubs such as fuchsias — should have their crowns covered. Put a 6- to 9-in (15- to 23-cm) layer of mulch, such as straw, sharp sand, or bark chips, around and over the crown of the plants in late fall. Anchor this material with a few rocks, if necessary. Clear away the mulch in early spring.

In cold or exposed areas, do not cut down the dead top growth of herbaceous perennials in the fall. Instead, wait until spring to do this pruning job — the old stems will provide some winter protection for the delicate, dormant shoots in the crown. It is also a good idea to leave the deadheading of susceptible shrubs, such as hydrangeas, until the spring, since the broad clusters of dead flowers form a useful insulation layer and a sort of "umbrella" against snow.

Often, the damaging effects of frosts are caused not so much by the low temperature as by the speed at which the frost melts when early morning sun strikes it. The unfurling flower buds of camellias are notoriously susceptible to petal scorch in late winter, especially when the plant is positioned in a spot that catches the morning sun. The best solution is to plant such species either in a spot with full shade or continuous dappled shade, or against a west-facing wall, where the rate of melting will be slower.

Surprisingly, a layer of ice over new shoots actually protects them from extreme cold. If you find a prized tender shrub covered in thick white frost, spray it gently with cold water before the sun strikes; it will reduce the chance of permanent harm. Never spray with warm or hot water, however.

If shrubs, trees, or evergreen perennials do become damaged by cold or other winter-weather conditions, leave them alone until the spring when new growth starts to appear. Pruning in winter will often promote the premature emergence of tender growth, which can then be damaged further by a late frost. If the entire plant looks dead, don't despair — wait until the summer before you dig it out, since, given time, new growth may appear from ground level. The so-called hardy fuchsias, for instance, invariably die down to the ground every winter, but vigorous shoots burst out from the crown in spring. Trim off the deadwood as soon as new shoots appear.

The best frost protection is to plant only species adapted to your climate. Refer to the temperature zone map on pages 170–171 to identify which zone you are in, and then purchase only plants rated hardy for that area. Keep plants well fed with a complete fertilizer, since that enhances cold hardiness. But don't fertilize after midsummer so that the plants can harden off by fall and enter dormancy at the natural season.

Protection against snow

As with ice, snow can actually insulate tender plants against extreme cold — that is why many alpine plants are able to survive on even the coldest mountains. However, a heavy load of snow can cause physical damage to plants. The branches of evergreen trees and shrubs can be broken under the weight. And those branches that are bent down but do not break may not resume their original position when the snow melts — in fact, the shape of a compact, formal plant, such as a dwarf or prostrate conifer, can be ruined.

If you live in an area where heavy snow is common during the winter, bind the branches of evergreens with garden string or rope from late fall to spring. If the branches get weighed down before you have a chance to bind them, immediately shake or brush loose snow away and tie the branches.

Gently brush snow off cold frames or greenhouse roofs, since a prolonged covering will dramatically reduce the light levels inside and may even break the glass.

PROTECTING PLANTS FROM STRONG WINDS

1 Burlap secured between wooden posts or stakes makes an adequate temporary screen to protect newly planted shrubs from undue wind gusts, which would loosen the roots.

2 Special windbreak materials, made from durable high-density plastic, can be attached to conventional fence posts to provide an effective, permanent windbreak.

Protection against water loss

One of the most serious threats to plants during frosty weather is dehydration. Although there may be an abundance of water, in the form of snow and ice, none of it is available to the plants. Protect plants by spraying them with an antidessicant (available at most garden centers). By temporarily sealing some of the plant's surface, it reduces water loss, as well as water needs. In addition, take advantage of any midwinter thaw to water plants thoroughly.

Protection against wind

High winds can damage plants any time of the year, causing the roots to become dislodged from the soil by rocking and growth to become lopsided by bud death on the exposed side.

Check all newly planted specimens after a storm and press down the root ball, if necessary. Ensure that young trees and standard-trained shrubs are securely staked; replace ties as needed.

In an exposed garden, provide protection for floppy or unstable plants by erecting a windbreak of some kind. It can be a permanent feature, such as a hedge or fence, or a temporary barrier to be removed once the plants have developed a strong root system.

Do not use solid materials, such as a wall of wood or bricks, for a windbreak — currents of air will blow over the top, swirling as they go, often creating worse turbulence behind the barrier. Instead, choose a material that will allow some air to pass through it, but at a reduced speed. Woven wooden fencing, slatted snow fencing, sheets of burlap, or even wire mesh will do an excellent job.

Commercial windbreak material, however, gives the best protection of all. It is usually made from lightweight, highly durable plastic. The mesh construction is designed to reduce wind speed by about 50 percent to a distance of four times the height of the barrier, and by 33 percent to a distance of eight times its height. As well as reducing physical damage by high winds, such windbreak materials also lessen the wind-chill factor.

Plastic windbreak mesh is easy to erect — staple it directly to wooden posts spaced at about 10-ft (3-m) intervals, following the manufacturer's instructions. More elaborate fastenings may be advised for permanent windbreaks, but these are usually simple to install.

Protection against rain

Excess rainfall can cause waterlogging of the soil, but the only

SPECIAL RAIN PROTECTION

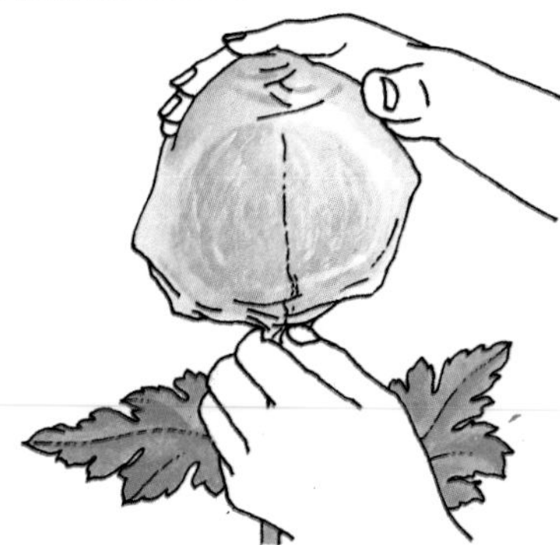

1 Protect the petals of chrysanthemums grown for exhibition by "bagging" them in plastic bags. Use two bags, putting one inside the other. Puncture holes at the base of the outer one to allow any water that soaks through to drain away.

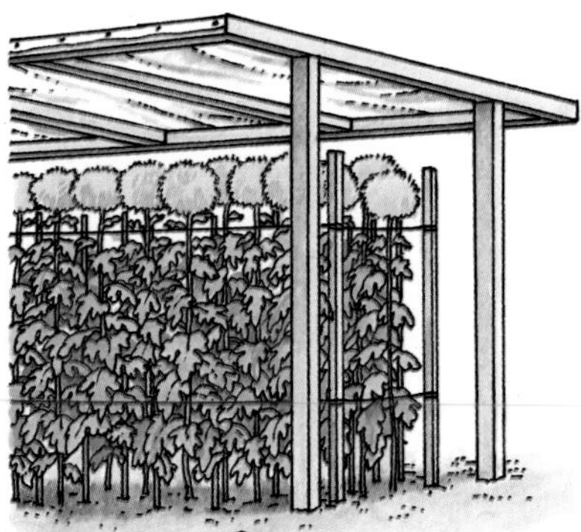

2 Construct an open-sided framework of lumber and heavy-duty plastic — with a slightly sloping roof — to prevent heavy rain from spoiling the blooms of exhibition plants. Don't cover the plants until the buds show color.

3 Prevent water from accumulating in the leaf rosettes of alpine plants by securing a small pane of glass on pieces of sturdy wire a few inches (centimeters) above the ground. Tilt the glass slightly so that rainwater runs off.

way of preventing this problem is by good soil preparation and cultivation — curative measures are generally impossible.

Tiny plants, such as the true alpines and many rock garden types that hate being soaked by heavy rain — their rosette leaves collect water, resulting in rotting at the neck — can be covered with a small sheet of glass supported on sturdy wire. Tilt the glass slightly to one side so that rainwater runs off and away from the delicate plants. Put a good surface layer of sharp sand around alpine plants to drain away any surplus water from their collars.

Perfect blooms can be individually protected with paper bags or umbrellalike roofs.

Shield strawberries from splashing rain by tucking clean straw beneath the ripening fruits and around the plants — unprotected fruits can be ruined by mud thrown up by heavy rain. Alternatively, make circular strawberry mats — collars of plastic film or roofing felt that fit under and around each individual plant.

Protection against animals

Dogs and cats can soil the garden, scrape up and trample plants, and dig holes in seedbeds; moreover, their urine can burn grass and other plants. The best means of coping with these problems is to train your own pets to use a small plot of unused garden, away from the lawn and flower beds. Commercial repellent dusts and sprays may also keep pets — and other animals — away from a particular area or group of plants, though the effects are rarely long lasting.

Many birds eat seeds and seedlings. The best method of protecting a seedbed is to insert low stakes around the perimeter, tie black thread to one of them and loop it in a crisscross pattern over the bed. Alternatively, nylon mesh or netting can be spread over the bed, supported on stakes. Erect a fruit cage over berry bushes to keep birds off, making sure there are no holes in the construction — a single trapped bird can do a great deal of damage.

Bird-scaring devices, such as scarecrows, owl decoys, and foil pans or strips hung from stakes, may be used to limit bird damage, and several chemical bird repellents are also available, but none of these methods is fully effective.

GUARDING AGAINST ANIMAL DAMAGE

1 In rural areas, the bark of young trees and woody shrubs is often gnawed by rabbits, voles, or deer. Protect it with cylindrical plastic tree guards or enclose the trunk in a cylinder of wire mesh.

2 Commercially available animal repellents are sold in granular, aerosol, or powder form. They may be used to deter pets and other animals, including some birds, from approaching particular garden plants.

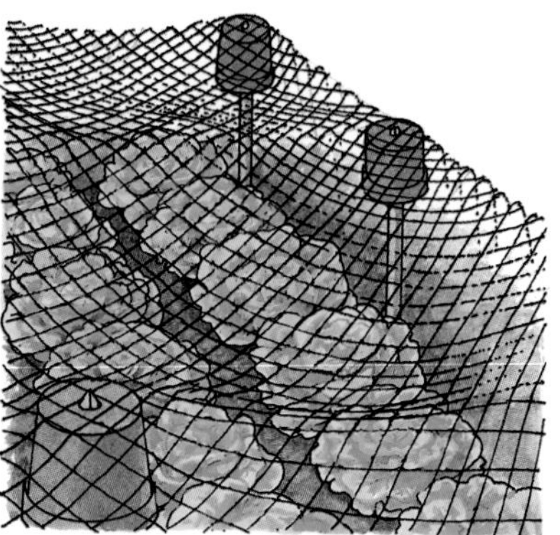

3 Groundhogs and squirrels are troublesome in vegetable patches. Cover the plot with strong netting supported on canes topped with upturned plastic pots. Weigh down the edges with planks.

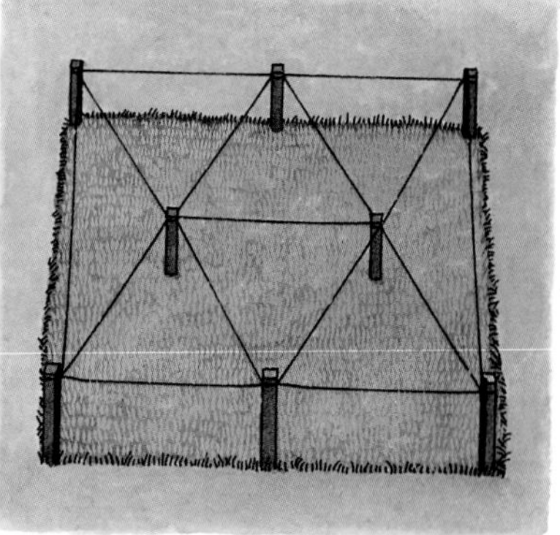

4 Deter birds from seedbeds or reseeded lawn patches by stretching black thread in a crisscross pattern between short stakes — most seed-eating birds won't take the risk of getting trapped.

The bark of young trees and woody shrubs may be gnawed by rabbits, voles, or deer. Such damage can kill trees or seriously stunt their growth, and secondary fungal infections can also develop in the wounds. Plastic tree guards can be purchased, the design varying enormously, according to the manufacturer — all are cylindrical, usually perforated with holes to allow the bark to breathe and prevent condensation, and range from about 1 ft (30 cm) long to 3 ft (90 cm) long or more.

You can make your own tree guards from chicken wire or wire mesh bent into a cylinder and wrapped around the tree. Don't rest the guard directly against the trunk of the tree.

Rabbits can be kept away from young vegetables by covering the plot with netting, though a determined rabbit will get through all but strong wire mesh. A high fence — 5 ft (1.5 m) or higher — encircling the garden should serve as a deterrent to rabbits and deer, but you will have to check constantly for holes. To prevent rabbits from burrowing underneath, bury wire mesh under the fence to a depth of at least 1 ft (30 cm).

Groundhogs are experts at penetrating such protective barriers, but can usually be controlled with catch-and-release traps. Regular spring-type traps are the best way to limit mice, which sometimes attack both seeds and bulbs. Avoid the use of poisoned baits — they pose too great a danger to other wildlife, pets, and small children. Squirrels are virtually impossible to curb; the only effective safeguard against their damage to ripe fruits, as well as shrubs and trees, is to cover valuable plants with netting.

Pruning

Correct pruning benefits the health and well-being of trees and shrubs, as well as improves their appearance. The vast majority of woody plants respond to pruning by producing fresh growth from immediately below the cut, so that, in effect, a well-clipped plant is continually being rejuvenated. The flowers and fruits that grow on the young shoots of most regularly pruned trees and shrubs are more reliable, prolific, and often larger than those found on plants that have not been cut back. Similarly, shrubs with colored bark show the brightest, freshest tints; trees such as eucalyptus continue to produce attractive juvenile foliage; and trees such as paulownia bring forth their enormous, exotic-looking leaves only if cut back hard periodically.

Proper timing is vital, and a mistake can lead to the loss of a whole year's flowers. The best time of year for pruning depends mainly on individual flowering habits; with few exceptions, those plants that blossom on the new season's growth are cut back immediately after they bloom. Weather is also a factor. Pruning in early fall can result in soft, new growth, unable to withstand winter cold, while cutting back in frosty conditions can lead to dieback — branches dying from their cut tips. A few plants, such as cherry, are vulnerable to disease at certain times of the year, and so should not be pruned during these periods.

You'll need to decide roughly how much to remove, exactly which stems or branches to cut, and where to make each cut. By choosing these pruning points with care, you can ensure that new growth occurs in the desired direction. Maintenance pruning helps to tidy up crowded, thin, dead, or diseased wood.

Perfect roses Stunning summer displays depend on a rigorous spring-pruning program.

PRUNING ROSES

Probably no aspect of gardening causes as much needless anxiety as pruning — particularly the annual cutting back of roses.

The method of pruning differs slightly for each of the main categories of roses — hybrid teas, floribundas, polyanthas, miniatures, climbers, ramblers, and shrub roses — and they undoubtedly perform best when treated appropriately. But most roses flower well after only light pruning, as long as you follow the three basic steps outlined here.

Roses are pruned to maintain a healthy, well-shaped plant and to encourage the development of flowering shoots. Pruning methods vary because cultivated roses don't all replace their old and exhausted stems in quite the same way, nor do they all flower on wood of the same age.

Basic pruning principles apply to all roses whatever their classification — bush, shrub, climbing, or rambling — and serve as the starting point for all surgery.

Pruning equipment

Sharp pruning shears cut most stems. Many experienced gardeners prefer two-bladed models, but single-bladed pruning shears with an anvil action are adequate if the blade is sharp. Cut thick stems with a saw or loppers; use a sharp knife to trim the edges around rough cuts. Always wear sturdy gloves for protection.

When to prune

Most modern roses — notably hybrid teas, floribundas, and large-flowered climbers — bloom most heavily on the current season's canes. Cutting them back

▼ **Pruning tools** Essential equipment (clockwise from top) includes pruning saws, double-bladed pruning shears, loppers, single-bladed pruning shears, pruning knife, and gloves.

heavily in early spring actually encourages a better show of flowers a few months later. Although fall pruning is sometimes recommended, it is not a good practice in regions with cold winters; waiting until buds begin to swell in early spring allows you to identify (and remove) any dead canes.

Many old-fashioned roses, however, whose bushes flower once in late spring, bloom on canes produced during the previous growing season. Pruning them hard in early spring removes most of their potential for flowering in the following months. Instead, prune them right after they flower.

Deadheading

A form of pruning carried out during the flowering season, deadheading encourages a second blooming among repeat-flowering roses. For roses that flower just once, it will prevent the plant from redirecting its energy to the development of seed. Don't deadhead roses that produce showy hips — the display will be lost.

With hybrid teas, cut off faded blossoms above a strong outward-facing bud. Later in the season, cut back to the first bud below the flower; at the season's end, take off the flower stalk. With floribundas, remove the whole spent flower cluster, then cut back to the first bud. To prevent them from spreading disease to other plants, dispose of these prunings.

Correct pruning cuts

Two kinds of cuts are used in pruning. When removing a complete stem — for instance, the weaker of two stems that cross — cut close to the base, then trim off any stumps. To shorten a stem, cut to just above an outward-facing growth bud or eye. Choosing such an eye ensures that the center of the bush won't be cluttered by crisscrossing stems. Vigorous types, such as hybrid teas, can be pruned hard — cut almost to the ground — each year. With ramblers and climbers, cut to an eye or bud that will grow in a direction suitable for training along a support.

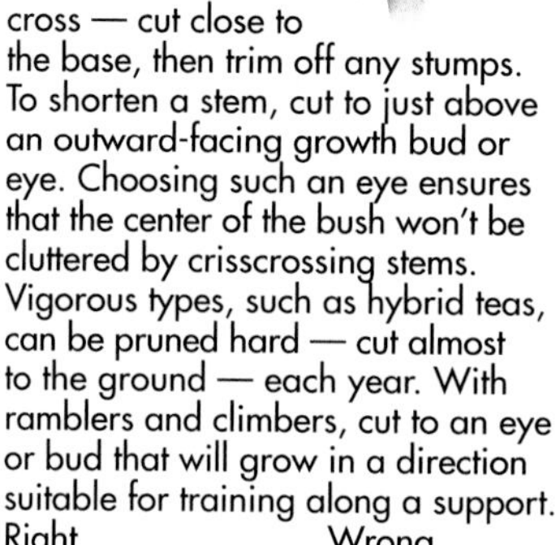

Right Wrong

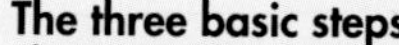

The three basic steps

There are three pruning steps that apply to all roses, whether established or newly planted. Follow them routinely whenever you are planting or pruning. Many roses will need very little further attention.

1 Remove all dead, damaged, or diseased stems. Cut back to just above a bud on healthy wood or take out the stem completely, cutting back to a junction with a healthy stem or even the rootstock itself.

2 Remove weak or thin stems. These are unlikely to produce flowers, yet they will take away strength that the plant could put into other, better growth. Cut back to a joint with a healthy, strong-growing stem or to the rootstock.

3 Take out the least vigorous of stems that cross or rub. Either remove the whole stem or prune back to a growth bud below the point where the two stems cross. With ramblers and climbers, cut out some overcrowding stems and remember that training and tying will be needed to avoid rubbing. Always paint cuts with white glue to protect roses against stem borers.

ROSE CLASSIFICATION

	TYPE	GROWTH HABIT	FLORAL CHARACTERISTICS	POPULAR EXAMPLES
BUSH ROSES	**HYBRID TEAS**	Bushy, compact, 2-4 ft (60-120 cm)	Large, elegant, double, high-centered, to 4 in (10 cm) across, one or few per stem	'American Pride,' 'Crimson Glory,' 'Honor,' 'Fragrant Cloud,' 'Peace,' 'Tiffany'
	FLORIBUNDAS	Bushy, small, 2-3 ft (60-90 cm)	Cluster-flowering, 2½ in (6 cm) across, double or semidouble	'Angel Face,' 'Eye Paint,' 'Goldilocks,' 'Iceberg'
	POLYANTHAS	Bushy, small, to 2 ft (60 cm)	Cluster-flowering, to ¾-1½ in (2-4 cm) across	'Cecile Brunner,' 'The Fairy'
	MINIATURES	Bushy, dwarf, 8-12 in (20-30 cm)	Mostly double, up to 1 in (2.5 cm) across	'Angel Darling,' 'Gold Coin,' 'Popcorn,' 'Stars 'n' Stripes'
SHRUB ROSES	**MODERN SHRUB ROSES** Including Musks and Rugosas	Medium to large shrubs, 3-5 ft (1-1.5 m), dense, vigorous, many good for hedging	Single or clusters, each flower 2-3 in (5-8 cm) across, very free-flowering; showy hips	'Constance Spry,' 'Champlain,' 'Golden Wings,' 'Roseraie de l'Hay,' 'Fruhlingsgold'
	OLD GARDEN ROSES Including Albas, Bourbons, Chinas, Gallicas, and Hybrid Perpetuals	Medium to large shrubs, 3-6 ft (1-1.8 m), variable habit, often lax and open, suitable for general shrub plantings	Variable, according to parentage, double or single, some repeat- or perpetual-flowering, mostly 2-3 in (5-7.5 cm) across	'Rosa Mundi,' 'Mutabilis,' 'Konigin von Danemarck,' 'Paul Neyron,' 'Ferdinand Pichard,' 'Henri Martin,' 'Sombreuil'
	SPECIES/WILD ROSES	Medium to large, open shrubs, to 6-8 ft (1.8-2.5 m), often wiry or arching, good for mixed plantings	Usually single, with five petals, some semidouble or double, once-flowering; showy hips	*Rosa rugosa, R. rubrifolia, R. californica* 'Plena,' 'Canary Bird,' *R. moyesii, R. x harisonii*
OTHERS	**CLIMBERS** Including lower-growing Pillars	Scrambling, tall shrubs, 10-30 ft (3-9 m), permanent framework, little or no new basal growth	Large, borne singly or in small clusters, double, mostly 3-4 in (8-10 cm) across	'Blaze,' 'Don Juan,' 'Golden Showers,' 'Mermaid,' 'New Dawn,' 'Zephirine Drouhin'
	RAMBLERS	Scrambling, tall shrubs, 10-25 ft (3-7.5 m), with thin, flexible canes growing from base each year	Clusters or trusses, mostly single, small, to 1½ in (4 cm) across, best on year-old shoots	'American Pillar,' 'Dorothy Perkins,' 'Excelsa,' 'Veilchenblau,' 'Goldfinch,' 'Wedding Day'

Initial pruning

If you buy a plant that is not dormant and has not been cut back, or you are transplanting a bush, you should prune as follows.

Hybrid teas and hybrid perpetuals must be pruned hard to outward-facing buds about 4 in (10 cm) above the ground. Prune floribundas less hard, to buds about 6 in (15 cm) above the ground; reduce dwarf varieties to 3 in (7.5 cm) above the ground. Hybrid teas and floribundas grown as standards can be cut back even more moderately.

Prune miniature rose stems to about 2 in (5 cm) high. Cut back the stems of polyanthas, such as 'The Fairy,' by about one-third.

Old roses simply need the basic steps. Remove about 3 in (7.5 cm) from the tips of species and shrub roses, climbers, and ramblers.

▶ **Reward for pruning** Annual pruning will ensure abundant flowers.

NEWLY PLANTED HYBRID TEAS

1 Carry out the three basic pruning steps — remove dead, damaged, diseased, and weak stems, as well as any that cross or crowd the center of the bush.

2 Cut all stems down to 4 in (10 cm) from the ground, above an outward-facing bud. This pruning encourages an open, well-balanced bush.

▲ **Hybrid tea roses** Hard prune hybrid tea roses, such as 'Fragrant Cloud,' during the dormant season to produce a balanced bush with shapely blooms.

▲ **Floribunda roses** Reduce strong shoots on floribunda roses, such as 'Anne Harkness,' for a good framework bearing flowers throughout summer.

NEWLY PLANTED FLORIBUNDAS

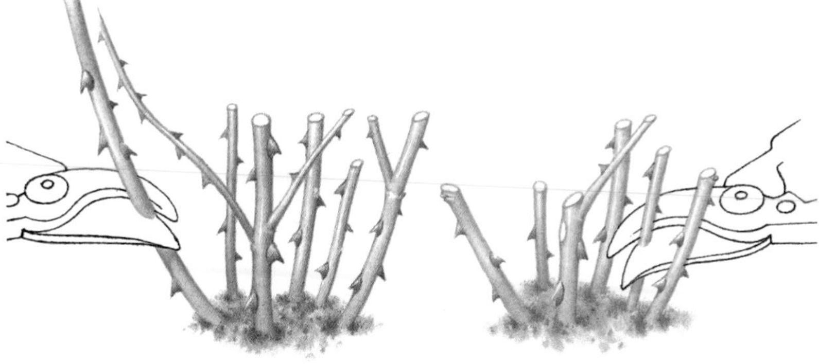

1 Carry out the three basic pruning steps. Floribundas are more vigorous and free-flowering than hybrid teas, and need less severe pruning.

2 Then cut remaining stems down to outward-facing buds at about 6 in (15 cm) above ground level. Always use sharp tools and make clean cuts.

Pruning bush roses

The hybrid teas, floribundas, polyanthas, and miniatures, together with the standards derived from these groups, make up a large category of roses that you should prune in virtually the same way.

Reduce the stems of hybrid teas and hybrid perpetuals by about one-third their length. This moderate pruning is adequate to encourage a good garden display of flowers. Hard pruning to within three buds of the base results in fewer but better flowers.

Hybrid teas grown for exhibition are normally hard pruned. The very vigorous kinds may occasionally need hard pruning to check tall growth, which might get damaged in high winds. In the fall, trim the top growth of tall bush roses to prevent injury.

1 A bush rose in need of pruning will have a mixture of wood — dead or old unproductive stems, diseased and weak stems, and some that cross.

▲ **Miniature roses** Usually miniature roses, such as 'Anna Ford,' need only light or moderate pruning. Reduce main stems by a quarter in early spring.

2 Cut back a dead stem to the point where it meets a healthy stem. Prune any part of a stem that is diseased to just above a bud on healthy wood.

3 Cut out thin or weak stems to their point of union with a strong stem, or with the rootstock, to allow more nourishment to reach vigorous wood.

4 Cut out stems that cross or rub. Remove the weaker of the two, cutting to a growth bud below where they cross, to prevent a crowded center.

5 Every spring, prune bush roses of average growth lightly to ensure a good display. In general, prune weaker varieties and thin shoots more severely than vigorous ones.

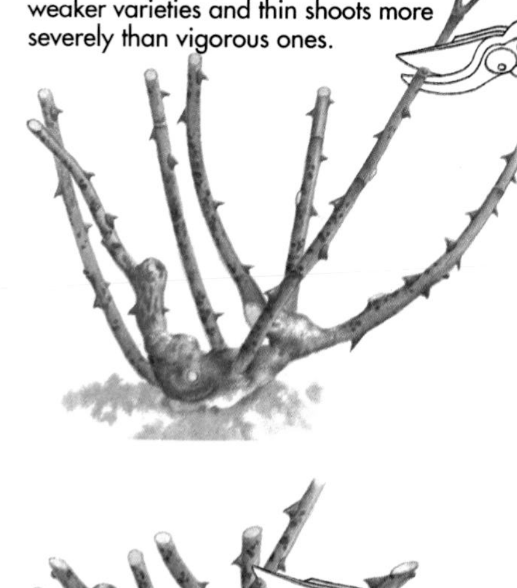

▲ **Bush roses** Prune polyanthas, such as 'The Fairy,' and floribundas less severely than hybrid teas. Cut back by about a quarter during dormancy.

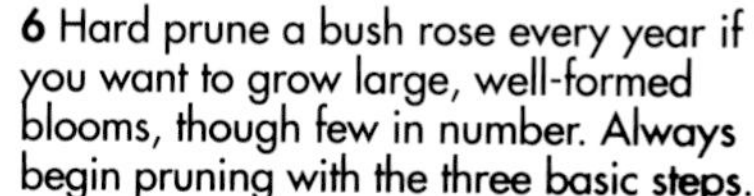

6 Hard prune a bush rose every year if you want to grow large, well-formed blooms, though few in number. Always begin pruning with the three basic steps.

Pruning shrub roses

Old and modern shrub roses, and the species roses, require only light pruning.

After completing the three basic pruning steps, check plants to see if any vigorous new shoots have developed from old stems. If so, cut back the old stem to the junction with the new shoot. Look for any exceptionally long stems that distort the shrub's balance. Cut these back by about one-third. Prune all laterals (the stems growing from the leaders) that flowered the previous summer to a strong bud about 4 in (10 cm) from the main stem. Lastly, cut back the tips of all main stems by 4-6 in (10-15 cm) to encourage side shoots, which will bear flowers during the following year.

▶ **Modern shrub roses** These flower best on side shoots. Tip main stems and laterals of shrub roses, such as 'Constance Spry,' to encourage growth of sublaterals.

▲ **Old garden roses** Most, including Gallicas, such as 'Président de Sèze,' flower on shoots of the previous season. Prune lightly, tipping the main shoots after flowering.

▼ **Species roses** Prune very lightly to maintain shape. Do not deadhead hip-bearing types, such as the Albas, the Moyesiis, and this *Rosa rugosa*.

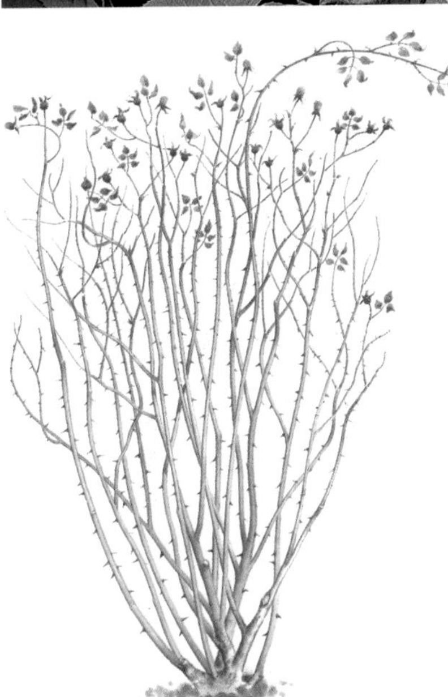

1 A shrub rose ready for pruning. First, remove all dead and diseased stems.

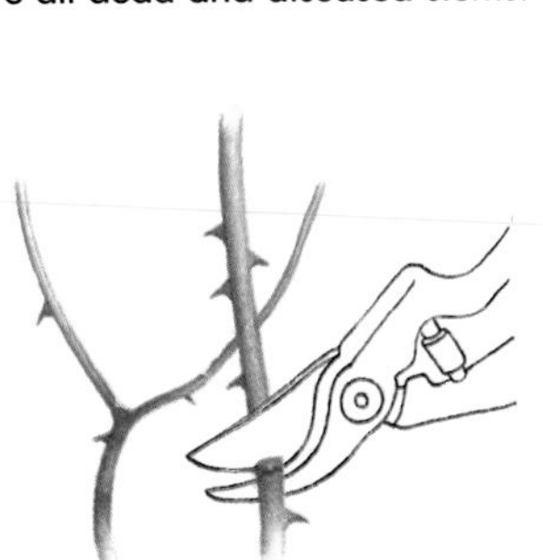

2 Cut back all long shoots by about one-third to prevent them from drooping.

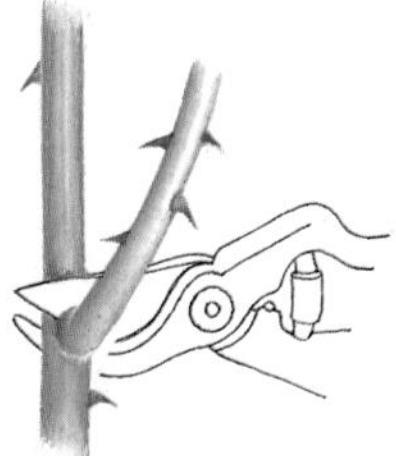

3 Cut old, exhausted stems back to the junction with new, healthy laterals.

4 From the base, cut out dead stems and any that cross in the center.

5 Finally, lightly tip all remaining stems to promote strong lateral growth.

Pruning climbers

The pruning of the vigorous climbing roses and the shorter-growing pillar roses needs to go hand in hand with training them. These roses flower on the previous season's wood. Most do not send out shoots readily from the base — new wood appears higher up on the old stems of the leaders.

In summer, trim stems that have borne flowers back to a new bud. In winter, cut back main stems (or leaders) to vigorous new shoots. However, if no new growth has formed during the growing season, cut back leaders and laterals by about half. As far as possible, train new shoots to grow horizontally — this practice will stimulate the growth of flower-bearing side shoots.

1 With climbers, prune most heavily in early spring, just before bud break. Remove spindly wood, but retain a framework of new shoots for the current season's bloom.

◀ **Pruning climbers** Prune climbers, such as 'Paul's Lemon Pillar,' in early spring. Cut out old stems and replace with new laterals.

2 Prune again in summer after the climber has flowered. Trim back flowered twigs to selected new buds. Don't let hips form — they drain the rose's energy.

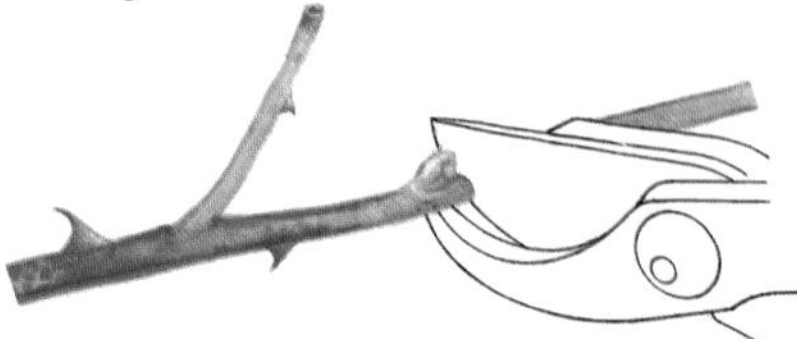

3 In early spring, remove old wood, cutting back the leaders to strong new shoots.

4 If no new shoots have grown from a leader, prune it and its laterals by about half to encourage new side shoots.

Pruning ramblers

The ramblers are lax-growing scramblers that produce a single but profuse crop of flowers in summer. The long, flexible canes that develop from the base bear flowers in their second year.

Begin pruning after flowering by carrying out the three basic steps. For those ramblers that produce new canes from the base, cut old flowered canes right out from the rootstock and tie in new canes to replace them. In some ramblers, the new stems spring not from the base, but from some point along an old stem. With these, cut back the old cane to the point where the new stem is growing away. Tie it in place.

The tangling vigor of ramblers can make pruning difficult. Cut out old canes in sections rather than in one piece.

1 Prune ramblers after flowering or as soon as new canes sprout freely.

2 Cut back flowered stems to the base, or junction with a new cane.

▲ **Pruning ramblers** True ramblers, such as 'Albertine,' have one glorious display, on canes produced the previous year. Flowered stems must be removed annually and replaced by new ones.

PRINCIPLES OF PRUNING

Pruning is a means of maintaining shape and vigor by removing weak, crossed, diseased, or dead growth from shrubs and trees.

Large shrubs and climbers with straggly, untended, or diseased branches look unattractive and often fail to produce a good display of flowers or fruits. Though regular pruning may not be essential for many shrubs, you can improve their growth by cutting away old branches to let light into the center of the plant. Some shrubs will bring forth larger — though generally fewer — flowers if pruned each year. Dead or diseased branches should be cut away immediately to prevent the spread of infection.

Three tools are used in pruning: pruning shears for removing shoots and small stems; loppers, for large stems; and a pruning saw, for large branches. A sharp knife may also be needed for trimming large wounds.

When shortening branches, cut just above an outward-facing bud or shoot. Cut diagonally, parallel with the angle of the bud or shoot. When removing entire branches, cut back to the raised "collar" around the base, then trim the area with a knife. Don't paint with a commercial pruning seal, since this treatment can encourage rot rather than prevent it.

Shrubs that have been hard pruned — especially when you cut them back every year — benefit from a 2-in (5-cm) layer of mulch. Use garden compost or composted manure. Also, apply a slow-release, complete fertilizer.

Young shrubs, whether they are evergreen or deciduous, seldom require pruning except for the removal of crossing branches or injured shoot tips. Frost-damaged or dead shoots should be cut back to healthy wood in spring. Young conifers may occasionally fork, in which case the weaker of the two leading shoots should be cut out at the base in early or midspring. Sometimes a young shrub produces a fast-growing main stem; cut it back to induce branching.

Dead or straggly wood

Most shrubs require pruning to remove damaged wood, which may involve only the removal of a small piece of injured branch. This task can be done at any time of year — for example, after a long, straggly branch has developed, or when a branch has broken in a storm. Or, if you prefer, routinely examine all the shrubs in your garden every spring.

Remove any dead or damaged wood, cutting back to a healthy, outward-facing shoot or bud. Then take off shoots that are particularly weak, cutting right back to a main branch. If any branches have grown straggly and unsightly, prune them by half to a strong shoot or bud facing outward.

Do not remove any well-formed, healthy wood, or you are likely to cut off many of the buds that would produce flowers later.

Popular shrubs that need this type of pruning include camellias, rockroses, daphnes, euonymuses, hebes, shrubby cinquefoils *(Potentilla)*, and viburnums.

◀ **Thinning out** Fast-growing shrubs, such as forsythias, produce numerous shoots from the base every year. Unless removed, old stems will crowd the shrub and impede flowering.

Overgrown plants

Some shrubs, particularly broad-leaved evergreens, can go without pruning for many years, until they become overgrown or bare at the base. Then, in spring, cut all the main branches down to within a few inches of the ground with a pruning saw or bow saw (do not use this technique for needled evergreens, however).

Mulch with garden compost or composted manure and apply a balanced, complete fertilizer at the rate recommended on the product label. The shrub won't flower again until the next year.

Popular shrubs that may require this treatment include the cherry laurels *(Prunus laurocerasus* and *P. lusitanica)*, daisy bushes *(Olearia)*, pernettyas and pieris, and the deciduous mock oranges *(Philadelphus)*.

Flowers on new shoots

A number of shrubs flower mainly on shoots that have grown in the current season. To restrict their size, or to encourage larger but fewer flowers, prune them in spring, as they begin to grow.

Cut all last year's shoots back to two or three buds or shoots from their base. Unless you want to remove a branch completely, do not cut back into the older wood, as this intrusion might prevent new shoots from developing.

After pruning, mulch with a 2-in (5-cm) layer of garden compost or well-composted manure and apply a balanced, complete fertilizer at the rate recommended on the product label.

Shrubs that can be pruned by this method include *Buddleia davidii*, caryopterides, ceratostigmas, coluteas, *Cytisus* × 'Porlock,' fuchsias, indigos *(Indigofera)*, deciduous California lilacs *(Ceanothus)*, lippias, passionflowers *(Passiflora)*, potato vines *(Solanum crispum)*, santolinas, Spanish brooms *(Spartium)*, most spireas, and *Tamarix pentandra*.

Flowers on last year's shoots

Certain shrubs flower on shoots grown the previous year. These can be pruned each year immediately after they finish flowering — whether in spring, summer, or fall. The pruning is aimed at keeping the shrub in bounds, or promoting larger but fewer flowers.

Cut each shoot that has borne flowers back to two or three shoots or buds from its junction with the parent stem. The new shoots will produce flowers in the next season.

REMOVING DEAD AND STRAGGLY WOOD

1 A mature shrub may look untidy when a few branches grow longer than the rest, or when random branches die out. Cosmetic pruning can be carried out at any time of year to improve the shrub's overall appearance.

2 First, prune any dead or damaged wood and very weak stems all the way back to the strong, healthy growth. Then shorten branches that have grown straggly and unsightly. Cut them back by half to an outward-facing bud or shoot.

CUTTING DOWN OVERGROWN SHRUBS

1 Regular pruning of most broad-leaved evergreens is unnecessary — they often grow slowly. If they do outgrow their space, however, most can be cut down to encourage compact growth.

2 Begin pruning an old, overgrown shrub by clearing away the top growth with loppers — an essential tool for pruning thick branches that are beyond the capacity of ordinary pruning shears.

3 Once access to the base of the shrub is established, saw off all the branches close to the ground, leaving short stumps from which new shoots will appear. Do not cover wounds with pruning seal.

PRUNING SHRUBS THAT FLOWER ON NEW SHOOTS

1 *Buddleia davidii* is one of the most popular shrubs that flowers on shoots grown in the current year. Pruned annually, it will produce large flower spikes.

2 In late winter or early spring, prune the previous year's shoots back to two or three buds from their base. Unless you want to remove a branch entirely, do not cut back into the older, thicker, darker-colored wood, as it may not readily sprout new shoots. The pruned shrub will have a low framework of branches from which shoots will grow rapidly to produce flowers in summer.

Buddleia alternifolia, ornamental brambles *(Rubus)*, brooms (*Cytisus*, except *C.* × 'Porlock'), deutzias, kerrias, *Prunus glandulosa*, *Prunus triloba*, *Spiraea* × *arguta*, and weigelas can all be pruned by this method.

Removing old wood

There are shrubs, most notably the common *Hydrangea macrophylla*, that benefit from having some of the oldest growth removed almost at ground level each year.

In the spring, cut out all 3-year-old stems. These tend to be rough looking, and they have both sublateral and lateral branches. Make the cuts within 1-2 in (2.5-5 cm) of the ground. You can also cut away some of the 2-year-old stems. These may have lateral branches, but they will have no sublaterals.

Other shrubs that profit from this method of pruning when they have become overgrown include barberries *(Berberis)*, beauty bushes *(Kolkwitzia amabilis)*, clethras, cotoneasters, flowering currants *(Ribes sanguineum)*, forsythias, genistas, shrubby cinquefoils *(Potentilla)*, snowberries *(Symphoricarpos)*, abelias, Himalayan honeysuckles *(Leycesteria)*, and weigelas.

PRUNING SHRUBS THAT FLOWER ON LAST YEAR'S SHOOTS

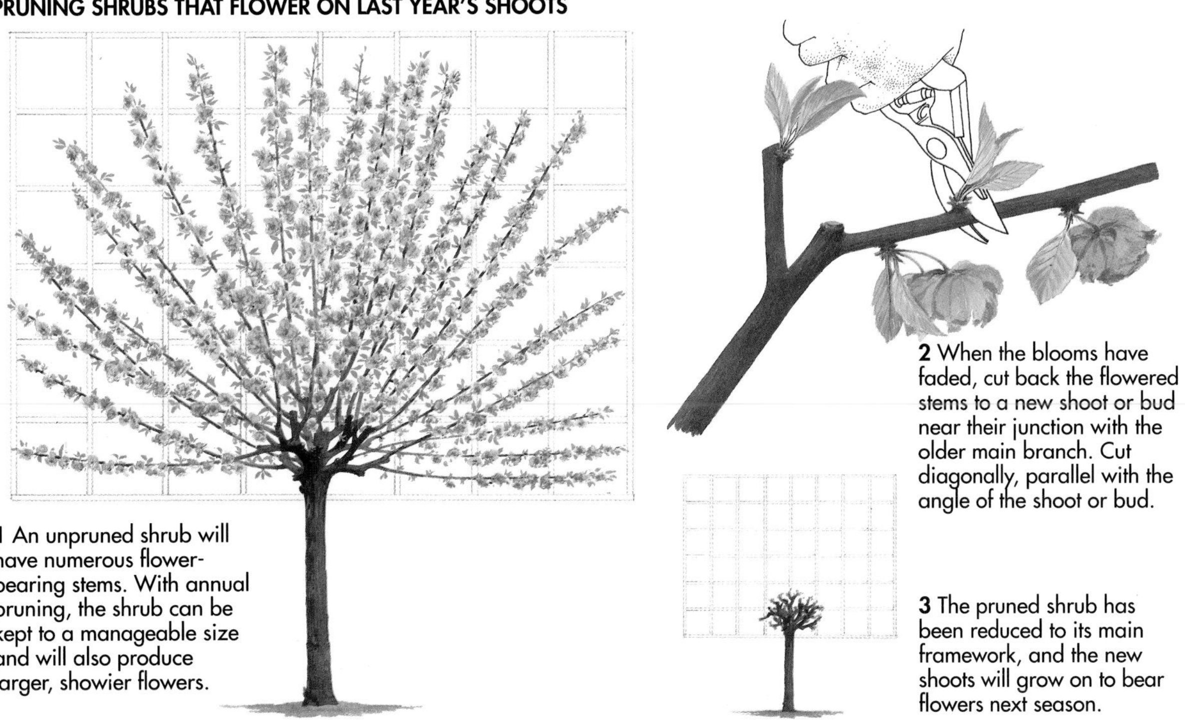

1 An unpruned shrub will have numerous flower-bearing stems. With annual pruning, the shrub can be kept to a manageable size and will also produce larger, showier flowers.

2 When the blooms have faded, cut back the flowered stems to a new shoot or bud near their junction with the older main branch. Cut diagonally, parallel with the angle of the shoot or bud.

3 The pruned shrub has been reduced to its main framework, and the new shoots will grow on to bear flowers next season.

CLEARING OLD WOOD FROM THE CENTER

2 In spring, cut away almost to ground level the stems that are more than three years old — those with sublaterals as well as laterals. Some 2-year-old stems can also be removed.

1 An unpruned shrub, such as this *Hydrangea macrophylla*, has many old stems with lateral and sublateral branches. They are overcrowding the space and preventing light from penetrating to the center of the plant.

3 One-year-old, and some 2-year-old, growths are left to flower in summer. The center is now open to sun.

Controlling climbers

Leave most woody climbers unpruned until they get too large, then cut them back after they have flowered. Prune nonflowering climbers in spring or summer.

Self-clinging climbers, such as ivies *(Hedera)* or climbing hydrangeas *(Hydrangea petiolaris)*, can be trimmed as necessary on the wall. Climbers that prefer to twine their stems around objects, such as honeysuckles *(Lonicera japonica* and *L. periclymenum)* and clematises, should be detached from their supports. Then remove all side growths, leaving just the main stems.

If the main stems look very old, cut them out and in their place tie some of the younger ones — either shoots growing from ground level or from low down on the old stems.

Other woody climbers that require this pruning once they are established include actinidia vines, *Clematis armandii*, *Clematis macropetala*, *Clematis montana*, Russian vines, trumpet creepers *(Campsis)*, ornamental grape vines *(Vitis)*, and Virginia creepers *(Parthenocissus)*.

RESTRICTING CLIMBERS

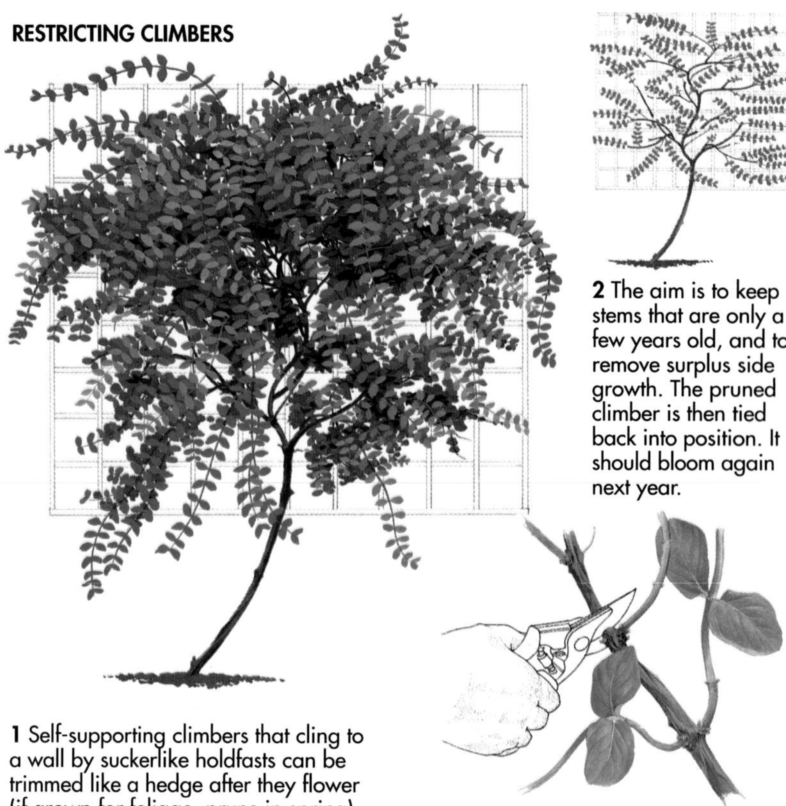

1 Self-supporting climbers that cling to a wall by suckerlike holdfasts can be trimmed like a hedge after they flower (if grown for foliage, prune in spring).

Climbing shrubs that grow on trellises or wires should be removed carefully from their supports before pruning is begun, after flowering.

2 The aim is to keep stems that are only a few years old, and to remove surplus side growth. The pruned climber is then tied back into position. It should bloom again next year.

3 If the main stems are very old, cut them back to where the young shoots are growing near the base.

PRUNING POPULAR SHRUBS

Deciduous shrubs in particular need regular pruning to keep them healthy and well-balanced, but their specific requirements vary.

Shrubs are grown for the beauty of their flowers or foliage, for the quality of their fruits, for their brightly colored winter stems or branches, for their characteristic shape or outline, or for a combination of all of these. The purpose of regular pruning and trimming is to make the most of these attributes; the timing depends on the shrub's flowering habits.

Not all shrubs need annual pruning — many, especially when grown as single specimens, require only occasional light trimming to maintain their shape. The necessity for periodic pruning can also be reduced by care and forethought at the time of planting, by determining the eventual size and shape of the shrub, and by allowing ample room for growth. Overcrowded shrubs must be drastically pruned each year to prevent them from becoming weakened and misshapen as they compete for the available root space, light, nutrients, and water.

The health and vigor of a shrub are maintained by correct pruning. It is important to remove all dead or injured wood as soon as you notice it. The longer deadwood is allowed to remain on a shrub, the greater is the risk of disease spores entering it, multiplying, and eventually spreading to healthy tissue. In severe cases, extensive damage and even death of the whole shrub may occur. Branches that cross or rub against one another are also potentially harmful, and should be cut away before diseases can enter through the wounds that result from this action.

Thin, weak growths are of little use, especially if they are produced in the center of a bush, where they are starved of light and air. Well-ripened branches stand up better to harsh weather and to disease. Consequently, the purpose of pruning is also to keep the center of a shrub fairly open so that light and air can circulate freely around the branches.

Make pruning cuts cleanly, leaving no ragged edges, torn bark, or bruising and crushing of the stems, since any of these irregularities will result in the tissues dying. The branch will heal more rapidly if the cut is made almost horizontally across it. As the buds are the only points from which further growth can develop along a stem, pruning cuts should be as close as possible to a bud without damaging it. Start the cut on the side opposite to the bud and finish immediately above it so that the cut slopes downward away from the bud. This technique ensures that water runs off the cut without rotting the bud.

Cut unwanted or damaged shoots flush with the main stem from which they arise — never leave a short length of branch, or snag, as it may die back or produce unwanted clusters of short stems. Trim off the edges of any large pruning cuts with a sharp knife. Leave the wound unpainted — paints, shellacs, and other dressings only serve to keep the wood moist and therefore more receptive to fungal spores.

Colored-leaved and variegated shrub varieties, such as *Spiraea* × *bumalda* 'Goldflame,' sometimes show shoots that lack the characteristic color — golden-leaved varieties in particular tend to produce a few all-green shoots from time to time. These must be removed completely as soon as they appear, since they are frequently more vigorous than the plant's regular shoots and will ruin its visual effect.

◄ **Winter stems** Many willows and dogwoods are grown for their brightly colored bare stems in winter. As on this scarlet willow, coloration is most prominent on young stems; prune hard in alternate years for new growth.

Buddleia alternifolia (Butterfly bush)

A graceful shrub, with long, weeping branches, which produces lavender-blue flower sprays on the previous year's shoots.

As soon as the blooms fade, cut back the flowered stems to strong new shoots. On young plants, keep most of the older wood for the first few years to build up a good framework. As the shrub ages, cut back harder.

Caryopteris x *clandonensis* (Bluebeard)

This bushy, thin-stemmed shrub bears small bright blue flowers on the current year's shoots. It becomes straggly unless pruned each spring.

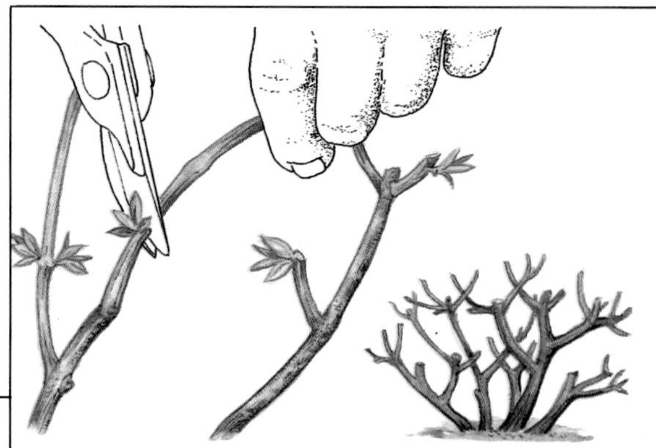

In later winter or early spring, cut back all of the previous year's shoots to new shoots about 1 in (2.5 cm) from the old wood. Remove all dead, weak, and straggly or overcrowded shoots from the base.

Ceanothus species and hybrids

Evergreen California lilacs need no regular pruning, but deciduous types should be pruned each spring.

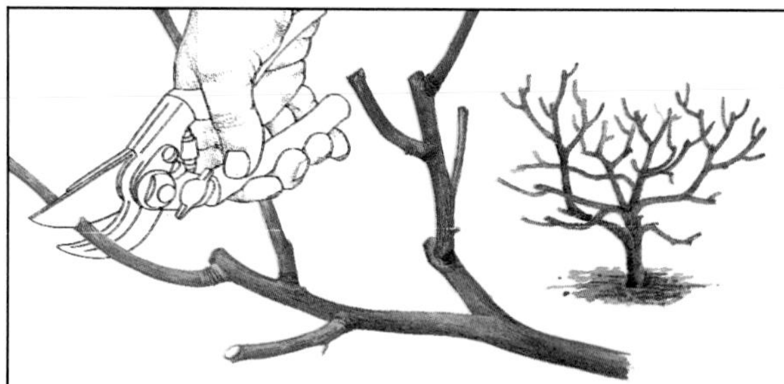

In midspring, cut back the previous year's shoots of all deciduous *Ceanothus* species, varieties, and hybrids to two or three pairs of buds from the base. On young plants, prune more lightly until the shrub has built up a strong framework.

With the evergreen California lilacs, merely shorten leggy, untidy stems by about half after flowering; cut back late-flowering types the following spring.

***Ceratostigma willmottianum* (Chinese plumbago)**

Shrubby Chinese plumbago does not need regular pruning, but can be constrained by severe pruning in spring.

Overgrown plants can be cut back to within 1-3 in (2.5-7.5 cm) of the ground in early spring to midspring. Cut all the stems, both old and new. The new shoots that spring up will flower in the fall.

The related *Ceratostigma plumbaginoides* dies down each winter, and so needs no pruning.

***Chaenomeles* (Quince species and hybrids)**

Free-standing Japanese quinces *(japonicas)* need no regular pruning, but wall-trained plants must be kept within bounds.

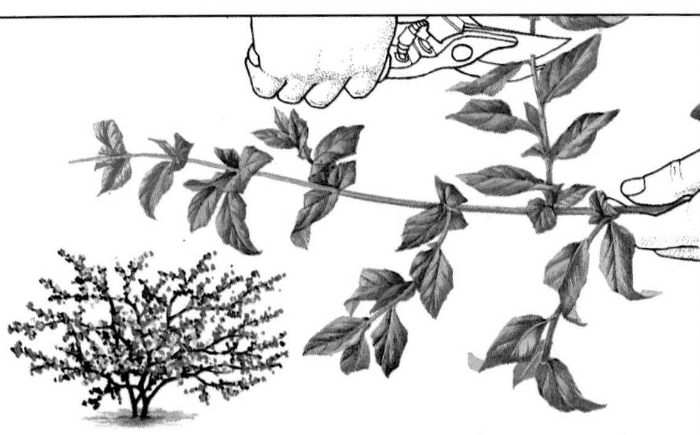

When they are grown against a wall or fence, tie in the leaders of Japanese quinces each year until the space is completely filled. In midspring to late spring, after the flowers have faded, pinch or cut back all the young shoots not wanted for training to four or five leaves from the older wood.

***Cornus alba* and *C. stolonifera* (Dogwood varieties)**

These dogwoods are grown chiefly for their colored stems in the fall and winter; young shoots produce the best effects.

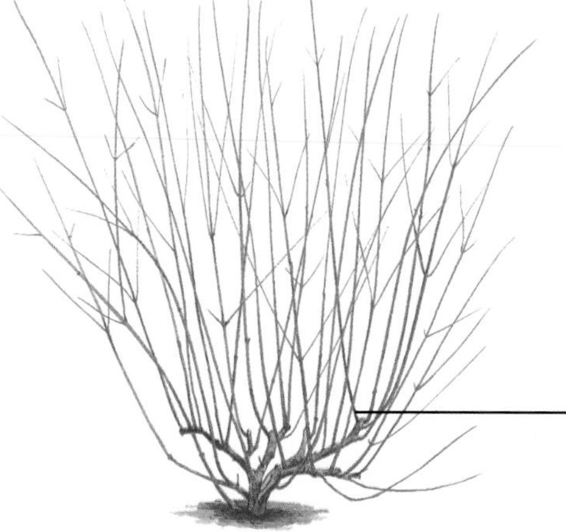

In early spring, hard prune the previous year's shoots, cutting back to a few in (cm) from the base. To renovate an old bush, remove some stems completely and cut back strong shoots to a framework 1 ft (30 cm) high.

Cytisus (Broom species and hybrids)

Most garden types of broom flower on shoots of the previous year. Prune annually to prevent them from becoming leggy.

Pruning must be started early in the plant's life, before the main branches become old. In summer, after flowering has finished, remove the growths that bore flowers, cutting back to young shoots. Never prune old wood, as new growth rarely sprouts.

Deutzia species and hybrids

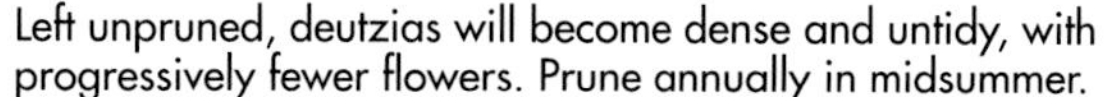

Left unpruned, deutzias will become dense and untidy, with progressively fewer flowers. Prune annually in midsummer.

After the flowers fade, thin out weak stems completely at ground level in order to admit light and air into the center. Cut back the stems that have flowered to a point low down where new shoots are developing.

Forsythia species and hybrids

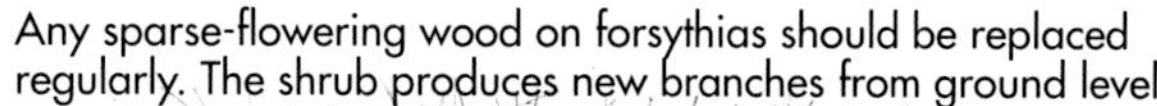

Any sparse-flowering wood on forsythias should be replaced regularly. The shrub produces new branches from ground level.

Once the shrub is 3 years old, take out old branches every year or two after flowering. On a neglected bush *(shown)*, cut out half of the old stems to encourage new shoots, then remove the rest the following year.

Fuchsia magellanica (Hardy fuchsia)

Though the rootstocks of this attractive shrub are hardy, top growth often dies back to near ground level each winter.

Where growth is killed, buds appear from near soil level in spring. At this time, prune dead shoots to just above a new bud. When branches survive, prune laterals to one or two buds from their base.

Hypericum calycinum (St.-John's-wort)

This St.-John's-wort is usually grown as a low ground cover. Pruning is made quicker and easier by using grass shears.

In very late winter or early spring, cut back the old shoots to within 2-3 in (5-7.5 cm) of the base. At the same time, clear away dead leaves and garden debris from between the twiggy stems. Young shoots will develop quickly and flower in summer.

Hypericum (St.-John's-wort shrubby species and hybrids)

Prune tall-growing hypericums, such as *Hypericum* 'Hidcote,' in early spring to remove dead and spindly wood.

Cut back dense or straggly wood to where young shoots are appearing. They will form a new framework, but won't give their best show of flowers until the following year. In future years, shorten all strong branches.

Indigofera (Indigo species)

With shrubby indigo, winter frosts may do the pruning for you; if not, it can be cut back hard each spring.

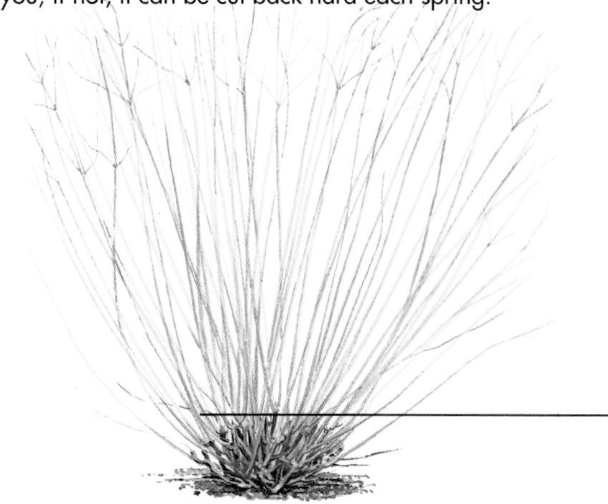

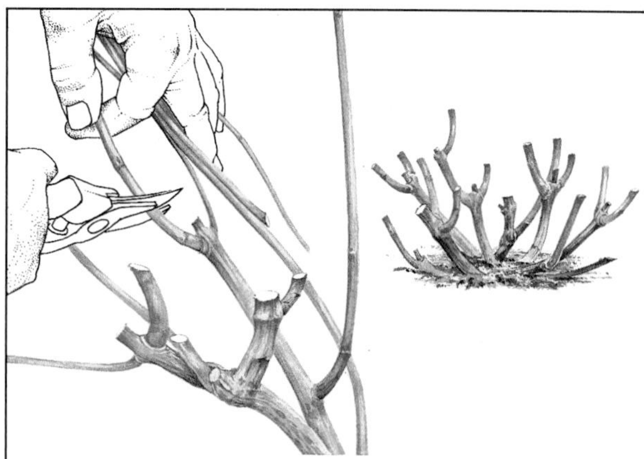

If shoots are killed down to ground level in winter, simply remove the deadwood in late winter or early spring. Cut back living stems almost to their junction with older wood. New shoots flower the same year.

Jasminum nudiflorum (Winter jasmine)

If left to itself, winter jasmine soon becomes a dense and unsightly tangle of growths, with relatively few flowers.

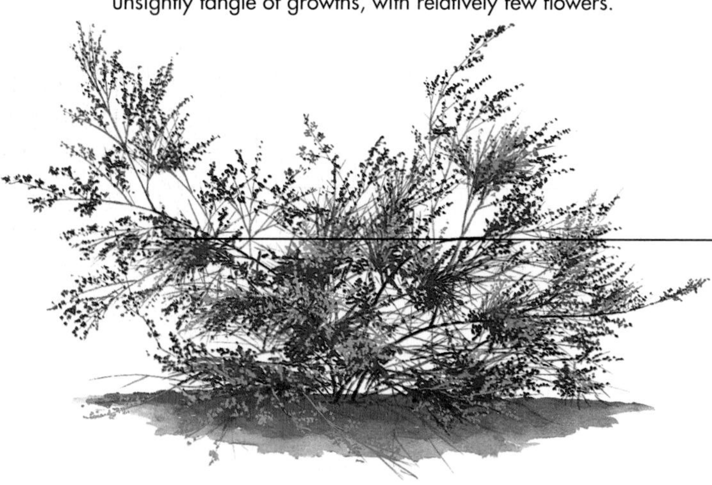

In early spring, cut back the shoots that have flowered to two or three buds from their junction with the main branches. Cut away all dead and weak growths to allow air to circulate. With white jasmine *(Jasminum officinale)*, just remove any crowded or dead stems.

Kerria japonica (Japanese kerria)

This kerria produces new shoots from ground level each year; these flower the next season and then often die back.

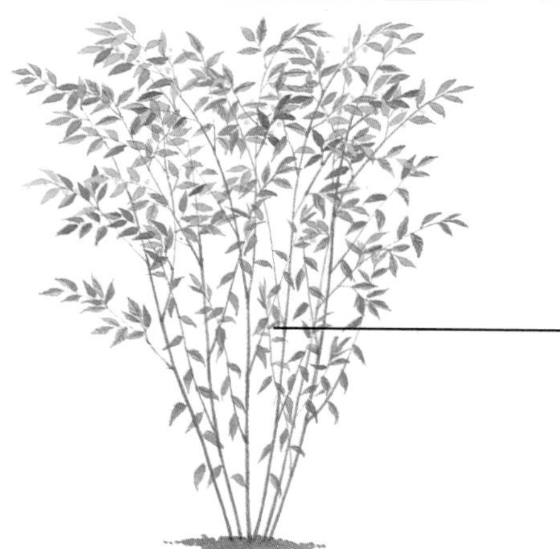

Remove the old flowered stems when the blooms fade in late spring or early summer. Cut right back to near the ground or, on stronger stems, to where healthy new shoots are developing.

Lavandula angustifolia (English lavender)

Without pruning, lavender becomes leggy and bare-stemmed. It is best trimmed annually with either pruning shears or grass shears.

In early spring to midspring, cut down the dead flower spikes plus about 1 in (2.5 cm) of top growth. Do not cut into old wood, as dieback can result. To tidy plants for winter, old flowers can be cut off in fall.

Leycesteria formosa (Flowering nutmeg)

This shrub produces strong shoots from the base, which flower [illegible] same year, and gives a display of pea-green winter

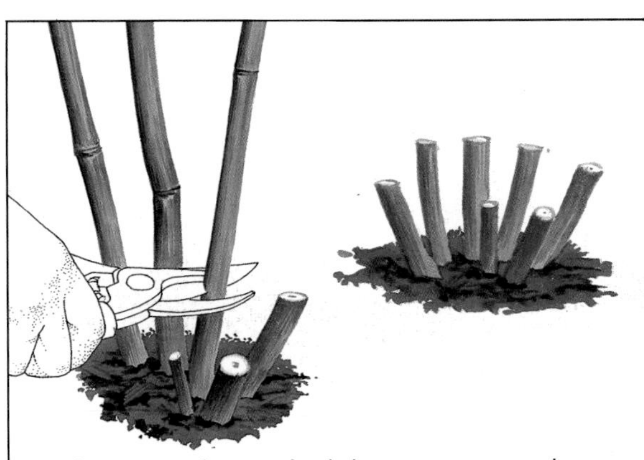

With a young plant, cut back the previous year's shoots to within two or three buds of the base in early spring. For an old, neglected plant, use loppers to cut the oldest wood down to ground level.

Lippia citriodora (Lemon-scented verbena)

Lippias may develop a permanent woody framework in mild areas, but branches often die back in winter.

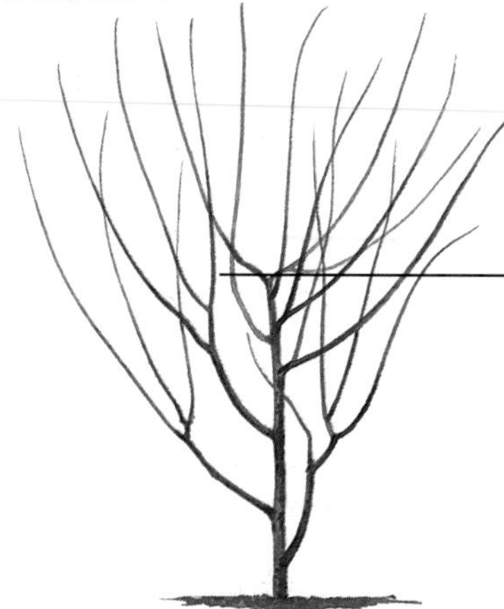

Shorten main branches that survive the winter to within 1 ft (30 cm) of the central stem in late spring. Cut back side shoots to within 2-3 in (5-7.5 cm) of the main branches. Prune frost-killed stems back to healthy buds.

Philadelphus (Mock orange species and hybrids)

Old mock orange plants invariably become dense and untidy, so prune them after flowering in midsummer.

Remove all dead and weak growth completely. Then cut back old stems to where young shoots are growing. Very old branches can be cut right down to ground level, so that no remaining growth is more than 5 years old.

Rhus (Sumac species and varieties)

The ferny leaves of sumacs turn fiery orange in the fall, but the best display is achieved only by regular pruning.

In late winter, cut the previous year's growths back to within 4 in (10 cm) of the old wood. By this method, a low, well-structured framework will gradually be built up, bearing very large and attractive leaves.

Ribes sanguineum (Flowering currant)

If a flowering currant becomes too large, it can be cut back hard immediately after blooming, generally in midspring.

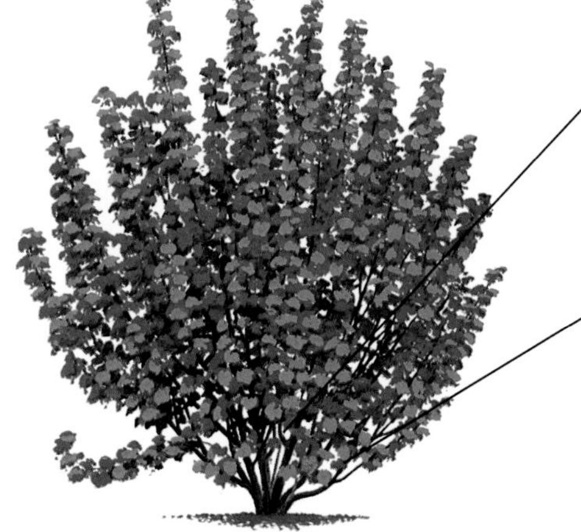

Cut the old stems back hard to live buds near the ground *(top left)*. Last year's shoots only need to be shortened to strong shoots lower down *(above left)*. In future years, remove one-third of the older stems.

Rubus **species and hybrids**

Rubus cockburnianus is grown for its white winter stems. Those remaining after pruning will flower the next summer.

In midsummer, cut out the stems that have flowered. Other species can be pruned in the same way, either after flowering or after fruiting. *R.* x *tridel* and *R. deliciosus,* however, need a framework of older wood.

Salix alba **(White willow varieties)**

Varieties of the white willow are often grown for their winter display of brightly colored young stems.

To produce a fresh crop of stems, cut them all back almost to their base every second year in late winter, as the buds are breaking. Or, cut half the stems every year. Red or yellow shoots will sprout from the stumps.

Sambucus **(Elderberry species and varieties)**

Elderberries grown for their foliage (not flowers or fruits) can be cut back hard to produce large, colorful young leaves.

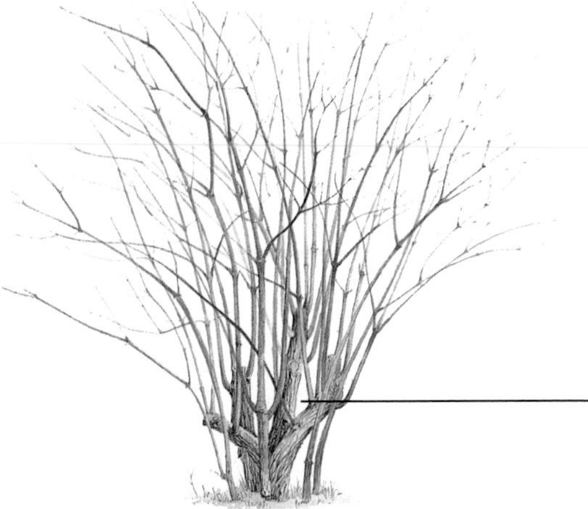

In early winter to midwinter, cut all stems close to the ground, if possible; otherwise, to 2-3 in (5-7.5 cm) from their base. Cut out weak shoots completely. Use a pruning saw to cut thicker shoots.

Santolina (Lavender cotton species and varieties)

All santolinas tend to become straggly with age and to lose their compact shape unless they are pruned annually.

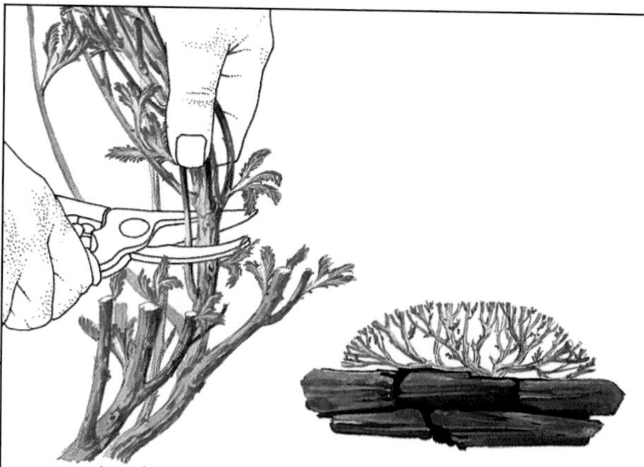

Prune hard in midspring, cutting back each long growth to where clusters of young shoots appear near the base. Flowers will form on the young shoots. Clip hedging plants in spring and summer.

Sorbaria (False spirea species)

Most species of sorbaria produce many suckers, which have to be removed to keep the plant within bounds.

Between early winter and late winter, prune all stems back hard — to within 4-9 in (10-23 cm) of the base. Vigorous new shoots will develop quickly and produce larger leaves and flower heads.

Spartium junceum (Spanish broom)

Old Spanish brooms can become very dense and cluttered, but annual pruning helps to form a more compact plant.

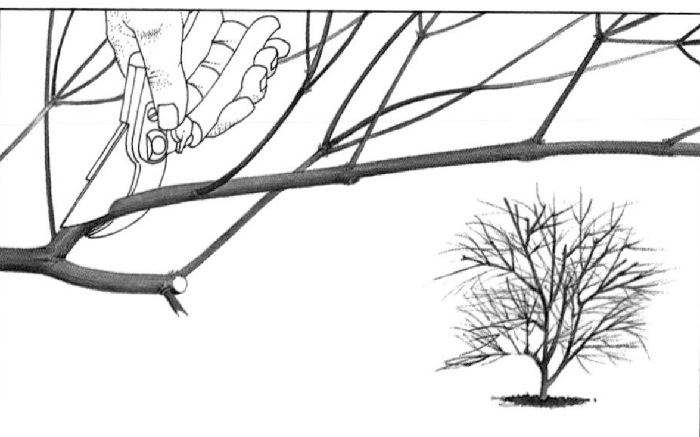

Renovate old plants in early spring by cutting back hard into old wood — as far back as you wish. In later years, prune the previous season's growths to within 1 in (2.5 cm) of the older wood. Very young plants should have the previous year's growth cut by half.

Spiraea x _arguta_ (Bridal wreath)

Some spireas, including *S.* x *arguta* and *S. thunbergii,* produce flowers on stems that grew the previous year.

Renovate an old plant after the flowers fade, usually in late spring. Cut back old stems to where younger shoots are growing *(top left)*. On all plants, cut away the part of the stem that has flowered *(above left)*.

Spiraea japonica (Japanese spirea)

Other spireas, including *S. japonica* and *S.* x *bumalda,* flower on the current year's shoots.

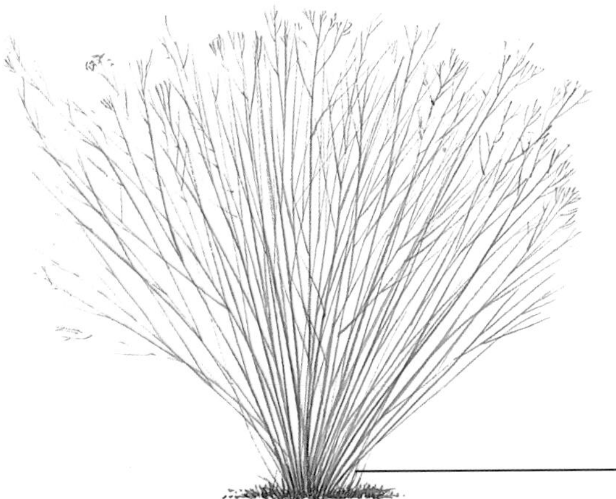

In late winter or early spring, prune strongest stems to within 2-3 in (5-7.5 cm) of the ground and cut out all weak stems. New shoots will spring up to flower in midsummer to late summer. Remove spent flowers and shoots with all-green leaves from colored varieties.

Stephanandra tanakae (Tanaka stephanandra)

This shrub is grown for its fall leaves and colored winter stems. Pruning lets in light and produces bright new stems.

After the plant has flowered in early summer or midsummer, cut back the flowered stems to the strong, young shoots sprouting lower down the stem, or right down to the ground. Remove weak stems completely.

Tamarix (Salt cedar species)

In good conditions, tamarisks may develop into straggly, top-heavy shrubs, so they need regular pruning.

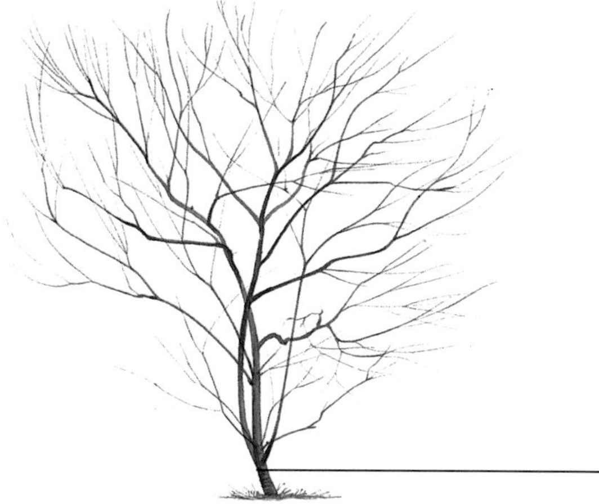

Prune summer-flowering species *(T. pentandra* and *T. ramosissima)* in late winter. Cut last year's growths to 2 in (5 cm) from the old wood. On an old, overgrown plant, cut strong stems to 2 in (5 cm) from their base and remove dead, weak, and straggly shoots. Prune spring-flowering species *(T. tetrandra* and *T. parviflora)* after blooms fade. Shorten lax stems; remove weak ones.

Weigela florida and hybrids

Weigelas can quickly become dense and crowded, with fewer blooms, so prune them annually after they flower in summer.

Prune back flowered stems to where young shoots are developing lower down. Cut out dead and weak growths. With an old, neglected plant, the oldest branches can be cut down nearly to the ground.

Wisteria species and varieties

In summer, the long leaders of wisterias must be trained in the direction you want this vigorous wall shrub to spread.

To encourage flowering spurs, cut back unwanted growths to 6-12 in (15-30 cm) from their base. In winter, shorten them further — to two or three buds from their base. Or, to provide more flower buds, work over the plant every few weeks throughout summer, pinching back all growths not needed for extending the coverage. Pinch back the shoots to 4 in (10 cm), and later pinch back any extension growth to two leaves — each shoot may be pinched back three times during the season. Then no winter pruning is needed.

TREE SURGERY

In general, ornamental trees do not require regular pruning, but they may become too large or get damaged during a storm and need remedial attention.

Left alone, most trees normally develop into a well-proportioned shape that is characteristic of the particular species. In certain circumstances, however, you may wish to modify their shape or size by pruning. A tree growing in a confined space, for example, may become unbalanced. Or, one that grows close to a house may have to be restricted to prevent structural damage to the building.

There are several other reasons for pruning a tree — for instance, after a storm, it may be necessary to tidy up broken branches to restore the tree's appearance and to prevent fungal diseases from entering the wounds.

On shallow, rocky soils tall trees may become unstable and therefore need to be kept in check. Trees that have been planted too close together often look better if they are thinned out as they mature, either by cutting down some of them or by removing a few branches from each.

In addition, some gardeners like to encourage artificial growth habits in their trees — a form of topiary on a large scale — perhaps to make an otherwise rather ordinary tree into a real eye-catcher, or to establish a different atmosphere in the garden.

A mature tree won't be harmed by the sudden loss of a single limb; in fact, the tree's energy will be diverted to branches elsewhere. If a branch has to be removed for some reason — it may simply be growing at an awkward angle or too close to a utility line, for example — don't be afraid to take it off. You must cut it back to the "collar" — the swollen ridge of bark surrounding the base of the branch.

Legal requirements

Before cutting *any* tree down, regardless of whether it stands on private property, check with your local government. Some communities have ordinances requiring you to receive permission before removing any trees. There may even be a penalty for violating such a community ordinance.

Generally, there is no restriction of responsible, properly conducted pruning, since that should contribute to the tree's health.

The correct tools

The branches and trunks of living trees consist of wood and bark, the density and hardness of which vary among species. Even when trees are dormant, this wood is relatively moist and has different physical properties from the dried lumber used in carpentry.

For this reason, carpentry saws are not suitable for living tree surgery of any kind — their teeth are too fine and closely set, and soon get clogged with damp sawdust, making for unnecessarily strenuous work.

Small branches can be trimmed with pruning shears, but any branch thicker than a finger should be cut with loppers, a pruning saw, or a bow saw.

If you are experienced in their use, chain saws can provide a

◀ **Winter pruning** A pole pruner is invaluable for trimming high branches without the need for a ladder. The cutting head (which, in some models, is much like pruning shears) can remove surplus twigs from mature fruit trees. Their elimination will divert the plant's energy into producing fruiting spurs.

TREE-PRUNING HAND TOOLS

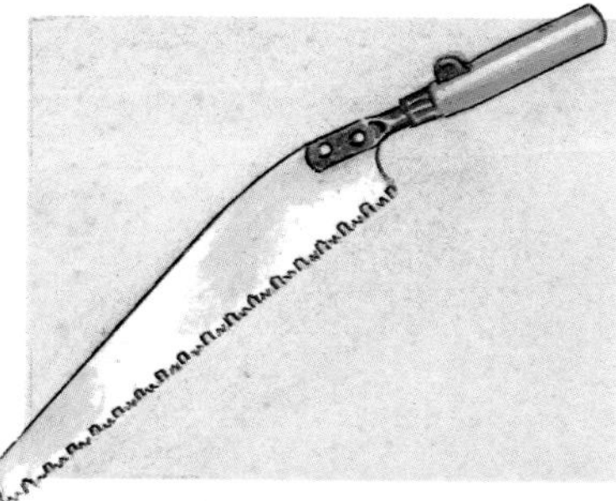

▲ **A straight pruning saw** is ideal for cutting branches 1-5 in (2.5-13 cm) thick. The teeth cut on the pull stroke — the strongest stroke if you are working at shoulder height. This saw has interchangeable handles.

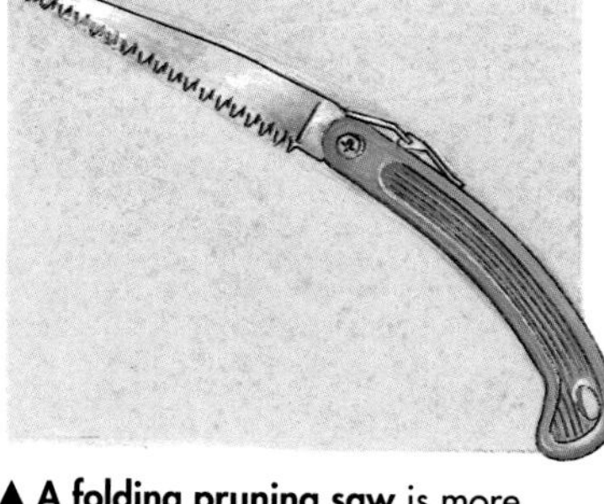

▲ **A folding pruning saw** is more portable than any other type and is safe when not in use, as the teeth are shielded inside the handle. The blade is short and suitable for branches 1-3 in (2.5-7.5 cm) in diameter.

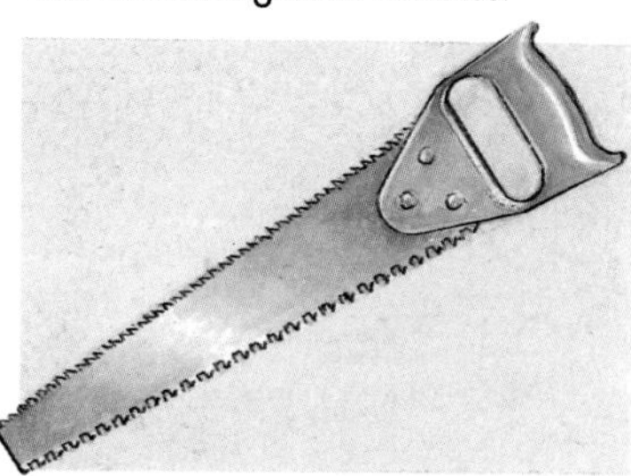

▲ **A duplex pruning saw** can be used for both coarse and fine work. Take care not to slice desirable branches with the unused edge. The blade is long and will cut quite large branches.

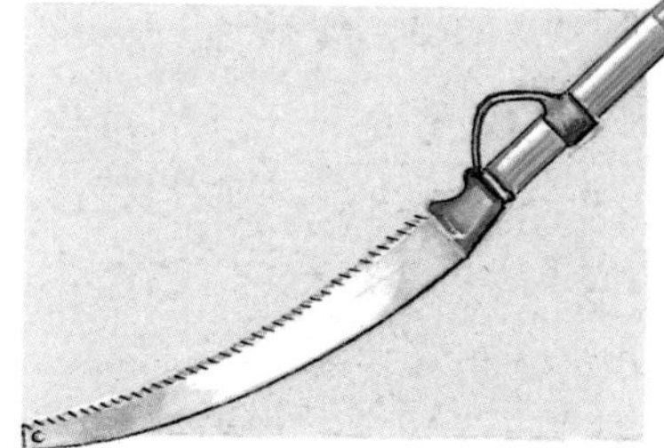

▲ **An orchard saw** has a slender, curved blade. This shape affords easier access to branches that are in confined spaces; the teeth cut deeply into the wood on the pull stroke with relatively little effort.

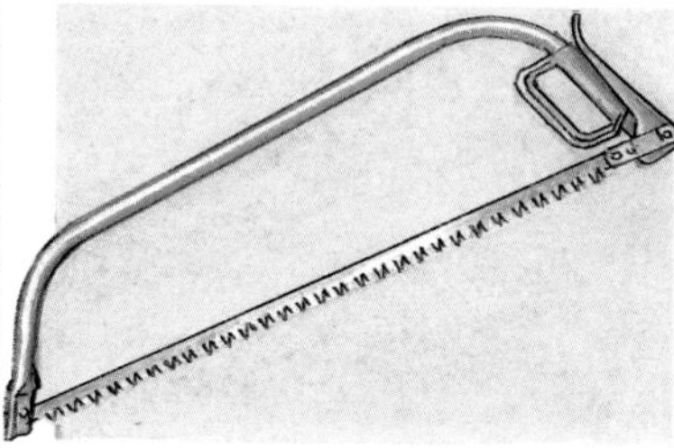

▲ **A bow saw** is the best tool for cutting trunks, boughs, and logs. The coarse teeth cut on both push and pull strokes. The bow-shaped handle gives the blade clearance to cut about 8 in (20 cm) deep.

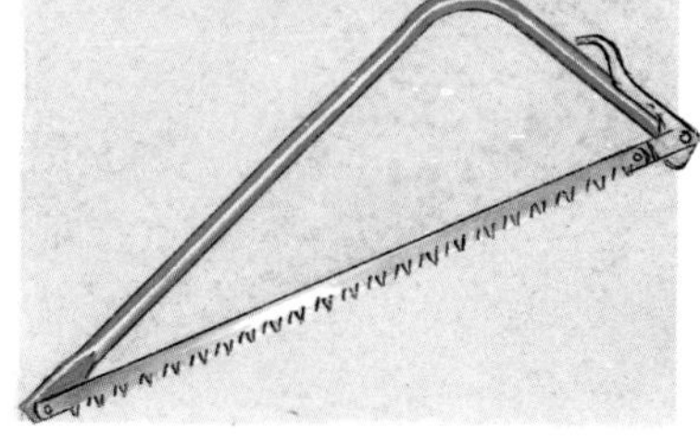

▲ **A triangular bow saw** serves the same purpose as a bow saw, but its pointed nose allows better access to closely packed branches. It is less suitable for cutting trunks, boughs, or logs over 5 in (13 cm) in diameter.

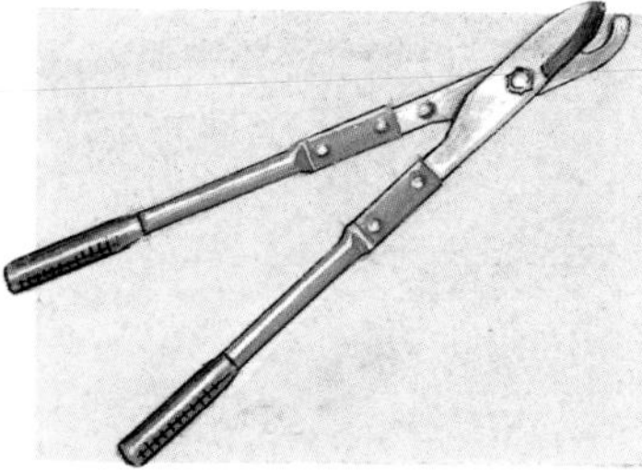

▲ **Loppers** are excellent for cutting branches that are too large or tough for pruning shears, but not large enough for a saw. The handles are about 1-1½ ft (30-45 cm) long and provide good leverage on the blades.

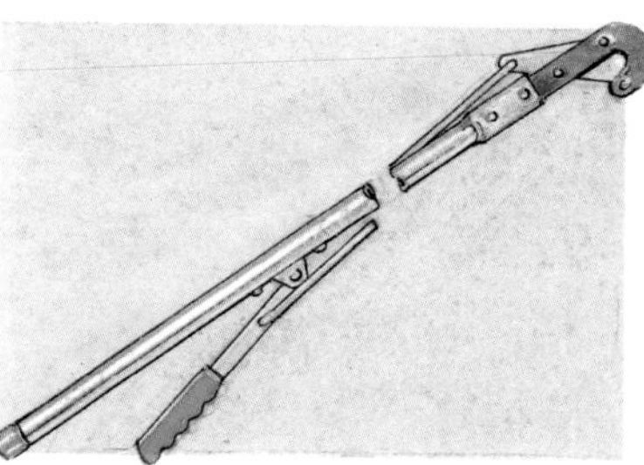

▲ **Pole pruners** reach high branches up to 1 in (2.5 cm) in diameter without a ladder. Some have one-piece poles; others have poles of interlocking pieces; lengths range from 6 ft (1.8 m) to 12 ft (3.6 m).

much quicker and less laborious solution to tree pruning, but they are far too dangerous for use by a casual, inexperienced gardener. For a novice, any job too big for a sharp handsaw is probably best left to a professional arborist.

To gain access to the upper branches of a large tree, you will need a sturdy ladder. Aluminum ladders are lighter to carry around the garden than wooden ones, and those with serrated rungs provide extra protection against slipping if you are wearing muddy shoes or boots.

Caution: For safety, tie the top of the ladder to the tree with rope before starting work. Get someone to hold the ladder from below until you have secured it at the top. Beware of overhead power lines when you carry a ladder around a tree, especially if the ladder is made of metal.

Dealing with branches

As with all garden plants, dead, diseased, or damaged branches must be removed from trees once they are spotted. If you fail to do so, the result can be further unsightly dieback or even the death of the entire tree. Any branch that crosses and rubs against another when the wind blows should also be taken off, since damaged bark can lead to cankers and other forms of decay.

To gain more access under a tree and to allow more sunlight to reach plants growing below it, cut back some of the lower branches to the main trunk or to a large bough. If you wish to reduce the overall weight of the tree's crown to minimize the chance of storm damage, sever some of the upper branches. Their elimination will also reduce the amount of shade cast by the tree.

Remove heavy branches in two pieces, taking the weight off the tip before attempting to make a final cut close to the trunk. The most important reason for doing it this way is to prevent the possibility of the bark tearing away from the main trunk as the branch falls — such a wound will take a long time to heal, and may become infected. To reduce further the chance of the bark tearing, make the first cut to all branches on the underside, then saw down into the first cut to complete the job.

Painting tree wounds with a

REMOVING A TREE BRANCH

1 Detach the bulk of the branch about 1½ ft (45 cm) from the main trunk or bough. Cut first on the underside of the branch, then make a second cut from the top of the branch to sever it.

2 Find the "collar," the ridge of bark that surrounds the branch's base. You will make the cut just to the outside of this collar (indicated by the dotted line), thus enabling the resulting wound to heal.

3 To remove the stump without tearing off a strip of bark, first undercut the stump as you did above, just outside the collar, then saw through from above.

4 Smooth the surface of the cut with a sharp knife and trim any ragged edges. Do not paint the wound — it may only encourage decay.

DEALING WITH SUCKERS

Suckers are shoots that spring from the base of a tree, and are very common on grafted trees. If not removed, they drain energy from the tree. On grafted trees, suckers may overtake and replace the desirable cultivar grafted onto the rootstock. Wearing gloves, tear them away from the rootstock *(left)*. So-called water sprouts can grow from pruning wounds. In fall, use pruning shears to cut them flush with the trunk *(right)*.

commercial dressing is counterproductive. Trees have a natural ability to isolate the damaged tissue. Wound dressings rarely seal a wound completely; instead, they keep its surface moist, and so, more prone to decay. In addition, most of them are toxic to the tree's cambium — the shallow layer of living cells inside the bark where all the tree's new growth occurs. As a result, dressings not only enhance decay, they can actually discourage healing.

To minimize damage to the tree's bark and the living tissue underneath, use only sharp tools. Make the cut at the right spot — just outside the raised collar of wood that is surrounding the base of each limb. The tree should heal before decay organisms succeed in penetrating the wound.

Boughs and trunks

You may decide to cut the tree's main trunk for cosmetic purposes or to eradicate diseased and insecure wood. If you do so, special care must be taken.

Heartwood at the center of a trunk or bough can rot before any outward symptoms are evident, and this inner decay seriously weakens the tree — it can fall during high winds and damage surrounding property. If large, flattish, fan-shaped fungal growths, known as bracket fungi, appear on the bark, they signal that internal rotting is at an advanced stage, and the bough or trunk must be felled.

Root pruning

Trees often have substantial roots that extend beyond the spread of the top growth. These can cause damage to the foundations of buildings and walls, and to paths and drains. The larger the root system grows, the more vigorous is the top growth, which may be undesirable in a small garden.

To limit the tree's spreading branches and its ever-increasing height, winter root pruning is a useful practice. To be successful, however, it must begin when the tree is still small and then become a regular part of maintenance. You may also wish to prune roots to prepare a tree for replanting elsewhere the following year.

Start when the tree has reached a height and spread of about 10 ft (3 m). Dig out a trench around the tree, about 5 ft (1.5 m) away from

THE ART OF POLLARDING

1 Pollarding is a special pruning technique adopted either as a means of restricting the crown of a mature tree, or of developing an unusual, often formal growth shape. The tree should have almost reached its ultimate desired height before you begin pollarding in late winter.

2 Using a bow saw, lop the entire crown of the tree, leaving just short stumps with lots of dormant growth buds. Or, cut out selected branches and reduce the others to desired lengths or shapes — like bonsai, pollarding techniques are largely a matter of personal taste.

3 In spring, tufts of new shoots will grow from the cuts. These may have colorful bark and will bear lush foliage. In 1 to 3 years, or as soon as the new shoots have outgrown the desired space, prune back to the original wounds. After repeated pollarding, the stumps become gnarled.

the trunk, putting the soil to one side. Try not to damage small roots with your spade, but aim to expose all the thickest outward-growing roots. Using a pruning saw, sever only the largest roots. Finally, refill the trench with the original soil and press it in firmly.

As the tree grows, it needs a stronger anchor. It is unwise to sever all the large roots at once. Instead, divide the circle around the tree into four sections, and excavate no more than two opposite ones at once. This way, the tree always has enough roots to protect it against the wind.

Pollarding

Repeated severe lopping of a tree's crown, cutting back to the established main trunk or to main branches, is known as pollarding. The effect produced is that of a single tight ball of leafy growth at the top of the tall trunk or tufts of fresh growth along a framework of gnarled branches. When pollarding, the cuts are always made at the same point; protective calluses then form at the cut stumps.

Pollarded trees have a unique, almost grotesque appearance and can be used to great effect in a formal garden. This type of pruning is also useful where trees are planted close to a building and a broad-spreading crown would occupy too much space. Street trees are frequently pollarded to allow the free passage of traffic beneath their crowns.

Linden trees *(Tilia)* are favorite subjects for pollarding, since they rapidly regenerate a head of lush, green, leafy growth after being cut back. Colored-stemmed varieties of the white willow — *Salix alba* 'Britzensis' (scarlet) and *S. a.* 'Vitellina' (bright yellow) — produce their brightest bark when pollarded annually.

CUTTING DOWN A SMALL TREE

1 Take heed of the legal note on page 151. Ensure that the area all around the tree is clear of people or valued possessions — keep young children and pets safely indoors. Start by tying a sturdy rope to the crown of the tree. Get a strong helper to maintain a firm pull on the rope in the required direction of fall, standing beyond the danger zone — the tree will fall toward your helper.

Make the first cut **(1)** 3 ft (1 m) or so up on the side facing your helper, sawing horizontally one-third of the way through the trunk. Then saw out a wedge of wood by cutting downward at an angle of 30-45° to the horizontal into the back of the first cut **(2)**. At this point, the tree should still stand securely on its own, but your helper must maintain a firm grip on the rope. Make the final cut on the side

behind the direction of fall **(3)**. Saw downward at an angle of 30° to the horizontal toward the inner edge of the wedge cavity. As the tree loses its balance it will fall into the wedge. As soon as the tree starts to fall, quickly move away and allow your helper to guide the falling tree with the rope. Clear away the debris, then sever the roots and lever out the stump.

Garden tools and safety

The old saying that "a craftsman is only as good as his tools" applies as much to gardening as to any other activity. Having the right tools for the job, keeping them in good condition, and using them correctly can mean the difference between a quick, easily accomplished task and an arduous one, inefficiently done. Top-quality stainless steel tools, well cared for, can last for years, if not a lifetime. In the long run, buying the best tools you can afford is more satisfying and economical than buying a series of cheap but short-lived ones.

Before purchasing tools, check that the handles are comfortable, and that large tools suit your size and strength; border spades, for example, hold smaller, lighter loads. Clean tools after every use and oil metal parts occasionally, especially before winter storage. Store tools somewhere clean, dry, and secure.

Common sense dictates that sharp tools as well as power tools should be handled with care. Thoughtless acts, such as filling a gasoline mower with the engine running or plugging too many electrical extension cords together, can cause accidents.

Keep tools and equipment out of reach of children, and garden chemicals, especially herbicides and pesticides, away from both children and pets. Remember that young children can climb on one object to reach another. Make sure chemicals are clearly labeled and in their original containers, never in soft-drink or other bottles, for example. Safety with chemicals extends beyond the garden, too. Don't flush unwanted chemicals down the drain or pour them on the ground, but take them to your community toxic-waste disposal site instead.

Tools of the trade Having the right tools takes the backache out of gardening.

GARDEN TOOLS & EQUIPMENT

A multitude of hand and power tools are advertised as labor-saving devices. Some are essential; others may be a waste of money and time.

Certain tools are essential for all gardening jobs; others are needed only for more specialized tasks. It is inadvisable, however, to invest in gadgets that are useful only on rare occasions, or in heavy-duty equipment for the average garden (the latter can be rented more cheaply on a daily basis).

Buying a small number of traditional good-quality tools that will last a lifetime is better value for money than spending your entire budget on so-called bargain products, which are often inferior in use and may break down or wear out quickly.

Hand tools

Almost every gardener will need a spade, fork, rake, hoe, trowel, and a pair of pruning shears. If a lawn forms a large part of your garden, a lawn rake, half-moon edging tool, and edging and grass shears will be as useful as the essential mower. Hedge shears will be needed for trimming a hedge (power shears or hedge trimmers are a more expensive option).

Well-known brand names are the safest buys, but you will have to decide whether a particular product is suitable for your needs. Handle the tool before you buy it, checking its weight, strength, and comfort — one brand or model may be ideal for a tall or very strong person, while another may be better for a short or less powerful person. Pruning shears in particular must feel comfortable in your palm — there are many different grip sizes and shapes to choose from, and inappropriate ones will give you blisters after prolonged use.

Spades and garden forks usually have high-carbon steel heads and are given a coat of paint to protect them from rusting. Once the paint wears off, regular wiping with an oily cloth will keep the head in good order. Stainless steel and chromium-plated types are available at extra cost; provided the surface is not scratched and pitted, they will maintain their shine for many years. Polished surfaces are easier to push into the soil than pitted, rusty ones.

Tool handles are commonly metal or wooden. Both are durable and should be strong enough for normal garden use. Spade and fork handles may also be made of plastic now, and can be replaced, if necessary. Plastic is strong, splinter-free, and durable, and therefore it is not used simply for frugality. The handle should be securely attached to the shaft and the shaft should be securely attached to the head. The rivets or bolts must be flush with the surface and should feel smooth.

Caring for your tools

Clean all tools thoroughly after use — never put them away caked with mud or grass clippings. Wipe metal surfaces with an oily cloth and coat bare wood with light machine or mineral oil occasionally. Don't store tools on a concrete floor — they will become damp

◀ **Heavy-duty two-handed pruning shears,** also known as loppers, are useful for cutting thick-stemmed, woody shrubs and small trees. The handles provide leverage and allow access to the center of a dense plant. Use a bow saw for larger branches.

and rusty. Hang them by their handles on hooks secured to the shed or garage wall. Treat wooden handles with respect — if splintered, they can be dangerous.

Sharpen the blades of pruning shears and hedge shears regularly — blunt blades make the cutting action tiring and produce ragged cuts that, in turn, can lead to plants becoming diseased.

Special hand tools

If age or physical fitness is not on your side — or if you have a disability — certain gardening jobs may be difficult or impossible. There are, however, several tools on the market that can make a particular job more manageable, or render an otherwise impossible one within your capability. The following information refers only to normal production tools, not to any specially adapted equipment made to order for an individual disability.

Star-wheeled cultivators can be used to cultivate light soils. They consist of revolving spiked disks mounted on a frame that incorporates a hoe blade. The unit is attached to a long handle and is pushed over the soil surface, producing a fine tilth while, at the same time, cutting down small weeds. Depth of cultivation is regulated by the angle at which the handle is held. This implement requires the use of one hand only.

Two-handled spades make soil lifting easier. A second D-shaped handle is mounted midway down the shaft, allowing you to pull the spade head upward from a standing or sitting position rather than having to bend down to reach the base of the shaft.

Long-handled grippers consist of a pair of boards fixed to the ends of two long handles, mounted together on a scissorlike hinge. They can be used to gather up garden debris without bending.

Long-handled weeders are useful for extracting weeds from inaccessible places, and they eliminate the need for bending. There are spring- or lever-operated models that will pick up the weeds once loosened from the soil.

Loppers are a powerful type of pruning shear; they are able to cut branches up to about 1¼ in (30 mm) in diameter. The handles are generally 18 or 22 in (45 or 55 cm) long, allowing you to reach into the center of the plant.

Pole pruners give easy access to tree branches at heights up to 20 feet. The pole may be in one piece or consist of two or more interlocking sections for convenient storage. A cutting head at one end is operated with a pull rope, and the head of many models is also equipped with a saw. Fruit harvesters are a modification of this tool — metal fingers at the end of the pole pick the fruit, which can then be dropped into a basket.

Bow saws often provide the best means of cutting large branches or trunks. A replaceable blade is tensioned across a broad, bow-shaped handle, giving clearance to cut trunks up to 1 ft (30 cm) in diameter.

Grass hooks, scythes, and sickles, consisting of shaped blades attached to short or long handles, are useful for cutting down long, coarse grass and weeds.

Sod lifters have a large rounded blade attached to a long handle, angled appropriately to undercut and lift sod pieces.

Tools for the disabled

Special tools and equipment may be available for disabled gardeners, including a kneeling bench with sturdy metal handles to facilitate movement to and from a kneeling position, and wheelbar-

► **Digging made easy** A foot-pedal spade eliminates the need for bending and strength when you are digging. A pedal attached to the base of the spade shaft makes it easier to push the blade into the soil. The shaft is mounted to the blade via a pivot — by pulling backward on the handle, soil is thrown forward automatically. If needed, a fork head can be fitted in place of a spade.

rows that can be hitched onto wheelchairs. Lightweight aluminum hand tools are molded in one piece, with special grips for finger and thumb.

Power tools

Garden power tools formerly meant just lawn mowers and chain saws. In recent years, though, there has been an expansion of powered labor-saving appliances that have simplified almost the whole range of gardening chores.

Like lawn mowers, the advantage of the new power tools over traditional hand tools is the speed and ease with which they perform strenuous, time-consuming tasks.

A prime example is the gasoline-powered garden tiller, or rototiller, which certainly reduces the backbreaking work of turning the soil. The types whose blades are mounted at the rear are particularly easy to use, and some can be guided with only one hand.

However, the rototiller also illustrates the limitations of many power tools. It can't dig as deep as a spade or fork, since typically the blades reach only 4-6 in (10-15 cm) below the frame. And because a garden tiller digs always to the same level, repeated use may also create a layer of hardpan in the soil just below that level.

▲ **String trimmers** are useful gadgets, suitable for trimming lawn edges and cutting grass around obstacles. Wear safety goggles, sturdy shoes, and — if needed — ear protection.

Power sources

The power source for all garden tools is usually either gasoline or electricity. Electric tools are generally cheaper and are useful in small- to average-sized gardens; the need for extension cords restricts their range. Effective battery-powered models for many tools are now being developed.

Gasoline-powered tools usually have a higher price tag, and are aimed at larger gardens. The initial expense of a gasoline-powered tool should be judged against its longer working life. Manufacturers admit that generally gasoline appliances last 10 to 15 years, while equivalent electric models last 5 to 10 years.

To operate an electrically powered tool safely, it is essential that you use the correct outdoor extension cord. There are many different sizes, or gauges, of cord available, and you must make sure that the length and gauge of cord you select can carry the amperage your motor requires. (The amperage rating for a tool's motor will be given on the tool itself.) If you use an extension cord of insufficient size, or if you link a series of extension cords together, the resulting drop in voltage can cause a tool's motor to overheat and possibly burn out. For instance, a 15-amp tool requires a 14-gauge, 25-ft (7.5-m) cord, but if you need to reach further than 50 ft (15 m) with the same tool, you must use a 12-gauge cord.

You should be aware that gasoline tools are more mechanically complex, so bills for parts and labor can be higher than for those that run on electricity. In addition, electric models are simpler to start, and don't have a fuel tank to refill. Seasonal maintenance is also simpler.

Weight is another factor that you should consider. Electric models tend to be constructed mostly of lightweight plastic, making them easy to lift and manage.

Gasoline-powered models are built of metal parts that protect them against the corrosive fuel they burn; as a result, these tools can be very heavy. If normal use requires that a tool has to be lifted or held in the air for any length of time (such as with a hedge trimmer or chain saw), make sure you will be able to safely control the extra weight of it when it has a full tank of gas. Some tools are specially balanced to counteract the engine weight. Otherwise, they would be too unwieldy.

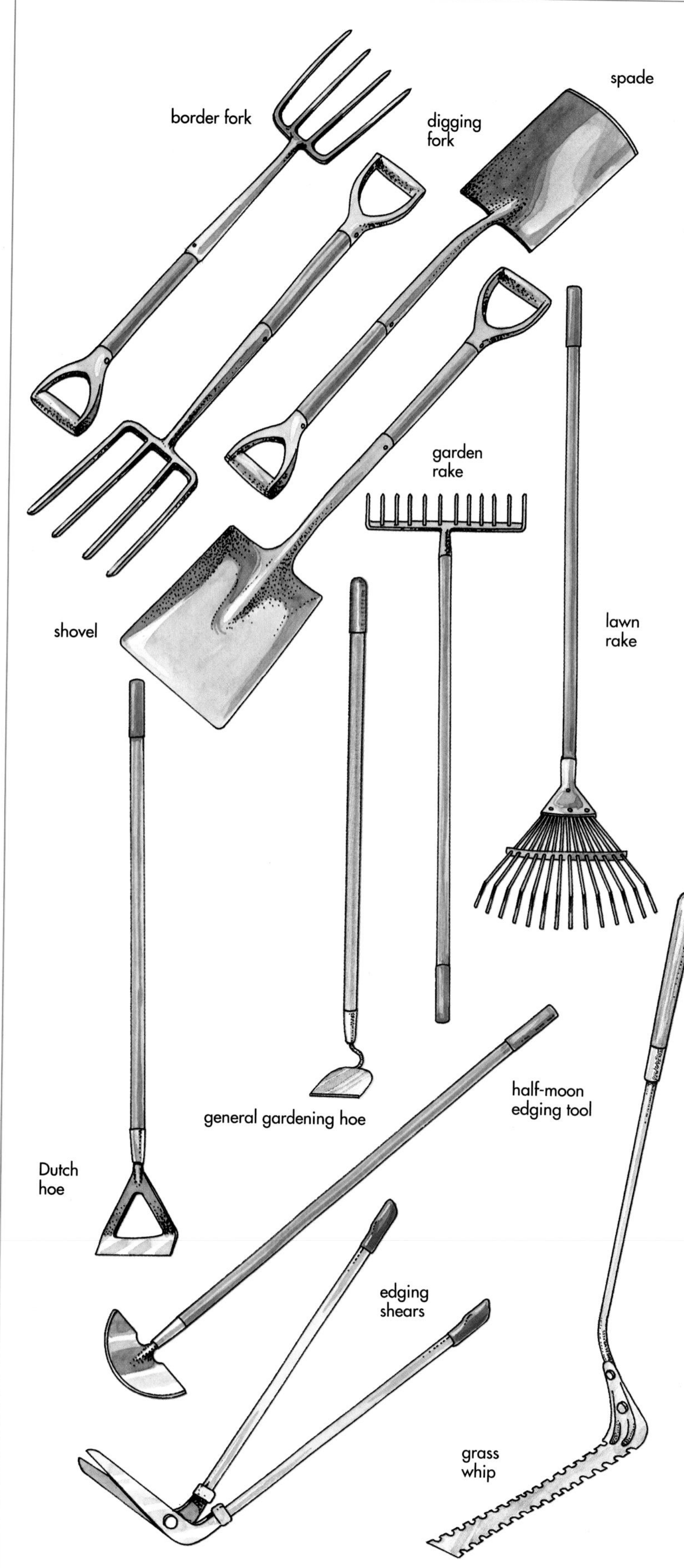

LONG-HANDLED TOOLS

Garden forks are sold under a variety of names, depending on their size — digging or border, for instance — but these names do not correspond to standard specifications. Forks are used primarily for breaking up and preparing the soil prior to planting or sowing, but are also useful for moving debris or compost, and for general cultivation and lawn aeration. Border forks are smaller than digging forks and are used for more shallow cultivation of planted areas. Most digging forks have square tines, tapering to a point. Don't buy forks with flat tines — they bend easily.
Spades may also be called digging or border, depending on their size. They are used for deep soil preparation and for making large planting holes.
Shovels are similar to spades, but have the sides of the blade curved upward to form a scoop. They are used for shifting sand, soil, or other materials.
Hoes are used to cut down small weeds growing among other plants and for breaking up crusted soil surfaces. The Dutch, or "scuffle," hoe has an open triangular steel blade attached to a long shaft and is used with a push-pull action — it furnishes the quickest means of clearing weeds. The general gardening hoe has a backward-angled blade secured by a swan-necked stem to a long shaft. It is used for loosening heavy weed growth and, when tipped at an angle, for making seed drills. Shafts are generally made of lightweight wood.
Rakes consist of a row of metal, wooden, or plastic tines — prongs — mounted on a horizontal head attached to a long handle. They are used for general seedbed preparation and soil leveling. Lightweight alloy shafts make easier work of raking, but cost more than ordinary ash handles. Lawn rakes are designed for removing moss and dead grass. Their heads are fan shaped, with springy wire, bamboo, rubber, or plastic tines. Lawn rakes can also be used for collecting fallen leaves.
Half-moon edging tools have a rounded blade and are used for cutting a new, straight edge in turf at the perimeter of a lawn.
Edging shears are convenient for trimming grass blades along the lawn edges. The blades are angled in such a way that you can cut the grass from a standing position without the need to bend over.
Grass whips are used for scything down tall grass and weeds. Though the cut they give is rough, they can prepare the way for the smoother finish of a lawn mower.

SMALL HAND TOOLS

Hand trowels are used for setting out small plants and for digging out weeds. Avoid those that have a thin neck — it may bend during use.
Hand forks, short- or long-handled, are used for weeding and cultivating the soil around plants. They may have three or five tines, which can be curved or flat — the latter are generally recommended.
Hand cultivators, with three or five hooked tines, are used for loosening compacted soil. Three-tined models are best for heavy soil.
Onion hoes are used for general surface cultivation between rows of seedlings or other small plants.
Pruning shears resemble pliers. They are hand-held, spring-loaded shears used for cutting small stems up to ½ in (1.2 cm) in diameter. Some have one blade that cuts against an anvil head, others have blades that cut with a scissor action. They range in size from small flower gatherers to large, heavy-duty types, but one general-purpose pair should be adequate.
Hedge shears are used for trimming hedges. The blade edges may be straight or serrated — the former are easiest to sharpen, but the latter are better for cutting woody stems.
Grass shears are used for the lighter work of trimming long grass. Since they are spring-loaded, they may be operated with one hand, and are quite efficient, though their use involves stooping.
Pruning saws, which come in various shapes and sizes (including folding models), are excellent for pruning or cutting back woody branches that are too large for pruning shears but not large enough to warrant the use of a bow saw. Some have fine teeth on one cutting edge and coarse teeth for rougher work on the other.
Bulb planters are handy for planting bulbs, especially in grass or among other plants. They consist of a metal cylinder with a serrated cutting edge that is pushed into the soil by means of a handle.
Planting lines, consisting of a reel of string fastened at each end to a stake, are used for marking out seed drills and straight edges.
Dibbles are convenient for making planting holes. They may be pencil-sized sticks used for inserting small plants or cuttings, or larger versions up to 1 in (2.5 cm) in diameter for planting vegetables.
Dandelion weeders have a blade mounted at the end of a long, stout neck, so that it can cut, then pry out the whole root of perennial weeds, such as dandelions.
Cape Cod weeders cut like a hoe, but because of their size, are much better adapted to close, delicate work.

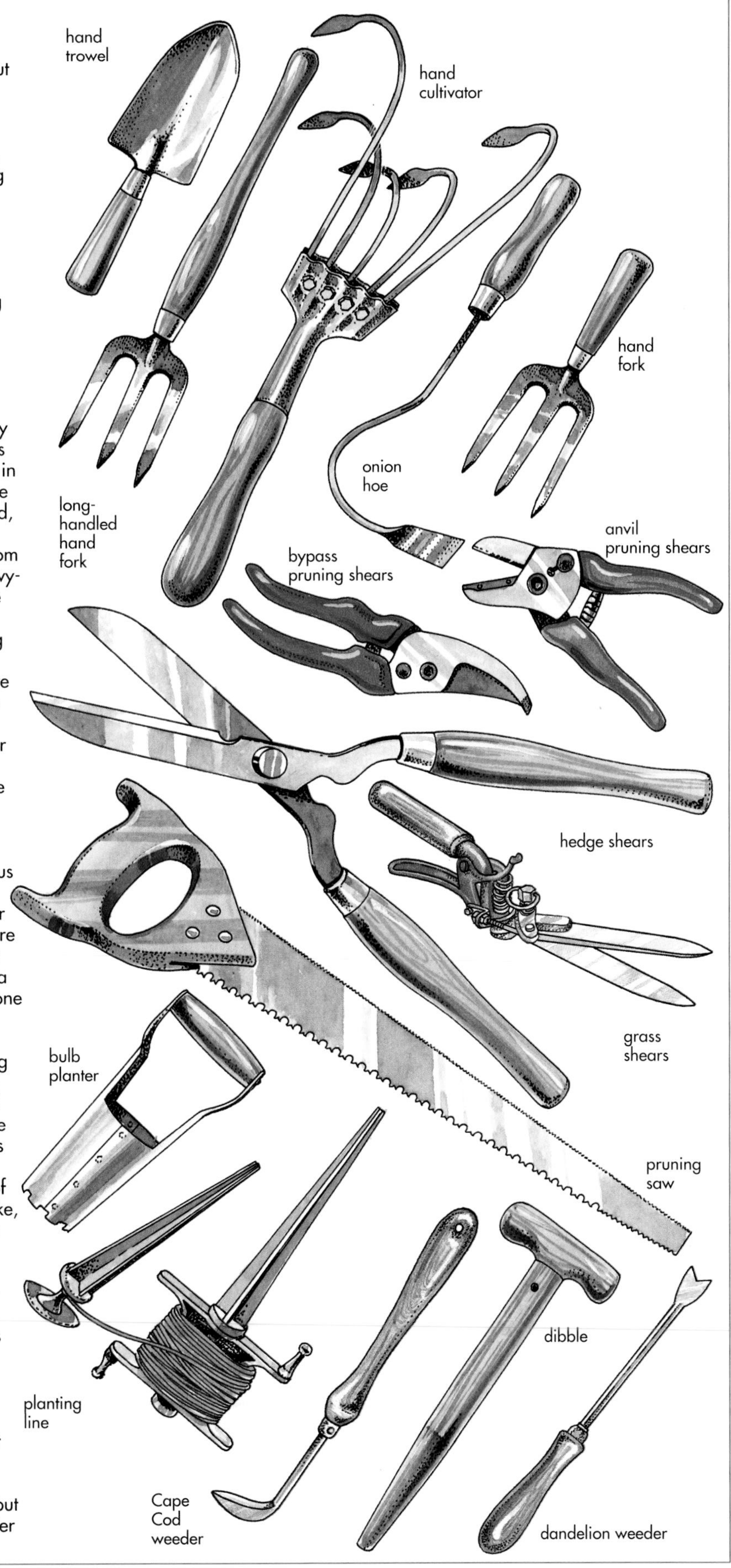

POWER TOOLS

Hedge trimmers should have reciprocating blades — two blades that move at the same time. Those trimmers that have just one blade vibrate uncomfortably. Some trimmers have teeth on both sides of the blades and some have teeth along just one edge — the latter are not as versatile.

Generally, the closer the teeth, the cleaner the finish. Close teeth are fine for maintaining Lawson cypress hedges, but wider-gapped teeth are more suitable if you want to prune woody stems and branches.

Power hedge trimmers are the source of many accidents, so safety is vital. Machines fitted with shutoff switches have a two-step starting procedure, which prevents the machine from being activated accidentally. Make sure the motor will turn off when you relieve pressure on the power switch.

Chain saws of professional size and power are best left to professionals. Smaller electric models are useful for removing small- to medium-sized branches and for felling thin-stemmed or young trees. Like hedge trimmers, chain saws should have a two-step starting procedure and turn off when you release the power switch.

String trimmers, also called nylon-cord trimmers, are popular with gardeners because they perform several tasks. The machines are ideal for cutting grass where lawn mowers can't reach, such as around pathways and near buildings and trees. They will also edge a lawn, though not as neatly as some edging tools.

Some trimmers are equipped with devices to feed the nylon string. As the string can snap while the tool is running, this mechanism prevents interruption of your work.

Garden tillers come with the tines either in front of or behind the wheels. Front-tine tillers are cheaper, but harder to control and less effective than rear-tine tillers.

Power shredders help recycle your garden refuse — woody tree and shrub prunings, for instance — by reducing it into shredded matter ready for the compost pile. Electric and gasoline models are expensive, but do begin the process of creating high-grade compost.

Hand trimmers are one of the easiest means of trimming lawn edges, and they give a very clean cut. Some types can be fitted with an extension rod so that you do not have to stoop.

Battery-powered hand trimmers require regular recharging — you could run out of power in the middle of a task. They are not suitable for yards bigger than 30 sq yd (sq m).

Lawn mowers See page 40.

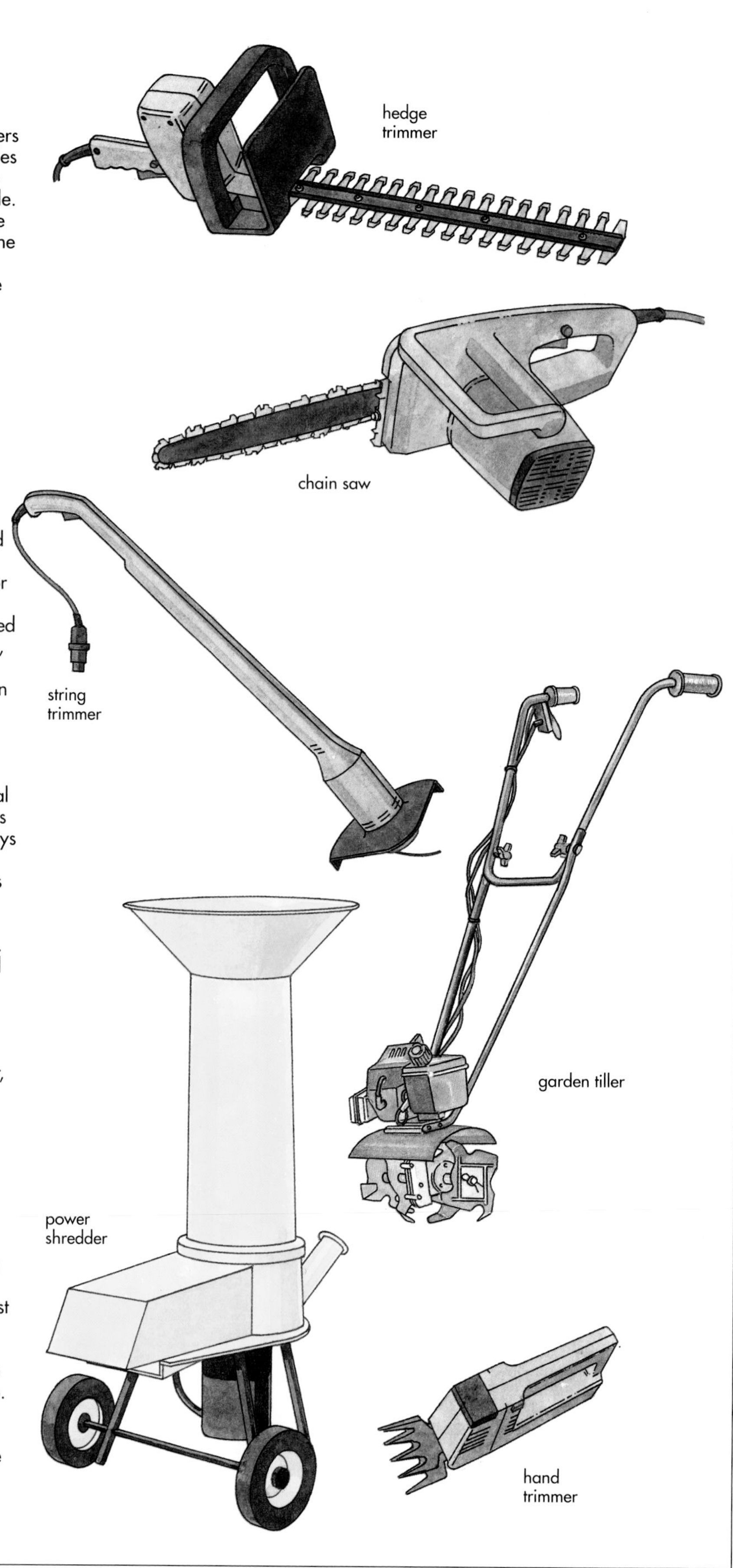

GARDEN SAFETY

Many gardening activities are potentially hazardous. Simple precautions can safeguard you and your family.

Thousands of accidents occur in gardens every year, and statistics show that all age groups, irrespective of gardening experience, are involved. Almost all of these accidents are avoidable; gardening can be as safe as any other leisure activity so long as a few basic precautions are taken.

General precautions

Unless you are in very good physical condition or engage in manual labor daily, take plenty of time with strenuous jobs, such as digging or pushing a reel lawn mower. Give yourself frequent breaks to do something more leisurely. Never set yourself a massive task — such as digging the entire vegetable plot in one afternoon — you could end up with muscle or back pain for weeks afterward.

Choose gloves appropriate for the job in order to protect your hands from thorns, splinters, and rough or sharp materials. Wear sturdy shoes or boots at all times, preferably with steel-reinforced toes. Don't garden in bare feet or in sandals. Remember that overexposure to sunshine can have serious consequences — wear a hat if you intend to stay out in the sun all day, and protect your face and arms with sunblock.

Additional safety gear should be worn for particularly hazardous activities. When cutting brick or flagstone with a chisel and hammer, for example, protect your eyes with safety goggles. Always read the label completely before applying any pesticide or herbicide, and have the number of the nearest poison-control center handy in case of accidents. Wear rubber gloves for handling chemicals, as well as any other protective gear recommended on the pesticide or herbicide label. Don't spray chemicals on a windy day, and take care to stand upwind of the target when spraying.

▲ **Safety first** Use all power tools, such as hedge trimmers, with care. Hold them with both hands and keep the cord across your shoulder or clipped to a belt. Don't lean over a hedge from a wobbly stepladder.

◀ **Pool covers** Stretch strong, rigid wire mesh over ponds and ornamental pools to prevent children and pets from falling in. Aquatic plants will soon grow through and above the mesh.

Safety with hand tools

Take your time and do not rush jobs — accidents happen much more often when you hurry.

Hold pruning shears firmly in the palm of your hand, getting a good grip before you make cuts. Different-sized models are available to suit your particular hand size — choose the right one to avoid getting blisters or pinching your skin between the pivot or spring mechanism. Use a pruning saw to cut large stems — never struggle with pruning shears because you can blister your hand and strain the tool. Wear gloves if your skin is soft or if you are pruning thorny plants. Secure the

PROTECTIVE CLOTHING

1 Wear strong gardening gloves when pruning thorny or woody plants, especially roses. Gloves also provide some protection against blisters in the palm of your hand if you have soft skin.

2 Choose sturdy shoes or boots, preferably with steel-reinforced toes, when digging or using equipment. Never stab a fork into the soil — place the tines on the soil surface, then push the fork into the ground with your foot.

3 When using string trimmers, wear safety goggles and long boots for protection from the rotating cord, which can fling stones and other objects. Ear protection will reduce the high-pitched noise of the cord.

4 Put on sturdy gloves and footwear when doing any construction work around the garden. Also, wear safety goggles to protect your eyes when cutting paving stones with a chisel, or chipping stone or concrete.

safety catch on pruning shears when they are not in use.

If you are cutting long grass with shears, check that there are no concealed electric cords or other objects in the way, then proceed carefully. Take similar care when wielding a scythe or grass whip, and make cutting strokes away from yourself to avoid injuring your legs. Wear long sleeves and gloves when dealing with coarse weeds, which may include nettles and brambles.

Ensure that the blades of all cutting tools are closed together when not in use. Because of the leverage of their long handles, loppers are particularly dangerous; you can easily lose a finger if you handle them carelessly.

When digging with a garden fork, place the tines on the ground first, then push into the soil with your foot. Never stab the fork into the ground — you could put it through your foot.

Do not leave a rake or a garden fork lying on the ground with its tines pointing upward — if you step on the tines, the handle may catapult into your face.

Safety with power tools

Electricity is a safe power source, but careless use can damage tools and cause injury.

Extension cords must be in good condition, with an undamaged outer covering. They should be as short as possible, free from kinks, and absolutely dry. When using cords stored on a reel, unroll them to their full length before plugging in power tools — heavy electrical loads can cause coiled cords to overheat.

Always plug power tools and extension cords into a GFCI (ground-fault circuit interrupter) outlet to protect from electric shocks. Never plug several tools into the same socket, or join cords together with tape — use properly connected extension cords. The third — or grounding — prong on a plug should never be removed.

Don't use power tools in wet conditions or drag the cord through water. If there are several people in the garden, keep the cord away from paths where it may be stepped on or crossed by wheelbarrows or vehicles. If the cord pulls taut while you are working, switch off the tool immediately — it may be caught in a door or snagged somewhere.

Put an extension cord across your shoulder when operating an electric lawn mower or hedge trimmer to reduce the risk of cutting through it or tripping over it. Watch out for other objects that could be run over as well — including your own toes, especially when working on a slope. Always wear protective footwear — modern mowers won't slice into tough leather, but you could lose a toe in an accident if you are so foolish as to mow the lawn while wearing sneakers.

When working with an unfamiliar tool for the first time, read the manufacturer's instructions carefully before plugging it in. Do not wear loose clothing when using tools with rotating or oscillating parts, and pull back long hair that may get caught in moving parts. Ensure that the chuck is tight and that the chuck key has been removed before starting an electric drill. And don't set a drill down until it is unplugged and the chuck has stopped rotating.

Safety with water

Adults are unlikely to find water a hazard in the garden, except with regard to the use of electricity. Young children, however, can drown in quite shallow water.

Encourage youngsters to play away from ornamental ponds or water barrels. Use strong, rigid wire mesh to cover all expanses of water if you have small children — green-coated mesh is fairly unobtrusive. Always keep the top of a water barrel or tank covered with a strong lid — preferably one that is locked in place.

Swimming pools should be surrounded by a fence with a lock on the gate. Keep the gate locked even when the pool is empty.

ELECTRICAL SAFETY

1 Outdoor GFCI outlets should be fitted with a weatherproof faceplate, which you can close securely when the outlet is not in use. Outside power lines must be enclosed in a conduit along their entire length; consult local electrical codes for any requirements for buried cables.

2 To avoid cutting through an extension cord when using an electric lawn mower, keep the cord to one side, or put it over your shoulder, so that it is always trailing behind you. Loosely knot the mower and extension cords together to prevent them from separating as you work.

3 When you run a cord across a patio or walkway, ensure that it can't rub against a wall. Make a roller from a wooden stake and a piece of PVC drainpipe or a dish-detergent bottle to keep the cord clear of sharp edges. Avoid getting kinks in the cord.

Safety with chemicals

Store chemicals — pesticides, fungicides, herbicides, disinfectants, fertilizers, motor oil, and gasoline — out of reach of children. A cupboard under lock and key or a high shelf in a locked shed is ideal. Never store chemicals in a hot place, such as a greenhouse, where they may catch fire or give off toxic fumes.

Flammable liquids, such as gasoline and oil, should be stored in metal cans — plastic ones are suitable only for short-term transportation of such liquids — and the quantity restricted to no more than a couple of gallons. It is preferable to keep them in a brick or concrete garage, which will help to contain an explosive fire, rather than in a wooden shed.

Always store chemicals in their original container so that they are accurately labeled — most chemicals are sold with clear instructions on the label for their correct use and for emergency situations. Never put a chemical in an unmarked bottle — or worse still, in an incorrectly labeled container, such as an old soft-drink bottle. Wash out all equipment thoroughly after using chemicals.

Mix up only as much of a chemical solution as you will need for one application. Wash your hands after handling any chemical.

Do not store diluted chemicals nor pour them on the ground or down the drain. Instead, dispose of any excess either by applying it to one of the other approved target plants listed on the label, or by taking it to the toxic-waste disposal at the nearest landfill or resource-recovery plant (if there is such a facility near you). Take used motor oil to your nearest service station for safe disposal.

Lead-contaminated soils

Parents of infants may want to test their garden soil for its lead

LIFTING HEAVY WEIGHTS

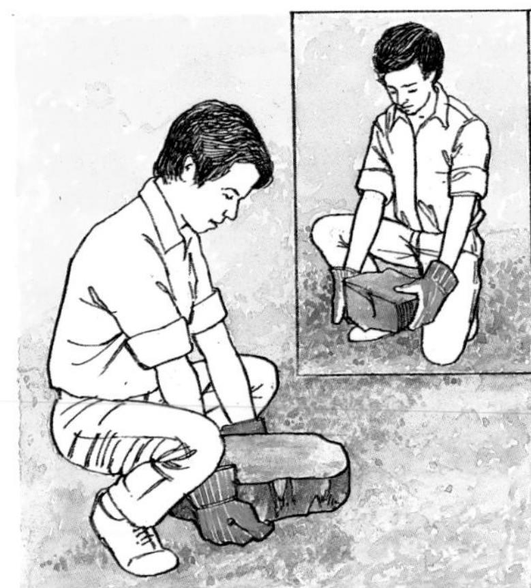

1 Lifting heavy weights can cause back or groin injury if done incorrectly. Crouch down to the object with feet apart and one foot alongside the load. Keep your back straight and let your leg muscles do the lifting work.

2 Never attempt to lift awkward-shaped or very heavy items by yourself. To minimize the actual height to which the load must be lifted, use rope or sturdy straps as handles. Again, let your leg muscles do the lifting.

3 When taking a heavy sack from a truck or loading platform it is best to carry it on your back. Get a firm grip with both hands and keep your back straight by raising the top of your head slightly and by tucking in your chin.

USING LADDERS SAFELY

1 When moving a ladder, rest it on one shoulder and lift it by the rung just below your normal reach. Find the correct balance before moving.

2 When extended, a ladder should stand at a 75° angle. If, for example, the ladder reaches 12 ft (4 m) up a wall, it should stand 3 ft (1 m) from the wall. Extension ladders with a closed length of up to 15 ft (4.5 m) must be overlapped by two rungs; longer ones, by three or four rungs.

3 Ladders over 10 ft (3 m) tall should be secured either at the top or at the bottom. Lash them to a firm object — never to a pipe or gutter. Alternatively, ask someone to stand on the bottom rung to steady the ladder.

POISONOUS PLANTS

Teach children not to pick or eat any berries, seeds, leaves, or flowers unless they are known to be harmless. The following plants are toxic — some causing stomachache, others being deadly — so do not eat any part:

Anemones *(Anemone* species)
Autumn crocuses *(Colchicum* species)
Black locust *(Robinia pseudoacacia)*
Boxwoods *(Buxus* species)
Buttercups *(Ranunculus* species)
Cherry laurel *(Prunus laurocerasus)*
Columbines (*Aquilegia* species)
Daffodils (*Narcissus* species — bulbs are toxic)
Daturas *(Datura* species)
Foxgloves (*Digitalis purpurea)*
Hemlocks *(Conicum* species)
Hollies *(Ilex* species)
Ivies *(Hedera* species)
Larkspurs (*Delphinium* species)
Lilies of the valley (*Convallaria majalis*)
Lupines (*Lupinus* species)
Monkshoods (*Aconitum* species)
Nightshade (*Solanum* species — unripe berries are highly toxic)
Oleander *(Nerium oleander* — all parts are highly toxic)
Pokeweed *(Phytolacca americana)*
Potatoes (only green tubers, leaves, and fruits are toxic)
Privets *(Ligustrum ovalifolium)*
Rhubarb *(Rheum* — leaves only)
Spindlebush *(Euonymus europaeus)*
Spurges *(Euphorbia* species)
Sumacs *(Rhus* species)
Sweet peas *(Lathyrus* species)
Tomatoes (leaves and stems only)
Wisteria (beanlike seeds are toxic)
Yews *(Taxus* species)

content, especially if your house was built before the 1980s (it may have been coated originally with lead-based paint), if you live on a busy street (automobile exhaust was formerly a source of lead), or if you live in an apple-growing region (lead arsenate was once a standard orchard spray).

Lead is most dangerous to infants, both because they are more sensitive to it and because, in the course of their play, they are liable to ingest soil.

Homegrown vegetables can pose a special risk, since root crops, and to a lesser extent, greens, absorb lead. You can ingest the lead when you eat.

A test for lead is relatively inexpensive and can be performed by most soil laboratories or your local Environmental Protection Agency. If your soil contains more than 500 parts per million (ppm) of lead, your doctor should monitor your child through periodic blood tests. If you have more than 1,000 ppm of lead in your soil, you should consult your community health board about remedial measures. Generally, these involve nothing more elaborate than tilling the affected area and covering it with sod or dense shrubbery.

HEDGE TRIMMING SAFETY

When trimming a tall hedge, work off a scaffold board supported by two stepladders or trestles. Position the steps as close to the hedge as possible and on firm, level ground. Boards 2 in (50 mm) thick and 8 in (200 mm) wide can safely span a gap up to 5 ft (1.5 m).

The Gardeners' Calendar

Container-grown plants can be planted at any time of year — but what about bulbs and seeds? Which are the best months to prune, feed, or mulch? This calendar pinpoints the essential tasks of the seasons and suggests plants to provide color throughout the year.

Early spring to midspring

Lawns Rake the lawn vigorously and mow it with lawnmower blades set high. Aerate a badly drained lawn and brush sandy compost into the holes left by removal of cores. Sow seed of cool-season grasses, such as bluegrasses, fescues, and ryegrasses. In the North, it is a good time to lay sod. Unwanted crabgrass seeds sprout when soil temperatures reach 65-70° F; stop them by applying a preemergent herbicide — but keep these herbicides off newly seeded lawns, as they will prevent grass seed from germinating.

Trees and shrubs Remove winter protection from tender shrubs. Plant or transplant conifers, evergreen shrubs, and all bare-rooted trees and shrubs. Continue to prune winter-flowering shrubs once their blooms have faded. Also prune species that flower in late summer and lightly shear winter heathers. Prune tree and shrub branches killed by winter cold or wind. Using a hoe, remove weeds in between shrubs and under hedges. Apply a dressing of general-purpose fertilizer around the base of shrubs, then lay down a mulch of garden compost, shredded bark, or well-rotted manure.

Roses Prune established plants. Apply a rose fertilizer and then spread a mulch of garden composted manure around the base of plants.

Perennials Remove winter protection from tender perennials, then fertilize established beds and apply a thick mulch. Finish dividing and replanting established plants. As weather grows milder and the soil dries, plant out young perennials that you started indoors. Propagate summer-flowering chrysanthemums from new shoots that sprout on the root clumps that you stored over winter. In midspring, sow perennials in a seedbed for next year's flowering. Prepare the ground for outdoor-flowering chrysanthemums.

Annuals Finish preparing the ground for seeds. Allow a couple of weeks for the soil to settle and then sow hardy annuals. Scatter slug pellets, if needed. Sow half-hardy annuals indoors for planting out in early summer. Start begonia tubers in boxes of moist potting soil supplied with moderate bottom heat. In midspring, plant out sweet peas.

Bulbs Deadhead early spring flowering bulbs as they fade. Remove dead leaves of bearded irises and apply fertilizer to surrounding soil. Divide snowdrops. Fertilize other spring-flowering bulbs as soon as their foliage begins to emerge. Begin planting gladioli and acidantheras, setting out groups of bulbs every 10 to 14 days. In cold areas, plant De Caen anemones for summer flowering. Plant hardy indoor bulbs outside once they have finished flowering; discard those grown in water and pebbles. Spread a light mulch of leaf mold or well-rotted compost over lily beds. Protect young lily shoots from frost by covering them with upended canning jars at night.

Flower color, early spring: Dutch and species crocuses, *Iris reticulata*, polyanthuses, saxifrages, anemones, primroses, spring snowflakes, *Tulipa kaufmanniana*, forsythias, camellias, flowering currants, Japanese quinces, *Daphne mezereum*, hyacinths, and *Magnolia stellata*.

Flower color, midspring: Daffodils, tulips, grape hyacinths, lilies of the valley, wood anemones, aubretias, alyssums, arabises, gentians, brooms, magnolias, ornamental crab apples, barberries, and spireas.

Midspring to late spring

Lawns Mow lawns weekly at recommended heights. Fertilize lawns. In the South, sow warm-season grasses — common Bermuda grass, Bahia grass, carpet grass, and centipede grass. Apply selective herbicides in all regions. In late spring, watch for moths fluttering close to turf in the evening; these are a sign of armyworms in the South and sod webworms in the North. Treat both with an insecticide recommended in your region.
Trees and shrubs Prune forsythias, weigelas, and other spring-flowering shrubs once they have finished blooming. Mulch trees and shrubs if you have not already done so.
Roses Watch for yellowing leaves speckled with black — the first symptom of black spot. If roses become infected, spray at recommended intervals with a fungicide approved in your region, and dispose of diseased foliage as it falls away from the bush. Continue until all signs of disease have disappeared. Apply a rose fertilizer.
Perennials Plant outdoor-flowering chrysanthemums early; remove center tip a week later to encourage bushy growth. Pinch growing tips of New York asters, goldenrod, heleniums, and other vigorous plants. Mulch beds and borders; weed them regularly. Provide support for tall plants, such as delphiniums and sea hollies.
Annuals Plant out half-hardy annuals after danger of frost has passed, and feed them with half-strength solution of a liquid fertilizer, such as seaweed extract. Thin seedlings of hardy annuals.
Biennials Sow Canterbury bells, foxgloves, sweet Williams, and wallflowers.
Bulbs Continue to deadhead early-flowering bulbs, but allow foliage to yellow and wither before removing it — now is the time when plants are storing food for next year's bloom. Stake tall lilies as flower buds form. In late spring in milder zones, plant out dahlia tubers. If you need extra space, lift spring-flowering bulbs that have finished blooming.
Flower color Pulsatillas, stars-of-Bethlehem, wallflowers, spurges, forget-me-nots, pyrethrums, sunroses, Spanish gorse, azaleas, rhododendrons, wisterias, laburnums, and clematises.

Early summer to midsummer

Lawns During hot, dry weather, keep mower blades high and mow less frequently.
Trees and shrubs Remove faded azalea and rhododendron flowers. Continue pruning shrubs as they finish flowering. Train the new growth on climbing plants. During dry spells, water young shrubs and trees.
Roses Prune spring-blooming old-fashioned roses. Deadhead hybrid teas and floribundas. Apply fertilizer. Treat for mildew, Japanese beetles, and aphids, if necessary. Continue to spray for black spot, if needed.
Perennials Water thoroughly in dry weather. When bloom ends, cut down early-flowering species to 3 in (7.5 cm) above ground. For large chrysanthemum blooms, reduce stems to six or eight per plant. Fertilize.
Annuals Support tall annuals. Remove faded flower heads. Sow late summer-flowering annuals, such as candytufts, cornflowers, and marigolds. Plant annuals, using them to fill window boxes, baskets, and other containers, as well as borders. Water sweet peas and container plants frequently.
Biennials Continue to sow spring-flowering biennials: forget-me-nots, wallflowers, Canterbury bells, and sweet Williams. Remove second-year plants when flowering ends.
Bulbs Lift and divide daffodils and tulips when leaves start to yellow. In mild areas, plant De Caen anemones for the fall. You can also plant fall-flowering bulbs: nerines, colchicums, and fall-flowering crocuses. On dahlias, pinch out tips of leading shoots in early summer, then water, mulch, and apply general-purpose fertilizer to them; keep an eye out for pests. In midsummer, tie in young shoots of dahlias and remove faded flowers; stake taller varieties. Cut back stems of tall bearded irises after flowering. Stake gladioli and acidantheras, either individually or with one stake per clump.
Flower color, early summer: Delphiniums, sweet Williams, Canterbury bells, lupines, bearded irises, alliums, stocks, pinks, peonies, roses, honeysuckles, potentillas, rockroses, and lilacs.
Flower color, midsummer: Sweet peas, nasturtiums, phloxes, petunias, lavenders, roses, clematis hybrids, and hydrangeas.

Midsummer to late summer

Lawns Mow regularly but infrequently — perhaps once every 2 or 3 weeks during hot weather. In the North, grass will go dormant unless you water it — turning brown now but greening again with the return of cool, moist weather in the fall. In the West and the South, turf may need irrigation during these months to survive; deep, infrequent watering is best. Fertilize warm-season grasses, if needed. Throughout the country, be alert in hot, humid weather for the appearance of brown circles that are several inches to several feet in diameter—these indicate brown patch. Treat the areas with a fungicide approved in your area, and limit applications of high-nitrogen fertilizer. Summer's end is the ideal time to seed or reseed a lawn in the North.

Trees and shrubs Water periodically during dry spells. Clip lavender bushes after flowering. Cut back wisteria.

Roses Prune ramblers after flowering. Continue to deadhead hybrid teas and floribundas. Regular, deep watering is essential for roses during hot, dry weather. In cold-winter zones, don't fertilize after mid-August .

Perennials Ensure that perennials never dry out, particularly fall-flowering species such as New York asters, goldenrod, and heleniums. Lift and divide bearded irises if clumps show signs of dying out at center. Deadhead all faded flowers not needed for their seeds. Keep chrysanthemums well supported and tied in; continue to disbud.

Annuals Deadhead regularly and water well during dry spells. In the South, sow a second crop of annuals at summer's end, if desired.

Biennials Deadhead spent blooms regularly and water well. Remove the plants as they finish flowering.

Bulbs Plant crocus corms as soon as they are available from garden centers. Replant in their final positions any bulbs that you previously lifted and stored to make room for annuals. Continue to deadhead and tie in dahlias; rub out young buds on side shoots.

Flower color Early-flowering chrysanthemums, begonias, heleniums, marigolds, lobelias, sunflowers, lilies, gladioli, hibiscuses, fuchsias, buddleias, and St.-John's-worts.

Early fall to midfall

Lawns The return of rains brings renewed growth of broadleaf weeds in most areas — spray with an approved selective herbicide. Set mower blades lower than summer height. In the West and the North, September is also a good time for sowing or fertilizing cool-season grasses. In the Southwest, remove thatch from summer lawns of warm-season grasses and sow cool-season grasses for winter lawns. Fertilize lawns in the North; Southern lawns with warm-season grasses have less need of fertilizer at this time. Aerate and topdress existing lawns.

Trees and shrubs Early fall is an excellent time to transplant evergreen trees or shrubs; wait until midfall for deciduous types. After storms, resecure climbers and young trees.

Roses Deadhead to encourage late flowers. Tie in new shoots on climbers. Watch for diseases. Transplant and relocate any bushes you set too close together in the spring.

Perennials Now is a good time to plant perennials (notably peonies) in any zone, but especially in hot-weather regions. Early fall is also the time to lift and divide most perennial flowers — keep them well watered. Deadhead and cut down all dead stems.

Annuals Clear away annuals as they finish flowering. Apply high-nitrogen fertilizer to ornamental cabbage.

Biennials Plant out biennials grown from seed in separate beds.

Bulbs Plant these spring-flowering bulbs as soon as you can buy them or when your mail-order shipment arrives: narcissi, anemones, scillas, grape hyacinths, and Dutch, English, and Spanish irises. Pot indoor bulbs, such as precooled hyacinths, daffodils, and tulips, for flowering in winter and spring; store them in a cool, shaded place. Water dahlias when dry.

Flower, leaf, and berry color Dahlias, agapanthuses, gladioli, Japanese anemones, goldenrod, crocosmias, autumn cyclamens, colchicums, sedums, fall-flowering snowflakes, tamarisks, caryopterides, mountain ashes, chrysanthemums, larches, ornamental grasses, oaks, maples, cotoneasters, pansies, abelias, viburnums, and hawthorns.

The Temperature Zone Map

Selecting plants that are adapted to your climate is half the secret of successful gardening. A plant that is well suited to its surroundings will flourish with a minimum of help, while a plant transplanted to an inhospitable site will struggle no matter how much care you give it.

Your best tool for identifying such plants is the temperature zone map shown here. Developed by the United States Department of Agriculture (USDA) as an aid to gardeners and nurseries, it divides Canada and the United States, including the Hawaiian Islands, into 11 zones. Most American and Canadian nurseries and mail-order companies have adopted the USDA map as a standard reference.

Each zone is based on an average minimum temperature, which is an index of the local winter's severity. In most cases this temperature is the crucial factor in determining whether a plant will survive in a given region. Most plant descriptions — in catalogs or on plant labels, for example — indicate the zones in which a specific plant will thrive. For instance, the common flowering dogwood will be listed as hardy from zones 6 to 9. Once you have identified the zone you are in, buy only plants that are recommended for that zone — then you can be reasonably confident that your purchases will be adapted to the local climate.

However, plant hardiness can also be influenced by certain local conditions. A garden located at the top of a 1,000-ft (300-m) mountain, for example, will usually have temperatures several degrees colder than one in the surrounding plains. And because water collects heat from the sun, a garden that is located on the shore of a pond will be both warmer in winter and cooler in summer than a garden just down the road.

Such local peculiarities and microclimates may force an adjustment in your use of the temperature zone map. If you have further questions about plant hardiness in your area, contact your local Cooperative Extension or Agricultural Service.

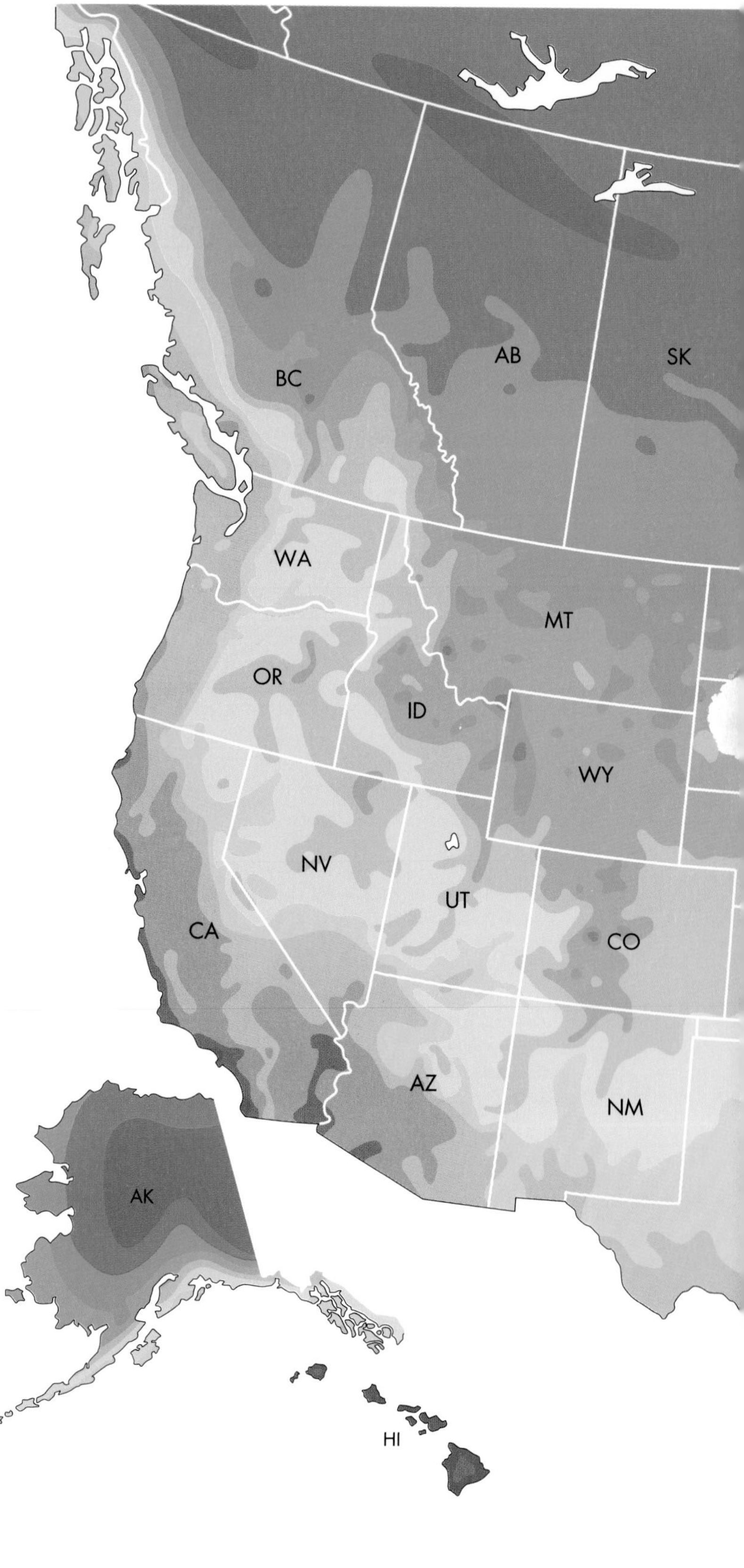

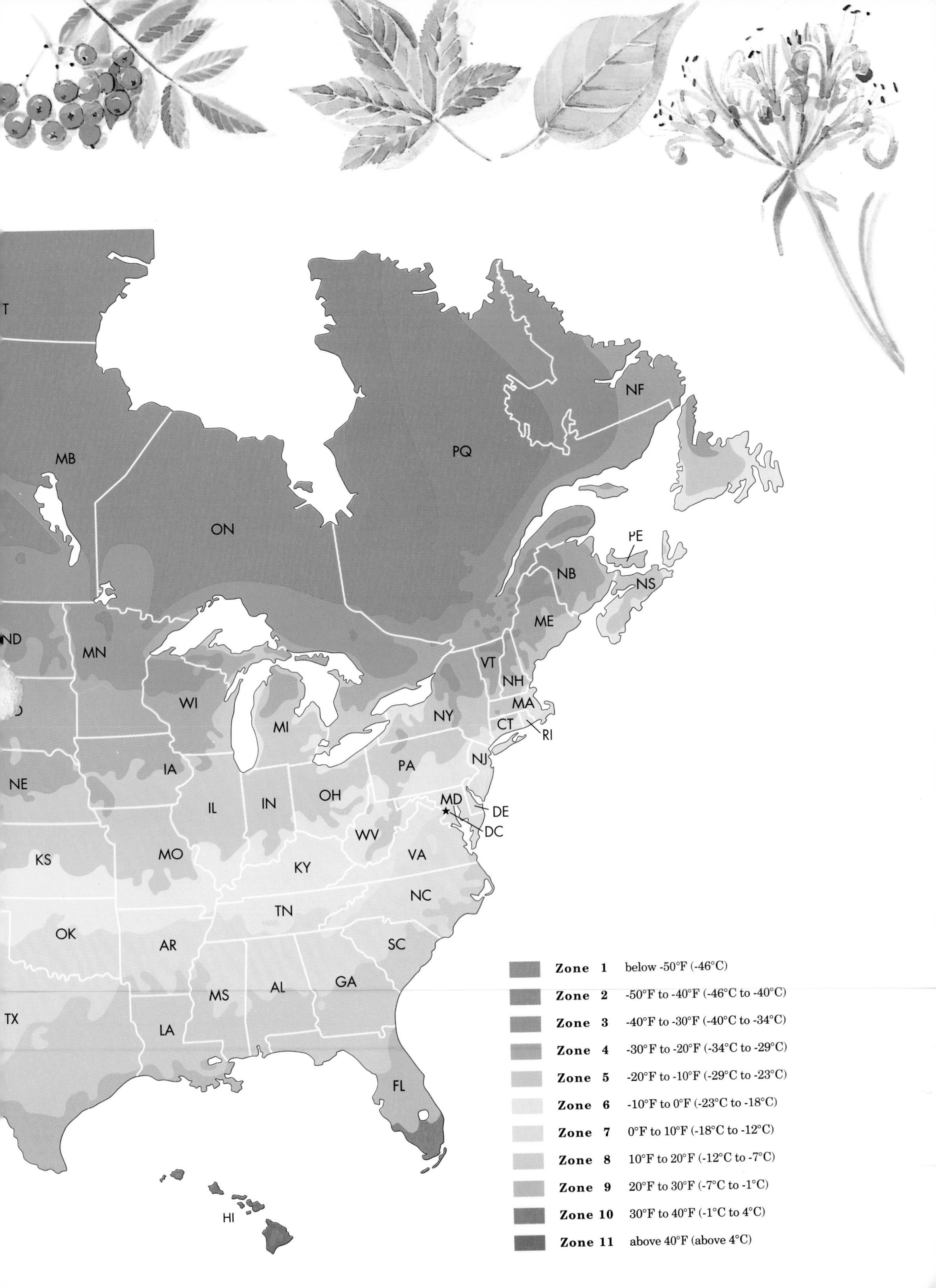

MB
ON
PQ
NF
PE
NB
NS
ME
ND
MN
VT
NH
MA
WI
NY
CT
RI
MI
NJ
PA
IA
NE
IL
IN
OH
MD
DE
DC
WV
KS
MO
VA
KY
NC
TN
OK
AR
SC
MS
AL
GA
TX
LA
FL
HI
Zone 1 below -50°F (-46°C)
Zone 2 -50°F to -40°F (-46°C to -40°C)
Zone 3 -40°F to -30°F (-40°C to -34°C)
Zone 4 -30°F to -20°F (-34°C to -29°C)
Zone 5 -20°F to -10°F (-29°C to -23°C)
Zone 6 -10°F to 0°F (-23°C to -18°C)
Zone 7 0°F to 10°F (-18°C to -12°C)
Zone 8 10°F to 20°F (-12°C to -7°C)
Zone 9 20°F to 30°F (-7°C to -1°C)
Zone 10 30°F to 40°F (-1°C to 4°C)
Zone 11 above 40°F (above 4°C)

Midfall to late fall

Lawns Keep height of mower blades low for final cut. Watch for yellow patches sprouting cottony white mold — it is snow mold, often caused by excess nitrogen fertilization. Control by aerating the lawn and applying a fungicide approved in your area.
Trees and shrubs Plant deciduous and evergreen species; cover newly planted or tender shrubs if frost threatens. If very cold, bring tender container shrubs indoors. Prune conifers. Fertilize established trees.
Roses Take cuttings of species, ramblers, and some floribundas. Prune climbing roses. In cold regions, protect hybrid teas by mounding soil 9 in (23 cm) over crowns; remove climbers from trellis, and lay them, covered, on the ground.
Perennials Tidy borders, cut back plants, and remove old stems and leaves. Divide and replant overgrown perennials that have finished flowering. As outdoor-flowering chrysanthemums go dormant, lift root clumps and store in boxes of old soil in a frost-free place for use as source of cuttings in early spring; keep ventilated and slightly moist. Bring other tender plants indoors. When temperatures drop, cover tender plants and those in exposed sites.
Annuals Finish clearing annuals.
Biennials Replant remaining flowers. Keep one-year plants free of wet fallen leaves.
Bulbs Continue planting spring-flowering bulbs, such as tulips, lilies of the valley, hardy lilies, snowdrops, *Iris reticulata,* miniature daffodils, crocuses, and chionodoxas. Divide overgrown clumps of lilies; cut off their stems as they fade. Feed bearded irises with potash. Cut down dahlias, lift the tubers, and store them. Also cut down stems of gladioli, lift the bulbs, and store them in a frost-free place. Check bulbs potted in early fall for indoor display; move those with 1-in (2.5-cm) shoots to a frost-free place.
Flower, leaf, and berry color, midfall: Colchicums, *Amaryllis belladonna*, New York asters, maples, strawberry trees, shrub roses, Japanese quinces, sumacs, ornamental cherries, and Virginia creepers.
Flower, leaf, and berry color, late fall: Chinese lanterns, mountain ashes, *Skimmia japonica*, pyracanthas, barberries, pernettyas, viburnums, and snowberries.

Winter

Lawns If ground is not frozen, rake off fallen leaves. In warmer regions of the Southwest, begin fertilization in late winter.
Trees and shrubs Prune trees and deciduous summer-flowering shrubs such as clematis, buddleia, potentilla, and hardy fuchsia. Prune winter-flowering shrubs once they have finished blooming; apply general-purpose fertilizer and mulch around their bases. Continue planting deciduous species during mild spells; otherwise, heel in young plants to protect them. Cut suckers growing from the bases of trees. In the North, water trees and shrubs deeply during winter thaws.
Roses Begin to prune floribunda and hybrid tea roses in mild regions.
Perennials Order plants and seeds for spring. During mild spells in zones 7 to 11, lift and divide lupines, New York asters, delphiniums, and other hardy border plants that have been left for 3 years or more. Apply general-purpose fertilizer to other hardy perennials. Examine stored chrysanthemum clumps for rot; air them on mild, dry days. Press soil down firmly around any plants that have been lifted by frost.
Annuals In mild weather, dig soil and add soil amendments. Order seeds for sowing in late winter and early spring. In late winter, sow half-hardy annuals in a cold frame or greenhouse.
Biennials Keep overwintering plants free of debris. After frosts, press soil down around any plants that have been loosened. In late winter, apply a general-purpose fertilizer.
Bulbs Move potted daffodil, hyacinth, and tulip bulbs with shoots indoors; make sure they do not dry out. Check stored dahlia tubers: if they show signs of mold, spray with an approved fungicide; if they are withering, soak them in tepid water overnight. As crocus buds emerge in late winter, protect them from hungry birds by stretching dark cotton, supported on sticks, across the bed. Pot lily bulbs indoors for early display.
Flower, leaf, and berry color Christmas roses, snowdrops, crocuses, winter aconites, winter sweets, Chinese witch hazels, cotoneasters, winter-flowering heathers, hollies, winter-flowering jasmines, euonymuses, *Mahonia bealii, Lonicera fragrantissima,* and cornelian cherries.

INDEX

ACKNOWLEDGMENTS

Photo credits
Heather Angel 10, 131(b), 133(t,c), 134(t). Black & Decker 159. Linda Burgess 79(b). Simon Butcher/Eaglemoss 11. Brian Carter 132(t). Eric Crichton 25, 32(b), 34(b), 45, 56(b), 89, 97, 99, 103, 105, 109, 163(t). Robert Estall 163 (b). Garden Picture Library 39, (Brigitte Thomas) 2-3, (Steve Wooster) 62. John Glover 35(t), 45, 52. Jerry Harpur 32(t), 33, 34(t). J. Stephenson 31. Neil Holmes 85, 87. Jerry Howard/Positive Images 68. Lamontagne 54(t,b), 55(b), 59, 77, 79(t), 80, 119. Andrew Lawson 17, 53, 74, 75, 91, 128, 151. Tania Midgley 12(t), 156. Philippe Perdereau 81, 131(t). Photos Horticultural 12(c,b), 35(b), 55(t), 56(t,c), 57(t,c), 63, 68, 69(t), 86, 115, 123, 135, 157. Nick Rebbeck 9(tl). Barry L. Runk/Grant Heilman Photography, Inc. 9(br). Harry Smith Collection 21, 88, 95, 131(c), 132(b), 133(b), 134(b), 139. Chris Stephens/Eaglemoss 129. The Soil Survey 9(c,bl). John Suett/Eaglemoss front cover. Brigette Thomas, back cover. Michael Warren/Eaglemoss 69(b), 70–71. Elizabeth Whiting and Assoc. 81, (Karl-Dietrich Buhler) 94, (Jerry Harpur) 4–5, 8 (Harpur/design: Cobblers Garden) 6, (Spike Powell) 30. Wolf Tools 158.

Illustrations
Sophie Allington 152, 153(bl), 154. David Ashby 162 (except as noted below). Sylvia Bokor 72(tr), 86(t,br), 112, 113 (t,tl), 114(tc), 118(tl,tc,tr). Elisabeth Dowle 26, 27 (l,tr,trc, br), 28, 104–108, 140(c), 141(t), 143(b). Terry Evans 78–79. Ian Garrard/Reader's Digest 136–138, 144–150. Will Giles 10, 82–83. Christine Hart-Davies 18–19, 22–24, 36, 37(t, bl,cr,br), 38, 41(tr), 42, 43(tr,bl,bc,br), 44(tl, tc,bl,bc), 46–48, 51(except br), 60, 61, 64–66, 74–76, 86(bl), 87, 89–92, 96–98, 100–102, 110–111, 115–117, 118(br), 120–122. Ron Hayward 164(tl,tr,br), 165(tr,b), 166. John Hutchinson 160 & 161(except as noted below). Ed Jacobus 170–171. Marianne Markey 51(br), 153(tl,tr,cl,cr,br), 160(gardening hoe, grass whip), 161(Cape Cod weeder, dandelion weeder, grass shears), 162(garden tiller), 165(tl,tc). Sean Milne/Reader's Digest 52. Stan North 113 (tl,tr,b), 114(tl,b). Charles Pickard/Reader's Digest 130–34. Reader's Digest 140(t,b), 141(c,b), 142, 143(t,c), 144, 153 (tl,tr,cl,cr). Ray Skibinski 9, 13–15, 16, 27(brc), 37(bc), 40, 41(tl,b), 43(tl,tc), 44(tr,br), 50, 164(bl). Charlotte Wess 167–169, 172. Ann Winterbotham 124–126. Cathy Wood 70, 72.